CHARTER & ORDINANCES

OF THE

CITY OF MILWAUKEE,

WITH THE

CONSTITUTION OF THE STATE,

AND

ACTS OF THE LEGISLATURE,

RELATING TO THE CITY,

INCLUDING

A LIST OF OFFICERS,

AND THE

RULES AND REGULATIONS

OF THE

COMMON COUNCIL.

PUBLISHED BY ORDER OF THE COMMON COUNCIL.

DECEMBER 5, 1856.

MILWAUKEE:
DAILY NEWS BOOK AND JOB STEAM PRINTING ESTABLISHMENT, MASON STREET.
1857.

MILWAUKEE CITY OFFICERS.

MAYOR,	JAMES B. CROSS.
President of Board,	JACKSON HADLEY.
Clerk,	ROBERT WHITEHEAD.
Deputy Clerk,	JOHN A. SEGER.
Treasurer,	HERMAN SCHWARTING.
Comptroller,	JOHN B. EDWARDS.
City Attorney,	WILSON GRAHAM.
Marshal,	CHARLES C. MEYER.
City Printers,	J. R. SHARPSTEIN, SCHŒFFLER & WENDT.
Police Justice,	CLINTON WALWORTH.
Chief of Police,	WILLIAM BECK.
City Engineer,	WILLIAM S. TROWBRIDGE.
Inspector of Wood and Hay,	ERNST F. HERZBERG.
Sealer of Weights and Measures,	JESSE M. VAN SLYCK.
Superintendent of Bridges,	PATRICK MARKEY.

BOARD OF ALDERMEN.

First Ward.

J. HADLEY,
C. BAAST,
L. MARNELL.

Second Ward.

J. A. HOOVER,
AUG. GREULICH,
J. C. DICK.

Third Ward.

TIM. O'BRIEN,
JNO. SHORTELL,
M. DELANEY.

Fourth Ward.

A. H. JOHNSTON,
JNO. PLANKINTON,
J. TAYLOR.

Fifth Ward.

H. MILMAN,
J. H. CORDES,
J. HUMPHREY.

Sixth Ward.

H. HÆRTEL,
FERD. KUEHN,
JOHN KLEIN.

Seventh Ward.

G. S. MALLORY,
EDWARD BUTTON,
F. J. JUNG.

STANDING COMMITTEES.

Finance—Hærtel, Mallory and Kuehn.
Judiciary—Mallory, Hadley and Taylor.
Police—Shortell, Klein and Dick.
Fire Department—Hoover, O'Brien and Humphrey.
Schools—Hadley, Mallory and Greulich.
Printing—Greulich, Kuehn and Marnell.
Harbor—Hadley, Hærtel, Mallory, Taylor, O'Brien, Humphrey and Hoover.
License—Milman, Baast and Delaney.
Bridges—Taylor, Hadley, Kuehn, Hoover, O'Brien, Button and Humphrey.
Gas Light—Jung, Hoover, Plankinton, Delaney, Hadley, Cordes and Hærtel.
Old Tax—Kuehn, Johnston, Cordes, Baast, O'Brien, Dick and Jung.
Rail Road—Hadley, Greulich, Shortell, Taylor, Cordes, Hærtel and Button.

SCHOOL COMMISSIONERS.

JACKSON HADLEY, President. R. WHITEHEAD, Secretary.

First Ward—J. Hadley, L. Marnell, Silas Chapman.
Second Ward—I. A. Lapham, James Flynn, C. J. Kern.
Third Ward—E. O'Neil, John Horan, Jno. S. Mitchell.
Fourth Ward—S. C. Elmore, J. A. Seger, J. Taylor.
Fifth Ward—Andrew Mitchell, E. De Wolf, C. A. Larkin.
Sixth Ward—C. E. Jenkins, Ben. Church, Ferd. Kuehn.
Seventh Ward—James Johnson.

COMMISSIONERS OF SURVEY.

I. A. Lapham, S. B. Grant, E. Eldred, A. Mitchell, I. E. Goodall, Otis B. Hopkins.

WARD OFFICERS.

ASSESSORS.

First Ward, . . . Stephen Hoff,
Second Ward, . . J. Kluppak,
Third Ward, . . . John D. Dolan,
Fourth Ward, . . A. Ely,
Fifth Ward, . . . F. Conrad,
Sixth Ward, . . . Adam Hein,
Seventh Ward, . . C. R. Austin.

JUSTICES OF THE PEACE.

First Ward, . . . —— ——
Second Ward, . . . C. F. Bode,
Third Ward, . . . Wm. Holland,
Fourth Ward, . . R. N. Austin,
Fifth Ward, . . . O. Parsons,
Sixth Ward, . . . R. N. Messenger,
Seventh Ward, . . Albert Smith.

CONSTABLES.

First Ward, . . . John Scheffel,
Second Ward, . . Charles Neuman,
Third Ward, . . . John H. Ryan,
Fourth Ward, . . H. M. Beecroft,
Fifth Ward, . . . Aug. Meyer,
Sixth Ward, . . . George Fisher,
Seventh Ward, . . G. Luther.

RAIL ROAD COMMISSIONERS.

First Ward, . . . B. Skidmore,
Second Ward, . . George Abert,
Third Ward, . . . Thos. Eviston,
Fourth Ward, . . John A. Seger,
Fifth Ward, . . . C. H. Larkin,
Sixth Ward, . . . Adam Pœrtner,
Seventh Ward, . . John Jennings.

FIRE DEPARTMENT.

Chief Engineer, . . . John C. Goodrich,
First Ass't Engineer, John Lowther,
Second Ass't Engineer, Henry Vehrkins,
Third Ass't Engineer, N. B. Brooks.

CONSTITUTION

OF THE

STATE OF WISCONSIN.

PREAMBLE.

We, the people of Wisconsin, grateful to Almighty God for our freedom, in order to secure its blessings, form a more perfect government, insure domestic tranquility, and promote the general welfare, do establish this constitution. **Preamble.**

ARTICLE I.

DECLARATION OF RIGHTS.

SECTION 1. All men are born equally free and independent, and have certain inherent rights: among these are life, liberty, and the pursuit of happiness. To secure these rights, governments are instituted among men, deriving their just powers from the consent of the governed. **Equality of rights, and how secured.**

SEC. 2. There shall be neither slavery nor involuntary servitude in this state, otherwise than for the punishment of crime, whereof the party shall have been duly convicted. **Slavery not to exist in state.**

SEC. 3. Every person may freely speak, write and publish his sentiments on all subjects, being responsible for the abuse of that right, and no laws shall be passed to restrain or abridge the liberty of speech or of the press. In all criminal prosecutions or indictments for libel, the truth may be given in evidence; and if it shall appear to the jury that the matter charged as libelous be true, and was published with good motives and for justifiable ends, the party shall be acquitted; and the jury shall have the right to determine the law and the fact. **Liberty of speech and of the press; evidence in case of libel.**

Right of the people to consult and petition.

SEC. 4. The right of the people peaceably to assemble to consult for the common good, and to petition the government or any department thereof, shall never be abridged.

Right of trial by jury.

SEC. 5. The right of trial by jury shall remain inviolate; and shall extend to all cases at law, without regard to the amount in controversy; but a jury trial may be waived by the parties in all cases, in the manner prescribed by law.

Bail.

SEC. 6. Excessive bail shall not be required, nor shall excessive fines be imposed, nor cruel and unusual punishments inflicted.

Rights of the accused.

SEC. 7. In all criminal prosecutions, the accused shall enjoy the right to be heard by himself and counsel; to demand the nature and cause of the accusation against him; to meet the witnesses face to face; to have compulsory process to compel the attendance of witnesses in his behalf; and in prosecutions by indictment or information, to a speedy public trial by an impartial jury of the county or district wherein the offence shall have been committed; which county or district shall have been previously ascertained by law.

Presentment or indictment in criminal cases.

No person to be twice tried for same offence, &c.

When accused may be bailed; writ of habeas corpus.

SEC. 8. No person shall be held to answer for a criminal offence, unless on the presentment or indictment of a grand jury, except in cases of impeachment, or in cases cognizable by justices of the peace, or arising in the army or navy, or in the militia when in actual service in time of war or public danger; and no person for the same offence shall be put twice in jeopardy of punishment, nor shall be compelled in any criminal case to be a witness against himself. All persons shall, before conviction, be bailable by sufficient sureties, except for capital offences, when the proof is evident or the presumption great; and the privilege of the writ of habeas corpus shall not be suspended unless, when, in cases of rebellion or invasion the public safety may require.

Remedy for wrongs how should be obtained.

SEC. 9. Every person is entitled to a certain remedy in the laws, for all injuries or wrongs which he may receive in his person, property, or character; he ought to obtain justice freely, and without being obliged to purchase it; completely and without denial; promptly and without delay, conformably to the laws.

SEC. 10. Treason against the state shall consist only in levying war against the same, or in adhering to its enemies, giving them aid and comfort. No person shall be convicted of treason unless on the testimony of two witnesses to the same overt act, or on confession in open court. Treason.

SEC. 11. The right of the people to be secure in their persons, houses, papers, and effects, against unreasonable searches and seizures shall not be violated, and no warrant shall issue but upon probable cause, supported by oath or affirmation, and particularly describing the place to be searched and the persons or things to be seized. Searches and seizures.

SEC. 12. No bill of attainder, ex post facto law, nor any law impairing the obligation of contracts, shall ever be passed; and no conviction shall work corruption of blood, or forfeiture of estate. Attainder, expost facto laws, &c.

SEC. 13. The property of no person shall be taken for public use without just compensation therefor. Private property.

SEC. 14. All lands within the state are declared to be allodial, and feudal tenures are prohibited. Leases and grants of agricultural land, for a longer term than fifteen years, in which rent or service of any kind shall be reserved, and all fines and like restraints upon alienation, reserved in any grant of land, hereafter made, are declared to be void. Tenure of lands, and leases and fines.

SEC. 15. No distinction shall ever be made by law between resident aliens and citizens, in reference to the possession, enjoyment, or descent of property. Rights of citizens and aliens to property equal.

Sec. 16. No person shall be imprisoned for debt arising out of, or founded on a contract, expressed or implied. No imprisonment for debt.

SEC. 17. The privilege of the debtor to enjoy the necessary comforts of life, shall be recognized by wholesome laws, exempting a reasonable amount of property from seizure or sale for the payment of any debt or liability hereafter contracted. Exemption of property from sale for debt.

Rights of worship and of conscience, &c.

SEC. 18. The right of every man to worship Almighty God according to the dictates of his own conscience, shall never be infringed, nor shall any man be compelled to attend, erect, or support any place of worship, or to maintain any ministry, against his consent. Nor shall any control of, or interference with the rights of conscience be permitted, or any preference be given by law to any religious establishments, or mode of worship. Nor shall any money be drawn from the treasury for the benefit of religious societies, or religious or theological seminaries.

Religious tests and competency of witnesses.

SEC. 19. No religious tests shall ever be required as a qualification for any office of public trust, under the state, and no person shall be rendered incompetent to give evidence in any court of law or equity, in consequence of his opinions on the subject of religion.

Subordinat'n of military to civil power.

SEC. 20. The military shall be in strict subordination to the civil power.

Writs of error.

SEC. 21. Writs of error shall never be prohibited by law.

Free government how maintained.

SEC. 22. The blessings of a free government can only be maintained by a firm adherence to justice, moderation, temperance, frugality, and virtue, and by frequent recurrence to fundamental principles.

ARTICLE II.

BOUNDARIES.

Boundaries of state.

SECTION 1. It is hereby ordained and declared that the state of Wisconsin doth consent and accept of the boundaries prescribed in the act of congress entitled "an act to enable the people of Wisconsin territory to form a constitution and state government, and for the admission of such state into the Union," approved August sixth, one thousand eight hundred and forty-six, to wit: Beginning at the north-east corner of the state of Illinois, that is to say, at a point in the centre of Lake Michigan where the line of forty-two degrees and thirty minutes of north latitude crosses the same; thence, running with the boundary line of the state of Michigan, through Lake Michigan, Geeen Bay, to the mouth of the Menomonee river ; thence up the channel of the said river to the Brule river ; thence up said last-mentioned river to Lake Brule ; thence along the southern shore of Lake Brule, in a direct line to the centre of the channel between Middle and South islands, in the Lake of the Desert ; thence in a direct line to the head waters of the Montreal river, as marked upon the survey made by captain Cram ; thence down the main channel of the Montreal river to the middle of Lake Superior ; thence through the centre of Lake Superior to the mouth of the St. Louis river ; thence up the main channel of said river to the first rapids in the same, above the Indian village, according to Nicollet's map ; thence due south to the main branch of the river St. Croix ; thence down the main channel of said river to the Mississippi ; thence down the centre of the main channel of that river to the north-west corner of the state of Illinois ; thence due east with the northern boundary of the state of Illinois, to the place of beginning, as established by " an act to enable the people of the Illinois territory to form a constitution and state government, and for the admission of such state into the Union on an equal footing with the original states," approved April 18th, 1818. [*Provided, however, That the following altera- [*Not assented to by Congress.] tion of the aforesaid boundary be, and hereby is, proposed to the congress of the United States as the preference of the State of Wisconsin, and if the same shall be assented and agreed to by the congress of the United States then the same shall be and forever remain obligatory on the State of Wisconsin, viz: leaving the aforesaid boundary line at the foot of the rapids of the St. Louis river; thence in a direct line, bearing south-westerly to the mouth of the Iskodewabo, or Rum river, where the same empties into the Mississippi river ; thence down the main channel of the said Mississippi river, as prescribed in the aforesaid boundary.]

Propositions of Congress accepted and confirmed.

SEC. 2. The propositions contained in the act of Congress, are hereby excepted, ratified and confirmed, and shall remain irrevocable without the consent of the United States, and it is hereby ordained that this state shall never interfere with the primary disposal of the soil within the same, by the United States, nor with any regulations congress may find necessary for securing the title in such soil to *bona fide* purchasers thereof; and no tax shall be imposed on land, the property of the United States; and in no case shall non-resident proprietors be taxed higher than residents. *Provided*, That nothing in this constitution, or in the act of Congress aforesaid, shall in any manner prejudice or affect the right of the state of Wisconsin to five hundred thousand acres of land granted to said state, and to be hereafter selected and located by, and under the act of congress, entitled "an act to appropriate the proceeds of the sales of the public lands, and grant pre-emption rights," approved September fourth, one thousand eight hundred and forty-one.

Proviso.

ARTICLE III.

SUFFRAGE.

Who are qualified electors.

SECTION 1. Every male person, of the age of twenty-one years or upwards, belonging to either of the following classes, who shall have resided in the state for one year next preceding any election, shall be deemed a qualified elector at such election:

1. White citizens of the United States.

2. White persons of foreign birth, who shall have declared their intention to become citizens, conformably to the laws of the United States on the subject of naturalization.

3. Persons of Indian blood, who have once been declared by law of congress to be citizens of the United States, any subsequent law of congress to the contrary notwithstanding.

4. Civilized persons of Indian descent, not members of any tribe. *Provided*, That the legislature may at any time,

extend by law, the right of suffrage to persons not herein enumerated; but no such law shall be in force until the same shall have been submitted to a vote of the people at a general election, and approved by a majority of all the votes cast at such election.

SEC. 2. No person under guardianship, non compos mentis, or insane, shall be qualified to vote at any election: nor shall any person convicted of treason or felony be qualified to vote at any election unless restored to civil rights. Who not.

SEC. 3. All votes shall be given by ballot, except for such township officers as may by law be directed or allowed to be otherwise chosen. Votes to be by ballot.

SEC. 4. No person shall be deemed to have lost his residence in this state by reason of his absence on business of the United States, or of this state. Absence.

SEC. 5. No soldier, seaman, or marine, in the army or navy of the United States, shall be deemed a resident of this state in consequence of being stationed within the same. Soldiers, seamen and marines.

SEC. 6. Laws may be passed excluding from the right of suffrage all persons who have been or may be convicted of bribery or larceny, or of any infamous crime, and depriving every person who shall make, or become directly or indirectly interested in any bet or wager depending upon the result of any election, from the right to vote at such election. Persons may be excluded from right of suffrage for crimes and wagers.

ARTICLE IV.

LEGISLATIVE.

SECTION 1. The legislative power shall be vested in a senate and assembly. Legislative power.

SEC. 2. The number of the members of the assembly shall never be less than fifty-four, nor more than one hundred. The senate shall consist of a number not more than one-third, nor less than one-fourth of the number of the members of the assembly. Number of members of senate and assembly.

SEC. 3. The legislature shall provide by law for an enu- Census, and of the apportionment of members. meration of the inhabitants of the state, in the year one thousand eight hundred and fifty-five, and at the end of every ten years thereafter; and at their first session after such an enumeration, and also after each enumeration made by the authority of the United States, the legislature shall apportion and district anew the members of the senate and assembly, according to the number of inhabitants, excluding Indians not taxed, and soldiers and officers of the United States army and navy.

Members of assembly how and when chosen, and districts how formed. SEC. 4. The members of the assembly shall be chosen annually by single districts, on the Tuesday succeeding the first Monday of November, by the qualified electors of the several districts; such districts to be bounded by county, precints, town, or ward lines, to consist of contiguous territory, and be in as compact form as practicable.

Senators how and when elected and classed. SEC. 5. The senators shall be chosen by single districts of convenient contiguous territory, at the same time and in the same manner as members of the assembly are required to be chosen, and no assembly district shall be divided in the formation of a senate district. Senate districts how formed and numbered. The senate districts shall be numbered in regular series, and the senators chosen by the odd numbered districts shall go out of office at the expiration of the first year, and the senators chosen by the even numbered districts shall go out of office at the expiration of the second year, and thereafter the senators shall be chosen for the term of two years.

Qualification of members. SEC. 6. No person shall be eligible to the legislature who shall not have resided one year within the state, and be a qualified elector in the district which he may be chosen to represent.

Each house to judge of its members; what to constitute a quorum. SEC. 7. Each house shall be the judge of the elections, returns and qualifications of its own members, and a majority of each shall constitute a quorum to do business; but a smaller number may adjourn from day to day, and may compel the attendance of absent members, in such manner and under such penalties as each house may provide.

SEC. 8. Each house may determine the rules of its own proceedings, punish for contempt and disorderly behavior, and, with the concurrence of two-thirds of all the members elected, expel a member; but no member shall be expelled a second time for the same cause. To determine its rules, punish for contempts and expel.

SEC. 9. Each house shall choose its own officers, and the senate shall choose a temporary president, when the lieutenant-governor shall not attend as president, or shall act as governor. To choose its own officers.

SEC. 10. Each house shall keep a journal of its proceedings, and publish the same, except such parts as require secrecy. The doors of each house shall be kept open except when the public wellfare shall require secrecy. Neither house shall, without the consent of the other, adjourn for more than three days. To keep and publish a journal; to sit with open doors, and how may adjourn.

SEC. 11. The legislature shall meet at the seat of government, at such time as shall be provided by law, once in each year, and not oftener, unless convened by the governor. Legislature where and how often to meet.

SEC. 12. No member of the legislature shall, during the term for which he was elected, be appointed or elected to any civil office in the state, which shall have been created, or the emoluments of which shall have been increased, during the term for which he was elected. No member eligible to civil office created during his term.

SEC. 13. No person being a member of congress, or holding any military or civil office under the United States, shall be eligible to a seat in the legislature; and if any person shall, after his election as a member of the legislature, be elected to congress, or be appointed to any office, civil or military, under the government of the United States, his acceptance thereof shall vacate his seat. Who ineligible, and of subsequent disability.

SEC. 14. The governor shall issue writs of election to fill such vacancies as may occur in either house of the legislature. Writs of election to fill vacancies.

Members privileged from arrest and service of civil process.

SEC. 15. Members of the legislature shall, in all cases except treason, felony, and breach of the peace, be privileged from arrest; nor shall they be subject to any civil process, during the session of the legislature, nor for fifteen days next before the commencement and after the termination of each session.

Not liable for words spoken in debate.

SEC. 16. No member of the legislature shall be liable in any civil action or criminal prosecution whatever, for words spoken in debate.

Style of laws.

SEC. 17. The style of the laws of the state shall be, "The people of the state of Wisconsin, represented in senate and assembly, do enact as follows:" and no law shall be enacted except by bill.

Private and local bills.

SEC. 18. No private or local bill, which may be passed by the legislature, shall embrace more than one subject, and that shall be expressed in the title.

Bills may originate in either house.

SEC. 19. Any bill may originate in either house of the legislature; and a bill passed by one house may be amended by the other.

Yeas and nays.

SEC. 20. The yeas and nays of the members of either house, on any question, shall, at the request of one-sixth of those present, be entered on the journal.

Compensation of members.

SEC. 21. Each member of the legislature shall receive for his services, two dollars and fifty cents for each day's attendance during the session, and ten cents for every mile he shall travel in going to and returning from the place of the meeting of the legislature, on the most usual route.

Boards of supervisors may be vested with certain powers.

SEC. 22. The legislature may confer upon the boards of supervisors of the several counties of the state, such powers, of a local, legislative, and administrative character, as they shall from time to time prescribe.

But one system of town and county government.

SEC. 23. The legislature shall establish but one system of town and county government, which shall be as nearly uniform as practicable.

SEC. 24. The legislature shall never authorize any lottery, or grant any divorce. Lotteries and divorces

SEC. 25. The legislature shall provide by law that all stationery required for the use of the state, and all printing authorized and required by them to be done for their use, or for the state, shall be let by contract to the lowest bidder; but the legislature may establish a maximum price. No member of the legislature, or other state officer, shall be interested, either directly or indirectly, in any such contract. Stationery and printing to be let to lowest bidder.

SEC. 26. The legislature shall never grant any extra compensation to any public officer, agent, servant or contractor, after the services shall have been rendered or the contract entered into. Nor shall the compensation of any public officer be increased or diminished during his term of office. Extra compensation not to be granted, nor compensation to be increased or diminished.

SEC. 27. The legislature shall direct by law in what manner and in what courts suits may be brought against the state. Suits against the State.

SEC. 28. Members of the legislature, and all officers, executive and judicial, except such inferior officers as may be by law exempted, shall, before they enter upon the duties of their respective offices, take and subscribe an oath or affirmation to support the constitution of the United States, and the constitution of the state of Wisconsin, and faithfully to discharge the duties of their respective offices to the best of their ability. Oath of office, by whom to be taken.

SEC. 29. The legislature shall determine what persons shall constitute the militia of the state, and may provide for organizing and disciplining the same, in such manner as shall be prescribed by law. Militia.

SEC. 30. In all elections to be made by the legislature, the members thereof shall vote *viva voce*, and their votes shall be entered on the journal. Elections by legislature, viva voce.

ARTICLE V.

EXECUTIVE.

Executive power vested in governor and his term of office.

SECTION 1. The executive power shall be vested in a governor, who shall hold his office for two years. A lieutenant governor shall be elected at the same time, and for the same term.

Who eligible as governor and lieutenant governor

SEC. 2. No person, except a citizen of the United States, and a qualified elector of the state, shall be eligible to the office of governor or lieutenant governor.

When and how chosen.

SEC. 3. The governor and lieutenant governor shall be elected by the qualified electors of the state, at the times and places of choosing members of the legislature. The persons respectively having the highest number of votes for governor and lieutenant governor, shall be elected. But in case two or more shall have an equal and the highest number of votes for governor or lieutenant governor, the two houses of the legislature, at its next annual session, shall forthwith, by joint ballot, choose one of the persons so having an equal and the highest number of votes for governor or lieutenant governor. The returns of election for governor and lieutenant governor shall be made in such manner as shall be provided by law.

Powers of the governor

SEC. 4. The governor shall be commander-in-chief of the military and naval forces of the state. He shall have power to convene the legislature on extraordinary occasions; and in case of invasion, or danger from the prevalence of contagious disease at the seat of government, he may convene them at any other suitable place within the state. He shall communicate to the legislature, at every session, the condition of the state, and recommend such matters to them for their consideration, as he may deem expedient. He shall transact all necessary business with the officers of the government, civil and military. He shall expedite all such measures as may be resolved upon by the legislature, and shall take care that the laws be faithfully executed.

Sec. 5. The governor shall receive, during his continuance in office, an annual compensation of one thousand two hundred and fifty dollars. His compensation.

Sec. 6. The governor shall have power to grant reprieves, commutations, and pardons, after conviction, for all offences, except treason and cases of impeachment, upon such conditions, and with such restrictions and limitations as he may think proper, subject to such regulations as may be provided by law relative to the manner of applying for pardons. Upon conviction for treason, he shall have the power to suspend the execution of the sentence until the case shall be reported to the legislature, at its next meeting, when the legislature shall either pardon, or commute the sentence, direct the execution of the sentence, or grant a further reprieve. He shall annually communicate to the legislature each case of reprieve, commutation, or pardon granted, stating the name of the convict, the crime of which he was convicted, the sentence and its date, and the date of the commutation, pardon, or reprieve, with his reasons for granting the same. His power as to reprieves, pardons, &c.

Sec. 7. In case of the impeachment of the governor, or his removal from office, death, inability from mental or physical disease, resignation, or absence from the state, the powers and duties of the office shall devolve upon the lieutenant governor, for the residue of the term, or until the governor, absent or impeached, shall have returned, or the disability shall cease. But when the governor shall, with the consent of the legislature, be out of the state in time of war, at the head of the military force thereof, he shall continue commander-in-chief of the military force of the state. When his powers and duties to devolve on lieutenant governor.

Sec. 8. The lieutenant governor shall be president of the senate, but shall have only a casting vote therein. If during a vacancy in the office of governor, the lieutenant governor shall be impeached, displaced, resign, die, or from mental or physical disease become incapable of performing the duties Lieutenant governor to be president of senate; when secretary of state to act as governor.

of his office, or be absent from the state, the secretary of state shall act as governor until the vacancy shall be filled, or the disability shall cease.

Compensation of lieutenant governor.

SEC. 9. The lieutenant governor shall receive double the per diem allowance of members of the senate, for every day's attendance as president of the senate, and the same mileage as shall be allowed to members of the legislature.

Power and duty of governor relative to bills; proceedings on bills returned by governor.

SEC. 10. Every bill which shall have passed the legislature shall, before it becomes a law, be presented to the governor. If he approve, he shall sign it; but if not, he shall return it, with his objections, to that house in which it shall have originated, who shall enter the objections at large upon the journal, and proceed to reconsider it. If, after such reconsideration, two-thirds of the members present shall agree to pass the bill, it shall be sent, together with the objections, to the other house, by which it shall likewise be reconsidered, and if approved by two-thirds of the members present, it shall become a law. But in all such cases, the votes of both houses shall be determined by yeas and nays, and the names of the members voting for or against the bill shall be entered on the journal of each house respectively. If any bill shall not be returned by the governor within three days (Sundays excepted) after it shall have been presented to him, the same shall be a law, unless the legislature shall, by their adjournment, prevent its return; in which case it shall not be a law.

ARTICLE VI.

ADMINISTRATIVE.

Election of secretary of state, treasurer and attorney general and their term of office.

SECTION 1. There shall be chosen by the qualified electors of the state, at the times and places of choosing the members of the legislature, a secretary of state, treasurer, and an attorney general, who shall severally hold their offices for the term of two years.

Duties of secretary of state and his

SEC. 2. The secretary of state shall keep a fair record of the official acts of the legislature and executive department of the state, and shall, when required, lay the same and all matters relative thereto before either branch of the legislature. He shall be *ex-officio* auditor, and shall perform such other duties as shall be assigned him by law. He shall receive as a compensation for his services, yearly, such sum as shall be provided by law, and shall keep his office at the seat of government. compensation.

SEC. 3. The powers, duties, and compensation of the treasurer and attorney general shall be prescribed by law. Same of treasurer and attorney general.

SEC. 4. Sheriffs, coroners, registers of deeds, and district attorneys shall be chosen by the electors of the respective counties, once in every two years, and as often as vacancies shall happen. Sheriff's shall hold no other office, and be ineligible for two years next succeeding the termination of their offices. They may be required by law to renew their security from time to time; and in default of giving such new security, their offices shall be deemed vacant. But the county shall never be made responsible for the acts of the sheriff. The governor may remove any officer in this section mentioned, giving to such officer a copy of the charges against him, and an opportunity of being heard in his defence. Sheriffs coroners, registers of deeds and district attorneys, how chosen and term of office, &c.; may be removed by governor.

ARTICLE VII.

JUDICIARY.

SECTION 1. The court for the trial of impeachments shall be composed of the senate. The house of represantatives shall have the power of impeaching all civil officers of this state, for corrupt conduct in office, or for crimes and misdemeanors; but a majority of all the members elected shall concur in an impeachment. On the trial of an impeachment against the governor, the lieutenant governor shall not act as a member of the court. No judicial officer shall exercise his office after he shall have been impeached, until his acquittal. Before the trial of an impeachment, the members of the court shall take an oath or affirmation truly and impartially to try Of impeachments, and mode of proceeding therein, and extent of judgment.

the impeachment, according to evidence ; and no person shall be convicted without the concurrence of two-thirds of the members present. Judgment in cases of impeachment shall not extend further than to removal from office, or removal from office and disqualification to hold any office of honor, profit, or trust, under the state ; but the party impeached shall be liable to indictment, trial and punishment according to law.

Judicial power where vested.

SEC. 2. The judicial power of this state, both as to matters of law and equity, shall be vested in a supreme court, circuit courts, courts of probate, and in justices of the peace. The legislature may also vest such jurisdiction as shall be deemed necessary in municipal courts, and shall have power to establish inferior courts in the several counties, with limited civil and criminal jurisdiction : *Provided*, That the jurisdiction which may be vested in municipal courts shall not exceed, in their respective municipalities, that of circuit courts in their respective circuits, as prescribed in this constitution ; and that the legislature shall provide as well for the election of judges of the municipal courts as of the judges of inferior courts, by the qualified electors of the respective jurisdictions. The term of office of the judges of the said municipal and inferior courts shall not be longer than that of the judges of the circuit courts.

Election and term of office of judges of municipal and inferior courts.

Jurisdiction and powers of supreme court.

SEC. 3. The supreme court, except in cases otherwise provided in this constitution, shall have appellate jurisdiction only, which shall be co-extensive with the state ; but in no case removed to the supreme court, shall a trial by jury be allowed. The supreme court shall have a general superintending control over all inferior courts ; it shall have power to issue writs of habeas corpus, mandamus, injunction, quo warranto, certiorari, and other original and remedial writs, and to hear and determine the same.

Circuit judges to be judges of su-

SEC. 4. For the term of five years, and thereafter until the legislature shall otherwise provide, the judges of the several circuit courts shall be judges of the supreme court, four of whom shall constitute a quorum, and the concurrence of a majority of the judges present shall be necessary to a decision. The legislature shall have power, if they should think it expedient and necessary, to provide by law, for the organization of a separate supreme court, with the jurisdiction and powers prescribed in this constitution, to consist of one chief justice and two associate justices, to be elected by the qualified electors of the state, at such time and in such manner as the legislature may provide. The separate supreme court, when so organized, shall not be changed or discontinued by the legislature; the judges thereof shall be so classified that but one of them shall go out of office at the same time, and their term of office shall be the same as is provided for the judges of the circuit court. And whenever the legislature may consider it necessary to establish a separate supreme court, they shall have power to reduce the number of circuit judges to four, and subdivide the judicial circuits, but no such subdivision or reduction shall take effect until after the expiration of the term of some one of the said judges, or until a vacancy occur by some other means.

preme court; what number to constitute a quorum.

Separate supreme court may be established, &c.

SEC. 5. The state shall be divided into five judicial circuits, to be composed as follows: The first circuit shall comprise the counties of Racine, Walworth, Rock, and Green. The second circuit, the counties of Milwaukee, Waukesha, Jefferson, and Dane. The third circuit, the counties of Washington, Dodge, Columbia, Marquette, Sauk, and Portage. The fourth circuit, the counties of Brown, Manitowoc, Sheboygan, Fond du Lac, Winnebago, and Calumet. And the fifth circuit shall comprise the counties of Iowa, Lafayette, Grant, Crawford, and St. Croix; and the county of Richland shall be attached to Iowa, the county of Chippewa to the county of Crawford, and the county of La Pointe to the county of St. Croix, for judical purposes, until otherwise provided by the legislature.

Judicial circuits.

Number of circuits may be increased and limits altered.

SEC. 6. The legislature may alter the limits, or increase the number of circuits, making them as compact and convenient as practicable, and bounding them by county lines, but no such alteration or increase shall have the effect to remove a judge from office. In case of an increase of circuits, the judge or judges shall be elected as provided in this constitution, and receive a salary not less than that herein provided for judges of the circuit court.

Judge to be elected for each circuit and to reside therein.

Designation of chief justice and classification of judges.

SEC. 7. For each circuit there shall be a judge chosen by the qualified electors therein, who shall hold his office as is provided in this constitution, and until his successor shall be chosen and qualified ; and after he shall have been elected, he shall reside in the circuit for which he was elected. One of said judges shall be designated as chief justice, in such manner as the legislature shall provide. And the legislature shall, at its first session, provide by law, as well for the election of, as for classifying the judges of the circuit court, to be elected under this constitution in such manner that one of said judges shall go out of office in two years, one in three years, one in four years, one in five years, and one in six years, and thereafter the judge elected to fill the office shall hold the same for six years.

Jurisdiction and powers of circuit courts.

SEC. 8. The circuit courts shall have original jurisdiction in all matters, civil and criminal, within this state, not excepted in this constitution, and not hereafter prohibited by law, and appellate jurisdiction from all inferior courts and tribunals, and a supervisory control over the same. They shall also have the power to issue writs of habeas corpus, mandamus, injunction, quo warranto, certiorari, and all other writs necessary to carry into effect their orders, judgments, and decrees, and give them a general control over inferior courts and jurisdictions.

Vacancies how filled.

SEC. 9. When a vacancy shall happen in the office of judge of the supreme or circuit courts, such vacancy shall be filled by an appointment of the Governor, which shall continue until a successor is elected and qualified ; and when elected, such successor shall hold his office the residue of the unexpired term. There shall be no election for a judge or judges at any general election for state or county officers, nor within thirty days either before or after such election.

Judges not to be elected at general election.

SEC. 10. Each of the judges of the supreme and circuit courts shall receive a salary, payable quarterly, of not less than one thousand five hundred dollars annually ; they shall receive no fees of office, or other compensation than their salaries ; they shall hold no office of public trust, except a judicial office, during the term for which they are respectively elected, and all votes for either of them, for any office except a judicial office, given by the legislature or the people, shall be void. No person shall be eligible to the office of judge, who shall not, at the time of his election, be a citizen of the United States, and have attained the age of twenty-five years, and be a qualified elector within the jurisdiction for which he may be chosen.

Salary of judges.

Disqualified from holding other office and who eligible.

SEC. 11. The supreme court shall hold at least one term annually, at the seat of government of the state, at such time as shall be provided by law, and the legislature may provide for holding other terms, and at other places, when they may deem it necessary. A circuit court shall be held at least twice in each year, in each county of this state, organized for judicial purposes. The judges of the circuit court may hold courts for each other, and shall do so when required by law.

Terms of supreme and circuit courts and interchange of judges.

SEC. 12. There shall be a clerk of the circuit court chosen in each county organized for judicial purposes, by the qualified electors thereof, who shall hold his office for two years, subject to removal, as shall be provided by law. In case of a vacancy, the judge of the circuit court shall have the power to appoint a clerk, until the vacancy shall be filled by an election. The clerk thus elected or appointed, shall give such

Clerks of the circuit court, and clerk of the supreme court.

security as the legislature may require; and when elected, shall hold his office for a full term. The supreme court shall appoint its own clerk, and the clerk of a circuit court may be appointed clerk of the supreme court.

Removal of judges.

SEC. 13. Any judge of the supreme or circuit court may be removed from office by address of both houses of the legislature, if two-thirds of all the members elected to each house concur therein, but no removal shall be made by virtue of this section, unless the judge complained of shall have been served with a copy of the charges against him, as the ground of address, and shall have had an opportunity of being heard in his defence. On the question of removal, the ayes and noes shall be entered on the journals.

Judge of probate.

SEC. 14. There shall be chosen in each county, by the qualified electors thereof, a judge of probate, who shall hold his office for two years, and until his successor shall be elected and qualified, and whose jurisdiction, powers and duties shall be prescribed by law: *Provided, however,* That the legislature shall have power to abolish the office of judge of probate in any county, and to confer probate powers upon such inferior courts as may be established in said county.

Office may be abolished.

Justices of the peace, their term of office and classification

SEC. 15. The electors of the several towns, at their annual town meetings, and the electors of cities and villages, at their charter elections, shall in such manner as the legislature may direct, elect justices of the peace, whose term of office shall be for two years, and until their successors in office shall be elected and qualified. In case of an election to fill a vacancy occurring before the expiration of a full term, the justice elected shall hold for the residue of the unexpired term. Their number and classification shall be regulated by law; and the tenure of two years shall in no wise interfere with the classification in the first instance. The justices thus elected shall have such civil and criminal jurisdiction as shall be prescribed by law.

Sec. 16. The legislature shall pass laws for the regulation of tribunals of conciliation, defining their powers and duties. Such tribunals may be established in and for any township, and shall have power to render judgment, to be obligatory on the parties, when they shall voluntarily submit their matter in difference to arbitration, and agree to abide the judgment, or assent thereto in writing. Tribunals of conciliation.

Sec. 17. The style of all writs and process shall be, "The state of Wisconsin." All criminal prosecutions shall be carried on in the name and by the authority of the same; and all indictments shall conclude against the peace and dignity of the state. Style of writs and how criminal prosecutions conducted, &c.

Sec. 18. The legislature shall impose a tax on all civil suits commenced or prosecuted in the municipal, inferior, or circuit courts, which shall constitute a fund to be applied toward the payment of the salary of judges. Tax on civil suits.

Sec. 19. The testimony in causes in equity, shall be taken in like manner as in cases at law; and the office of master in chancery, is hereby prohibited. Testimony in equity, &c.

Sec. 20. Any suitor in any court of this state, shall have the right to prosecute or defend his suit either in his own proper person or by an attorney or agent of his choice. Suitors may prosecute or defend in person or by attorney.

Sec. 21. The legislature shall provide by law for the speedy publication of all statute laws, and of such judicial decisions made within the state, as may be deemed expedient. And no general law shall be in force until published. Legislature to provide for publication of laws and decisions; and no law to be in force until published.

Sec. 22. The legislature at its first session after the adoption of this constitution, shall provide for the appointment of three commissioners, whose duty it shall be to inquire into, revise and simplify the rules of practice, pleadings, forms, and proceedings, and arrange a system adapted to the courts of record of this state, and report the same to the legislature, subject to their modification and adoption; and such commission shall terminate upon the rendering of the report, unless otherwise provided by law. Legislature to appoint commissioners to revise practice, &c.

Judicial powers may be vested in certain persons.

SEC. 23. The legislature may provide for the appointment of one or more persons in each organized county, and may vest in such persons such judicial powers as shall be prescribed by law: *Provided,* That said power shall not exceed that of a judge of the circuit court at chambers.

ARTICLE VIII.

FINANCE.

Rule of taxation to be uniform.

SECTION 1. The rule of taxation shall be uniform, and taxes shall be levied upon such property as the legislature shall prescribe.

How money to be paid out of treasury.

SEC. 2. No money shall be paid out of the treasury, except in pursuance of an appropriation by law.

Credit of the State not to be given for private purposes.

SEC. 3. The credit of the state shall never be given or loaned in aid of any individual, association, or corporation.

State not to contract debt except in certain cases.

SEC. 4. The state shall never contract any public debt, except in the cases and manner herein provided.

Annual tax to be levied to defray state expenses.

SEC. 5. The legislature shall provide for an annual tax sufficient to defray the estimated expenses of the state for each year; and whenever the expenses of any year shall exceed the income, the legislature shall provide for levying a tax for the ensuing year, sufficient, with other sources of income, to pay the deficiency, as well as the estimated expenses of such ensuing year.

For what purpose, to what extent and how public debt may be contracted.

SEC. 6. For the purpose of defraying extraordinary expenditures, the state may contract public debts; but such debts shall never in the aggregate exceed one hundred thousand dollars. Every such debt shall be authorized by law, for some purpose or purposes to be distinctly specified therein; and the vote of a majority of all the members elected to each house, to be taken by yeas and nays, shall be necessary to the passage of such law; and every such law shall provide for levying an annual tax sufficient to pay the annual interest of such debt, and the principal within five years from the passage of such law, and shall specially appropriate the proceeds of such taxes to the payment of such principal and interest; and such appropriation shall not be repealed, nor the taxes be postponed or diminished until the principal and interest of such debt shall have been wholly paid.

SEC. 7. The legislature may also borrow money to repel invasion, suppress insurrection, or defend the state in time of war; but the money thus raised shall be applied exclusively to the object for which the loan was authorized, or to the re-payment of the debt thereby created.

When legislature may borrow money and how to be applied

SEC. 8. On the passage in either house of the legislature, of any law which imposes, continues, or renews a tax, or creates a debt or charge, or makes, continues, or renews an appropriation of public or trust money, or releases, discharges, or commutes a claim or demand of the state, the question shall be taken by yeas and nays, which shall be duly entered on the journal; and three-fifths of all the members elected to such house, shall in all such cases be required to constitute a quorum therein.

Passage of laws imposing taxes, &c., to be by yeas and nays, and three-fifths of each house to constitute a quorum.

SEC. 9. No scrip, certificate, or other evidence of state debt whatsoever, shall be issued, except for such debts as are authorized by the sixth and seventh sections of this article.

When only state scrip may be issued.

SEC. 10. The state shall never contract any debt for works of internal improvement, or be a party in carrying on such works; but whenever grants of land, or other property, shall have been made to the state, especially dedicated by the grant to particular works of internal improvement, the state may carry on such particular works, and shall devote thereto the avails of such grants, and may pledge or appropriate the revenues derived from such works in aid of their completion.

State not to contract debt for internal improvement, but may apply the avails of grants &c., to that purpose.

ARTICLE IX.

EMINENT DOMAIN AND PROPERTY OF THE STATE.

SECTION 1. The state shall have concurrent jurisdiction on all rivers and lakes bordering on this state, so far as such rivers or lakes shall form a common boundary to the state,

Concurrent jurisdiction of state.

Navigable rivers to be common highways.

and any other state or territory now or hereafter to be formed and bounded by the same. And the river Mississippi, and the navigable waters leading into the Mississippi and St. Lawrence, and the carrying places between the same, shall be common highways, and forever free, as well to the inhabitants of the state as to the citizens of the United States, without any tax, impost, or duty therefor.

Lands and other property of the territory to vest in the state.

SEC. 2. The title to all lands, and other property, which have accrued to the territory of Wisconsin, by grant, gift, purchase, forfeiture, escheat, or otherwise, shall vest in the state of Wisconsin.

Ultimate property of lands in the people of the state, and when no heirs to escheat to the people.

SEC. 3. The people of the state, in their right of sovereignty, are declared to possess the ultimate property in and to all lands within the jurisdiction of the state; and all lands, the title to which shall fail from a defect of heirs, shall revert or escheat to the people.

ARTICLE X.

EDUCATION.

State superintendent of public instruction, how elected, and his compensation.

SECTION 1. The supervision of public instruction shall be vested in a state superintendent, and such other officers as the legislature shall direct. The state superintendent shall be chosen by the qualified electors of the state, in such manner as the legislature shall provide; his powers, duties and compensation shall be prescribed by law: *Provided,* That his compensation shall not exceed the sum of twelve hundred dollars annually.

What to constitute school fund, to be set apart and how interest applied.

SEC. 2. The proceeds of all lands that have been or hereafter may be granted by the United States to this state, for educational purposes, (except the lands heretofore granted for the purposes of a university,) and all moneys, and the clear proceeds of all property, that may accrue to the state by forfeiture or escheat, and all moneys which may be paid as an equivalent for exemption from military duty, and the clear proceeds of all fines collected in the several counties for any breach of the penal laws, and all moneys arising from any grant to the state, where the purposes of such grant are not specified, and the five hundred thousand acres of land to which the state is entitled by the provisions of an act of congress, entitled "an act to appropriate the proceeds of the sales of the public lands, and to grant pre-emption rights," approved the fourth day of September, one thousand eight hundred and forty-one, and also the five *per centum* of the nett proceeds of the public lands to which the state shall become entitled on her admission into the union, (if congress shall consent to such appropriation of the two grants last mentioned,) shall be set apart as a separate fund, to be called the school fund, the interest of which, and all other revenues derived from the school lands, shall be exclusively applied to the following objects, to wit:

1. To the support and maintenance of common schools in each school district, and the purchase of suitable libraries and apparatus therefor.

2. The residue shall be appropriated to the support and maintenance of academies and normal schools, and suitable libraries and apparatus therefor.

District schools to be established by law, and to be free and not sectarian.

SEC. 3. The legislature shall provide by law for the establishment of district schools, which shall be as nearly uniform as practicable, and such schools shall be free and without charge for tuition to all children between the ages of four and twenty years, and no sectarian instruction shall be allowed therein.

Annual tax to be raised for support of schools, and amount thereof.

SEC. 4. Each town and city shall be required to raise, by tax, annually, for the support of common schools therein, a sum not less than one-half the amount received by such town or city respectively for school purposes, from the income of the school fund.

Income of school fund; how to be distributed, and when

SEC. 5. Provision shall be made by law for the distribution of the income of the school fund among the several towns and cities of the state, for the support of common distribution not to be made. schools therein, in some just proportion to the number of children and youth resident therein, between the ages of four and twenty years, and no appropriation shall be made from the school fund to any city or town, for the year in which said city or town shall fail to raise such tax, nor to any school district for the year in which a school shall not be maintained at least three months.

State university to be established; what to constitute university funds and how the interest is to be applied.

SEC. 6. Provision shall be made by law for the establishment of a state university, at or near the seat of state government, and for connecting with the same from time to time such colleges in different parts of the state, as the interests of education may requre. The proceeds of all lands that have been or may hereafter be granted by the United States to the state for the support of a university, shall be and remain a perpetual fund to be called the "university fund," the interest of which shall be appropriated to the support of the state university, and no sectarian instruction shall be allowed in such university.

Commissioners for the sale of the school and university lands and the investment of the funds.

SEC. 7. The secretary of state, treasurer, and attorney general shall constitute a board of commissioners for the sale of the school and university lands. and for the investment of the funds arising therefrom. Any two of said commissioners shall be a quorum for the transaction of all business pertaining to the duties of their office.

Lands to be sold after appraisal and unpaid purchase money to be secured.

SEC. 8. Provision shall be made by law for the sale of all school and university lands, after they shall have been appraised, and when any portion of such lands shall be sold, and the purchase money shall not be paid at the time of the sale, the commissioners shall take security by martgage upon the land sold for the sum remaining unpaid, with seven per cent. interest thereon, payable annually at the office of the treasurer. The commissioners shall be authorized to execute a good and sufficient conveyance to all purchasers of such lands, and to discharge any mortgages taken as security, when the sum due thereon shall have been paid. The commissioners shall have power to withhold from sale any portion of such lands when they shall deem it expedient, and shall invest all moneys arising from the sale of such lands, as well as all other university and school funds, in such manner as the legislature shall provide, and shall give such security for the faithful performance of their duties as may be required by law. Commissioners may withhold lands from sale and shall invest moneys, &c.

ARTICLE XI.

CORPORATIONS.

SECTION 1. Corporations without banking powers or privileges may be formed under general laws, but shall not be created by special act, except for municipal purposes, and in cases where, in the judgment of the legislature, the objects of the corporation cannot be attained under general laws. All general laws or special acts enacted under the provisions of this section may be altered or repealed by the legislature at any time after their passage. Corporations other than banking how to be formed; all corporation laws may be altered or repealed.

SEC. 2. No municipal corporation shall take private property for public use against the consent of the owner, without the necessity thereof being first established by the verdict of a jury. Private property when not to be taken by municipal corporations.

SEC. 3. It shall be the duty of the legislature, and they are hereby empowered to provide for the organization of cities and incorporated villages, and to restrict their power of taxation, assessment, borrowing money, contracting debts, and loaning their credit, so as to prevent abuses in assessments and taxation, and in contracting debts by such municipal corporations. Legislature to provide for organization of cities and villages and to restrict their power of taxation, &c.

SEC. 4. The legislature shall not have power to create, authorize, or incorporate, by any general or special law, any bank or banking power or privilege, or any institution or corporation, having any banking power or privilege whatever, except as provided in this article. Not to create or authorize banks or banking except as provided in next section.

Banks how may be created.

SEC. 5. The legislature may submit to the voters at any general election, the question of "bank or no bank," and if at any such election a number of votes equal to a majority of all the votes cast at such election on that subject shall be in favor of banks, then the legislature shall have power to grant bank charters, or to pass a general banking law, with such restrictions and under such regulations as they may deem expedient and proper for the security of the bill holders: *Provided,* That no such grant or law shall have any force or effect until the same shall have been submitted to a vote of the electors of the state at some general election, and been approved by a majority of the votes cast on that subject at such election.

ARTICLE XII.

AMENDMENTS.

How constitution may be amended.

SECTION 1. Any amendment or amendments to this constitution may be proposed in either house of the legislature, and if the same shall be agreed to by a majority of the members elected to each of the two houses, such proposed amendment or amendments shall be entered on their journals with the yeas and nays taken thereon, and referred to the legislature to be chosen at the next general election, and shall be published for three months previous to the time of holding such election. And if in the legislature so next chosen, such proposed amendment or amendments shall be agreed to by a majority of all the members elected to each house, then it shall be the duty of the legislature to submit such proposed amendment or amendments to the people, in such manner and at such time as the legislature shall prescribe, and if the people shall approve and ratify such amendment or amendments by a majority of the electors voting thereon, such amendment or amendments shall become part of the constitution: *Provided,* That if more than one amendment be submitted, they shall be submitted in such manner that the people may vote for or against such amendments separately.

SEC. 2. If at any time a majority of the senate and assembly shall deem it necessary to call a convention to revise or change this constitution, they shall recommend to the electors to vote for or against a convention at the next election for members of the legislature; and if it shall appear that a majority of the electors voting thereon have voted for a convention, the legislature shall at its next session provide for calling such convention. When and how convention to revise or change constitution may be called.

ARTICLE XIII.

MISCELLANEOUS PROVISIONS.

SECTION 1. The political year for the state of Wisconsin shall commence on the first Monday in January in each year, and the general election shall be holden on the Tuesday succeeding the first Monday in November in each year. Political year when to commence; when general election to be held.

SEC. 2. Any inhabitant of this state who may hereafter be engaged, either directly or indirectly, in a duel, either as principal or accessary, shall forever be disqualified as an elector, and from holding any office under the constitution and laws of this state, and may be punished in such other manner as shall be prescribed by law. Inhabitants of state engaged in a duel to be disqualified as electors and from holding office.

SEC. 3. No member of congress, nor any person holding any office of profit or trust under the United States, (postmasters excepted,) or under any foreign power; no person convicted of any infamous crime in any court within the United States, and no person being a defaulter to the United States, or to this state, or to any county or town therein, or to any state or territory within the United States, shall be eligible to any office of trust, profit, or honor in this state. Who ineligible to office in this state.

SEC. 4. It shall be the duty of the legislature to provide a great seal for the state, which shall be kept by the secretary of state; and all official acts of the governor, his approbation of the laws excepted, shall be thereby authenticated. Great seal of state to be provided and to be kept by secretary, &c.

SEC. 5. All persons residing upon Indian lands within any county of the state, and qualified to exercise the right of Persons residing on Indian lands where may vote. suffrage under this constitution, shall be entitled to vote at the polls which may be held nearest their residence, for state, United States, or county officers: *Provided*, That no person shall vote for county officers out of the county in which he resides.

Elective officers of legislature. SEC. 6. The elective officers of the legislature, other than the presiding officers, shall be a chief-clerk, and a sergeant-at-arms, to be elected by each house.

When county not to be divided without vote of the people. SEC. 7. No county with an area of nine hundred square miles or less, shall be divided, or have any part stricken therefrom, without submitting the question to a vote of the people of the county, nor unless a majority of all the legal voters of the county voting on the question, shall vote for the same.

How county seat to be removed. SEC. 8. No county seat shall be removed until the point to which it is proposed to be removed, shall be fixed by law, and a majority of the voters of the county, voting on the question, shall have voted in favor of its removal to such point.

How certain officers to be elected or appointed. SEC. 9. All county officers whose election or appointment is not provided for by this constitution, shall be elected by the electors of the respective counties, or appointed by the boards of supervisors, or other county authorities, as the legislature shall direct. All city, town, and village officers, whose election or appointment is not provided for by this constitution, shall be elected by the electors of such cities, towns and villages, or of some division thereof, or appointed by such authorities thereof, as the legislature shall designate for that purpose. All other officers whose election or appointment is not provided for by this constitution, and all officers whose offices may hereafter be created by law, shall be elected by the people, or appointed as the legislature may direct.

Legislature may declare when offices SEC. 10. The legislature may declare the cases in which any office shall be deemed vacant, and also the manner of filling the vacancy where no provision is made for that purpose, in this constitution. vacant and the manner of filling same.

ARTICLE XIV.

SCHEDULE.

SECTION 1. That no inconvenience may arise by reason of a change from a territorial to a permanent state government, it is declared that all rights, actions, prosecutions, judgments, claims, and contracts, as well of individuals as of bodies corporate, shall continue as if no such change had taken place, and all process which may be issued under the authority of the territory of Wisconsin, previous to its admission into the union of the United States, shall be as valid as if issued in the name of the state. All rights to continue and process to be as valid as if no change in government.

SEC. 2. All laws now in force in the territory of Wisconsin, which are not repugnant to this constitution, shall remain in force until they expire by their own limitation, or be altered or repealed by the legislature. Existing laws to remain in force until they expire or are altered.

SEC. 3. All fines, penalties, or forfeitures, accruing to the territory of Wisconsin, shall enure to the use of the state. Fines, &c., accruing to the territory to enure to use of state.

SEC. 4. All recognizances heretofore taken, or which may be taken before the change from territorial to a permanent state government, shall remain valid, and shall pass to, and may be prosecuted in the name of the state, and all bonds executed to the governor of the territory, or to any other officer or court, in his or their official capacity, shall pass to the governor or state authority, and their successors in office, for the uses therein respectively expressed, and may be sued for and recovered accordingly; and all the estate or property, real, personal, or mixed, and all judgments, bonds, specialties, choses in action, and claims or debts of whatsoever description, of the territory of Wisconsin, shall enure to and vest in the state of Wisconsin, and may be sued for and recovered in the same manner and to the same extent, by the Recognizances and bonds executed to officers to remain valid; and all property of the territory to vest in the state.

state of Wisconsin, as the same could have been by the territory of Wisconsin. All criminal prosecutions and penal actions, which may have arisen, or which may arise before the change from a territorial to a state government, and which shall then be pending, shall be prosecuted to judgment and execution in the name of the state. All offences committed against the laws of the territory of Wisconsin, before the change from a territorial to a state government, and which shall not be prosecuted before such change, may be prosecuted in the name and by the authority of the state of Wisconsin, with like effect as though such change had not taken place ; and all penalties incurred shall remain the same as if this constitution had not been adopted. All actions at law, and suits in equity, which may be pending in any of the courts of the territory of Wisconsin, at the time of the change from a territorial to a state government, may be continued and transferred to any court of the state which shall have jurisdiction of the subject matter thereof.

Criminal suits and offences to be prosecuted and civil actions to be continued.

Existing officers to continue in office until superseded.

SEC. 5. All officers, civil and military, now holding their offices under the authority of the United States, or of the territory of Wisconsin, shall continue to hold and exercise their respective offices until they shall be superseded by the authority of the state.

Seat of government and first session when and where to be held.

SEC. 6. The first session of the legislature of the state of Wisconsin shall commence on the first Monday in June next, and shall be held at the village of Madison, which shall be and remain the seat of government until otherwise provided by law.

Existing county and town officers to hold over until removed or superseded.

SEC. 7. All county, precinct, and township officers, shall continue to hold their respective offices, unless removed by the competent authority, until the legislature shall in conformity with the provisions of this constitution, provide for the holding of elections to fill such offices respectively.

Copy of constitution, &c. to be trans-

SEC. 8. The president of this convention shall immediately after its adjournment, cause a fair copy of this constitution, together with a copy of the act of the legislature of this territory, entitled "An act in relation to the formation of a state government in Wisconsin, and to change the time of holding the annual session of the legislature," approved October 27th, 1847, providing for the calling of this convention; and also a copy of so much of the last census of this territory as exhibits the number of its inhabitants, to be forwarded to the President of the United States, to be laid before the congress of the United States at its present session. mitted to the president.

SEC. 9. This constitution shall be submitted at an election to be held on the second Monday in March next, for ratification or rejection, to all white male persons of the age of twenty-one years, or upwards, who shall then be residents of this territory and citizens of the United States, or shall have declared their intention to become such in conformity with the laws of congress on the subject of naturalization; and all persons having such qualifications shall be entitled to vote for or against the adoption of this constitution, and for all officers first elected under it. And if the constitution be ratified by the said electors, it shall become the constitution of the state of Wisconsin. On such of the ballots as are for the constitution, shall be written or printed the word "yes;" and on such as are against the constitution, the word "no." The election shall be conducted in the manner now prescribed by law, and the returns made by the clerks of the boards of supervisors or county commissioners (as the case may be) to the governor of the territory, at any time before the tenth day of April next. And in the event of the ratification of this constitution, by a majority of all the votes given, it shall be the duty of the governor of this territory to make proclamation of the same, and to transmit a digest of the returns to the senate and assembly of the state, on the first day of their session. An election shall be held for governor and lieutenant governor, treasurer, attorney-general, members of the state legislature, and members of congress, on the second

Constitution to be submitted for ratification or rejection; who entitled to vote thereon, &c.

First election for governor, &c., when to be held.

Monday of May next, and no other or further notice of such election shall be required.

Congressional districts.

SEC. 10. Two members of congress shall also be elected on the second Monday of May next; and until otherwise provided by law, the counties of Milwaukee, Waukesha, Jefferson, Racine, Walworth, Rock and Green, shall constitute the first congressional district, and elect one member; and the counties of Washington, Sheboygan, Manitowoc, Calumet, Brown, Winnebago, Fond du Lac, Marquette, Sauk, Portage, Columbia, Dodge, Dane, Iowa, La Fayette, Grant, Richland, Crawford, Chippewa, St. Croix and La Pointe, shall constitute the second congressional district, and shall elect one member.

First elections, how to be conducted and returns made, &c.

SEC. 11. The several elections provided for in this article shall be conducted according to the existing laws of the territory: *Provided,* That no elector shall be entitled to vote, except in the town, ward, or precinct where he resides. The returns of election for senators and members of Assembly, shall be transmitted to the clerk of the board of supervisors, or county commissioners, as the case may be, and the votes shall be canvassed, and certificates of election issued, as now provided by law. In the first senatorial district, the returns of the election for senator shall be made to the proper officer in the county of Brown; in the second senatorial district, to the proper officer in the county of Columbia; in the third senatorial district, to the proper officer in the county of Crawford; in the fourth senatorial district, to the proper officer in the county of Fond du Lac; and in the fifth senatorial district, to the proper officer in the county of Iowa. The returns of election for state officers and members of congress, shall be certified and transmitted to the speaker of the assembly at the seat of government, in the same manner as the votes for delegate to congress are required to be certified and returned by the laws of the territory of Wisconsin, to the secretary of said territory, and in such time that they may be received on the first Monday in June next ; and as soon as the legislature shall be organized, the speaker of the assembly and the president of the senate shall, in the presence of both houses, examine the returns, and declare who are duly elected to fill the several offices hereinbefore mentioned, and give to each of the persons elected a certificate of his election.

Senate and Assembly districts.

SEC. 12. Until there shall be a new apportionment, the senators and members of the assembly shall be apportioned among the several districts, as hereinafter mentioned, and each district shall be entitled to elect one senator or member of the assembly, as the case may be.

The counties of Brown, Calumet, Manitowoc and Sheboygan, shall constitute the first senate district.

The counties of Columbia, Marquette, Portage and Sauk, shall constitute the second senate district.

The counties of Crawford, Chippewa, St. Croix and La Pointe, shall constitute the third senate district.

The counties of Fond du Lac and Winnebago, shall constitute the fourth senate district.

The counties of Iowa and Richland, shall constitute the fifth senate district.

The county of Grant shall constitute the sixth senate district.

The counnty of La Fayette shall constitute the seventh senate district.

The county of Green shall constitute the eighth senate district.

The county of Dane shall constitute the ninth senate district.

The county of Dodge shall constitute the tenth senate district.

The county of Washington shall constitute the eleventh senate district.

The county of Jefferson shall constitute the twelfth senate district.

The county of Waukesha shall constitute the thirteenth senate district.

The county of Walworth shall constitute the fourteenth senate district.

The county of Rock shall constitute the fifteenth senate district.

The towns of Southport, Pike, Pleasant Prairie, Paris, Bristol, Brighton, Salem and Wheatland, in the county of Racine, shall constitute the sixteenth senate district.

The towns of Racine, Caledonia, Mount Pleasant, Raymond, Norway, Rochester, Yorkville and Burlington, in the county of Racine, shall constitute the seventeenth senate district.

The third, fourth and fifth wards of the city of Milwaukee, and the towns of Lake, Oak Creek, Franklin and Greenfield, in the county of Milwaukee, shall constitute the eighteenth senate district.

The first and second wards of the city of Milwaukee, and the towns of Milwaukee, Wauwatosa and Granville, in the county of Milwaukee, shall constitute the nineteenth senate district.

The county of Brown shall constitute an assembly district.

The county of Calumet shall constitute an assembly district.

The county of Manitowoc shall constitute an assembly district.

The county of Columbia shall constitute an assembly district.

The counties of Crawford and Chippewa shall constitute an assembly district.

The counties of St. Croix and La Pointe shall constitute an assembly district.

The towns of Windsor, Sun Prairie, and Cottage Grove, in the county of Dane, shall constitute an assembly district.

The towns of Madison, Cross Plains, Clarkson, Springfield, Verona, Montrose, Oregon and Greenfield, in the county of Dane, shall constitute an assembly district.

The towns of Rome, Dunkirk, Christiana, Albion and Rutland, in the county of Dane, shall constitute an assembly district.

The towns of Burnett, Chester, Le Roy and Williamstown, in the county of Dodge, shall constitute an assembly district.

The towns of Fairfield, Hubbard and Rubicon, in the county of Dodge, shall constitute an assembly district.

The towns of Hustisford, Ashippun, Lebanon and Emmet, in the county of Dodge, shall constitute an assembly district.

The towns of Elba, Lowell, Portland and Clyman, in the county of Dodge, shall constitute an assembly district.

The towns of Calamus, Beaver Dam, Fox Lake and Trenton, in the county of Dodge, shall constitute an assembly district.

The towns of Calumet, Forest, Auburn, Byron, Taychedah and Fond du Lac, in the county of Fond du Lac, shall constitute an assembly district.

The towns of Alto, Metoman, Ceresco, Rosendale, Waupun, Oakfield and Seven Mile Creek, in the county of Fond du Lac, shall constitute an assembly district.

The precincts of Hazel Green, Fairplay, Smeltzer's Grove and Jamestown, in the county of Grant, shall constitute an assembly district.

The precincts of Plattville, Head of Platte, Centerville, Muscoday and Fennimore, in the county of Grant, shall constitute an assembly district.

The precincts of Pleasant Valley, Potosi, Waterloo, Hurricane and New Lisbon, in the county of Grant, shall constitute an assembly district.

The precincts of Beetown, Patch Grove, Cassville, Millville and Lancaster, in the county of Grant, shall constitute an assembly district.

The county of Green shall constitute an assembly district.

The precincts of Dallas, Pedlar's Creek, Mineral Point and Yellow Stone, in the county of Iowa, shall constitute an assembly district.

The precincts of Franklin, Dodgeville, Porter's Grove, Arena and Percussion, in the county of Iowa, and the county of Richland, shall constitute an assembly district.

The towns of Watertown, Aztalan and Waterloo, in the county of Jefferson, shall constitute an assembly district.

The towns of Ixonia, Concord, Sullivan, Hebron, Cold Spring and Palmyra, in the county of Jefferson, shall constitute an assembly district.

The towns of Lake Mills, Oakland, Koskonong, Farmington and Jefferson, in the county of Jefferson, shall constitute an assembly district.

The precincts of Benton, Elk Grove, Belmont, Willow Springs, Prairie, and that part of Shullsburgh precinct north of town one, in the county of La Fayette, shall constitute an assembly district.

The precincts of Wiota, Wayne, Gratiot, White Oak Springs, Fever River, and that part of Shullsburgh precinct south of town two, in the county of La Fayette, shall constitute an assembly district.

The county of Marquette shall constitute an assembly district.

The first ward of the city of Milwaukee shall constitute an assembly district.

The second ward of the city of Milwaukee shall constitute an assembly district.

The third ward of the city of Milwaukee shall constitute an assembly district.

The fourth and fifth wards of the city of Milwaukee shall constitute an assembly district.

The towns of Franklin and Oak Creek, in the county of Milwaukee, shall constitute an assembly district.

The towns of Greenfield and Lake, in the county of Milwaukee, shall constitute an assembly district.

The towns of Granville, Wauwatosa and Milwaukee, in the county of Milwaukee, shall constitute an assembly district.

The county of Portage shall constitute an assembly district.

The town of Racine, in the county of Racine, shall constitute an assembly district.

The towns of Norway, Raymond, Caledonia and Mount Pleasant, in the county of Racine, shall constitute an assembly district.

The towns of Rochester, Burlington and Yorkville, in the county of Racine, shall constitute an assembly district.

The towns of Southport, Pike and Pleasant Prairie, in the county of Racine, shall constitute an assembly district.

The towns of Paris, Bristol, Brighton, Salem and Wheatland, in the county of Racine, shall constitute an assembly district.

The towns of Janesville and Bradford, in the county of Rock, shall constitute an assembly district.

The towns of Beloit, Turtle and Clinton, in the county of Rock, shall constitute an assembly district.

The towns of Magnolia, Union, Porter and Fulton, in the county of Rock, shall constitute an assembly district.

The towns of Milton, Lima and Johnstown, in the county of Rock, shall constitute an assembly district.

The towns of Newark, Rock, Avon, Spring Valley and Center, in the county of Rock, shall constitute an assembly district: *Provided*, That if the legislature shall divide the town of Center, they may attach such part of it to the district lying next north as they may deem expedient.

The county of Sauk shall constitute an assembly district.

Precincts numbered one, three and seven, in the county of Sheboygan, shall constitute an assembly district.

Precincts number two, four, five and six, in the county of Sheboygan, shall constitute an assembly district.

The towns of Troy, East Troy and Spring Prairie, in the county of Walworth, shall constitute an assembly district.

The towns of Whitewater, Richmond and Lagrange, in the county of Walworth, shall constitute an assembly district.

The towns of Geneva, Hudson and Bloomfield, in the county of Walworth, shall constitute an assembly district.

The towns of Darien, Sharon, Walworth and Linn, in the county of Walworth, shall constitute an assembly district.

The towns of Delavan, Sugar Creek, La Fayette and Elkhorn, in the county of Walworth, shall constitute an assembly district.

The towns of Lisbon, Menomonee and Brookfield, in the county of Waukesha, shall constitute an assembly district.

The towns of Warren, Oconomewoc, Summit and Ottowa, in the county of Waukesha, shall constitute an assembly district.

The towns of Delafield, Genesee and Pewaukee, in the county of Waukesha, shall constitute an assembly district.

The towns of Waukesha and New Berlin, in the county of Waukesha, shall constitute an assembly district.

The towns of Eagle, Muckwanego, Vernon and Muskego, in the county of Waukesha, shall constitute an assembly district.

The towns of Port Washington, Fredonia and Clarence, in the county of Washington, shall constitute an assembly district.

The towns of Grafton and Jackson, in the county of Washington, shall constitute an assembly district.

The towns of Mequon and Germantown, in the county of Washington, shall constitute an assembly district.

The towns of Polk, Richfield and Erin, in the county of Washington, shall constitute an assembly district.

The towns of Hartford, Addison, West Bend and North Bend, in the county of Washington, shall constitute an assembly district.

The county of Winnebago shall constitute an assembly district.

The foregoing districts are subject, however, so far to be altered that when any new town shall be organized, it may be added to either of the adjoining assembly districts.

SEC. 13. Such parts of the common law as are now in force in the territory of Wisconsin, not inconsistent with this constitution, shall be and continue part of the law of this state until altered or suspended by the legislature. Common law now in force to continue until altered.

SEC. 14. The senators first elected in the even numbered senate districts, the governor, lieutenant-governor, and other state officers first elected under this constitution, shall enter upon the duties of their respective offices on the first Monday of June next, and shall continue in office for one year from the first Monday of January next. The senators first elected in the odd numbered senate districts, and the members of the assembly first elected, shall enter upon their duties respectively on the first Monday of June next, and shall continue in office until the first Monday in January next. Senators, &c. first elected, when to enter upon the duties of their office, and how long to continue in office.

SEC. 15. The oath of office may be administered by any judge or justice of the peace, until the legislature shall otherwise direct. Oath of office by whom administered.

RESOLUTIONS.

Resolved, That the congress of the United States be, and is hereby requested, upon the application of Wisconsin for admission into the Union, so to alter the provisions of an act of congress entitled "an act to grant a quantity of land to the territory of Wisconsin, for the purpose of aiding in opening a canal to connect the waters of Lake Michigan with those of Rock River," approved June eighteenth, eighteen hundred and thirty-eight ; and so to alter the terms and conditions of the grant made therein, that the odd numbered sections thereby granted and remaining unsold, may be held and disposed of by the state of Wisconsin, as part of the five Resolution relative to Lake Michigan and Rock river canal lands. Odd numbered sections to constitute part of 500,000 acres.

hundred thousand acres of land to which said state is entitled by the provisions of an act of Congress, entitled "an act to appropriate the proceeds of the sales of the public lands, and to grant pre-emption rights," approved the fourth day of September, eighteen hundred and forty-one; and further, that the even numbered sections reserved by congress may be offered for sale by the United States for the same minimum price, and subject to the same rights of pre-emption as other public lands of the United States.

Even numbered sections to be offered at minimum price, &c.

Excess price of those sold to be refunded.

Resolved, That congress be further requested to pass an act whereby the excess price over and above one dollar and twenty-five cents per acre, which may have been paid by the purchasers of said even numbered sections which shall have been sold by the United States, be refunded to the present owners thereof, or they be allowed to enter any of the public lands of the United States, to an amount equal in value to the excess so paid.

Odd numbered sections to be sold, &c.

Resolved, That in case the odd numbered sections shall be ceded to the state as aforesaid, the same shall be sold by the state in the same manner as other school lands: *Provided,* That the same rights of pre-emption as are now granted by the laws of the United States shall be secured to persons who may be actually settled upon such lands at the time of the adoption of this constitution: *And provided further,* That the excess price over and above one dollar and twenty-five cents per acre, absolutely or conditionally contracted to be paid by the purchasers of any part of said sections which shall have been sold by the territory of Wisconsin, shall be remitted to such purchasers, their representatives or assigns.

Excess price of those sold to be remitted.

Grant of the 500,000 acres and the five per centum to be applied to the use of schools.

Resolved, That congress be requested, upon the application of Wisconsin for admission into the Union, to pass an act whereby the grant of five hundred thousand acres of land to which the state of Wisconsin is entitled by the provisions of an act of congress entitled "an act to appropriate the proceeds of the sales of the public lands, and to grant pre-emption rights," approved the fourth day of September, eighteen hundred and forty-one, and also the five per centum of the nett proceeds of the public lands lying within the state, to which it shall become entitled on its admission into the Union, by the provisions of an act of congress, entitled "an act to enable the people of Wisconsin territory to form a constitution and state government, and for the admission of such state into the Union," approved the 6th day of August, eighteen hundred and forty-six, shall be granted to the state of Wisconsin for the use of schools, instead of the purposes mentioned in said acts of congress respectively.

Resolved, That the congress of the United States be, and hereby is requested, upon the admission of this state into the Union, so to alter the provisions of the act of congress, entitled "an act to grant a certain quantity of land to aid in the improvement of the Fox and Wisconsin rivers, and to connect the same by a canal in the territory of Wisconsin," that the price of the lands reserved to the United States shall be reduced to the minimum price of the public lands.

Minimum price of lands in Fox and Wisconsin river grant, reserved to U. S. to be reduced.

Resolved, That the legislature of this state shall make provision by law for the sale of the lands granted to the state in aid of said improvements, subject to the same rights of pre-emption to the settlers thereon, as are now allowed by law to settlers on the public lands.

Legislature to provide for sale of canal lands subject to pre-emption rights of settlers thereon.

Resolved, That the foregoing resolutions be appended to and signed with the constitution of Wisconsin, and submitted therewith to the people of this territory, and to the congress of the United States.

Resolutions to be signed and submitted to the people and to congress.

We, the undersigned, members of the convention to form a constitution for the state of Wisconsin, to be submitted to the people thereof for their ratification or rejection, do hereby certify that the foregoing is the constitution adopted by the convention.

Certificate and names of members of the convention.

In testimony whereof, we have hereunto set our hands, at Madison, the first day of February, A. D. eighteen hundred and forty-eight.

MORGAN L. MARTIN,

President of the convention and delegate from Brown county.

THO'S MCHUGH, *Secretary.*

Calumet,

G. W. Featherstonhaugh,

Columbia,

James T. Lewis,

Crawford,

Daniel G. Fenton.

Dane,

William H. Fox,
Charles M. Nichols,
William A. Wheeler.

Dodge,

Stoddard Judd,
Charles H. Larrabee,
Samuel W. Lyman.

Fond du Lac,

Samuel W. Beall,
Warren Chase.

Grant,

Orsamus Cole,
George W. Lakin,
Alexander D. Ramsey,
William Richardson,
John Hawkins Rountree.

Green,

James Biggs.

Iowa,

Charles Bishop,
Stephen Hollenbeck,
Joseph Ward.

Jefferson,

Jonas Folts,
Milo Jones,
Theodore Prentiss,
Abraham Vanderpool.

La Fayette,

Charles Dunn,
John O'Connor,
Allen Warden.

Milwaukee,

John L. Doran,
Garret M. Fitzgerald,
Albert Fowler,
Byron Kilbourn,
Rufus King,
Charles H. Larkin,
Morritz Schœffler.

Portage,

William H. Kennedy.

Racine,

Albert G. Cole,
Stephen A. Davenport,
Andrew B. Jackson,
Frederick S. Lovell,
Samuel R. McClellan,
James D. Reymert,
Horace T. Sanders,
Theodore Secor.

Rock,
Almerin M. Carter,
Joseph Colley,
Paul Crandall,
Ezra A. Foote,
Louis P. Harvey,
Edward V. Whiton.

Sheboygan,
Silas Steadman.

Walworth,
Experience Estabrook,
George Gale,
James Harrington,
Augustus C. Kinne,
Hollis Latham,
Ezra A. Mulford.

Waukesha,
Squire S. Case,
Alfred L. Castleman,
Peter D. Gifford,
Eleazer Root,
George Scagel.

Washington,
James Fagan,
Patrick Pentony,
Harvey G. Turner.

Winnebago,
Harrison Reed.

CHARTER
OF THE
CITY OF MILWAUKEE.

To consolidate and amend the act to incorporate the City of Milwaukee, and the several acts amendatory thereof.

The People of the State of Wisconsin, represented in Senate and Assembly, do enact as follows :

CHAPTER I.

CITY AND WARD BOUNDARIES.

CHAP. I.

Name and powers.

SECTION 1. All the district of country in the county of Milwaukee, contained within the limits and boundaries hereinafter described, shall be a city by the name of "Milwaukee," and the people now inhabiting, and those who shall hereafter inhabit within the district of country herein described, shall be a municipal corporation, by the name of the "City of Milwaukee," and shall have the general powers possessed by municipal corporations at common law ; and in addition thereto, shall possess the powers hereinafter specifically granted, and the authorities thereof shall have perpetual succession, shall be capable of contracting and being contracted with, of suing and being sued, pleading and being impleaded, in all courts of law and equity ; and shall have a common seal and may change and alter the same at pleasure.

SEC. 2. The territory included within the following boundaries and limits, shall constitute the City of Milwaukee, to wit : beginning on the shore of Lake Michigan, where it is

CHAP. I.

Boundaries.

intersected by the section line dividing sections fifteen and twenty-two, of township seven, north of range twenty-two east; running thence west along said line, to the south-east corner of the south-west quarter of said section fifteen; thence north along the quarter section line, to the north-east corner of the south-east quarter of the south-west quarter of said section fifteen; thence west to the north-west corner of said quarter section; thence south to the south-west corner of said quarter section; thence west along said line, dividing sections fifteen and twenty-two, to the west line of said township seven; thence south along said line, to the south line of said township; thence east along said line to the Lake shore, in the southerly part of Milwaukee bay; thence from a point therein in range with the south side of the south pier of the Government harbor, the line shall diverge and run south-easterly in a direct line to and along the south side of said pier, to the further extremity thereof, and five hundred feet beyond, and from thence due east to the eastern boundary of the State in Lake Michigan; thence north to a point opposite to the place or point of beginning; thence west to the place or point of beginning.

Division of wards.

SEC. 3. The said City shall be divided into five Wards, as follows: all that part of said district which lies east of the middle of the Milwaukee river and north of the middle of Wisconsin street shall be the First Ward, and all that part of the said district which lies west of the middle of Milwaukee river, and north of the middle of Cedar street, and its extension to the west line of the city, shall be the Second Ward; all that part of the said district which lies east of the middle of the said river, and south of the middle of Wisconsin street, shall be the Third Ward, and all that part of the said district which lies west of the middle of said river, and south of the middle of Cedar street, and within sections numbered twenty-nine and thirty, shall be the Fourth Ward; and the residue of said City shall be the Fifth Ward.

CHAPTER II.

ELECTIONS.

SECTION 1. The annual election for Ward and City officers shall be held on the first Tuesday of March, of each year, at such place in each Ward as the Common Council shall designate, and the polls shall be kept open from nine o'clock in the forenoon till five in the afternoon, and ten days previous notice shall be given by the Common Council of the time and place of holding such elections, and of the City and Ward officers to be elected. Annual election.

SEC. 2. The elective officers shall be a Mayor, Treasurer, Marshal, and Police Justice, for the City, and three Aldermen, one Assessor, one Constable, and one Justice of the Peace for each Ward. All other officers necessary for the proper management of the affairs of said City shall be appointed by the Common Council. All elective officers, except Justices of the Peace, shall, unless otherwise provided, hold their respective offices for one year and until their successors are elected and qualified: Provided, however, the Common Council shall have power, for due cause, to expel any of their own number, and to remove from office any officer or agent under the city government, due notice having been first given to the officer complained of. Justices of the Peace shall hold their respective offices for two years and until their successors are elected and qualified. Elective officers. Council may appoint others. Term of service. Justice of the Peace.

SEC. 3. Whenever a vacancy shall occur in the office of Mayor or Aldermen, such vacancy shall be filled by a new election, which shall be ordered and held within ten days after such vacancy shall occur. Any vacancy happening in any other office shall be filled by the Common Council. The person elected or appointed to fill a vacancy, shall hold his office and discharge the duties thereof for the unexpired term, and with the same rights, and subject to the same liabilities as the person whose office he may be elected or appointed to fill. Vacancies.

CHAP. II.

Plurality elects.

Tie vote.

SEC. 4. All elections by the people shall be by ballot, and a plurality of votes shall constitute an election. When two or more candidates for an elective office shall receive an equal number of votes for the same office, the election shall be determinad by the casting of lots in the presence of the Common Council, at such time and in such manner as they shall direct.

Qualifications of voters.

SEC. 5. All persons entitled to vote for County or State officers, and who shall have resided in the city for one year preceding the election, and for ten days within the Ward where they offer to vote, shall be entitled to vote for any officer to be elected under this law, and to hold any office hereby created.

Aldermen to be inspectors of elections.

SEC. 6. The elections in said city shall be held and conducted by the Aldermen of each Ward, who shall be the inspectors of elections, and shall take the usual oaths or affirmations as prescribed by the general laws of this State to be taken by the judges and inspectors of elections, and shall have the power to appoint clerks of such elections, and to administer the necessary oaths. Said elections shall be held and conducted in the same manner and under the same penalties, and vacancies in the board of inspectors thereof filled, as required by the laws of this State regarding elections.

Oaths to persons offering to vote when challenged.

SEC. 7. If either of the inspectors shall suspect that any person offering a vote does not possess the qualifications of an elector, or if such vote be challenged by an elector, the inspector, before receiving the vote of any such, shall require him to take the following oath:—"You do solemnly swear (or affirm, as the case may be) that you are twenty-one years of age, that you are a citizen of the United States (or have declared your intentions to become a citizen conformably to the laws of the United States on the subject of naturalization) that you have resided within this city one year, and within this ward ten days next preceding this election, and that you have not voted at this election, and that you have made no bet or wager, or become directly or indirectly interested in any bet or wager depending on the result of this election ;" and if the person offering to vote shall take such oath, his vote shall be received. And if such person shall take such oath falsely, he shall be deemed guilty of a wilful and corrupt perjury, and upon conviction thereof upon indictment, shall suffer the punishment provided by law for persons guilty of perjury. If any person who is not a qualified voter, shall vote at any election, or if any person qualified shall vote in any other ward than the one in which he resides, or shall vote more than once at any one election, he shall be liable to indictment, and on conviction thereof, shall forfeit and pay a sum not exceeding one hundred dollars, or less than twenty-five dollars. It shall be the duty of the inspectors to keep a list of the names of all persons whose votes may be challenged as aforesaid, and who shall swear in their votes, and if any inspector shall knowingly and corruptly receive the vote of any person not authorized to vote, or shall make out false returns of an election, or any clerk shall not write down the name of every voter as he votes, or shall wilfully make untrue and incorrect count and tallies of votes, each and every such inspector and clerk shall be liable to indictment, and on conviction thereof, shall severally forfeit and pay a sum not exceeding five hundred dollars, nor less than one hundred dollars. All such indictments shall be tried in the circuit court of the county of Milwaukee.

Penalty for illegal voting

Sec. 8. When an election shall be closed, and the number of votes for each candidate or person voted for shall be counted and ascertained, the said inspectors shall make return thereof, stating therein the number of votes for each person, for each and every office, and shall deliver, or cause to be delivered, such returns to the clerk of the Common Council, who shall forthwith give notice to each of the Aldermen elected, of their respective elections. Within one week after any election the Common Council shall meet and canvass

Returns made to the Clerk.

CHAP. II. said returns and declare the result as it appears from the same.

Special elections. SEC. 9. Special elections to fill vacancies, or for any other purpose, shall be held and conducted by the Aldermen of each ward, in the same manner and the returns thereof shall be made in the same form and manner as general or annual elections, and within such time as may be prescribed by ordinance.

Removals vacate offices. SEC. 10. Any officer removing from the city, or any ward officer removing from the ward for which he was elected, or any officer who shall neglect or refuse for ten days after notice of his election or appointment, to enter upon the discharge of the duties of his office, shall be deemed to have vacated his office, and the Common Council shall proceed to fill such vacancy, as herein prescribed.

Election of Aldermen. SEC. 11. There shall be elected at the first election under this act, one Alderman for each ward, who shall hold his office for two years, and two Aldermen who shall hold their office for one year.

SEC. 12. At every annual election thereafter, there shall be elected one Alderman in each ward, who shall hold his office for two years, and one who shall hold his office for one year.

SEC. 13. The votes for the Alderman who shall hold his office for two years, shall be deposited in a separate ballot box; and the votes for Aldermen holding their office for one year, and all other elective officers, shall be on one ballot and deposited in a separate ballot box.

SEC. 14. There shall be written or printed, or partly written or printed, at the head of the votes for the Alderman for two years, the words, "Alderman for two years;" and at the head of the vote for Aldermen for one year, "Aldermen for one year."

Aldermen members of Board of Supervisors. SEC. 15. The Aldermen in each ward elected for two years, shall be in the order of their election, members of the

County Board of Supervisors, with all the rights, duties and liabilities of the Chairman of the Board of Supervisors of the several towns.

May substitute others.

SEC. 16. By consent of a majority of the Aldermen of any ward, the Alderman for two years may substitute either of the other Aldermen in his place in said Board of Supervisors, for such time as may be named by him in writing.

Term of office.

SEC. 17. All the city and ward officers now in office, shall hold their respective offices, until their successors shall be elected or appointed under this act; and the term of every officer, elected under this law, shall commence on the second Tuesday of March of the year for which he is elected; and shall, unless herein otherwise provided, continue for one year, and until his successor is elected and qualified.

SEC. 18. All duties herein required of the Common Council and Aldermen in regard to elections, shall be performed, so far as may be necessary, by the present Common Council and Aldermen in regard to the first election, and the organization of the city government under this law.

New election in case of failure.

SEC. 19. Should there be a failure by the people to elect any officers herein required to be elected on the day designated, the Common Council may order a new election to be held, ten days notice of the time and place of holding the election being first given.

CHAPTER III.

OFFICERS—THEIR POWERS AND DUTIES.

Oaths and bonds of officers.

SEC. 1. Every person elected or appointed to any office under this act, shall, before he enters upon the duties of his office, take and subscribe an oath of office and file the same, duly certified by the officer taking the same, with the clerk of the city; and the treasurer, clerk, marshal, constables, and such other officers as the Common Council may direct, shall severally, before they enter upon the duties of their respective offices, execute to the city of Milwaukee, a bond with at least two sureties, who shall swear that they are each worth the penalty specified in said bond, over and above all debts, exemptions or liabilities, and said bonds shall contain such penal sum, and such conditions as the Common Council may deem proper; and they may from time to time require new or additional bonds, and remove from office any officer refusing or neglecting to give the same.

Mayor.

SEC. 2. The Mayor shall, when present, preside over the meetings of the Common Council, and take care that the laws of the State and the ordinances of the City are duly observed and enforced, and that all other executive officers of the City discharge their respective duties; he shall from time to time give the Common Council such information, and recommend such measures as he may deem advantageous to the City. The Mayor shall be the chief executive officer and head of the Police of the City; and in case of a riot, or other disturbance, he may appoint as many special or temporary constables as he may deem necessary. The Mayor shall have a vote only in case of a tie.

President of Council.

SEC. 3. At the first meeting of the Common Council each year, they shall proceed to elect, by ballot, one of their number President, and in the absence of the Mayor, the said President shall preside over the meetings of the Common Council; and during the absence of the Mayor from the City, or his inability, for any reason, to discharge the duties of his office, the said President shall exercise all the powers, and discharge all the duties of the Mayor. In case the Mayor and President shall be absent at any meeting of the Common Council, they shall proceed to elect a temporary presiding officer, who, for the time being, shall discharge all the duties of the Mayor. The President, or temporary presiding officer, while presiding over the Board, or performing the duties of the Mayor, shall be styled Acting Mayor, and any acts performed by them shall have the same force and validity as if performed by the Mayor.

Clerk.

SEC. 4. The Clerk shall be elected by ballot by the Common Council; he shall keep the corporate seal, and all papers and records of the City; and keep a record of the proceedings of the Common Council, at whose meetings it shall be his duty to attend; and copies of all papers filed in his office, and transcripts from the records of the Common Council, certified by him under the corporate seal, shall be evidence in all courts, in like manner as if the original were produced; he shall draw and countersign all orders on the treasury, in pursuance of any order or resolution of the Common Council, and keep a full and accurate account thereof, in books provided for that purpose. The Clerk shall have power and authority to administer oaths or affirmations.

Attorney.

SEC. 5. The Attorney shall perform all professional services incident to the office, and when required, shall furnish written opinions upon any subject submitted to him by the Common Council or its committees.

Treasurer.

SEC. 6. The Treasurer shall receive all monies belonging to the City, and keep an accurate and detailed account thereof in such manner as the Common Council shall from time to time direct. The Treasurer shall exhibit to the Common Council, at least fifteen days before the annual election, or sooner if required by them, a full and detailed account of all receipts and expenditures after the date of the last annual report, and also of the state of the treasury, which account shall be filed with the Clerk.

Marshal.

SEC. 7. The Marshal shall perform such duties as shall be prescribed by the Common Council for the preservation of the public peace, and the collection of license moneys and fines; he shall possess the power of constable at common law, or by the laws of this Strte, and receive like fees, but shall not serve civil process, except where the city is a party.

Other officers.

SEC. 8. The Common Council shall have power from time to time, to requre other and further duties to be performed by any officer whose duties are herein prescribed; and

CHAP. III. to appoint such other officers as may be necessary to carry into effect the provisions of this act, and to prescribe their duties, and to fix the compensation of all officers elected or appointed by them ; such compensation shall be fixed by resolution at the time the office is created, or at the commencement of the year, and shall not be increased or diminished during the term such officer shall remain in office.

Compensation of officers.

City printers

SEC. 9. The Common Council at their first meeting in each year, or as soon thereafter as may be, shall designate not more than two daily papers printed in said City, one in English and one in German, in which shall be published all ordinances and other proceedings and matters required by this act, or by the by-laws or ordinances of the Common Council, to be published in a public newspaper.

Affidavit of publication.

SEC. 10. The City printer or printers, immediately after the publication of any notice, ordinance or resolution, which by this act is required to be published, shall file with the Clerk of the City a copy of such publication, with his or their affidavit or the affidavit of his or their foreman, of the length of time the same has been published, and such affidavit shall be conclusive evidence of the publication of such notice, ordinance or resolution.

Penalty for detention of property.

SEC 11. If any person having been an officer in said City, shall not within ten days after notification and request, deliver to his successor in office all property, books, papers and effects of every description, in his possession, belonging to said City, or pertaining to the office he may have held, he shall forfeit and pay to the use of the City, one hundred dollars, besides all damages caused by his neglect or refusal so to deliver ; and such successor may recover the possession of such books, papers and effects, in the manner prescribed by the laws of this State.

Aldermen not to be parties in contract.

SEC. 12. No Alderman shall be a party to, or interested in any job or contract with the City or any of the wards, and any contract in which any Alderman may be so interested, shall be null and void ; and in case any money shall have been paid on any such contract, the Common Council may sue for and recover the amount so paid, from the parties to such contract and the Alderman interested in the same.

Officers of the peace.

SEC. 13. The Mayor or Acting Mayor, Sheriff of Milwaukee county, and each and every Alderman, Justice of the Peace, Marshal, Constable and Watchman, shall be officers of the peace, and may command the peace, and suppress in a summary manner, all rioting and disorderly behavior within the limits of the City ; and for such purposes may command the assistance of all bystanders, and if need be, of all citizens and military companies ; and if any person, bystander, military officer, or private, shall refuse to aid in maintaining the peace when so required, every such person shall forfeit and pay a fine of fifty dollars ; and in cases where the civil power may be required to suppress riotous or disorderly behavior, the superior or senior officer present, in the order above mentioned in this section, shall direct the proceedings.

Police Justice.

SEC. 14. The Police Justice shall possess all the authority, power and rights of a Justice of the Peace, except that he shall in no case entertain any civil proceeding to which the City is not a party ; and shall have sole exclusive jurisdiction to hear all complaints and conduct all examinations and trials in criminal cases within the City, cognizable before a Justice of the Peace ; but warrants returnable before the Police Justice may be issued in criminal cases by any other Justice in the City, but no fee shall be received therefor by such Justice. The Police Justice shall have exclusive jurisdiction in cases in which the City is a party, and he shall have the same power and authority, in case of contempt, as a court of record : *Provided,* That nothing herein contained shall be deemed to divest the Circuit Judges of their authority as conservators of the peace, nor to affect in any manner the jurisdiction or powers of the County or Circuit Court of Milwaukee county. In case of the absence, sickness or other inability of the Police Justice, or for any sufficient reason, the Mayor, by warrant, may authorize any other Justice of the Peace within said City, to perform the duties of Police Justice, and it shall thereupon be the duty of the Mayor to inform the Attorney and Marshal of such substitution, and make report thereof to the Common Council, and they may confirm or set aside such appointment, or appoint some other Justice of the Peace; and the Justice so appointed shall for the time being possess all the authority, power, and rights of the Police Justice.

SEC. 15. The Police Justice shall quarterly report to the Common Council a list of all proceedings instituted before him, in behalf of the City, and the disposition thereof; and shall, at the same time, account and pay over the amount of all penalties and costs collected, which may by law accrue to the City. He shall be entitled to receive from the county of Milwaukee an annual salary of not less than four hundred dollars, nor more than eight hundred dollars, for his services in criminal cases; and shall receive from the City of Milwaukee such compensation as the Common Council may deem proper.

Surveyor.

SEC. 16. There shall be elected by the Common Council, a City Surveyor, who shall be a practical Surveyor and Engineer. He shall keep his office at some convenient place within said City, and the Common Council shall prescribe his duties, and fix the fees and compensation for any service performed by him. All surveys, profiles, plans or estimates made by him for the City, or either of the wards, shall be the property of said City, and shall be carefully preserved in the office of the Surveyor, open to the inspection of parties interested, and the same, together with all books and papers appertaining to said office, shall be delivered over by the Surveyor, at the expiration of his term of office, to his successor or the Common Council.

Comptroller.

His duties. § 17–29 inclusive.

SEC. 17. The Common Council shall appoint a City Comptroller, whose duty it shall be to make out the amount paid by, and chargeable to the general city fund and to the several ward funds, for personal taxes for the year 1849 refunded, and for over payment of taxes accruing under the law authorizing the collection of taxes, approved 24th January, 1851.

SEC. 18. After the assumption of the ward debts by the city, said Comptroller shall report to the Common Council the amount of indebtedness of the several wards to the city, and what amount of taxes it will be necessary to levy annually in each ward, and for what number of years, to reimburse the city the amount paid by the same, on account of the indebtedness of the several wards.

SEC. 19. He shall make out a list of all the outstanding city bonds, to whom, when, and where payable, and the rate of interest they may respectively bear, and recommend such action to the Common Council, as will secure the punctual payment of the principal and interest of such bonds.

SEC. 20. He shall report annually, on or about the first of April, to the Common Council, an estimate of the expenses of the city, and of the several wards, and likewise the revenue, necessary to be raised for the current year; and the fiscal year of the city shall commence on the first day of April.

SEC. 21. He shall make, or cause to be made, estimates of the expense of any work to be done by the city, and countersign all contracts, made in behalf of the city, and certificates of work by any committee of the Common Council, or by any city officer.

SEC. 22. He shall examine all estimates of work to be done by the street commissioners of the several wards and countersign all contracts and certificates of work entered into or given by them; and no contract entered into, or certificate

CHAP. III. issued, shall be of any validity unless countersigned by the comptroller.

SEC. 23. He shall keep a list of all certificates issued in each ward, and before the levy by the Common Council of the annual tax, shall report to the Council a schedule of all the lots or parcels of land within the several wards, which, under this act, may be subject to any special tax or assessment, and also the amount of such special tax or assessment which it may be necessary to levy on such lot or parcel of land, with a full statement of the several acts done and performed in reference to such special taxes or assessments: which said schedule shall be verified by the affidavit of the comptroller, and shall be *prima facie* evidence of the facts therein stated in all cases wherein the validity of such special tax or assessment shall come in question. The Common Council shall, if from such report they deem such special tax legal and just, cause the same to be levied, in pursuance of the provisions of this act.

SEC. 24. He shall report monthly to the Common Council the amount of work done, or for which contracts have been entered into, chargeable to the several wards and to the general city fund, and set forth what proportion the same will bear to the annual estimate made by him, for the work to be performed and revenue to be raised.

SEC. 25. If, on or before the first day of December of any year, the amount expended or to be expended chargeable to any of the ward or city funds, (adding thereto the current expenses estimated for the remainder of the fiscal year and chargeable to such fund,) shall be equal to three-fourths of the tax authorized to be raised, or revenue estimated for such fund, he shall at once report the same to the Common Council; and he shall not countersign any contracts chargeable to such fund, until the amount of taxes actually collected be ascertained; and during the remainder of the fiscal year, he shall not countersign any contracts, the expense of which shall exceed the revenue actually collected for the fund to which such expense is properly chargeable.

SEC. 26. The Comptroller may negotiate, between the first of April and the collection of taxes for the same year, such temporary loans for the different funds, anticipating the revenue of the current year, as he shall deem expedient; and such loans shall be subject to the approval of the Common Council.

SEC. 27. He shall examine the report, books, papers, vouchers and accounts of the Treasurer, and from time to time, shall perform such other duties as the Common Council may direct.

SEC. 28. All claims and demands against the City before they are allowed by the Common Council, shall be audited and adjusted by the Comptroller.

SEC. 29. The Comptroller shall keep a record of all his acts and doings, which record shall be open to the inspection of all parties interested. He shall not be directly or indirectly interested in any contract or job to which the City or either of the wards is a party.

CHAPTER IV.

THE COMMON COUNCIL—ITS GENERAL POWERS AND DUTIES.

SECTION 1. The Mayor and Aldermen shall constitute the Common Council, and the style of all ordinances shall be, "The Mayor and Common Council of the City of Milwaukee do ordain," &c. The Common Council shall meet at such time and place as they, by resolution, shall direct. A majority of the Aldermen shall constitute a quorum. Style. Meetings. Quorum.

SEC. 2. The Common Council shall hold stated meetings, and the Mayor may call special meetings, by notice to each of the members, to be served personally, or left at their usual place of abode. The Common Council shall determine the rules of its own proceedings, and be the judge of the elec- Special meetings. Compel attendance.

 tion and qualification of its own members, and have power to compel the attendance of absent members.

Powers of Common Council.

SEC. 3. The Common Council shall have the management and control of the finances, and of all the property of the City; and shall likewise, in addition to the power herein vested in them, have full power and authority to make, enact, ordain, establish, publish, enforce, alter, modify, amend and repeal all such ordinances, rules and by-laws, for the government and good order of the City, for the suppression of vice, for the prevention of crime and for the benefit of the trade, commerce and health thereof, [and] as they shall deem expedient, declaring and imposing penalties, and to enforce the same against any person or persons who may violate any of the provisions of such ordinance, rules or by-laws; and such ordinances, rules and by-laws are hereby declared to be and have the force of law; Provided, That they be not repugnant to the Constitution and laws of the United States or of this State; and for these purposes, shall have authority by ordinances, resolutions, or by-laws:

Licenses.

1. To license and regulate the exhibitions of common showmen or shows of any kind, or the exhibitions of caravans, circuses, or theatrical performances, billiard tables, bowling saloons, and to provide for the abatement and removal of all nuisances under the ordinances, or at common law; and to grant licenses, and regulate groceries, taverns, victualing houses, and all persons vending or dealing in spirituous, vinous or fermented liquors: *Provided*, That the license for so dealing in, or vending spirituous or fermented liquors, shall be thirty dollars a year, and that no license shall be granted for a less term than one year.

Games of chance.

2. To restrain and prohibit all descriptions of gaming, and fraudulent devices and practices, and all playing of cards, dice, or other games of chance, for the purpose of gaming in said City, and to restrain any person from vending, giving,

Liquors.

or dealing in spirituous, fermented or vinous liquors, unless duly licensed by the Common Council. CHAP. IV.

3. To prevent any riots, noise, disturbance, or disorderly assemblages, suppress and restrain disorderly houses or groceries, and houses of ill-fame, and to authorise the destruction of all instruments used for the purpose of gaming. Riots, &c.

4. To compel the owner or occupant of any grocery, cellar, tallow chandler shop, soap factory, tannery, stable, barn, privy, sewer, or other unwholesome, nauseous house or place, to cleanse, remove or abate the same, from time to time, as often as it may be deemed necessary for the health, comfort, and convenience of the inhabitants of said City. Nuisances.

5. To direct the location and management of slaughter houses and markets, and to establish rates for and license venders of gunpowder, and regulate the storage, keeping and conveying of gunpowder or other combustible materials. Markets. Powder.

6. To prevent the encumbering of the streets, sidewalks, lanes or alleys, with carriages, carts, wagons, sleighs, boxes, lumber, firewood, or any other material or substances whatever. Obstructions in streets.

7. To prevent horse racing, immoderate riding or driving in the streets, and to regulate the places of bathing and swimming in the waters within the limits of said City. Racing. Bathing.

8. To restrain the running at large of cattle, swine, sheep, poultry, and geese, and to authorize the distraining and sale of the same. Animals at large.

9. To prevent the running at large of dogs, and to authorize the destruction of the same in a summary manner when at large contrary to the ordinance. Dogs.

10. To prevent any person from bringing, depositing, or having within said City, any putrid carcass, or other unwholesome substance, and to require the removal of the same by any person who shall have upon his premises any such substance, or putrid or unsound beef, pork, fish, hides or skins of any kind ; and on default, to authorize the removal Unwholesome substances.

 thereof by some competent officers, at the expense of such person or persons.

Water, Lamps, Gas, Hacks, Carts &c. 11. To make and establish public ponds, pumps, wells, cisterns and reservoirs, and provide for the erection of water works, for the supply of water to the inhabitants, to erect lamps, and regulate and license hacks, cabs, drays, carts and the charges of hackmen, cabmen, draymen, and cartmen in the City ; and to provide for lighting the streets, public grounds, and public buildings with gas or otherwise.

Health, burial grounds 12. To establish and regulate boards of health, provide hospital and cemetery grounds, regulate the burial of the dead, and the return of the bills of mortality, and to exempt burial grounds set apart for public use, from taxation.

Bread. 13. To regulate the assize and weight of bread, and to provide for the seizure and forfeiture of bread baked contrary thereto.

Sidewalks. 14. To prevent all persons riding or driving any ox, mule, cattle, or other animal, on the side-walks in said City, or in any way doing any damages to such side-walks.

Firearms. 15. To prevent the shooting of fire-arms or crackers, and to prevent the exhibition of any fire-works in any situation which may be considered by the Council dangerous to the City, or any property therein, or annoying any citizen thereof.

Drunkards. Obscenity. 16. To restrain drunkards, immoderate drinking, or obscenity in the streets or public places, and to provide for arresting, removing and punishing any person or persons who may be guilty of the same.

Runners. 17. To restrain and regulate runners and solicitors for boats, vessels, stages, public houses, or other establishments, and to regulate the police of the City.

Markets. 18. To establish public markets, and make rules and regulations for the government of the same ; to appoint suitable officers for overseeing and regulating such markets, and to restrain all persons from interrupting or interfering with the due observance of such rules and regulations.

19. To license and regulate butcher's stalls, shops and stands for the sale of game, poultry, butcher's meat, butter, fish, and other provisions.

Hay, Wood, and Lime.

20. To regulate the place and manner of weighing and selling of hay, and measuring and selling of fuel and lime, and to appoint suitable persons to superintend and conduct the same.

Clearing sidewalks

21. To compel the owners or occupants of buildings or grounds, to remove snow, dirt or rubbish from the side-walk, street or alley opposite thereto, and to compel such owner or occupant to remove from the lot owned or occupied by him, all such substances as the board of health shall direct; and in his default, to authorize the removal or destruction thereof by some officer of the City, at the expense of such owner or occupant.

Piers.

22. To regulate the construction of piers and wharves extending into Lake Michigan, within the limits of said City, and to prescribe and control the prices to be charged for pierage or wharfage thereon.

Quarantine.

23. To regulate, control, and prevent the landing of persons from boats or vessels, wherein are contagious or infectious diseases or disorders, and to make such disposition of such persons as to preserve the health of said City.

Auctions.

24. To regulate the time, place and manner of holding public auctions or vendues.

Watchmen.

25. To appoint watchmen and prescribe their duties.

Weights and measures.

26. To provide by ordinance for a standard of weights and measures, and for the punishment of the use of false weights and measures.

Ordinances.

SEC. 4. All laws, ordinances, regulations, resolutions and by-laws shall be passed by an affirmative vote of a majority of the Common Council, and shall be signed by the Mayor, and shall be published in the official papers of said City, before the same shall be in force, and within fifteen days thereafter they shall be recorded by the City Clerk, in books to be provided for that purpose ; but before any of the said laws, ordinances, regulations or by-laws shall be recorded, the publication thereof respectively within the said time, shall be proved by the affidavit of the foreman or publisher of such newspaper, and said affidavit shall be recorded therewith, and at all times shall be deemed and taken as sufficient evidence of the time and manner of such publication. No appropriation shall be made without a vote of a majority of the members of the Common Council in its favor, which vote shall be taken by the ayes and noes, and entered among the proceedings of the Council.

Appropriations.

Nuisances.

SEC. 5. The powers conferred upon the said Council to provide for the abatement or removal of nuisances, shall not bar or hinder suits, prosecutions or proceedings in the courts according to law. Depots, houses or buildings of any kind wherein more than ten pounds of gunpowder are deposited, stored or kept at any one time, gambling houses, houses of ill-fame, disorderly taverns, and houses or places where spirituous, vinous or fermented liquors are sold without the license required therefor within the limits of said City, are hereby declared and shall be deemed public or common nuisances.

Accounting of Officers.

SEC. 6. The Council shall examine, audit and adjust the accounts of the Clerk, Treasurer, School Commissioners, Street Commissioners, of each ward, Marshal, and all other officers and agents of the City, at such times as they may deem proper, and also at the end of each year and before the term for which the officers of the said City are elected or appointed, shall have expired. And the Common Council shall require each and every such officer and agent to exhibit his books, accounts and vouchers, for such examination and settlement, and if any such officer or agent shall refuse to comply with the orders of said Council in the discharge of their duties in pursuance of this section, or shall neglect or refuse to render his accounts or present his books and vouchers to said Council, it shall be the duty of the Common Council to declare the office of such person vacant. And the Common Council shall order suits and proceedings at law against any officer and agent of said City, who may be found delinquent or defaulting in his accounts, or in the discharge of his official duties; and shall make a full record of all such settlements and adjustments.

CHAPTER V.

FINANCES AND TAXATION.

Funds, how drawn out.

SECTION 1. All funds in the treasury, except School, State and County funds, shall be under the control of the Common Council, and shall be drawn out upon the order of the Mayor and Clerk, duly authorized by a vote of the Common Council, and all orders drawn upon the treasurer shall specify the purpose for which they were drawn, and shall be payable generally out of any funds in the treasury belonging to the City; and all such orders shall be received in payment of any tax or assessment levied by the authority of the City. All orders shall be payable to the order of the person in whose favor they may be drawn, and shall be transferable by endorsement.

Orders, what to be received.

SEC. 2. No order or warrant drawn by the authority of the City of Milwaukee upon ward or City funds previous to the taking effect of this act, nor any warrant or order drawn for any debt or liability contracted previous thereto shall be receivable by the City Treasurer on payment of any tax or assessment levied in pursuance of this act: *Provided, however,* That orders or warrants issued in payment of special taxes or improvements shall be receivable therefor.

City Bonds.

SEC. 3. The Common Council is hereby authorized, and it shall be their duty, to issue bonds of the City, bearing interest of not more than seven per centum, as the Common Council may determine, payable at such time or times as said

CHAP. V. Council may deem advisable, regard being had in the case of a ward debt to the probable time that will be required under the provisions herein made to pay off such indebtedness, in payment of the existing indebtedness of said City, and of the several wards thereof, contracted for general city or ward purposes.

Taxation, City.

SEC. 4. The said Council shall, annually, levy a tax upon all the property in said City subject to taxation, not exceeding one per cent. per annum, to pay off the present indebtedness of said City, until such indebtedness shall be finally extinguished; and they may levy a further tax not exceeding three-fourths of one per cent. to defray the current expenses of the City.

Taxations, Ward.

SEC. 5. The Common Council shall annually levy a tax, not exceeding one per cent., upon the property liable to taxation, of any ward that is indebted, to pay off the indebtedness of such ward, assumed by the City under the provisions of this chapter, until an amount shall have been collected by the City from such tax, sufficient to pay off the indebtedness of such ward assumed by the City, at which time such tax shall cease.

SEC. 6. The Common Council shall annually levy upon the property liable to taxation in each ward, a tax not exceeding one per cent. per annum, to defray the current expenses of such ward.

Aldermen to certify ward debts to the Council.

SEC. 7. The Aldermen of any ward shall certify to the Council any debts contracted by such ward for the current year, and thereupon the said Council shall (if such debt be a proper claim against such ward,) allow such debt, and direct the Mayor and Clerk to issue to the proper person orders of the City to the amount of the debt allowed: *Provided,* The said Council shall in no case allow any such debt, if such allowance will cause the whole amount of orders so issued to meet the indebtedness of such ward, to exceed the amount of tax which may be levied and collected under the provisions of this chapter, to meet the expenses of the current year, assuming as a basis the tax list of such year, if then made out, and if not, then the tax list of the preceding year.

Aldermen not to contract debts greater than the amount of tax.

SEC. 8. No Alderman of any ward shall contract debts against such ward in any one year, to an amount greater than the amount of tax, which, under the provisions of this chapter, may be levied in such ward, to meet the current expenses of the year; and if any Alderman shall so contract debts to a greater amount than such tax, neither such ward nor the City shall be liable for the same, but the Alderman so contracting shall be liable therefor, as if the debt had originally been contracted by such Alderman personally: *Provided,* That no Alderman shall be held liable as aforesaid without proof of his assent as Alderman, to the contracting of the liability or debt by the ward.

CHAPTER VI.

OPENING OF STREETS, ALLEYS &C.

Laying out streets.

SECTION 1. The Common Council shall have power to lay out public squares, grounds, streets and alleys, and to widen the same as follows: Whenever ten or more freeholders residing in any ward shall, by petition, represent to the Common Council that it is necessary to take certain lands within the ward where such petitioners may reside, for public use, for the purpose of laying out public squares, grounds, streets, or alleys, or the enlarging or widening the same, the courses and distances, metes and bounds of the lands proposed to be taken, together with the names and residences of the owners of such premises, if the same shall be known to the petitioners, to be set forth in such petition, the Common Council shall thereupon cause notice of such application to be given to the occupant or occupants of such lands, if any there be, or if any portion of such lands shall not be in the actual occupation of any person, then the Common Council shall cause such notice, describing as near as may be, the

CHAP. VI. premises proposed to be taken, to be published in the official paper for four weeks, at least once in each week.

Notice of application for jurors.

SEC. 2. Such notice shall state, that on a certain day therein to be named, not less than ten days from the service of such notice, or the expiration of such publications, as the case may be, application will be made to Judge of the Circuit or County Court of Milwaukee county, for the appointment of twelve jurors, to view said premises, and to determine whether it will be necessary to take the same for the purpose specified in said petition.

Appointment of jurors.

SEC. 3. Upon the presentation of such application, and upon proof of the publication or service of the notice hereinbefore required, the said Judge shall thereupon appoint twelve reputable freeholders, residents of the City but not residents of the ward in which such premises may lie, nor interested in the result of such application. The said Judge shall thereupon issue his precept directed to said jurors, requiring them, within thirty days, to view said premises to be specified in said precept, and to make return under their hands, to the Common Council, whether, in their judgment, it is necessary to take said premises for the purpose specified in such application.

SEC. 4. If any of the jurors so appointed shall be disqualified from acting, or shall refuse to act, the Judge shall appoint others in their places, and a memorandum of such substitution shall be endorsed on the precept.

Duties of jurors.

SEC. 5. The said jurors at such times as they may agree upon, shall proceed in a body to view the premises in question, and shall hear such testimony as may be offered by any party interested, which testimony shall be reduced to writing by one of the jurors, and either of the jurors shall be authorized to administer the necessary oaths to witnesses.

Jurors report.

SEC. 6. After viewing the premises and hearing such testimony as may be offered, the jurors shall make a report of their proceedings, which shall be signed by them respectively, and which shall state whether in their judgement it is necessary to take the premises in question for the public use, which said report, testimony and precept, shall be returned to the Common Council within the time limited therein.

Damages.

SEC. 7. Should the jurors report that it is necessary to take such premises, the Common Council shall enter an order among their proceedings, confirming said report, and directing the same jurors within one month thereafter, or such further time as may be deemed proper, to again view said premises for the puropose of ascertaining and determining the amount of damages to be paid to the owner or owners of the property proposed to be taken, and also what lands or premises will be benefited by such taking, and to assess and return within the time limited, such damages and benefits to the Common Council.

SEC. 8. If there should be any building standing, in whole, or in part, upon the land to be taken, the jurors, before proceeding to make their assessment, shall first estimate and determine the whole value of such building to the owner, aside from the value of the land, and the injury to him in having such building taken from him; and secondly, the value of such building to him to remove.

Notice to Owner or Agent to be present.

SEC. 9. At least ten days personal notice of such determination shall be given to the owner or his agent, if known, and a resident of the City, or left at his usual place of abode. If not known, or a non-resident, notice to all persons interested shall be given by publication in the official paper, three successive weeks; such notice shall specify the building and the award of the jurors. It shall also require the parties interested to appear by a day to be therein named, or give notice of their election to the Common Council, either to accept the award of the jurors, and allow such building to be taken, with the land appropriated, or of their intention to remove such building at the value set thereon by the jurors to remove. If the owner shall agree to remove such building, he shall have such time for this purpose as the Common Council may allow.

Council may direct buildings to be sold.

SEC. 10. If the owner refuse to take the building at the value to remove, or fail to give notice of his election as aforesaid, within the time prescribed, the Common Council shall have power to direct the sale of such building at public auction, for cash, giving ten days notice of such sale. The proceeds shall be paid to the owner, or deposited to his use.

Assessment of damages.

SEC. 11. The said jurors, within the time limited, shall view and examine the premises proposed to be taken, and all such other premises as will in their judgemrnt be injured or benefited thereby ; after hearing such testimony as may be offered by any party interested, and which shall be reduced to writing by one of said jurors, they shall proceed to make their assessment and to determine and appraise to the owner or owners the value of the real estate so proposed to be taken, and the injury arising to them respectively, in consequence of the taking thereof, which shall be awarded to such owners respectively, as damages, after making due allowance therefrom for any benefit which such owners may respectively derive from such improvement. In the estimate of damages to the lands, the jurors shall include the value of the building or buildings, (if the property of the owner of such land,) as estimated by them as aforesaid, less the proceeds of the sale thereof, or if taken by the owner at the value to remove in such case they shall only include the difference between such value and the whole estimated value of such building or buildings.

Difference of benefits and damages to be paid or collected.

SEC. 12. If the damage to any person be greater than the benefits received, or if the benefit be greater than the damages, in either case the jurors shall strike a balance, and carry the difference forward to another column, so that the assessment will show what amount is to be received or paid by such owner or owners respectively, and the difference only, shall, in any case, be collected of them or payable to them.

SEC. 13. If the lands or building belong to different persons, or if the land be subject to lease, judgement, or mortgage, or if there be any estate in it less than an estate in fee, the injury done to such persons or interests, respectively may be awarded to them by the jurors, less the benefits resulting to them respectively from the proposed improvement.

In case of joint owners or mortgagees.

SEC. 14. Having ascertained the damages and expenses of the proposed improvement as aforesaid, the jurors shall thereupon apportion and assess the same, together with the costs of the proceedings upon the real estate by them deemed benefited in proportion to the benefits resulting thereto from the proposed improvement, as nearly as may be, and shall describe the real estate upon which their assessments may be made. The award of the said jurors shall be signed by them, and returned, together with the testimony taken, to the Common Council within the time limited in their order of appointment.

Award to be signed and returned to Council.

SEC. 15. The land required to be taken for the purposes mentioned in this act, shall not be appropriated until the damages awarded therefor to the owner thereof, shall be paid or tendered to the owner or his agent; or in case the said owner or agent cannot be found, or is unknown, deposited to his or their credit in some safe place of deposite: and then, and not before, such lands may be taken and appropriated for the purpose required; and the same shall thereafter be subject to all the laws and ordinances of the City, in the same manner as streets, alleys and public grounds, heretofore opened or laid out.

Land not to be taken till paid for.

SEC. 16. Where the whole of any lot or tract of land, or other premises, under lease, or other contract, shall be taken by virtue of this act, all the covenants, contracts or engagements between landlord and tenant, or any other contracting parties, touching the same or any part thereof, shall upon confirmation of such report, respectively cease and be absolutely discharged.

Contracts relative to lands, to cease when taken for public use.

CHAP. VI.

If part only is taken, contracts to be good, *pro rata*, as to the balance.

SEC. 17. When only part of a lot or tract of land, or other premises, so under lease, or other contract, shall be taken for any of the purposes aforesaid, all the covenants, contracts, or agreements respecting the same, upon the confirmation of such report, shall be absolutely discharged as to the part thereof so taken, but shall remain valid as to the residue thereof ; and the rents, considerations, and payments reserved, payble and to be paid for or in respect to the same, shall be so proportioned, so that the part thereof justly and equitably payable for such residue thereof, and no more, shall be paid or recoverable for in respect to the same.

Damages to be paid within 6 months, or proceedings to be void.

SEC. 18. The damages assessed shall be paid, or tendered, or deposited as herein required within six months from the confirmation of such assessment and report ; and if not so paid, tendered, or deposited, all the proceedings in any such case shall be void. The benefits so assessed, from the confirmation of said report, shall become and remain a lien upon the premises so determined by the jurors to be benefited by any opening or widening of such street, alley or public ground.

Benefits to remain a lien

In case of infants, &c.

SEC. 19. When any known owner of lands or tenements affected by any proceedings under this act shall be an infant, or labor under legal disability, the Judge of the Circuit Court of Milwaukee county, or in his absence the Judge of any Court of Record in said county, may, upon the application of the Common Council, or such party or his next friend, appoint a guardian for such party, and all notices required by this act shall be served upon such guardian.

New jurors may be appointed.

SEC. 20. After the jurors shall have made their report as to the necessity of taking any lands under this act, and the same shall have been confirmed, the Common Council shall have power to appoint new jurors in the place of any who shall neglect or refuse to serve, and the jurors before entering upon the discharge of their duties, shall severally take an oath before some competent officers, that they are freeholders of said City, and not interested in the premises proposed to be taken, and that they will faithfully and impartially discharge the trusts reposed in them.

Appeal from assessment.

SEC. 21. Any person whose property is taken, or against whom an assessment is made, may, within ten days from the return of the jurors to the Common Council, appeal from said assessment of damages or benefits to the Circuit Court of Milwaukee county, where such appeal shall be tried by the court and jury, as in ordinary cases. The Common Council shall have the same right of appeal.

Survey.

SEC. 22. Whenever any public ground, street or alley shall be laid out, widened or enlarged, under the provisions of this chapter, the Common Council shall cause an accurate survey and profile thereof to be made and filed in the office of the City Surveyor.

Cases under former Charter.

SEC. 23. In all cases where the return of a jury may have established the necessity of taking private property for the purpose of opening streets previous to the passage of this act, the Common Council may cause the damages and benefits arising therefrom to be assessed as required by this act, and for such purpose may summon a jury and do and perform all other acts in the same manner as if such proceedings had been originally instituted under this act.

Lands of G. Vliet and S. Brown excepted.

SEC. 24. The Common Council shall have no power under the provisions of this chapter to lay out any streets, alleys or public grounds, on the lands of Garret Vliet or Samuel Brown, in the north half of section nineteen and north-west quarter of section twenty, without consent of the said Garret Vliet and Samuel Brown as the case may be, as long as they are the owners thereof, and the same be used for farming purposes.

CHAP. VII.

CHAPTER VII.

CITY IMPROVEMENTS.

Aldermen to be Street Commissioners.

SECTION 1. The Aldermen of the several wards shall be street commissioners, in and for their respective wards, two of whom shall be a quorum ; one of their number, or some person appointed by them, shall be clerk of the board of commissioners, who shall keep a record of all their acts and doings, and shall keep and preserve all contracts, receipts and papers of the board. The several boards of street commissioners shall make report in detail to the Common Council, of their acts and doings, whenever required ; and at the expiration of each year, and before their term of office shall expire, shall submit all their acts and doings, books, records, papers, accounts, receipts and vouchers, to the Common Council for final settlement and adjustment.

Report.

Submit accounts.

Appeal from Street Commissioners.

SEC. 2. Any person deeming himself aggrieved by an act of the board of street commissioners, may, at any time appeal to the Common Council, who shall inquire into examine and correct the act or order complained of, as shall seem just and proper ; and the further action of the board in this respect, shall be regulated accordingly.

Powers of board.

SEC. 3. The said street commissioners shall have power to order and contract, for the making, grading, repairing and cleansing of streets, alleys, public grounds, reservoirs, gutters and sewers, within their respective wards, and to direct and control the persons employed therein.

Repair of sidewalks.

SEC. 4. Whenever the street commissioners shall deem it necessary to construct or repair any side-walk within their ward, they shall direct the owner or occupant of any lot adjoining such side-walk, to make or repair the same at his own proper cost and charge. If such work is not done in the manner and within the time prescribed, the commissioners shall cause the same to be done at the expense of the lots adjoining such side-walk.

Cost of surveying and estimating how to be paid.

SEC. 5. The cost and expense of surveying streets, alleys side-walks, sewers, and of estimating work thereon, and of repairing and cleansing streets and alleys, and of constructing and repairing reservoirs and sewers, shall be chargeable to and payable out of the fund of the proper ward; opening, graveling, grading, planking or paving streets and alleys to the centre thereof, shall be chargeable to and payable by the lots fronting on such street or alley. Sewers may be ordered by the street commissioners, and built at the expense of the lots or parcels of land benefitted thereby, which shall be apportioned among said lots or parcels of land by the street commissioners, with the assistance of the City Surveyor: *Provided, however,* That where sewers are constructed through alleys, no lots shall be assessed therefor except those situated in the block or blocks through which such sewers may be constructed; and where sewers are constructed through streets no lot shall be assessed therefor except those situated in the blocks fronting on such streets; and provided further, that in all cases where improvements or work of any kind are chargeable, by virtue of this section, upon lots benefitted, all such improvement across streets, alleys and public grounds shall be made and paid for out of the fund of the proper ward, in proportion to the width of the street, alley or public ground.

Sewers.

Estimate of work to be made.

SEC. 6. Whenever the commissioners shall determine to make any public improvement, as authorized by sections 3, 4 and 5, of this chapter, the[y] shall cause to be made an estimate of the whole expense thereof, and of the proportion to be assessed and charged to each lot, and in case of grading streets, alleys or side-walks, of the number of cubic yards to be filled in, or to be excavated in front of each lot; and such estimate shall be filed with the City Comptroller, for the inspection of the parties interested. The street commissioners shall give notice by advertisement, for ten days in one or more daily papers published in Milwaukee, to the owners or occupants of the lots or parcels of land fronting on any street,

Ten days notice to be given.

CHAP. VII. alley or sidewalk ordered to be graded, graveled, planked or paved, requiring them to do the work mentioned in such notice, within a reasonable time, therein to be specified; and if the said work shall not be done within such time, the said commissioners shall enter into contract for the doing thereof.

Deep cutting or extraordinary filling.

SEC. 7. Whenever the general interest of the City or ward requires deep cutting, or extraordinary filling in any street, and the owners of the lots or lands fronting on such deep cutting or filling, shall deem themselves aggrieved thereby and shall represent to the commissioners in writing, that the expense of such excavation or filling will exceed the benefit the same will be to the property assessed therefor, the street commissioners shall require the Marshal to summon five freeholders, not residents of the ward, nor owners of, nor interested in said lots or lands, who, after being sworn faithfully and impartially to discharge the trust reposed in them, shall examine the premises, and if, in their opinion, the cost of such work shall exceed the benefit derived therefrom, it shall be their duty to make report thereof to said commissioners in writing, and shall state therein what portion of such work shall be chargeable to such lots or parcels of land, and how much, or what portion shall be chargeable to the ward fund; and such proportion as shall be reported as properly chargeable to the lots or parcels aforesaid shall be assessed upon the same and levied and collected as other taxes and assessments, and the remainder shall be paid out of the ward fund:

Appeal must be made within fifteen days.

Provided, however, That the petition of no owner feeling himself aggrieved by an act of the street commissioners, shall be received unless the same shall be presented within fifteen days after the first publication of the notice requiring the same to be done: *And provided further*, That when it shall appear to the street commissioners, that lands belonging to non-residents, infants, or persons laboring under legal disability, who shall not be represented by any agent or guardian, or not benefited by the making of streets in front of such lots or lands, to the amount of the cost and expense thereof, it shall then be the duty of said commissioners to cause to be summoned a jury, as is herein provided.

Stagnant water.

SEC. 8. The street commissioners shall give notice to all owners or occupants of lots which may be deemed injurious to health by reason of stagnant water remaining thereon, in the official papers, for ten days, to abate such nuisance by draining or filling such lot within a reasonable time, therein to be specified, and if such nuisance shall not be abated or removed, within the time so specified, the street commissioners shall cause the same to be abated and removed at the expense of the property upon which the same may exist.

Wharves and dredging.

SEC. 9. The street commissioners shall have power to regulate and cause to be constructed, altered and maintained, wharves along the banks of the Milwaukee and Menomonee rivers, and shall have and exercise the same power and control over the said rivers, that they may by virtue of this act possess over streets and alleys. They shall also have power to cause the Milwaukee river to be dredged on each side thereof, not exceeding one hundred feet in width, and the expense of constructing, altering and maintaining such wharves and dredging the river shall be apportioned by the street commissioners among, and payable by the several lots or parcels of land extending to said river, in proportion to the work done opposite to such lot or parcel of land, to be estimated by the surveyor: *Provided*, however, that before causing such work to be done, the same notices shall be given as is required in the case of grading streets.

Contractors to receive certificates of work done

SEC. 10. After the completion and performance of any contract entered into by the street commissioners for work chargeable to lots or lands by virtue of this act, they shall give to the contractor or contractors, a certificate under their hand, stating therein the amount of work done by such contractor, the nature thereof and the description of the lot or parcel of land upon which the same is chargeable, which

CHAP. VII. said certificate may be transferred by endorsement thereon, and if the amount thereof shall not be paid before the time of making out the annual assessment roll, the same shall be assessed upon the said lots or parcels of land respectively, and collected for the use and benefit of the holder of such certificate, as other taxes on real estate are collected by virtue of this act; and if the notice to do the work required shall have been given as herein provided, no informality or error in the proceedings shall vitiate such assessment; *Provided*, that in no event where work is ordered to be done at the expense of any lot or parcel of land, shall either the city or any ward be held responsible for the payment thereof.

City award not to be liable.

Appeal to be made within 20 days.

SEC. 11. In all cases where work is ordered to be done by the owner of any lot, under the provisions of this chapter, such owner may make his appeal as herein before provided, at any time within twenty days after the publication of the notice required to be given, and until the expiration of such twenty days, no such order shall be executed.

Bayou in First Ward.

SEC. 12. The Aldermen of the first ward may cause the bayou in said ward to be filled, and shall cause the same to be done by contract, to be given to the lowest bidder in such manner as the Common Council shall by ordinance prescribe: *Provided*, however, that such contractor shall in no event hold the city or said ward responsible for the payment of any work he may do under said contract. It shall be the duty of the City Surveyor to make an estimate and report to the Common Council the amount of filling opposite to each lot abutting on or extending to said bayou, and the Common Council shall levy a tax upon the several lots so abutting in proportion to the amount of filling opposite to each lot as reported by the Surveyor, which in the aggregate shall be sufficient to defray the expense of such filling, including all costs and charges connected therewith, but in no case shall either said ward or the City be responsible for the payment of any liability that may be created in pursuance of this section. The tax so levied shall become a lien upon the several lots for such amount as shall be reported by said Surveyor and shall be collected as other taxes levied under this act.

CHAPTER VIII.

ASSESSING, LEVYING AND COLLECTING TAXES.

Property subject to tax.

SECTION 1. All property, real or personal, within the City, except such as may be exempt by the laws of this State shall be subject to taxation for the support of the City Government, and the payment of its debts and liabilities; and the same shall be assessed in the manner hereinafter provided; and the Assessors elected under this act, shall have and possess the same powers that are, or may be, conferred upon township Assessors, except so far as they may be altered by this act: *Provided, however,* That the Common Council may prescribe the form of assessment roll, and more fully define the duties of Assessors, and make such rules and regulations in relation to revising, altering or adding to such rolls, as they may from time to time deem advisable.

Assessment Rolls.

Duties of assessors.

SEC. 2. Within ten days after receiving notice of their election, the Assessors shall assemble at the Common Council chamber, and after taking their official oath, shall proceed to organize their body by electing one of their number chairman, who shall be authorized to administer such oaths as shall be required by this chapter; and within such time as the Common Council shall designate, the said Assessors shall make out a complete and accurate assessment roll, which shall contain a description, as near as may be, of all the lands, lots, or parcels of land within said City sufficient to identify the same; and also of all persons or bodies politic, liable to pay taxes on personal property; and opposite to each lot, or parcel of land, shall be affixed the value thereof, and opposite to the name of each person or body politic, shall be affixed the value of the personal property for which such person or body politic shall be assessed. Where there are buildings upon any lôt or parcel of land, the value of the same shall be set forth in a separate column. The Assessors may, if they deem it advisable, assess any lot or tract of land in such parcels or such sub-divisions as they may deem proper, but it shall not be necessary to enter the name of the owner opposite to any tract or parcel of land. Any act done by a majority of the Assessors shall have the same force and effect as if done by all the Assessors elected under this act.

Notice of completion of roll.

SEC. 3. When the same shall be completed, the Assessors shall give one week's notice thereof in the official papers and shall fix a time and convenient place where they will meet for the purpose of hearing any objections of parties deeming themselves aggrieved by such assessment; and after hearing the same, the Assessors shall make such alterations or revisions as justice or equity may require: *Provided*, the time of hearing such objections shall not be extended more than two weeks from the expiration of such notice.

SEC. 4. Within one week after the time limited for the hearing such objections, the board of Assessors shall return the said assessment roll to the Common Council, and they may confirm or refer the same back to the boardof Assessors.

Council may equalize roll.

The Common Council may supply omissions in said roll, and for the purpose of equalizing the same, may alter, add to, take from, and otherwise revise and correct the same: *Provided, however*, the Common Council shall not have power to increase the amount of said roll, except by the value of such real property as may have been omitted by the Assessors.

SEC. 5 When the assessment roll shall have been revised and corrected, the same shall be filed with the Clerk, and an order confirming the same shall be entered in the proceedings of the Common Council.

Levying of tax.

Thereupon the Common Council shall, by resolution, levy such sum or sums of money as may be sufficient for the several purposes for which taxes are herein authorized to be levied, but not exceeding the authorized per centage, particularly specifying the purpose for which the same are levied, and if not for general City purposes, the ward upon which the same are levied.

Taxes to be a lien on property.

SEC. 6. All taxes and assessments, general or special, levied under this act, shall be and remain a lien upon the lands and tenements upon which they may be assessed from the time of the confirmation of such assessment roll ; and on all personal property of any person or body politic assessed for personal taxes, from the delivery of the warrant for the collection thereof, until such tax shall be paid ; and no sale or transfer of such real or personal estate shall affect such lien.

Personal property may be sold for tax.

Any personal property belonging to the person taxed may be taken and sold for the payment of taxes upon personal property.

Tax List.

SEC. 7. As soon as said tax shall be levied, the Common Council shall cause the same to be copied in a book provided for that purpose, setting opposite to each tract of land, and to each person named, under proper columns, such sum or sums as may be levied upon such lot or against such person. The said copy shall be designated the tax list, and to it shall be appended a warrant signed by the Mayor and Clerk, and sealed with the corporate seal of said City, directed to the Treasurer, requiring and commanding him to collect the taxes and assessments in said list specified, in the manner prescribed by this act ; and in case said taxes and assessments shall not be paid within such time as in said warrant shall be specified, that then he shall proceed to sell the several lots or parcels of land, or those parts thereof, upon which said taxes or assessments shall remain unpaid, and to make due return to the Common Council within such time as shall be fixed in said warrant.

Form of warrant to Treasurer.

Tax list to be compared with roll and certified to by the Clerk.

SEC. 8. Such tax list, before being delivered to the Treasurer, shall be compared by the Clerk with the assessment roll, as confirmed ; to it he shall append his certificate, that the same has been so compared by him, and that the said assess-

CHAP. VIII. ment roll, and the whole thereof, has been copied into such tax list, and the said tax list, when so certified, shall be prima facie evidence in any court, that the lands and persons therein named were subject to taxation, and that the assessment was just and equal.

Treasurer's notice.

Form of notice.

SEC. 9. On receipt of such tax list, the Treasurer shall give one week's notice thereof in the official papers. Such notice shall specify that taxes on personal property shall be paid within twenty days from the first publication of said notice, and taxes and assessments on real estate, before the last day of December following; and that all tracts or parcels of land specified in said tax list, upon which the taxes and assessments shall not be paid by that day, will be sold at a certain time and place to be therein specified; and the publication of such notice shall be deemed a demand, and a neglect to pay the taxes and assessments within the time specified, shall be deemed a refusal to pay the same.

Enforcement of collection of personal tax.

Warrant to the Marshal.

Marshal's power to distrain.

SEC. 10. On the expiration of the twenty days mentioned in the preceding section, the Treasurer shall proceed to enforce the collection of the personal taxes in the manner specified in title 5 of the Revised Statutes, and if any of such personal taxes shall not be paid or collected in consequence of the neglect or delay of the Treasurer, the Common Council may sue for and recover the amount thereof from the said Treasurer and his sureties. In case the taxes on personal property shall not be paid within the time limited in the ninth section of this chapter, the Treasurer may issue his warrant directed to the City Marshal, requiring and commanding him within a certain time in such warrant to be specified, to proceed and collect such taxes on personal property as shall then remain unpaid. And the Marshal receiving such warrant shall be subject to all the liabilities, and shall have all the powers of levying, distraining and selling, that are herein given to the Treasurer, and shall be entitled to the fees for collecting which the Treasurer would have, had the tax been collected by him.

Sale of real estate for taxes.

SEC. 11. On the day and at the place designated in the Treasurer's notice, he shall commence by public auction the sale (and continue the same from day to day till the whole are disposed of,) of all tracts and lots, or parts thereof, upon which the taxes or assessments shall remain unpaid. The sale to be made for the smallest undivided portion of the lot or tract for which any person will take the same and pay the taxes and charges thereon. On receiving the amount of such taxes and charges, the treasurer shall issue to the purchaser, his or her heirs or assigns, a certificate containing the name of the purchaser, a description of the premises sold, the amount paid therefor, the rate of interest said certificate may bear, and the time when the right to redeem the same will expire. The Treasurer shall keep a record of the lots or tracts sold, the name of the purchaser, the date and amount of sale, the time, by whom, and for what sum the same was redeemed, and the time and to whom the same was conveyed if not redeemed.

Record of sales.

Second sale. Penalty for non-payment

SEC. 12. In case any purchaser at such tax sale shall neglect or refuse to pay the amount for which any lot or tract was sold, at such time as the Treasurer shall designate, he shall, on the day following, offer said lot or tract again for sale ; and any person bidding off, at any such sale, any lot or tract of land, and refusing or neglecting to pay for the same within the time designated, shall forfeit and pay to the City the sum of five dollars for each lot so purchased and not paid for, to be sued for and collected as other penalties under this act.

Redemption.

SEC. 13. Any lot or tract of land so sold, or any portion thereof, may be redeemed within three years from the day of sale, and at any time before the deed is executed, by the owner or any person interested therein, paying to the Treasurer the amount for which the same was sold, together with the interest at the rate of twenty-five per cent. per annum, and the legal charges thereon. If the estate of an infant or lunatic be sold, the same may be redeemed upon the like terms, at any time within one year after such disability shall be removed.

SEC. 14. Any tract or lot of land sold in pursuance of this act, or any part thereof, which shall not be redeemed within three years from the day of sale, shall be conveyed by the Treasurer to the purchaser, or his assigns as herein provided.

Assignment of tax certificates.

SEC. 15. The assignee of any tax certificate, by endorsement thereon, of any premises sold for taxes by virtue of this act, shall be entitled to receive a deed of such premises in his own name and with the same effect, as though he had been the original purchaser.

City to become purchaser of real or personal estate where no bid is made.

SEC. 16. If at any sale of real or personal estate for taxes or assessments, no bid shall be made for any parcel of land, or any goods and chattels, the same shall be struck off to the City ; and thereupon the City shall receive in the corporate name, a certificate of the sale thereof, and shall be vested with the same rights as other purchasers are. If the City shall become the purchaser of any personal property by virtue of this chapter, the Treasurer shall have the power to sell the same at public sale ; and in case the City shall become the purchaser of any real estate at any tax sale, the Treasurer is authorized to sell the certificates issued therefor, for the amount sold, and interest, and to endorse and transfer such certificate to the purchaser.

Omissions in assessment roll.

SEC. 17. If it shall appear to the Assessors that any lot or parcel of land was omitted in the assessment roll of either or both of the two preceding years and that the same was then liable to taxation, they will in addition to the assessment for that year, assess upon the lot or tract so omitted, for such year or years, that it shall have been so omitted, the just value thereof, noting the year when such omission occurred, and such assessment shall have the same force and effect as it would have had if made the year when the same was omitted; and the Common Council shall direct in addition to the tax for the current year, such tax to be levied upon such lot or tract as the same would have been chargable with, had not the same been so omitted, and such tax shall be collected as other taxes or assessments for the current year. All lands shall be subject to taxes that may have been omitted, in whosesoever hands they may have come.

Defect or informality. assessment.

Should the tax or assessment upon any parcel of land be set aside or declared void, by reason of any defect or informality in the assessing, levying, selling or conveying the same, but not affecting the equity and justice of the tax itself, the Common Council shall cause the tax or assessment so set aside or declared void to be re-levied in such manner as they shall by ordinance direct: *Provided,* That if the defect was in the assessment, the same shall again be assessed at such time as the Common Council may direct; and the said tax or assessment so re-assessed or re-levied shall be and continue a lien upon said lot or tract, and shall be collected as other taxes and assessments are collected under this act.

Tax deeds, prima facie evidence of validity of tax.

SEC. 18. All deeds purporting on their face to be executed on account of sale for taxes or assessment under this act, shall be, in all cases, prima facie evidence of the validity of such tax, and if the title conveyed by such deed shall come in question shall be prima facie evidence of all facts recited in such deeds, so far as they affect the validity of the title conveyed by such deed.

Immaterial errors or informality not to vitiate the tax.

SEC. 19. All the direction hereby given for the assessing of lands, and the levying and collection of taxes and assessments, shall be deemed only directory, and no error or informality in the proceedings of any of the officers entrusted with the same, not affecting the substantial justice of the tax itself, shall vitiate or in any way affect the validity of the tax or assessment.

Treasurer to receive moneys tendered for redemption.

SEC. 20. The Treasurer shall receive all moneys that may be legally tendered him for the redemption of lands sold for taxes, and he shall keep an account thereof, and pay the same over on demand, to the persons entitled to receive the same. He shall cancel all certificates so redeemed, and preserve the same in his office; and at the expiration of his term of office, he shall deliver over to his successor all redemption moneys in his hands, with the statement of the amount so received.

Liens upon land to be carried out in tax list.

SEC. 21. In all cases where, by the provisions of this act, any charge or assessment is made a lien upon land, the amount of such charge or assessment shall be carried out on the tax list in a separate column or columns, opposite the lot or tract upon which the same may be a lien; and the Treasurer may collect and sell, and do all other acts in regard thereto, in the same manner as if the amount of such lien was a general tax.

Fees of Treasurer.

SEC. 22. The Treasurer, in addition to such sum as the Common Council may allow him, shall be entitled to the following fees, to wit: five per cent. on all sums collected on personal tax, the same to be added to the amount of the personal tax of each person taxed; and in case of a distress and sale by him of goods and chattels, for the payment of any tax, he shall be entitled to such fees as are allowed Sheriffs on sales of goods under execution. For each certificate by him issued on sale of lands for payment of taxes or assessments, ten cents, to be added to the amount of such tax or assessment, and included in such certificate; for each lot redeemed, for which he shall issue a certificate, twenty-five cents, and five cents for each additional lot embraced in such certificate, to be paid by the person redeeming; for each tax deed executed by him, one dollar, and five cents for each additional lot or tract embraced in the same deed, to be paid by the person receiving the same.

Certain lands exempt.

SEC. 23. All those parts of sections nineteen, twenty, twenty-one, twenty-two, twenty-nine, thirty, thirty-one and thirty-two, included within said City limits, that are used for farming purposes, and not laid out into city lots or for town or city purposes, shall be exempt from all taxes and assessments authorized by this act, except for State, County, School and Poor purposes; but the Common Council may levy upon the lands so exempt, an annual tax of four mills on the dollar, one-half of which shall be applied to general City purposes, and the remainder to the ward in which the lands may lie.

Purchase from city of lots sold for taxes.

SEC. 24. Whenever any person shall bid off any lot offered for sale for taxes, which lot shall have been bid off in the name of the City for the taxes of any previous year, and shall, at the time of such subsequent sale, remain the property of the City, such person shall, before being entitled to his certificate of such sale, purchase of the City its certificate by paying the amount of principal, interest and charges thereon, and receive from the Treasurer an assignment thereof.

Where same lot is sold by both city and county Treasurer.

SEC. 25. When there shall be a sale by the County Treasurer and by the City Treasurer of any piece or parcel of land for taxes, in the same year, the purchaser of such piece or parcel who may be first in point of time may redeem the same from the subsequent purchaser, and in case he shall not redeem, the right of the last purchaser shall be held paramount in case of the execution of any tax deed therefor. If the first purchaser in point of time shall so redeem, it shall be the duty of the proper officer to make an entry in the sale book of the character in which such person may redeem, and the person so redeeming shall be substituted to all the rights of the holder of the certificate, so redeemed as aforesaid.

Plaintiffs in tax cases to deposit unpaid taxes before commencing a suit.

SEC. 26. No person shall be permitted to institute any proceeding to set aside any assessment or special tax hereafter levied or assessed upon any lot or tract of land, or to set aside any deed executed in consequence of the non-pay-

CHAP. VIII. ment of such taxes and of the sale of the premises therefor, unless such person shall first pay or tender to the proper party or deposite for his use with the Treasurer, the amount of all State, County and City taxes that may remain unpaid upon such lot or tract, together with the interest and charges thereon.

COUNTY AND STATE TAXES.

City Clerk to send roll to County Clerk

SEC. 27. Before the annual meeting of the Board of Supervisors of the County of Milwaukee, in the fall, it shall be the duty of the City Clerk to cause a copy of the assessment roll of said City for such year, to be transmitted to the Clerk of the Board of Supervisors, who shall lay the same before the Board of Supervisors at their meeting.

Equalization by Supervisors.

SEC. 28. The Board of Supervisors shall have the right of equalizing the assessment rolls of the town in said county and said City, as provided by law; but in such equalization, shall consider the assessment roll of said City as an entire roll, and shall not change the relative valuations of the different wards.

County tax, how levied.

SEC. 29. The said Board of Supervisors may levy a tax as now provided by law, but shall therein proceed without regard to the division of the City into wards, and shall cause the amount of taxes to be levied, and the purposes to be certified to the City Clerk, in the manner provided by the general laws of this State; and the said City Clerk shall make out a tax list for that purpose, separate from the tax list for City purposes, and shall deliver the same to the City Treasurer, as provided by law.

City Treasurer's duty relative to county tax.

SEC. 30. The Treasurer of the City, in giving bonds, collecting such tax, and making his return to the County Treasurer, and [and] in all other respects, shall conform to the general laws of the State, except that the return to the County Treasurer, shall be for the City and not for the wards.

CHAPTER IX.

FIRE DEPARTMENT.

Fire limits.

SEC. 1. The Common Council, for the purpose of guarding against the calamities of fire, shall have power, and it shall be their duty to prescribe the limits within which wooden buildings or buildings of other materials that shall not be considered fire proof, shall not be erected, placed or repaired, and to direct that all and any buildings within the limits prescribed, shall be made and constructed of fire-proof materials, and to prohibit the repairing or re-building of wooden buildings within the fire limits, when the same shall have been damaged to the extent of fifty per cent. of the value thereof, and to prescribe the manner of ascertaining such damage.

Powers of Common Council.

SEC. 2. The Common Council shall have power to prevent the dangerous construction and condition of chimneys, fire-places, hearths, stoves, stove-pipes, ovens, boilers and apparatus used in and about any building, and to cause the same to be removed or placed in a safe and secure condition, when considered dangerous.

To prevent the deposite of ashes in unsafe places ;

To require the inhabitants to provide as many fire-buckets and in such manner and time as they shall prescribe, and to regulate the use of them in time of fire ;

To regulate and prevent the carrying on of manufactories dangerous in causing or promoting fires ;

To regulate and prevent the use of fire-works and fire-arms ;

To compel the owners and occupants of buildings to have scuttles in the roofs, and stairs or ladders leading to the same ;

To authorize the Mayor, Aldermen, Fire-Wardens, and other officers of the City to keep away from the vicinity of any fire, all idle and suspected persons, and to compel all by-standers to aid in the extinguishment of fires and in the pres-

CHAP. IX. ervation of property exposed to danger thereat, and generally to establish such regulations for the prevention and extinguishment of fires as the Common Council may deem expedient.

Fire Engines and Companies. SEC. 3. The Common Council shall have power to purchase fire engines and other fire apparatus, and to authorize the formation of fire engine, hook and ladder, and hose companies, and to provide for the due and proper support and regulations of the same; and to order such Companies to be disbanded, and their meetings to be prohibited, and their apparatus to be delivered up. Each company shall not exceed seventy able bodied men between the ages of eighteen and fifty years, and may elect their own officers, and form their own by-laws, not inconsistent with the laws of this State, or the ordinances or regulations of said City, and shall be formed only by voluntary enlistments. Every member of each company hereby authorized to be formed, shall be exempt from highway work and poll tax, from serving on juries, and from military duty, during the continuance of such membership; and any person having served for the term of seven years, in either of said companies, shall be forever thereafter exempt from serving on juries, from poll tax and from military duty, except in cases of insurrection or invasion.

Exemption of firemen.

Meetings. SEC. 4. There shall be a meeting of the members of said companies, on the third Monday of March in each year, at such place as may be designated by the chief engineer, when they may nominate and recommend to the Common Council for appointment, one chief engineer, and three assistant engineers, and the Common Council shall thereupon confirm said nominations; and the persons so appointed shall perform such duties as the Common Council shall prescribe.

Officers.

Fire Wardens SEC. 5. At the same time, the members of said companies shall nominate, and the Common Council shall appoint the same, ten fire wardens, who shall perform such duties as the Common Council shall prescribe ; and they may at any time enter in, to, or upon, any house, store, barn, or other building or enclosure, for the purpose of inspecting the same.

Fines and penalties.

SEC. 6. One half of the nett proceeds of all fines and penalties recovered for the breach of any ordinance, by-law, or regulation, made in pursuance of this chapter, shall be paid to the fire department.

Arrests at fires.

SEC. 7. Whenever any person shall refuse to obey any lawful order of any Engineer, Fire Warden, Mayor or Alderman, at any fire, it shall be lawful for the officer giving such order, to arrest, or to direct orally, the marshal, constable, watchman or any citizen, to arrest such person and to confine him temporarily in any safe place until such fire shall be extinguished ; and in the same manner such officers, or any of them, may arrest, or direct the arrest and confinement of any person at such fire who shall be intoxicated, or disorderly ; and any person who shall refuse to obey any such lawful order or who shall refuse to arrest, or aid in arresting any person so refusing, shall be liable to such penalty as the Common Council may prescribe, not exceeding fifteen dollars.

Sack Company.

SEC. 8. The Common Council shall have power to organize a Sack Company, or continue in force any such company now organized, which shall be known as Sack Co. No. 1, to consist of not more than seventy members. Such company shall constitute a part of the fire department, and at fires shall be subject to the control of the chief engineer. The members of said company, either collectively or individually, are hereby authorized and empowered to act as a special police in and for the City of Milwaukee, and are hereby vested with all the powers and authority which now, [is] or may be hereafter vested in any police officer of said City, and shall be entitled to all the rights and immunities of members of the fire department. At fires they shall take charge of all property which may be exposed or endangered, and shall so far as it may be in their power, preserve the same from in-

Powers and duties.

jury or destruction. Said company may from time to time adopt such by-laws and regulations as they may deem necessary, not inconsistent with the laws of the State. The members of said company shall not be entitled to any pay or compensation for services rendered in their official capacity. They shall, in case of riot or disturbance of the peace, have free access to all licensed places of amusement in the city, and shall perform such services as may be necessary for the peace and good order of the same. The members of said company shall severally take an oath or affirmation that they will faithfully discharge their duties of the said office, and when any member of said company shall cease to be a member thereof by resignation, expulsion or otherwise, notice thereof shall be given to the city clerk and police justice, and they shall preserve a record of all the members of said company.

CHAPTER X.

MISCELLANEOUS PROVISIONS.

All work to be let by contract.

SECTION 1. All work for the City, or either of the wards, shall be let by contract to the lowest bidder, and due notice shall be given of the time and place of letting such contract.

Appropriation of money.

SEC. 2. No monies shall be appropriated for any purpose whatever, except such as are expressly authorized by this act.

Remission of penalties.

SEC. 3. No penalty or judgment recovered in favor of the City shall be remitted or discharged, except by a vote of two-thirds of all the Aldermen elect.

Suits to recover penalties.

SEC. 4. All actions brought to recover any penalty or forfeiture under this act, or the ordinances, by-laws, police or health regulations made in pursuance thereof, shall be brought in the corporate name of the City. It shall be lawful to declare generally in debt for such penalty or forfeiture, stating the clause of this act, or by-law, or ordinance, under which the penalty or forfeiture is claimed, and to give the special matter in evidence under it.

SEC. 5. In all prosecutions for any violation of any of the provisions of this act, or any by-law or ordinance, the first process shall be a summons, unless oath be made for a warrant as in other cases. Suits—how to be commenced.

SEC. 6. Execution shall issue forthwith on the rendition of the judgment unless the same be stayed or appealed according to the laws of this State. The execution shall require the defendant in any such action, in case no goods or chattels, lands, or tenements, whereof the judgment can be collected, be found, to be imprisoned in the jail of Milwaukee county for a term not exceeding six months, in the discretion of the justice or judge rendering judgment, unless the same be sooner paid. Executions.

SEC. 7. No person shall be an incompetent judge, justice, witness or juror by reason of his being an inhabitant of said City, in any proceeding or action in which the City shall be a party in interest.

SEC. 8. All ordinances, regulations, or resolutions now in force in the City of Milwaukee, and not inconsistent with this act, shall remain in force under this act until altered, modified, or repealed by the Common Council after this act shall take effect. Old ordinances.

SEC. 9. All actions, rights, fines, penalties, and forfeitures in suit or otherwise, which have accumulated under the several acts consolidated herein, shall be vested in and prosecuted by the corporation hereby created. Rights af action under old charter.

SEC. 10. If any election by the people or Common Council shall, for any cause, not be held at the time or in the manner herein prescribed, or if the Council shall fail to organize as herein provided, it shall not be considered reason for arresting, suspending or absolving said corporation, but such election or organization may be had on any subsequent day, by order of the Common Council; and if any of the duties enjoined by this act or the ordinances or by-laws of the City, to be done by any officer at any specified time, and the same Failures of election, &c.

CHAP. X. are not then done or performed, the Common Council may appoint another time at which the said acts may be done and performed.

Bridges. SEC. 11. Bridges shall be maintained and supported across the Milwaukee and Menomonee rivers, at the expense of the City, as follows: one from Water street in the first ward, to the foot of Cherry street in the second ward; one from the foot of Wisconsin street in the first and third wards, to Spring street in the fourth ward; one from the foot of Water street in the third ward to Ferry street in the Fifth ward; and one across the Menomonee river at the foot of West Water street. All of said bridges except the first shall contain draws sufficient for the passage of vessels.

Cherry St. Bridge. SEC. 12. It shall be the duty of the Common Council to levy a tax upon the taxable property in the first and third wards of said city, to defray the expenses of the first construction of the bridge at the foot of Cherry street, and it shall be the duty of the street commissioners of the second ward to cause all necessary grading to be done in order to make such bridge connect with the main land on the west side of the river, and to render the road thereto passable.

Damage to bridges. SEC. 13. The general laws for the preservation of bridges, and the punishment by such laws provided for the wilful and malicious injuries done thereto, are hereby extended to, and shall include all of said bridges, and shall apply to any wilful or malicious damage which may be done to either of them by any person or persons whatever, and the Common Council may from time to time make such by-laws or ordinances as they may deem necessary for the preservation of such bridges, and enforce the same by adequate penalties. In case of any damage being done to any of said bridges by any vessel or water craft, or by the master or any person in command thereof, such vessel or water craft may be proceeded against under the law to provide for the collection of demands against boats and vessels.

SEC. 14. When any suit or action shall be commenced against said City, the service thereof may be made by leaving a copy of the process by the proper officer with the Mayor, and it shall be the duty of the Mayor forthwith to inform the Common Council thereof, or take such other proceedings as by the ordinances or resolutions of said Council may be in such case provided.

Suits against City.

SEC. 15. The following property, now or at any time hereafter belonging to said City or either of the wards thereof, shall be exempt from levy and sale under or by virtue of any execution: engine houses, hook and ladder houses, together with the grounds and lots on which they are situated, and all fire engines, carriages, hooks, ladders, buckets, hose, or any other fire apparatus used by any company created or authorized by the Common Council of said City; school and market houses, and the furniture thereof, and furniture of Common Council and office rooms: *Provided*, That nothing herein contained shall exempt any of the aforesaid real or personal property from levy and sale, by virtue of any execution issued on judgments rendered in favor of any person or persons who may have furnished or sold any such fire apparatus to, or on the credit of said City. Nor shall any real or personal property of any inhabitants of said City, or of any individual or corporation, be levied on and sold by virtue of any execution, issued to satisfy or collect any debt, obligation, or contract of said City.

Property exempt from taxation.

Exception.

Individual Property not subject to execution for debts of City.

SEC. 16. The Common Council shall at its first meeting appoint five Commissioners, one from each ward, who, with the assistance of the City Surveyor, or such other assistant Surveyors as the Council may appoint, shall cause a new and accurate survey to be made of the lines and boundaries of all the streets, alleys, side-walks, public grounds, wharves and blocks, and shall cause to be established such permanent land-marks as they may deem necessary, and to cause an ac-

Commissioners of survey

CHAP. X. curate plot or plots thereof to be made and certified to by the said Surveyor and Commissioners, which shall be filed in the office of the City Surveyor, and a copy thereof shall be recorded in the office of the Register of Deeds of Milwaukee County.

SEC. 17. The survey and land marks so made and established shall be prima facie evidence of the lines and boundaries of all streets, alleys, side-walks, public grounds, wharves and blocks, in all cases in which they shall be drawn into controversy in all courts of this State.

Permanent grade.

SEC. 18. As soon as practicable after the completion of such survey, the Common Council shall cause to be established under the direction of the City Surveyor, the grade of all streets, side-walks and alleys in said City, and shall cause accurate profiles thereof to be made, one of which shall be filed in the office of the Register of Deeds of Milwaukee county; and should the grade so established be at any time hereafter altered, all damages, costs and charges arising therefrom shall be paid by the City to the owner of any lot or parcel of land, or tenement which may be affected or injured in consequence of the alteration of such grade.

City liable for alterations.

Commissioners of ordinances.

SEC. 19. The Common Council shall appoint one or more Commissioners, whose duty it shall be to report to the Common Council, within a reasonable time, a draft of all ordinances, by-laws, rules, regulations, and forms, that may be necessary to carry this act fully into effect, and more fully to define the powers and duties, and fix the compensation of the several officers created or authorized by this act. The said ordinances, by-laws, &c., when they shall have been adopted by the Common Council, shall be published in a convenient form, together with this act, and the same, when so published shall be admitted as evidence in any court within this State, of the passage and publication of such ordinances, without any further publication in the official paper.

SEC. 20. The market-house, and the lands appertaining thereto, in the first ward, shall be the property of said ward, and the Aldermen of said ward, or a majority of them, shall have the right to lease, manage and control the same, and shall have all authority in relation to said market-house which they now may have by virtue of any law of this State. The Common Council with the consent of a majority of said Aldermen, may pass ordinances applicable to the first ward alone, to control and regulate markets and the selling of meats and other provisions, and to confine the same to such limits as they may deem proper.

First Ward Market House.

SEC. 21. The said City may lease, purchase and hold real or personal estate sufficient for the convenience of the inhabitants thereof, and may sell and convey the same, and the same shall be free from taxation.

City, may hold real estate.

SEC. 22. Real estate exempted from taxation by the laws of the State shall be subject to special taxes as other real estate under this act.

SEC. 23. No general law of this State, contravening the provisions of this act, shall be considered as repealing, amending or modifying the same, unless such purpose be expressly set forth in such law.

General state laws not to repeal this act.

SEC. 24. On the petition of a majority of the inhabitants liable to pay poll tax of any district in any ward, and consisting of contiguous territory bounded by ward lines, or the centre of streets or alleys, the street commissioners of such ward may constitute such district a road district, and appoint any person named in such petition, or if no person be named, then any proper person, road-master for such district, and the person so appointed shall have all the powers of overseers of roads as provided in the title VI of the Revised Statutes, and shall report to the street commissioners when required: ***Provided, however,*** That no road-master shall receive more

Road districts.

CHAP. X. than one dollar for each day he is actually employed in the business of his office, and he shall receive such compensation out of the moneys collected on such poll tax, and that in no case shall any moneys be drawn either from the ward or City funds, for the compensation of road-masters or for any work performed by them or under their supervision.

Road masters.

School houses. Money to be borrowed.

SEC. 25. The Common Council may borrow on the faith of the City, a sum not exceeding four thousand dollars, for the purpose of completing and furnishing the public schools within the City, for a term not exceeding ten years, and at an interest not exceeding ten per cent., and may issue the bonds of the City therefor, and shall provide for the payment of the interest thereon. Should said sum not be sufficient to complete and furnish said schools, it shall be the duty of the Aldermen of the several wards, to complete and furnish the same out of the funds of their respective wards.

REPEALING CLAUSE.

Former acts repealed.

SEC. 26. An act to incorporate the City of Milwaukee, approved 31st January, 1846; an act relating to bridges in the City of Milwaukee, approved 2d February, 1846; an act relating to certain streets, in the City of Milwaukee, approved 2d February, 1846; an act to amend an act entitled an act to incorporate the City of Milwaukee, approved 4th of February, 1847; an act to authorize the levy of a special tax in the third ward, approved 11th March, 1848; an act to authorize the levy of a special tax in the fifth ward, approved 11th March, 1848; an act additional to an act to incorporate the City of Milwaukee, approved 10th of August, 1848; an act amendatory to an act entitled an act to authorize the levy of a special tax in the fifth ward of the City of Milwaukee, approved 19th of August, 1848; an act additional to an act to incorporate the City of Milwaukee, approved 19th of August, 1848; an act to amend an act entitled an act to incorporate the City of

Milwaukee, and acts amendatory thereto, approved 12th of March, 1849 ; an act in relation to the collection and return of taxes &c., for the year 1849, approved 24th of January, 1850 ; an act to authorize the construction of a wharf in the City of Milwaukee, approved 4th of February, 1850 ; an act to provide for the election of certain officers in the City of Milwaukee, approved 8th of February, 1850 ; an act giving criminal jurisdiction to justices of the peace in the 5th ward, approved 9th of February, 1850 ; an act to authorize the levy of a special tax in the third ward of the City of Milwaukee, approved 9th of February, 1850 ; an act to authorize the construction of wharves in the City of Milwaukee, approved 6th of March, 1851 ; an act to authorize the Aldermen of the third ward to pave certain streets in said ward, approved 13th of March, 1851 ; an act supplementary and amendatory to an act entitled an act to incorporate the City of Milwaukee, and acts amendatory thereto, approved 15th of March, 1851 ; an act to incorporate the City of Milwaukee, approved 15th of March, 1851, and an act in relation to streets, alleys and sewers in the City of Milwaukee, approved 15th of March, 1851, are hereby repealed ; but the repeal of said acts and parts of acts, shall not in any manner affect, injure or invalidate any contracts, acts, suits, claims or demands that may have been entered into, performed, commenced, or that may exist under or by virtue, or in pursuance of the said acts or any of them, but the same shall exist and be enforced and carried out as fully and effectually to all intents and purposes as if this act had not been passed. And all ordinances, resolutions, regulations, rules, by-laws and orders of the Common Council of said City, or parts thereof, not repealed, suspended, or made void by this act, shall continue and remain of the same force and effect *(and)* [as] if this act had not been passed, until altered, amended, repealed or suspended by the Common Council in pursuance of this act.

Repeal not to affect rights of action.

Ordinances to continue in force.

CHAP. X. SEC. 27. This act shall take effect from and after its passage; and not more than six day's notice shall be required of the first election to be held under this act, anything contained in the same to the contrary notwithstanding.

C. LATHAM SHOLES,
Speaker pro tem. of the Assembly.

E. B. DEAN, JR.,
President pro tem. of the Senate.

Approved, February 20, 1852.
LEONARD J. FARWELL.

ACTS OF THE LEGISLATURE,

AMENDATORY AND OTHERWISE,

RELATING TO THE

CITY OF MILWAUKEE.

ACTS OF THE LEGISLATURE.

AN ACT

In relation to Common Schools in the City of Milwaukee.

Be it enacted by the Council and House of Representatives of the Territory of Wisconsin.

SECTION 1. The several Common Schools which are now or hereafter may be established within the corporate limits of the City of Milwaukee, shall be under the general control and supervision of a Board of Commissioners, consisting of three persons from each ward of said City, to be appointed by the Mayor and Common Council thereof. Schools, how controlled.

SEC. 2. Within one week after the appointment of such Board of Commissioners, it shall be the duty of the individuals so appointed, to meet and organize, by the selection of President and Secretary, and to divide themselves by lot into three equal classes; the terms of office of the first class to expire within one year from the date of appointment; those of the second class to expire in two years, and those of the third class to expire in three years from such date. Organization of board of commissioners.

SEC. 3. It shall be the duty of the Mayor and Common Council of the City of Milwaukee, annually, to supply by appointment, the vacancies occasioned in the Board of School Commissioners by the expiration of the terms of office, and the persons so appointed shall hold their offices for three years, unless sooner removed, for misconduct or other sufficient cause, by a vote of two-thirds of the appointing Board Annual appointment. Time of office

SEC. 4. It shall likewise be the duty of the Mayor and Common Council of the City of Milwaukee, to supply by appointment any vacancies which may occur from time to Vacancies, how filled.

time in the Board of School Commissioners, by resignation or otherwise.

Duties of board.

SEC. 5. The Board of School Commissioners are authorized and required:

To establish schools.

1st. To establish and organize such and so many Common Schools within the corporate limits of the City of Milwaukee (including those now in operation) as they may deem requisite and expedient, and to alter or discontinue the same in their discretion.

Employ, remove and pay teachers

2d. To contract with and employ all teachers in the Common Schools; to remove any teacher for manifest incompetency, neglect of duty, or violation of contract; and out of the moneys appropriated and provided for School purposes, to pay the teachers' wages; to purchase or hire School Houses, and to improve the same, as they may deem proper; to purchase or lease suitable sites or lots, and to erect thereon good School Houses, and to enlarge, alter or repair such School Houses and their appurtenances as their judgment may dictate: *Provided*, That in no one year shall the sums expended for the various purposes, exceed the amount raised and appropriated in that year for the support and benefit of Common Schools.

Obtain school houses.

Books, apparatus, fuel.

3d. To select and introduce into the several Schools, uniform text books; to purchase, exchange, or repair necessary school apparatus; to furnish fuel, and to defray the contingent expenses of (*of*) the schools.

Tuition fees.

4th.† To fix the rate of tuition fees in said school, which rate shall not exceed one dollar and fifty cents per quarter of eleven weeks, for each scholar; and to exempt from the payment of such fees, or any portion of them, such persons as they may deem entitled to exemption by reason of their indigence, or for other sufficient cause.

Exemption.

† Virtually repealed by Art. X, Sec. 3, of the Constitution.

5th. To defray the necessary contingent expenses of the board, including the annual salary to the clerk, which shall not exceed one hundred dollars* : *Provided,* That the account of such expenses shall first be audited and allowed by the Mayor and Common Council of the City. Defray contingent expenses.

6th.† At the end of each term or quarter, to make out rate bills, containing the name of each person liable to pay tuition fees, and the amount for which such person is liable, and to deliver such rate bill with a warrant attached for its collection drawn by the Mayor, to a collector or constable designated by the board, who shall execute the same in like manner and with like effect with other warrants for the collection of taxes, and who shall previously execute to the Board of Commissioners, in their corporate capacity, a bond with one or more sureties, to be approved by said Commissioners, or a majority of them, conditioned for the faithful performance of his duty. Rate bills. Collector's bond.

7th.† To sue and recover, in their corporate capacity, the amount of the penalty prescribed in said bond, for the faithful performance of the duties of the collector, in case of any neglect or malfeasance on his part. Recovery on bond.

8th. To have, in all respects, the superintendence and management of the Common Schools of the City ; to adopt, and in their discretion, modify or repeal such by-laws, rules and regulations for their own government, and for the organization and management of the schools under their charge, and generally to adopt all such measures as shall be calculated to promote the good order, prosperity, and public utility of the Common Schools : *Provided,* That such by-laws, rules and regulations shall not conflict with the laws of the United States, and of the Territory of Wisconsin, or with the ordinances of the corporation of the City of Milwaukee ; and, *Provided further,* That such by-laws, rules, and regula- General supervisory duties.

* Amended.
† Virtually repealed by Art. X, Sec. 3, of the Constitution.

tions, before going into effect, shall be submitted to, and approved by the corporate authorities of the City of Milwaukee.

Visitation. Meetings. 9th. To visit the several schools, individually or as a body, as often as once a quarter ; to hold stated meetings of the board once a month or oftener, if by them deemed advisable ; to require at the quarterly or semi-annual meetings of the Board, the presence and reports of all the principal teachers ; to make an annual report on the first day of April, to the Mayor and Common Council of the City of Milwaukee, of the proceedings and acts of the Board of Commissioners and of the number and condition of all the Common Schools kept in said City during the year, the time they have severally been taught, the number of children taught in said schools respectively, and the numbers between the ages of five and sixteen, residing in the City on the 1st day of January preceding ; the amount of school moneys raised or received during the year, distinguishing the amount raised by taxes, and the amount received from rate bills, the manner in which such moneys have been expended and whether any portion remains unexpended, together with such other information as they may deem useful, or the Common Council may require at their hands ; and annually to determine and certify to the said Common Council, the sums in their opinion, necessary or proper to be raised for the purchase, lease, improvement of the sites of School Houses, the building, purchase, lease, or repair of School Houses and their appurtenances ; the purchase or improvement of school furniture, fixtures, books and apparatus, the payment of teachers' wages, the procurement of fuel, and the disposal of the contingent expenses of the several schools, distinguishing and specifying the sums, required for each object.

Report.

Estimate of expenses.

Title to property. Free from tax. Sec. 6. The title to the School Houses, sites, lots furniture, books, apparatus, appurtenances, and all other school property, shall be vested in the corporate authorities of the

City, and while used or appropriated to school purposes, such property shall not be liable to levy or sale under any warrant or execution, nor to taxation, or assignment for any purpose.

SEC. 7. It shall be the duty of the Mayor and Common Council of the City of Milwaukee, to raise annually, by tax on all real and personal property of the City, such sums of money as the Board of Commissioners shall certify to be necessary for the support and maintenance of the Common Schools in said City during such year, and in their discretion, such further sums as said Board of Commissioners may certify to be required for the purchase, erection, alterations, repair, or furniture of School Houses: *Provided,* That the aggregate amount so raised by tax for school purposes, shall not exceed, in any one year, one-fourth of one per cent. upon all taxable property in the City. School tax.

SEC. 8. All moneys raised by tax for school purposes, and all moneys received for tuition fees, shall be paid over to the Treasurer of the City of Milwaukee to be disbursed by him on the order of the Board of Commissioners, duly certified by their chairman and clerk, and no moneys so raised or received for Common Schools, shall be used or appropriated for any other purpose whatever. School fund.

SEC. 9. It shall be the duty of the clerk of the Board of School Commissioners to keep a record of the proceedings of said Board, and to perform such other duties as they may from time to time prescribe. Clerk's record.

SEC. 10. No school which is now, or may hereafter be established within the limits of the City, shall be entitled to any share of the moneys raised or received for school purposes, unless there shall be an actual average daily attendance of thirty scholars, nor unless the English language be taught therein as a branch of education, and such school conform in all respects to the rules and regulations which may be What schools may not share in the fund.

adopted by the Board of Commissioners for the government of the Common Schools of the City.

SEC. 11. The Board of School Commissioners shall, in their discretion, declare any school already established, or which may hereafter be established by any portion of the citizens within the corporate limits of the City, and in which not less than thirty children are taught, a Common School: *Provided*, The teacher in said school should, after examination by the Commissioners, be found qualified, and shall keep his school according to the provisions of this act, and in conformity with the rules and regulations established by the Board; and such school shall receive the same benefit from the funds raised for school purposes as any of the other schools authorized by this act.

SEC. 12. All laws or parts of laws which are inconsistent with the provisions of this act are hereby repealed.

SEC. 13. The first appointment of Commissioners under this act, shall be made within ninety days after it shall have become a law.

SEC. 14. This act shall take effect immediately after its passage.

Approved, February 3d, 1846.

AN ACT

To amend an Act entitled "An Act in relation to Common Schools in the City of Milwaukee," approved February 3, 1846, and to authorize the Board of School Commissioners of said City to settle with the Board of a certain School District in the Town of Milwaukee.

The People of the State of Wisconsin, represented in Senate and Assembly, do enact as follows:

Superintendent and Clerk.

SECTION 1. An act in relation to Common Schools in the City of Milwaukee, approved February 3, 1846, is hereby so amended as to authorize the Board of School Commissioners of the City of Milwaukee, to appoint a Superintendent of Schools, and fix his compensation, and to defray all necessary contingent expenses of the Board, including the salary of the Clerk and said Superintendent.

Settle with school districts.

SEC. 2. The Board of School Commissioners shall have authority to settle with the Board of a certain School District in the town of Milwaukee, over a part of which district the limits of said City have been extended, by "An act to consolidate and amend the act to incorporate the City of Milwaukee, and the several acts amendatory thereof," approved February 20th, 1852.

SEC. 3. This act shall take effect from and after its passage, and all acts and parts of acts contravening the provisions of this act are hereby repealed.

Approved, April, 1852.

AN ACT

To authorize the City of Milwaukee to borrow money and for other purposes.

Be it enacted by the Council and House of Representatives of the Territory of Wisconsin :

May borrow money. SECTION 1 That the Mayor and Common Council of the City of Milwaukee be and are hereby authorized, for the purposes hereinafter mentioned, to borrow, on the faith of said city, any sum or sums of money not exceeding, in the aggregate, fifteen thousand dollars, for any term or terms not less than ten years, and at such rate or rates of interest not exceeding ten per cent. per annum, as to them shall seem expedient.

Limit.

Purpose of loan. SEC. 2. That the whole of the moneys so borrowed shall be appropriated to the purchase of suitable sites, and to the construction of School Houses in the City of Milwaukee, and to no other purpose whatever.

Provision for payment. SEC. 3. It shall be the duty of the Mayor and Common Council of said City, and they are hereby authorized to levy and collect annually on the taxable property within said City, in addition to the taxes already authorized by law, a sum sufficient to pay and discharge the interest on such loan or loans as the same becomes due, and also such further sum as to them shall seem expedient, to constitute a sinking fund for the final liquidation of the principal of the loan or loans so made, as the same becomes due ; and the proceeds of every such tax shall be applied to the payment of the interest and principal of such loan or loans, and to no other purpose whatever.

Vote upon the loan. SEC. 4. This act shall take effect when a majority of the legal voters of said city, voting upon said question, shall vote in favor of the same, at any election called by the Mayor and Common Council for that purpose.

Approved, January 25, 1847.

AN ACT

To enable the City of Milwaukee to aid in the construction of a Rail Road from that City to the Mississippi River.

The People of the State of Wisconsin, represented in Senate and Assembly, do enact as follows :

SECTION 1. That the Common Council of the City of Milwaukee shall have authority to subscribe, in behalf of that city, to the capital stock of the "Milwaukee and Waukesha Rail Road Company," incorporated February 11, 1847, by the Legislature of Wisconsin Territory, or to the capital stock of any other Company which is now or may hereafter be incorporated for the purpose of constructing a rail road from the City of Milwaukee to the Mississippi river, to the amount of one hundred thousand dollars : *Provided, however,* that if, in the opinion of the Common Council, the interests of said City should hereafter require it, it shall have authority to increase its subscription to the said stock from time to time, until the aggregate amount of the subscription shall equal the amount of two hundred and fifty thousand dollars. Council may subscribe to stock $100,000. May increase to $250,000.

SEC. 2. In order to provide for the payment of the installments on the stock subscribed as aforesaid, the said Common Council may borrow, on the faith of the City, any sum or sums of money not exceeding in the aggregate the whole amount of the installments to become due on such stock, at a rate of interest not exceeding ten per centum per annum, and for a term not exceeding ten years ; and in order to provide for the payment of the installments becoming due on such stock, in case the same shall not have been provided for by law or otherwise, and also in order to provide for the pay- Loan to pay installments. Rate of interest.

Tax to meet loan. ment of interest and principal of any loan made in pursuance of this act, the said Common Council shall levy annually a tax on the real estate within the incorporated limits of the City, not exceeding one per cent., on the assessed value of such property : *Provided, however,* That if in any year the exigency of the case shall require it, such tax may be increased to any rate not exceeding two per cent. on such assessed value.

Railroad tax receipts. SEC. 3. Every person who shall pay such tax, shall be entitled to receive from the Treasurer of said City, a receipt therefor, specifying the sum paid and for what object, and such receipt or receipts shall, upon their surrender to the proper officer of said City, entitle the holder or assignee thereof to a transfer and assignment from said City of a share or shares of such capital stock, subscribed as aforesaid, equal in amount to the amount of such receipts : *Provided, however,* that in estimating the value of such shares, in case the installments on the same shall have been paid for with the proceeds of any loan herein authorized, interest on such installments shall be included.

Approved, March 12, 1849.

AN ACT

To authorize Thomas P. Williams and others to build a bridge.

The People of the State of Wisconsin, represented in Senate and Assembly, do enact as follows :

Bridge authorized to be built by T. P. Williams. SECTION 1. Thomas P. Williams and such other persons as shall associate with him, shall be and are hereby authorized to construct a bridge across the Milwaukee river in the City of Milwaukee, from the foot of Main or Milwaukee street, in the Third Ward, to the foot of Lake or some other street, in the Fifth Ward of said City.

SEC. 2. Said bridge shall be built and kept in repair by said Thomas P. Williams, his associates or assigns, and when completed, shall be and remain forever free, and no toll shall be required from any person or persons crossing the same. To be kept in repair; free of toll.

SEC. 3. Said bridge shall be so built as not to obstruct or encroach upon the channel of the Milwaukee river, by any permanent obstruction, and shall have a convenient draw or draws, (of a capacity not less than the draw of the Walker's Point bridge, from the foot of Water street, in the Fifth Ward of said City) capable of being so managed as to admit the passage of all boats, vessels and water-craft navigating, or which may hereafter navigate the Milwaukee river, without hindrance or unnecessary delay; and the owners of said bridge shall attend or cause the same to be attended, so as to pass and re-pass all boats, vessels, and water-craft, at all times, free of expense, and without unnecessary delay or interruption. Not to obstruct navigation. Draw.

SEC. 4. The said Thomas P. Williams, and associates or assigns, shall be liable for any damage that may occur to any person or persons, in consequence of any insufficiency of said bridge, or any bad management of the draw of the same. Liability for Damages.

SEC. 5. All laws in force for the protection of public bridges, and all laws that may hereafter be enacted for their protection, and all ordinances of the City of Milwaukee for the protection of bridges within the City, shall be applicable to said bridge.

Approved, March 2, 1849.

AN ACT

To authorize the Aldermen of the First Ward of the City of Milwaukee to levy a Special Tax to raise money for the purpose of erecting a Market House in said Ward.

The People of the State of Wisconsin, represented in Senate and Assembly, do enact as follows:

Bonds to be issued.

SECTION 1. The Aldermen of the first ward of the City of Milwaukee are hereby authorized to issue bonds to an amount not exceeding six thousand dollars, payable out of any funds belonging to the first ward of said City, not otherwise appropriated, in the treasury at the time said bonds become due; the bonds to be made payable at such time and place, and on such rate of interest, not exceeding ten per cent. per annum, as the Aldermen of said ward, or a majority of them, may deem proper and necessary to carry out the object, viz: to build a market house on lots five and six, in block fifty-five, in said first ward.

Tax to meet bonds.

SEC. 2. For the purpose of liquidating and paying the said bonds, the said Aldermen of the first ward of said City shall cause to be levied a special tax upon all the taxable property in said ward, not exceeding one per cent. in any one year, which tax shall be collected and paid over to the City Treasurer at the same time, and in the same manner and form as other taxes are collected and paid, and when so collected, the same shall not be appropriated or used for any other purpose whatever than paying the bonds provided for in the first section of this act.

Aldermen personally liable.

SEC. 3. Any Alderman voting to have the funds mentioned in this act, or any part thereof, appropriated or used for any other purpose than paying the bonds as provided for in the second section of this act, shall be held personally liable for the same; and any person having rights by virtue of the provisions of this act, may enforce the same by an action on the case.

SEC. 4. The said market house shall belong to and be the property of the first ward of the City of Milwaukee, and, together with the lots upon which the same shall be situated, shall be exempt from all taxes, and the same shall be under the management and control of the Aldermen of said ward, and the proceeds arising from the letting of the same, shall enure to the benefit of said ward. Markethouse to belong to First Ward.

SEC. 5. This act shall be submitted to the legal voters of the first ward, at the next annual charter election held after its passage, or at any special election which may be called by the Aldermen of said ward, of which ten days notice shall be given, by publishing the same in one or more newspapers published in the City of Milwaukee; and if a majority of the votes cast upon the question shall be "for the market house," then this act shall take effect and be valid; but if a majority of the votes so cast, shall be "against the market house," then this act shall be null and of no effect. Vote of the people upon the law.

Approved, March 27, 1849.

AN ACT

To authorize the levying and collection of certain special taxes, in the second and fifth wards of the City of Milwaukee.

The People of the State of Wisconsin, represented in Senate and Assembly, do enact as follows:

SECTION 1. The common council of the City of Milwaukee shall have power, and it shall be their duty, to levy such special taxes in the second and fifth wards of said city, as may be necessary to pay all sums due, or to become due upon contracts for grading side walks in the second ward, and for grading streets or side walks in the fifth ward of said city, entered into previous to the third Tuesday of May, 1851. Council to levy certain taxes in 2d and 5th wards.

To be levied on lots benefited. SEC. 2. Such taxes shall be levied upon the lots in front of which streets or side walks were made, upon the contracts referred to in the first section of this act, and shall be collected in the same manner as other taxes are authorized to be collected in said city. How collected.

Approved, March 4th, 1852.

AN ACT

In relation to the construction of an Act entitled "An Act to incorporate the City of Milwaukee," and the several Acts amendatory thereof, approved February 20th, 1852, and to confer certain powers on the Common Council of the City of Milwaukee.

The People of the State of Wisconsin, represented in Senate and Assembly, do enact as follows:

Temporary grades may be made. SEC. 1. Section 18, of Chapter 10, of an Act to consolidate and amend the act to incorporate the City of Milwaukee, and the several acts amendatory thereof, approved February 20, 1852, shall not be construed so as to prevent the Street Commissioners of the several Wards of the said City from ordering and causing to be done, the grading of any street within their ward, to a temporary grade, to be established by such street commissioners.

Council may issue bonds. SEC. 2. The Common Council of said City is hereby authorized to issue bonds of the city, bearing interest of not more than *ten per centum,* as the Common Council may determine, to pay the debt of the said city and the several wards thereof.

May choose persons to vote at elections of the M. & M. R. R. Co. SEC. 3. The said Common Council shall have the authority to elect, annually, one or more persons to cast at the election of the Directors of the Milwaukee and Mississippi Railroad Company, the number of votes to which the City of Milwaukee is entitled, by the number of shares of stock of said company which the said city may hold now or hereafter.

SEC. 4. This act shall take effect from and after its passage.

Approved, April 7th, 1852.

AN ACT

In relation to Auctioneers in the City of Milwaukee.

The People of the State of Wisconsin, represented in Senate and Assembly, do enact as follows:

SECTION 1. The Common Council of the City of Milwaukee are hereby authorized to regulate the business of auctioneers within said city, and grant licenses for the same. Council may regulate and license.

SEC. 2. Not less than five, nor more than fifty dollars, shall be the amount required for a license, and the Common Council shall have power to pass an ordinance, or ordinances, prescribing the penalty and proceedings for carrying on the business of auctioneers without such license. And the tax now by law to be paid, shall be paid into the City Treasury for the use of said city. Rate of license. Penalty. Tax to be paid to City.

Approved, April 16th, 1852.

AN ACT

To authorize the levying and collection of certain special taxes in the Second and Fifth Wards of the City of Milwaukee.

The People of the State of Wisconsin, represented in Senate and Assembly, do enact as follows:

SECTION 1. The Common Council of the City of Milwaukee shall have power, and it shall be their duty, to levy such special taxes in the second and fifth wards of said City, as may be necessary to pay all sums due or to become due, upon contracts for grading side-walks in the second ward, and for grading streets or side-walks in the fifth ward of said May levy special tax.

City, entered into previous to the third Tuesday of May, 1851.

On what taxes to be levied.

SEC. 2. Such taxes shall be levied upon the lots in front of which streets or side-walks were made, upon the contracts referred to in the first section of this act, and shall be collected in the same manner as other taxes are authorized to be collected in said City.

Approved, March 4, 1852.

AN ACT

To vacate a part of Fourth Street and certain alleys in the Fourth Ward in the City of Milwaukee.

The People of the State of Wisconsin, represented in Senate and Assembly, do enact as follows:

Street vacated.

SECTION 1. All that part of Fourth street lying south of the south line of Fowler street, and the alleys in block one hundred forty-two, one hundred forty-three, and the alleys running north and south through the south half of block one hundred forty-four, in the fourth ward in the City of Milwaukee, is hereby vacated.

SEC. 2. This act shall take effect from and after its passage.

Approved, March 24, 1852.

AN ACT

To authorize the City of Milwaukee to construct a Canal from the Milwaukee River to River Street, in the Fifth Ward of said City, and to levy a special tax to pay for the same.

The People of the State of Wisconsin, represented in Senate and Assembly, do enact as follows:

May construct a ship canal.

SECTION 1. The City of Milwaukee is hereby authorized to construct a Ship Canal from the Milwaukee River to River street in the fifth ward of said City ; said Canal to be nct less than eighty nor more than one hundred feet wide, and ten feet deep, and to run through block No. 68 and block No. 112, and part of block No. 111, to the alley running east and west in said block No. 111 ; thence to said River street, taking said Alley in said block No. 111, and also alleys in blocks No. 110 and 109, and not less than thirty nor more than forty feet on each side of said alleys and crossing the streets intervening between said River and said River street.

SEC. 2. Before the commencement of the construction of said Ship Canal, and taking the lands required for the same, the necessity of taking such lands for that purpose shall be established by a verdict of a jury in the same manner as is provided for laying out public squares, grounds, streets and alleys, in chapter six of "an act to consolidate and amend the act to incorporate the City of Milwaukee, and the several acts amendatory thereof," approved, February 20th, 1852, and the provisions of said chapter, as far as applicable, are hereby adopted as part of this act. **Necessity for taking lands must be established.**

SEC. 3. The Common Council may let out the contract for constructing said Canal in the same manner as is provided by law for making contracts for grading streets when owners refuse to grade, and shall report the same to the Common Council to be accepted or refused; if the said Common Council shall refuse to ratify such contract, the contract may then be let out in such manner as said Council may by ordinance direct: *Provided, however,* The said City or ward shall in no case be made liable for the payment of the costs of constructing said Canal, or for land taken for the same, or any expenses connected therewith, but the contractors and others shall rely solely upon the tax and assessment to be levied as hereinafter provided. **Contract, how let.**

SEC. 4. That any person whose land may be taken for the use of said Canal as aforesaid, may apply to the Common Council for payment, whereupon the said Council shall, by **Damages, how estimated.**

ordinance, direct the empanneling of a jury who shall proceed in such manner as in such ordinance shall be prescribed, and estimate the damages and benefits which the owners of lots in said blocks may sustain by reason of the taking of land for said Canal, and the benefits which the several owners of lots in said blocks may derive from the construction of such Canal, and shall apportion all the damages which may accrue to any person or persons as aforesaid over and above his benefits upon the several other lots in said block, according to the benefits which such other lots may derive from the same.

How taxes may be levied.

SEC. 5. The Common Council shall levy upon the several lots, and such parts of lots as are not taken for said Canal in said blocks, the costs of constructing said Canal according to the value of the same, as shall appear by the assessment rolls made last before such tax shall be levied; and shall also levy such amounts as shall be apportioned as aforesaid upon the several lots and parts of lots upon which the same may be so apportioned as aforesaid, and such taxes so levied as aforesaid shall be a lien upon such lots or parts of lots for which the said lots may be sold under the direction of the Common Council, in the same manner as is now provided by law for the sale of lots in said City for special taxes which shall be unpaid.

SEC. 6. The Common Council may, from time to time, pass such ordinances for carrying out the powers hereby vested in them and the object of this act, as they may deem necessary.

SEC. 7. Nothing contained in this act shall be so construed as to prevent the building of any bridges across the said Canal.

Approved, March 19, 1853.

AN ACT

To amend an act to authorize the City of Milwaukee to construct a Canal from the Milwaukee river to River Street, in the fifth ward of said City, and to levy a special tax to pay for the same, approved, March 19, 1853.

The People of the State of Wisconsin, represented in Senate and Assembly, do enact as follows:

Special tax.

SECTION 1. The act to authorize the City of Milwaukee to construct a Canal from the Milwaukee river to River street, in the fifth ward of said City, and to levy a special tax to pay for the same, approved, March 19th, 1853, is hereby so amended as to authorize the said City to construct such Canal from the said River to River street or any point east of the same, commencing at any point on said River between Virginia and Elizabeth streets, in said ward, which may be selected by the Aldermen of said ward, and the said Canal may be of any width not less than seventy nor more than two hundred feet: *Provided, however,* That said Canal shall follow the course of a street, or of the alleys running east and west, and that the line running through the middle of the Canal, from east to west, shall coincide with the line running through the centre of the street or of the alleys; and the cost of constructing such canal shall be levied on the lots adjacent to the same, and the damage which may accrue from the taking of any land, or street, or alley, for that purpose, shall be apportioned upon the several lots benefitted by the construction of such Canal, including, as well, lots in the neighborhood of such Canal as those immediately adjacent thereto.

Proviso.

Approved, July 12, 1853.

AN ACT

Authorizing the City of Milwaukee to loan its credit in aid of certain Railroads.

The People of the State of Wisconsin, represented in Senate and Assembly, do enact as follows:

Authority to loan the credit of the city.

SECTION 1. The Common Council of the City of Milwaukee are hereby authorized to loan the credit of said City, by issuing its bonds to aid in the construction of certain Railroads, leading from the said City, and particularly to the Green Bay, Milwaukee and Chicago Railroad Company, the Milwaukee and Fond du Lac Railroad Company, and the La Crosse and Milwaukee Railroad Company, companies duly incorporated and organized: *Provided*, That there shall not be loaned to either of the said companies an amount exceeding two hundred thousand dollars, nor in the aggregate an amount exceeding six hundred thousand dollars; *and provided further*, that no portion of the bonds issued in pursuance of this act, shall be issued or delivered, except upon the terms and conditions, and in the manner prescribed by this act.

Bonds, nature of.

SEC. 2. Every bond authorized by this act shall be for a term not less than ten nor more than twenty years, for a rate of interest not exceeding seven per cent. per annum, payable semi-annually, both interest and principal payable in the City of New York, and shall be signed by the Mayor of said City, and countersigned by the Clerk of the said Common Council, under the corporate seal of said City.

Shall execute bond to Treasurer.

SEC. 3. Before the issue to any such Railroad Company of any bonds mentioned in the first and second sections of this act, such Railroad Company shall execute to the Treasurer of the said City, for the use and benefit thereof, the bond of such company, under the authority of its Board of Directors, signed by their President, and countersigned by their Secretary; under the corporate seal of said company, in a penal sum, at least double the amount of the par value of the bonds proposed to be issued to such company, with the condition and covenants, that such company shall punctually pay and discharge the principal and interest moneys of such bonds as they shall severally become due, and shall also fully indemnify and save harmless the said city against all payments, liabilities, losses, damages and expenses, which it may incur or sustain in consequence of the issue and delivery of such bonds or any portion thereof.

Also mortgage.

SEC. 4. To secure the performance of the covenants and conditions of the bond mentioned in the preceding section, such company shall at the same time execute and deliver to the Treasurer of the said City, for the use and benefit thereof, a mortgage executed in due form of law, of the first section or division of the Railroad of the said railroad company, next to the City of Milwaukee, in length not less than twenty miles and not exceeding sixty miles; which mortgage shall convey such portion of such railroad, its equipments, real estate, buildings, personal property, and franchises, as well that thereafter to be acquired and constructed as that already acquired or constructed, and shall contain therein covenants of warranty of the title thereto, and shall be the first mortgage or lien upon said property, subject only to a first and prior mortgage of the same property, for a sum not exceeding ten thousand dollars per mile, for every mile of road embraced therein, to be ascertained by dividing the aggregate amount of the par value of the bonds secured by such prior mortgage, by the number of miles of the road embraced in the same.

Duty of Council before issuing bonds.

SEC. 5. It shall be the duty of the said Common Council, and they are hereby authorized to require and receive from any such railroad company, before the issue and delivery of any of the bonds mentioned in the first and second sections of this act, such further and additional security or securities, either personal or real, as may in the judgment of the Common Council be requisite to fully secure and indemnify said City against all liabilities on the bonds proposed to be issued to such railroad company, and in case of the default or neglect of any such railroad company to pay the whole or any part of the principal or interest moneys of the bonds issued to such company, the said Common Council shall have the power to collect or foreclose the bond and mortgage executed by such company to said City, and also to collect, sell or dispose of all and every security received from such company, and apply the proceeds thereof in payment of the interest or principal of such bonds, and said Common Council may from time to time surrender, release and discharge all and every such additional security, and receive such other securities in lieu thereof, as, in the judgment of the said Common Council, may be safe and proper. The Common Council shall not in the same ordinance or resolution, nor at the same meeting, authorize the issue or delivery of any of its bonds to other than said railroad company, nor shall any ordinance or proposition providing for the issue or delivery of such bonds, be submitted to the voters of said city for their approval, within fifteen days after any other ordinance or proposition providing for the issue or delivery of any bonds to the same or any other railroad company, shall have been submitted.

Ten miles of road must be constructed before issue of bonds.

SEC. 6. No bonds shall be delivered to any railroad company until at least ten miles of that portion of road mortgaged to the said City, by such company, to secure the payment of such bonds, shall have been constructed by such company, nor thereafter shall they be delivered faster than the work of construction of such portion of said road shall progress, nor shall there at any time have been delivered to such company more than five thousand dollars in value of bonds for every mile of such portion of road constructed, but such bonds may issue; *Provided*, other equivalent securities shall be furnished therefor or in lieu thereof.

SEC. 7. The faith of the City of Milwaukee is hereby irrevocably pledged for the full and punctual payment of the principal and interest of every such bond which shall be issued in pursuance of this act, and the Common Council of said City shall have the power to provide for the payment of the whole or any part of said principal and interest, and it shall be their duty to provide for the payment of any portion thereof, which shall not be paid or provided for by any railroad company, by levying and collecting from time to time such special tax or taxes on the real and personal property in said City liable to city taxes, as may be sufficient to pay and discharge the same, which taxes shall be levied and collected in the same manner as other city taxes.

Faith of city pledged.

SEC. 8. Before the issue or delivery of any bonds to any railroad company in pursuance of this act, the ordinance providing for such issue or delivery shall be submitted to and approved by the voters of the City of Milwaukee, at an election for that purpose to be called by the Common Council of said City, of which at least two weeks notice shall be given by publishing the same, together with a copy of such ordinance, in three daily newspapers published in said City, such election shall be held at the usual places of holding city elections, and shall be conducted, and the votes returned and canvassed in the same manner as at other city elections; the votes at such election shall be by ballot, on which shall be written or printed the words "for the railroad ordinance" or the words "against the railroad ordinance," and if a majority of the whole number of votes cast at such election shall be "for the railroad ordinance," then the bonds whose issue or delivery shall be provided for in such ordinance, may be issued and delivered, and not otherwise.

Question to be submitted to the voters of the city.

Approved, April 2, 1853.

AN ACT

In addition to "An Act authorizing the City of Milwaukee to loan its credit in aid of certain Railroads.

The People of the State of Wisconsin, represented in Senate and Assembly, do enact as follows:

Act extended

SECTION 1. The provisions of an act entitled "an act authorizing the City of Milwaukee to loan its credit in aid of certain Railroads," approved, April 2nd, A. D. 1853, are hereby extended, and shall include the Milwaukee and Watertown Railroad Company, and any other railroad company duly incorporated and organized, for the purpose of constructing railroads leading from the City of Milwaukee into the interior of the state, which, in the opinion of the Common Council, are entitled to aid from said City; *Provided,* That the amount of bonds which, under this act and the act of which this is amendatory, shall be issued to aid in the construction of any one railroad, shall not exceed two hundred thousand dollars; and provided that the aggregate amount of bonds which shall be issued under said acts shall not exceed one million of dollars.

Proviso.

Condition of issuing bonds

SEC. 2. No bonds shall be issued or delivered to any railroad company until the question of granting the credit of the City in aid of the construction of such railroad shall have been first submitted to and approved by the voters of the City of Milwaukee, in the manner provided in section eight of the act to which this is in addition, nor until all the other provisions of said act, relating to the securities to be given to said City, are fully complied with on the part of such railroad company.

Approved, July 12, 1853.

AN ACT

To authorize the Aldermen of the Third Ward of the City of Milwaukee to issue Ward Bonds for the purchase of real estate for the use of said Ward.

The People of the State of Wisconsin, represented in Senate and Assembly, do enact as follows:

SECTION 1. The aldermen of the third ward of the City of Milwaukee are hereby authorized and empowered to issue for and in the name of said ward, the bonds of said ward to an amount not exceeding ten thousand dollars, at a rate of interest not exceeding seven per cent., and made payable at any time within twenty years from the date thereof. Said bonds shall be signed by a majority of the aldermen of said ward, and countersigned by the city comptroller, the proceeds of which shall be applied to the purchase of real estate, and for the erection of a market house thereon, and such other buildings as the wants of the ward may require. **Empowered to issue bonds.**

SEC. 2. All purchases made by virtue of the preceding section shall be in the name and for the use of the third ward of the City of Milwaukee, and the land so purchased, and the improvements that may be made thereon, shall be exempt from taxation, and the aldermen of said ward, for the time being, acting in behalf of said ward, shall have control of the ground so purchased and of the improvement that may be made thereon, and may lease, rent, and regulate the same, and all moneys received by them from the proceeds thereof shall be paid over by them to the City Treasurer for the use and benefit of the third ward. **For the benefit of third ward.**

SEC. 3. To liquidate and to pay the interest on said bonds, the Mayor and Common Council of said City of Milwaukee shall cause to be levied a special tax upon all the taxable real and personal property in said third ward, not exceeding one per cent. in any one year, which tax shall be **Special tax.**

collected at the same time and in the same manner that other city taxes are collected, and when so collected, the same shall not be appropriated or used for any other purpose whatever than for paying the interest and principal of the bonds authorized to be issued by the first section of this act.

Mayregulate the sale of meats, &c. SEC. 4. The Mayor and Common Council of the City of Milwaukee may, by ordinance, provide for regulating the sale of meats, provisions, and vegetables, and confine the selling thereof in the third ward within such limits as they may deem proper.

Market house. SEC. 5. Before proceeding to erect a market house on said ground, the aldermen shall cause a plan and specification of the same to be drawn, and a copy thereof deposited in the office of the City Comptroller, and all contracts for building and improving the same shall be let to the lowest bidder. Previous to the letting, ten days notice shall be given through one or more of the daily papers published in the City of Milwaukee, and all contracts for building or otherwise improving said real estate so purchased, shall be signed by a majority of the aldermen of said third ward, and countersigned by the City Comptroller.

SEC. 6. This act shall take effect and be in force from and after its passage.

Approved, July 6, 1853.

AN ACT

To amend an Act entitled "An Act to consolidate and amend the Act to Incorporate the City of Milwaukee, and the several Acts amendatory thereof;" approved, February 20, 1852.

The People of the State of Wisconsin, represented in Senate and Assembly, do enact as follows:

City attorney and his duties. SECTION 1. At each annual election for city and ward officers, there shall be a City Attorney elected by the qualified voters of said city, whose duty it shall be to institute and conduct all suits and prosecutions in behalf of said city, and to perform all professional services incident to the office, and to furnish written opinions upon any matter submitted to him by the Common Council, or any of its committees.

Providing for election of city comptroller.

SEC. 2. At every such annual elections, there shall be elected by the qualified voters of the said city, a City Comptroller, who shall hold his office for the same term prescribed for Mayor and Treasurer, and shall perform all of the duties now prescribed by law for City Comptroller. Any vacancy occurring in the office of City Comptroller may be filled by the Common Council.

Rail road commissioner to be elected.

SEC. 3. There shall be elected annually in the City of Milwaukee, at the same time and in the same manner that other ward officers are elected, one Rail Road Commissioner for each ward, and the terms of office of such Rail Road Commissioners shall commence at the same time and continue for the same term as is now provided by law for Assessors in said city.

His duties and powers.

SEC. 4. It shall be the duty of such Rail Road Commissioners, and they are hereby authorized and empowered to attend the elections of Directors of any rail road company, in which the City of Milwaukee may own, or hold stock, or be entitled to vote upon stock; and such Commissioners shall severally be authorized and entitled to cast at such election such rateable number of the whole number of votes which the City of Milwaukee may be entitled to cast at such election as the assessed valuation of taxable property, in each ward, shall bear to the whole assessed valuation of taxable property in the said city.

Common Council shall determine the No. of votes said commissioner may cast.

SEC. 5. The Common Council of the said City of Milwaukee shall, at the meeting thereof, to be held in each year, to equalize and confirm the assessment roll of said city, or immediately after the assessment roll shall be confirmed by a resolution, determine the number of votes which each Rail Road Commissioner shall be entitled to cast, at the election of Directors of each rail road company in which the City of Milwaukee may own, hold, or be entitled to vote upon stock according to the fourth section of this Act; and shall cause such resolution to be entered in the proceedings of the Common Council, and shall furnish each of such Commissioners with a copy of such resolution, certified by the Clerk of said city, under the seal of the said city.

Common Council may establish the grades of streets, alleys &c.

SEC. 6. The Common Council of the said city, may, at such time as they may deem proper, establish the grade of all streets, alleys and side-walks in said city, and have accurate profiles thereof filed, as is provided in the eighteenth Section, of Chapter ten, of the Act to which this is amendatory, anything in said Act or the Acts to which this is amendatory, to the contrary notwithstanding.

Powers of Street Commissioners.

SEC. 7, The Street Commissioners of the several wards are hereby authorized to require, by such general regulations as they may choose to adopt, the owners or occupants of the several lots within their respective wards to cleanse and repair the side-walks, streets and alleys, opposite their respective lots, so far as to the centre of such streets and alleys, and to employ any person or persons, whose duty it shall be to make such repairs, and cleanse such streets, alleys and side-walks. Whenever such regulations shall not have been complied with, and at some period prior to the time of the delivery of the tax-list to the Treasurer under the Charter, it shall be the duty of the Street Commissioners to make a report to the Comptroller of the amount of tax properly chargeable against each lot for work done under this section, for any period not exceeding one year prior to such report, specifying the amount in gross, and such amount shall be a lien upon such lots, and be levied thereon as a special tax with all the legal consequences, both as to collection of taxes and sale of the lots prescribed in the Charter for special taxes.

SEC. 8. Section three, of Chapter two hundred and thirty-five, of the Session Laws of 1852, is hereby repealed.

SEC. 9. The corporate limits of the City of Milwaukee, are hereby enlarged, so as to include the south half of Section fifteen, and so much of the south half of Section sixteen, in Township seven, north of Range twenty-two, east, as lies east of the Milwaukee River; and the additional territory, so included, shall constitute part of the First Ward of said city. Limits enlarged.

SEC. 10. The salaries of the several officers of the said City of Milwaukee, hereinafter named, shall be as follows, viz: Comptroller, fifteen hundred dollars per annum; City Attorney, six hundred dollars per annum; City Marshal, eight hundred dollars per annum; City Clerk, one thousand dollars per annum. Salaries of officers fixed

SEC. 11. This Act shall take effect from and after its passage.

Approved, February 18, 1853.

AN ACT

To amend an Act entitled "An Act to consolidate and amend the Act to Incorporate the City of Milwaukee, and the several Acts amendatory thereof, approved, February 20th, 1852." Approved, February 18th, 1853.

The People of the State of Wisconsin, represented in Senate and Assembly, do enact as follows:

SECTION 1. The notice required by Section one of Chapter two, of Chapter fifty-six, of the Session Laws of 1852, so far as relates to the elections of the City Comptroller, City Attorney and Rail Road Commissioner, is hereby dispensed with, for the election to be held on the first Tuesday of March, 1853. Election of certain officers.

SEC. 2. This act shall take effect from and after its passage.

Approved, February 21, 1853.

AN ACT

To authorize the City of Milwaukee to aid in the construction of the Water Works in said City.

The People of the State of Wisconsin, represented in Senate and Assembly, do enact as follows:

Common Council may loan money.

SECTION 1. The Mayor and Common Council of the City of Milwaukee, are hereby authorized to loan the credit of said city, by issuing its bonds, to an amount not exceeding in the aggregate, seventy-five thousand dollars, to the "Lake Hydraulic Company," incorporated April 5, 1852, for the purpose of furnishing water to said city, and its inhabitants from Lake Michigan.

Bonds, how atttested.

SEC. 2. Said bonds shall be signed by the Mayor and countersigned by the Clerk of said city, under the corporate seal thereof; and shall be in sums of one thousand dollars each, for a term not less than ten nor more than twenty years, and shall bear interest at a rate not exceeding seven per cent. per annum, payable semi-annually.

Security of company.

SEC. 3. Before the issue or delivery of said bonds or any portion thereof, the said "Lake Hydraulic Company" shall execute and deliver to the said city, for the benefit thereof, the bond of the said company, executed under the authority of its Board of Directors, signed by their President and countersigned by their Secretary, under the corporate seal of said company, in the penal sum of one hundred and fifty thousand dollars, with the condition and covenants that said company shall punctually pay and discharge the principal and interest moneys of such and every of said bonds, and shall fully indemnify and save harmless the said city, against all payments, liabilities, issues, damages and expenses which it may incur or sustain in consequence of the issue and delivery of said bonds.

Mortgage.

SEC. 4. To secure the performance of the covenants and condition of such bond, said company shall at the same time execute and deliver to said city, in due form of law, a mortgage of the property of said company, as well that thereafter to be acquired or that already in possession, including real estate, fixtures, machinery, water pipes and reservoirs, and shall give such further and additional security as the Common Council may require, which other and additional security, said Common Council may, from time to time, at its direction, surrender or discharge in whole or in part.

SEC. 5. Said bonds shall not be issued or delivered except by virtue of an ordinance to be duly passed by a vote of a majority of the Aldermen of said city at a regular meeting of the Common Council.

This act to be submitted to the voters.

SEC. 6. This act shall not take effect until the same shall have been submitted to the legal voters of the City of Milwaukee at an election to be ordered for that purpose by the Common Council of said city, of which, at least two weeks notice shall be given by the publication thereof in the daily newspapers of said city, such election shall be held at the usual places of holding election in said city, and said election shall be conducted, and the votes returned and canvassed, in the same manner as at other city elections, at such election the votes shall be by ballot, on which shall be written or printed the words "For the Water Loan" or the words "Against the Water Loan," and if the majority of all the votes cast on that subject, shall be "For the Water Loan," this act shall be in force, and not otherwise.

Approved, March 23, 1853.

AN ACT

To authorize the Mayor and Common Council of the City of Milwaukee to issue bonds to raise money for the construction of a Harbor at the Straight Cut in said City.

The People of the State of Wisconsin, represented in Senate and Assembly, do enact as follows:

Authority to issue Bonds.

Amount.

SECTION 1. The Mayor and Common Council of the City of Milwaukee are hereby authorized and empowered to issue bonds of said city to an amount not exceeding fifty thousand dollars, bearing interest not to exceed seven per cent. per annum, and for a time not less than ten nor more than twenty years, to raise money to be expended under the direction of the Mayor and Common Council, in the construction of a Harbor at the Straight Cut in said city, as designated by Centre and Roe's survey, made in the year eighteen hundred and thirty-six, and also to provide for the payment of the interest on the amouut of bonds issued.

Power to excavate.

To use land.

SEC. 2. For the purpose of constructing such Harbor, the said Common Council shall have the power to open, excavate and dredge a new channel to the Milwaukee River into the deep water of Lake Michigan, through Centre street in the third ward, and for that purpose may take and use so much of said Centre street, and of any land adjoining, as may be necessary, and said Common Council shall have the power to erect, construct and maintain such docks, piers and other works in the Milwaukee River, and in Lake Michigan, as shall be necessary to keep open said channel, and to permit, at all times, a safe and convenient ingress and egress through the same to all vessels navigating the waters of said Lake.

Power to lay out ground.

SEC. 3. Said Common Council shall also have the power to take and lay out such portion of ground as may be selected for that purpose on either side of such new channel mentioned in the next preceding section, for public wharf or wharves.

SEC. 4. In case any land or lots shall be taken for the construction of such Harbor, or for the laying out of such wharf or wharves which shall not have been ceded for that purpose by the owner or owners thereof, the necessity of taking the same shall be first established by a verdict of a jury in the same manner as is provided for laying out public squares, grounds and streets in chapter six of an "Act to incorporate the City of Milwaukee, and the several Acts amendatory thereof," approved Feb. 20, 1852, and the compensation to be paid for the land taken for such new channel or harbor, and also for such public wharf or wharves, and the damages and benefit arising therefrom shall be assessed as required by said chapter six, and all the provisions of said chapter, so far as the same are applicable, are hereby adopted as part of this act. *Provided,* That no portion of the cost of the construction of that part of the harbor east of water line of the Lake shall be assessed as benefits.

Jury to establish the necessity.

Compensation.

Damages and benefits.

SEC. 5. It shall be the duty of the Common Council to cause accurate maps, plans and profiles of the proposed harbor and improvements, to be made and filed in the office of the Clerk of said city, and to let out the work by contracts to the lowest bidder, giving reasonable notice to invite proposals.

Contract with the lowest bidder.

SEC. 6. Before issuing any bonds as authorized in the first section of this act, the Common Council shall submit the question of such loan to the legal voters of the City of Milwaukee, at an election to be called for that purpose, of which at least ten days notice shall be given, at which election the votes shall be by ballot, which shall have written or printed thereon the words, "For the Harbor Loan," or the words, "Against the Harbor Loan," and if a majority of all the votes cast on that subject shall be "For the Harbor Loan," then the Common Council shall issue said bonds, and not otherwise.

Adoption submitted to the legal voters of the city.

Notice to be given of election.

Form of ballot.

SEC. 7. It shall be the duty of the Common Council, and it is hereby authorized, to provide for the payment of the interest and principal of any bonds which shall be issued under this act, and for that purpose it may levy a tax sufficient to pay the same, on the real and personal property of the City of Milwaukee.

Tax to be levied.

Approved, April 1, 1853.

AN ACT

To authorize the Common Council of the City of Milwaukee to levy a special tax in the Fourth Ward, to raise money for the purpose of grading and filling the public square, and the street surrounding it in said Ward.

The People of the State of Wisconsin, represented in Senate and Assembly, do enact as follows :

Special tax.

SECTION 1. The Common Council of the City of Milwaukee are hereby authorized to levy a special tax upon all the taxable property in the fourth ward of said city, sufficient to defray the expense of filling with earth the public square, and those portions of Third, Fourth and Sycamore streets, bounding said public square, (the cost or expense of which is chargeable to the said ward) to such a height as the Aldermen and Street Commissioners of said ward may order or direct, which tax shall be collected and paid over to the City Treasurer at the same time, and in the same manner and form as other taxes are collected and paid.

SEC. 2. This act shall take effect from and after its passage.

Approved, June 27, 1853.

AN ACT

To authorize the Mayor and Common Council of the City of Milwaukee to levy a special tax for the purposes therein mentioned.

The People of the State of Wisconsin, represented in Senate and Assembly, do enact as follows:

SECTION 1. The Mayor and Common Council of the City of Milwaukee are hereby authorized, if in their opinion it is right and proper, to levy a special tax in addition to the taxes levied in the year eighteen hundred and fifty-three, on the real and personal estate in the first ward of the City of Milwaukee, sufficient to pay the sum of eleven hundred and fifty dollars, it being a balance due, with the interest calculated for two years, for rebuilding the Chestnut street bridge across the Milwaukee River, in the winter of the year eighteen hundred and fifty-two, said tax to be levied and collected in the same manner that other taxes are levied and collected in said city, for said year. Special tax. 1st and 2d wards.

SEC. 2. This act shall be in force from and after its passage.

Approved, April 2, 1853.

AN ACT

To establish a code of procedure for the Police Court of the City of Milwaukee.

The People of the State of Wisconsin, represented in Senate and Assembly, do enact as follows :

SECTION 1. The term of office of the police justice shall be two years. He shall be *ex officio* a justice of the peace, with all the authority, powers, and rights of the same, ex- Powers &c.

cept that he shall in no case entertain any civil suit to which the city is not a party; and he shall have and possess the jurisdiction and powers conferred upon him by the charter of the City of Milwaukee, and the acts amendatory thereof.

May sue for and recover fines, penalties, &c.

SEC. 2. The City of Milwaukee, in its corporate name, may sue for and recover any and all fines, penalties, and forfeitures under said city charter, and the acts amendatory thereof; or under the ordinances, by-laws, or police or health regulations made in pursuance thereof, any general law of the State to the contrary notwithstanding; and such action shall be commenced by complaint substantially in the following form:

Form of complaint.

STATE OF WISCONSIN,
Milwaukee County, } ss.
CITY OF MILWAUKEE,

..............................., being duly sworn, complains on oath to the Police Justice of the City of Milwaukee, that ...., did, on the .... day of .... 18....., violate the .... section of an ordinance, by-law or resolution (describing it by its title), which said .... is now in force, as this complainant verily believes, and prays that said .... may be arrested, and held to answer to the said City of Milwaukee therefor.

Subscribed and sworn before me, this .... day of ...., 18..... ....

It shall be sufficient to give the number of the section or sections, and the title of the ordinances, by-laws, regulation or resolution, or of the law violated, in such complaint. And said complaint may be sworn to before any officer authorized to administer oaths in the courts of this State. Upon the filing of such complaint in the office of the Police Justice, he shall issue a warrant thereon, substantially as follows:

Warrant may issue.

Form of warrant.

STATE OF WISCONSIN,
CITY AND COUNTY OF MILWAUKEE, } *To the Sheriff, or any Constable of said County, or to the Marshal of the City of Milwaukee, greeting:*

WHEREAS, ... has this day complained to me in writing, on oath, that .... did, on the .... day of ...., 18....., violate the section or sections of an ordinance, by-law, regulation, or law (describing it by its title), which said .... is now in force and effect, as said complainant verily believes; therefore, in the name of the State of Wisconsin, you are hereby commanded to arrest the body of the said .... and him forthwith bring before the Police Justice of the said City, to answer to said City of Milwaukee, on the complaint aforesaid.

Given under my hand, this .... day of ...., 18..... ...., *Police Justice.*

Upon the return of the warrant, the court may proceed summarily with the case, unless it be continued by consent or for cause. If the cause be adjourned, the defendant, if required by the court so to do, shall recognize with surety for his appearance in such sum as the court shall direct; or, in default thereof, may be put in charge of the officer who made the arrest; or be committed to the common jail of Milwaukee county. The complaint made aforesaid shall stand in lieu of a declaration, and the plea of not guilty shall put at issue all subject matter which pertains to the defence of the action. **Course of proceeding.**

Sec. 3. A printed copy of an ordinance, by-law or resolution, passed by the Common Council and published in a newspaper, or in pamphlet or book form, shall be *prima facie* evidence of its due passage and publication, and may be received in evidence. After issue joined and before trial in all cases cognizable before the Police Justice, the defendant may demand a jury, of not more than twelve nor less than six men, and shall designate the number at the time of the demand. The proper officer whom the justice may direct shall thereupon make a list of twice the number of jurors demanded, who may be qualified to serve as jurors in courts of records of Milwaukee county, and the parties shall then alternately strike therefrom, the defendant commencing, so many names as will leave remaining the number demanded. The court shall thereupon issue a venire, commanding the officer **Defendant may demand jury.**

to summon those so remaining to appear before him, at such time as he may direct, to make a jury for the trial of the said action, and the court may compel their attendance by attachment. Either party may challenge any juror for cause, and deficiencies occasioned thereby or by any other cause, shall be supplied by talesmen, to be selected and summoned by the officer; if the defendant shall not demand a jury, the city or State may demand a like jury, as is above provided; and if no jury be demanded, it shall be deemed a waiver of a jury trial. If either party declines to strike from the list the names which he is entitled to strike, the court shall strike the same for such party. Each juror shall receive for his services fifty cents.

Witnesses and jurors to attend without payment of fees.

SEC. 4. Witnesses and jurors shall attend before the police court, in all city and criminal prosecutions, without the payment of fees in advance or a tender thereof, upon the process of the court duly served, and in default thereof, their attendance may be enforced by attachment. In case the jury, after being kept a reasonable time, should disagree, they shall be discharged without the payment of fees, and thereupon the court shall adjourn the cause to a day certain, and issue a new venire as aforesaid.

Justice may issue execution.

SEC. 5, In city prosecutions the finding of the court or jury, shall be either guilty or not guilty. If guilty, the court shall render judgment thereon against the defendant, for the fine, penalty or forfeiture contained in the ordinance, by-law or resolution for the violation of which the person or persons shall have been adjudged guilty, and for the costs of suit; but if not guilty, the costs shall be taxed against the city. Upon conviction and the non-payment of such judgment, the court may forthwith issue an executian, and shall determine and enter upon the docket the length of time the defendant shall be imprisoned, which, in no case, shall exceed six months, and also insert such time in the commitment or execution. Such execution may be in the following form:

STATE OF WISCONSIN, }
CITY AND COUNTY OF MILWAUKEE. } *To the Sheriff or any Constable of the County of Milwaukee, the City Marshal, and the keeper of the common Jail in said County:*

Form of execution.

WHEREAS, the City of Milwaukee, on the..............day of ....18...., recovered a judgment before the police court of said city, against............................for the sum of........... dollars, together with..........dollars costs of suit, for the violation of (here insert the number of section and title of the ordinance, as set forth in the complaint.) These are, therefore, in the name of the State of Wisconsin, to command you to levy distress on the goods and chattles of the said ....(excepting such as the law exempts,) and make sale thereof, according to law in such cases made and provided, to the amount of said sums, together with your fees, and twenty-five cents for this writ, and the same return to me in thirty days; and for want of such goods and chattles, whereon to levy, take the body of the said.................... and him convey and deliver to the keeper of the common jail in Milwaukee county. And the said keeper is hereby commanded to receive and keep in custody, in said jail, the said ...., for the term of..............., unless said judgment, together with all costs and jail fees are sooner paid, or he be discharged by due course of law.

Given under my hand and seal this..........day of............... 18.... ....[L. S.]

Police Justice.

The form of commitment may be substantially the same as that of the execution, leaving out all that relates to levy and sale, and return of the writ.

SEC. 6. The defendant in all city prosecutions, may appeal to the Circuit Court of Milwaukee county by filing an affidavit and bond, and complying with all the requirements of appeals in civil cases before Justices of the Peace: *Provided, however*, That such appeal shall be taken and perfected within twenty-four hours from the time that judgment is rendered in the suit. Upon any appeal being taken and allowed, the Police Justice shall stay all further proceedings in the case, and the defendant, if in custody, shall be discharged; and the Police Justice shall transmit the papers in the case so appealed, with a transcript of his docket, to the

Defendant may appeal.

Proviso.

Clerk of the Circuit Court, on or before the first day of the term thereof next after the appeal shall have been allowed.

Costs, how to be paid.

SEC. 7. The jail fees and officers fees for commitment in prosecutions in behalf of the city, shall be audited and allowed by the Common Council, when the same cannot be collected of the defendant before his discharge; and said Common Council may, by resolution, direct the Police Justice to discharge from the jail, any person confined for a judgment due said city, but such discharge shall not operate as a release of the judgment, unless said Common Council shall so direct in their resolution. Upon filing a certified copy of such resolution, attested by the Clerk of the Common Council, the Police Justice shall order such defendant discharged from custody, and make an entry of such discharge upon his docket; an execution may issue or be renewed by indorsement from time to time, before or after the return day thereof, and before or after the commitment of the defendant, until the judgment is satisfied or released; but after the defendant shall have been committed, no execution shall be issued against the body of the defendant, nor if previously issued, shall authorize the taking of the body of the defendant thereon.

SEC. 8. This act shall take effect from and after its passage, and all acts and parts of acts contravening any of the provisions of this act, are hereby repealed.

Approved, March 17, 1853.

AN ACT

To authorize the Mayor and Common Council of the City of Milwaukee to appropriate from a certain fund to the purposes therein named.

The People of the State of Wisconsin, represented in Senate and Assembly, do enact as follows:

SECTION 1. The Mayor and Common Council of the City of Milwaukee are hereby authorized and empowered to appropriate from any money in the treasury of said city received, or which may be received from the proceeds of any city bonds, which may be issued under and by virtue of an act entitled, "An Act to authorize the Mayor and Common Council of the City of Milwaukee to issue bonds to raise money for the construction of a Harbor at the Straight Cut in said City," approved April 1, 1854, an amount not exceeding one thousand dollars, to pay for repairs made or to be made on the government piers, or either of them, at the mouth of Milwaukee River. *Provided,* said repairs shall have been made, or shall be made hereafter, in accordance with a contract or contracts approved by said Mayor and Common Council, and on file in the office of the City Comptroller.

Authority to appropriate money.

Amount.

SEC. 2. This act shall take effect and be in force from and after its passage.

Approved, February 27, 1854.

AN ACT

To amend an Act entitled "An act to consolidate and amend the Act to incorporate the City of Milwaukee, and the several Acts amendatory thereof."

The People of the State of Wisconsin, represented in Senate and Assembly, do enact as follows:

SECTION 1. The twelfth section, chapter seven, of the Act entitled "An Act to consolidate and amend the Act to

Repealing sec. 12, chap. 7, of Charter.

J

incorporate the City of Milwaukee, and the several Acts amendatory thereof," approved February 20, 1852, is hereby repealed.

Aldermen acting in capacity of street commissioners may declare Bayou a public nuisance.

SEC. 2. The aldermen of the first ward of the City of Milwaukee, acting in their capacity as street commissioners in and for said ward, may, if they shall deem fit and proper, declare the ground, or tract of land, covered with water in said ward, and known as the Bayou, situated north of Oneida street, and between River street on the west, and blocks fifty-one, fifty-two, fifty-three and fifty-four on the east, and extending north to Division street, and beyond Division street, partly covering the lots in blocks one hundred and fifty-three, and one hundred and forty-eight, to be a public nuisance. And they may order the said Bayou or nuisance to be abated by filling, either the whole, or such part thereof as said aldermen may determine. And in case said nuisance be not abated by the owner or owners of said grounds or lots covered with water within the time limited in the order duly published by said street commissioners for that purpose, then said street commissioners may contract for the abatement of such nuisance by filling said grounds or lots in the same manner as they are now authorized and empowered by law, and the ordinance of said city, to abate nuisances in like cases. *Provided, however,* the said aldermen shall not declare the said Bayou a public nuisance, nor shall they order it filled, except the same be requested in a petition addressed to said aldermen, and signed by the inhabitants living on the lots adjacent thereto, and in the immediate vicinity of said Bayou.

In neglect of the owners to abate the nuisance, street commissioners may let the same by contract.

Not to be declared a nuisance unless petitioned for by inhabitants of lots adjacent

Expense of filling to be chargeable to the lots filled.

SEC. 3. The expense of filling said Bayou and abating said nuisance, shall, in no event, become a charge against the City of Milwaukee, or either of the wards therein, but the same shall be charged upon the grounds or lots so filled, and shall be certified to, assessed and collected in the same manner as the expenses of filling streets and lots, and abating nuisances, are now in the cases certified to, assessed and collected by law; and for the expense of filling that part of said Bayou lying between Oneida street on the south and Division street on the north, said aldermen, as street commissioners, shall issue certificates to the contractor, or portions of the same corresponding in width to the lots abutting on said Bayou, in blocks fifty-one, fifty-two, fifty-three and fifty-four, and extending across said Bayou to River street, wherever such portions of said Bayou shall be filled by said contractor, to the established grade, and duly certified to by the City Engineer.

Street commissioners to issue certificates.

SEC. 4. The south half of section fifteen, and so much of section sixteen, in township seven, north of range twenty-two east, as lies east of Milwaukee River, in the first ward of the City of Milwaukee, shall be included for the purposes of taxation, and shall be taxed in the same manner that other lands mentioned in section twenty-three, of chapter eight, of the Act of which this is amendatory, are taxed. *Provided, however*, that should any street or streets through said lands first above mentioned, be ordered graded, and the sidewalks thereon to be constructed, then the expense of constructing such street and side-walks shall be chargeable to such lands on either side of such street, and shall be certified to, asssessed and collected in the same manner as the expense of contracting streets and sidewalks in other parts of the city, is now charged and collected by law.

Certain lands to be taxed in the same manner as other lands mentioned in sec. 23, chap. 8, of Charter.

Streets and side-walks to be chargeable to lots same as in other parts of the city.

SEC. 5. This act shall take effect and be in force from and after its passage.

Approved, April 3, 1854.

AN ACT

To amend an Act entitled "An Act to consolidate and amend the Act to incorporate the City of Milwaukee, and the several Acts amendatory thereof."

The People of the State of Wisconsin, represented in Senate and Assembly, do enact as follows:

Authority to build a flume

SECTION 1. The Aldermen of the second ward of the City of Milwaukee shall have power to authorize the owner or owners of lot number one, in block number forty in said ward, and his, her or their heirs and assigns to construct and maintain a flume from the end of the canal on the north side of Poplar street, in said ward, to the mill, situated on said lot on the south side of said street.

Dimensions.

SEC. 2. Said flume shall be of such form and dimensions and shall be built in such manner as may be prescribed by the Aldermen of said ward, and shall be kept in repair and be so secured and arranged as not to impede or interfere with the free use of said street by the public.

SEC. 3. This act shall take effect and be in force from and after its passage.

Approved, March 23, 1854.

AN ACT

To amend an Act authorizing the City of Milwaukee to loan its credit in aid of certain Railroads, and the Acts amendatory thereof.

The People of the State of Wisconsin, represented in Senate and Assembly, do enact as follows:

Extension.

SECTION 1. The provisions of an act entitled "an act authorizing the City of Milwaukee to loan its credit in aid of certain rail roads," approved, April 2, 1853, and the acts amendatory thereto, are hereby extended, and shall include the

Southern Wisconsin Rail Road Company, or any other rail road company duly incorporated and organized for the purpose of constructing railroads to intersect and connect with any other railroad, having its terminus in said city, which, in the opinion of the Common Council, are entitled to aid from said city. *Provided*, that the amount of bonds which, under this act and the act of which this act is amendatory, shall be issued to aid in the construction of any one railroad, shall not exceed three hundred thousand dollars, and provided that the aggregate amount of bonds which shall be issued under said acts, shall not exceed fifteen hundred thousand dollars.

Amount of bonds.

To be submitted to the legal voters of the city.

SEC. 2. No bonds shall be issued or delivered to any railroad company until the question of granting the credit of the city in aid of the construction of such railroad shall have first been submitted to and approved by the voters of the City of Milwaukee in the manner provided in section eight of the act to which this is an addition, nor until all the other provisions of said act relating to the securities to be given to said city, are complied with, to the satisfaction of the Common Council.

Former acts repealed.

SEC. 3. All acts and parts conflicting with, or inconsistent with this act, are hereby repealed.

SEC. 4. This act shall be in force from and after its passage.

Approved, March 31, 1854.

AN ACT

To amend an Act entitled "An Act to consolidate and amend the Act to incorporate the City of Milwaukee, and the several Acts amendatory thereof."

The People of the State of Wisconsin, represented in Senate and Assembly, do enact as follows:

Amendment.

SECTION 1. The eleventh section of chapter ten of the act of which this is amendatory, is hereby amended, so as to read

Bridges across Milwaukee river from the foot of certain streets.

as follows: Bridges shall be maintained and supported across the Milwaukee and Menomonee rivers, at the expense of the city, as follows: One from Water street, in the first ward, to the foot of Cherry street, in the second ward; one from the foot of Division street, in the first ward, to Chestnut street in the second ward; one from the foot of Oneida street, in the first ward, to Wells street, in the fourth ward; one from the foot of Wisconsin street, in the first and third wards, to Spring street, in the fourth ward; one from the foot of Water street, in the third ward, to Ferry street, in the fifth ward; and one across Menomonee river, at the foot of West Water street. All of said bridges, except the first above mentioned, shall be turnable bridges, or shall contain draws sufficient for the passage of vessels. *Provided*, the bridges from the foot of Division street, in the first ward, to the foot of Chestnut street, in the second ward, shall not be used or extended as a railroad bridge.

Across Menomonee river.

Dock lines.

SEC. 2. The Common Council shall have power, by ordinance, to establish dock and wharf lines upon the banks of the Milwaukee and Menomonee rivers, restrain and prevent encroachments upon said rivers, and obstructions thereto; and to construct, alter, and maintain, or cause to be constructed, altered, and maintained, at the expense of the city, wharves along the banks of said rivers, where the same are not required by law to be constructed, and maintained at the expense of the owners of the lots bounded on said rivers; and also to cause the said Milwaukee river to be dredged at the expense of the city, for so much thereof as is not by law chargeable to the lots bounded on said river.

Milwaukee river to be dredged.

Authority to issue bonds.

SEC. 3. The Common Council of the City of Milwaukee is hereby authorized and empowered to issue bonds of the City in its corporate name, to be signed by the Mayor, and countersigned by the Clerk of said city, to an amount not exceeding fifty thousand dollars, and bearing interest at the rate of not more than seven per cent. per annum, as the Com-

Amount.

Rate of interest.

mon Council may determine, and payable twenty years from the date of their issues, said bonds and the proceeds thereof to be applied exclusively to pay the expense of dredging so much of the Milwaukee river, between the "Straight Cut," or Centre street, and the bridges at the foot of Cherry street, in the second ward, and the docking of its banks, as is not by law chargeable to the lots and lands bounded on said river; and the Common Council of said city are hereby authorized and directed to levy and collect annually on all the taxable property in said city, a tax sufficient to pay the annual interest on said bonds, in the same manner as other taxes are levied and collected by law, and finally to pay the principal, when it shall become due.

When payable.

Docking.

Tax to be levied.

SEC. 4. The Common Council may contract with the lowest or best bidder for the dredging and docking provided for in the last preceding section: *Provided, however,* they shall have power in their discretion to direct the street commissioners of the several wards to contract with the same or other persons for such dredging and docking as is chargeable to lots and lands, and may, in all things relating to such dredging and docking, order and direct the street commissioners of the several wards, as they shall deem proper, and for the best interests of the city, and the separate wards.

Contract with the lowest bidder

SEC. 5. The eighteenth section of chapter six of the act of which this is amendatory, is hereby so amended, as to give one year's time for the payment, tendering or depositing of the damages provided for in said section.

SEC. 6. This act shall take effect and be in force from and after its passage.

Approved, March 31, 1854.

AN ACT

Supplementary to an Act to amend an Act entitled "An Act to consolidate and amend the Act entitled 'An Act to incorporate the City of Milwaukee, and the several Acts amendatory thereof,'" approved March 31, 1854.

The People of the State of Wisconsin, represented in Senate and Assembly, do enact as follows:

Appropriate the proceeds of bonds.

SECTION 1. The Common Council of the City of Milwaukee are hereby authorized to appropriate from the proceeds of the bonds authorized to be issued by the act to which this is supplementary, an amount sufficient to pay for dredging the Milwaukee river, south of the Straight Cut. *Provided,* That the amount appropriated therefrom shall not exceed the sum of five thousand dollars.

Amount.

SEC. 2. This Act shall take effect and be in force from and after its passage.

Approved April 3, 1854.

AN ACT

To amend chapter six of an Act entitled "An Act to consolidate and amend the Act to incorporate the City of Milwaukee, and the several Acts amendatory thereof," approved February 20, 1852.

The People of the State of Wisconsin, represented in Senate and Assembly, do enact as follows:

Boundaries.

SECTION 1. The owner or owners of that tract of land lying in the second ward of the City of Milwaukee, bounded and described as follows:—Beginning at a point thirty-three (33) feet east of the south-west corner of the east half of the north-west quarter of section twenty (20), town seven (7), north of range twenty-two (22) east; thence north, in a direct line, one thousand twenty-one 1-100 feet, to the point of intersection with the southerly line of the Milwaukee and Fond du Lac Plank Road; thence south-easterly six hundred forty 8-10 feet, along said line of said plank road, to a point; thence south, in a direct line, five hundred ninety-six 5-10 feet, to the point of intersection with the south line of said quarter section; thence west, along said south line, four hundred sixty-two feet, to the place of beginning—and his or their heirs and assigns, are hereby authorized to lay out and enclose, within the same, such part thereof as he or they shall deem proper, as a private park and pleasure grounds, or garden for private use.

SEC. 2. The Common Council of the City of Milwaukee shall have no power to lay out, or open, and are hereby prohibited from laying out, or opening, any highway, street, alley, lane, or public grounds, in, through, or upon the said tract of land, described in the preceding section, without the consent, in writing, of all the owners thereof, first had and obtained, anything contained in the act to which this is amendatory, to the contrary notwithstanding. *Provided, however*, That the laying out of said private park and pleasure grounds, or garden, shall be commenced within one year from the date of the passage of this act, and the same shall be enclosed and improved, for the purposes herein mentioned, within five years from said date; otherwise, the privileges and immunities, hereby granted, shall be void, and the Common Council of said city shall have and possess the like power over said tract of land, as heretofore.

Council cannot open st.

Proviso.

SEC. 3. This act shall take effect and be in force from and after its passage.

Approved, January 24, 1854.

AN ACT

To authorize the City of Milwaukee to convey lot three, in block twenty-eight, in the Second Ward, to George Abert.

The People of the State of Wisconsin, represented in Senate and Assembly, do enact as follows:

SECTION 1. The City of Milwaukee is hereby authorized to convey to George Abert, lot number three, in block number twenty-eight, in the second ward of said city.

SEC. 2. The deed of conveyance of said lot shall be executed in the name of the City of Milwaukee, sealed with its corporate seal, and signed by the Mayor, and countersigned by the Comptroller of said city.

SEC. 3. This act shall take effect from and after its passage.

Approved, January 28, 1854.

AN ACT

To incorporate the Second Ward Cemetery Association in the City of Milwaukee.

The People of the State of Wisconsin, represented in Senate and Assembly, do enact as follows:

Body corporate.

SECTION 1. William Ferdinand Otto, Joachim F. Luck, Charles E. Jenkins, David Knab, Benjamin Church, William Reinhard, Jacob Oberman, and their associates, successors and assigns, are hereby constituted and declared to be a body politic and corporate, by the name and style of "The Second Ward Cemetery Association," and as such, shall have all the rights, powers, privileges and immunities, conferred on cemetery associations by chapter forty-eight of the Revised Statutes.

SEC. 2. All the property, real and personal, now held by the Second Ward Cemetery Association, as heretofore organized, shall become vested in, and shall belong to the said association hereby incorporated, and the said association shall succeed to and hold the title to lot six of the subdivision of the south-west quarter of section nineteen, in township seven north, and range twenty-two east, which was conveyed to the Second Ward Cemetery Association by William Ferdinand Otto, and Caroline, his wife, by deed bearing date December 31, 1850 ; *subject, however*, to the mortgage thereon, for the purchase money, executed by the said association to the said Otto. **Property held.**

SEC. 3. The affairs and property of said association shall be managed and conducted by a Board of three Trustees, a majority of whom shall constitute a quorum for the transaction of business, and shall have all the powers conferred upon trustees of cemetery associations by said chapter forty-eight of the Revised Statutes. They shall be elected annually, by the members of the association, and shall hold their office for one year, and until their successors be elected. They shall appoint one of their number President, and shall have power to elect a Secretary and Treasurer. **Officers of association.**

SEC. 4. The annual meeting of the association shall be held on the first Monday in February in each year, at such hour and place as the Board of Trustees may direct, in conformity with the by-laws. William Ferdinand Otto, Joachim F. Luck, and Benjamin Church, are hereby constituted trustees of the association, and shall hold their offices until the annual election in 1855, and until their successors shall be chosen. **Annual meeting.**

SEC. 5. The said association may take, by purchase, gift or otherwise, and hold such real and personal estate within the County of Milwaukee, as other cemetery associations may take and hold under the provisions of section seven of said chapter forty-eight of the Revised Statutes. **May hold real and personal property.**

SEC. 6. All persons who are, or hereafter shall be, owners of any lot or lots laid out for burial purposes in any land belonging to the said association, shall be members thereof.

SEC. 7. This act shall take effect from and after its passage.

Approved, February 3, 1854.

AN ACT

To vacate the plat of a certain block in the City of Milwaukee, therein named, and to authorize the owner thereof to re-plat the same.

The People of the State of Wisconsin, represented in Senate and Assembly, do enact as follows:

Block vacated.

SECTION 1. The plat of block number one hundred and sixty-one (161), in the second ward of the City of Milwaukee, heretofore made, by which said block is laid out into lots and alleys, is hereby vacated and set aside.

May re-plat the same.

SEC. 2. The owner or owners of all the lots in said block number one hundred and sixty-one (161), is, and are hereby authorized and empowered to re-plat said block, and lay the same out in such form as, in the judgment of such owner or owners, shall be most advantageous and most convenient for the public, and to cause a map thereof to be made, showing particularly how and in what manner the said block shall have been re-platted and laid out, the size and number of the lots, and the course and width of the alley or alleys through the same, which map shall be certified and authenticated according to law; and shall, in addition, have annexed to, or endorsed thereon, a certificate of the owner or owners of all the lots in said block, as now laid out, that such owner or owners approve of and assent to such new platting and laying out of said block, which certificate shall be duly acknowledged, and shall be filed and recorded, together with such map, in the office of the Register of Deeds of Milwaukee County.

SEC. 3. This act shall take effect from and after its passage.

Approved, February 14, 1854.

AN ACT

To authorize the Common Council of the City of Milwaukee to levy a Tax for Ward purposes in the City of Milwaukee.

The People of the State of Wisconsin, represented in Senate and Assembly, do enact as follows :

SECTION 1. The Common Council of the City of Milwaukee may, at the time of levying other city taxes for the year 1854, increase the amount to be raised for ward purposes; such increased amount shall not exceed eight mills on the dollar upon all the taxable property of said ward ; such tax to be collected at the same time and in the same manner that other city taxes are collected.

SEC. 2. This act shall be in force from and after its passage.

Approved, February 16, 1854.

AN ACT

To authorize the Board of Supervisors of the County of Milwaukee to issue Bonds for the purpose therein named.

The People of the State of Wisconsin, represented in Senate and Assembly, do enact as follows:

SECTION 1. The Board of Supervisors of the county of Milwaukee, is hereby authorized and empowered to issue bonds of said county to an amount not exceeding one hundred thousand dollars, bearing interest not to exceed seven

May issue bonds.

per cent. per annum, and for a time not less than ten nor more than twenty years; to raise money to be expended as hereinafter described, [in the purchase of grounds, and the construction of county buildings for said county,] and provide for the payment of interest on the amount of bonds issued.

General powers of Supervisors.

SEC. 2. The bonds issued under and by virtue of this act, shall be signed by the Chairman and countersigned by the Clerk of the Board of Supervisors, under the corporate seal of said county, and shall be in sums of not less than five hundred dollars each, with interest, payable annually, on the first day of May, in each year, at such place as said Board of Supervisors may determine.

SEC. 3. The Board of Supervisors of said county, may, at their annual, or at any special meeting called for that purpose, direct, by resolution, their Chairman to sign, and their Clerk to countersign, the whole amount of bonds authorized to be issued by this act, or such a part thereof as the Board may determine; and it shall be the duty of the County Treasurer to negotiate the bonds so directed to be issued, and to place the proceeds thereof in the treasury of said county; but before such Treasurer shall receive said bonds, or be entrusted with them for negotiation, he shall execute his bond to said county, with good and sufficient securities in the penal sum of double the amount of county bonds so to be entrusted to him at any one time; conditioned for the faithful performance of his duty, and a strict accountability for all money received by him from the sale of said county bonds, and the prompt payment of the same into the treasury of said county, which bond shall be approved by said Board of Supervisors and filed in the office of the Clerk of the Board of Supervisors, and said Board ot Supervisors shall fix, by resolution, the compensation of such Treasurer: *Provided, however,* he shall not receive, including all expenses, to exceed one per cent. on the amount of county bonds negotiated by him.

SEC. 4. Whenever the Board of Supervisors of said county shall determine to issue bonds authorized by this act, they may require the Treasurer of said county to give such additional security, as such Treasurer, as they may deem proper, which additional security shall be given and approved in the same manner as provided for in section 103 and 104 of Chapter 10 of the Revised Statutes; and in case said County Treasurer shall refuse or neglect to give such additional security for the space of twenty days after being duly notified in writing of such requirement by the Clerk of the Board of Supervisors, then such refusal or neglect shall be deemed a resignation of his office, and thereupon the Board of Supervisors may fill the vacancy in said office as provided in section 106 of Chapter 10 of the Revised Statutes; and it shall not be lawful for said County Treasurer to pay out or expend in any way the money raised by the county from the sale of said county bonds, except in the manner, and for the purposes described in this act, nor shall the fund thus raised be subject in any way to the payment of any claim against the County of Milwaukee, except as herein prescribed; and said County Board of Supervisors shall fix, by resolution, the compensation of said County Treasurer for receiving and disbursing the money raised under the provisions of this act: *Provided, however,* said County Treasurer shall not be entitled to, nor shall he receive to exceed one half of one per cent. on the amount of money placed in the treasury of said county by the provisions of this act, and disbursed by him in the manner herein provided.

SEC. 5. The Board of Supervisors, at a meeting called for that purpose, shall elect, *viva voce,* three Commissioners of county buildings, with powers and duties as named in the several sections of this act, who shall hold their office for the term of three years from the first day of April, in the year 1854, unless the county buildings herein referred to, shall be completed before that time, in which case their office Commissioners.

shall cease with the completion of said buildings: *Provided, however,* that no member of said Board of Supervisors, nor the Clerk thereof, shall be eligible to the office of commissioner, or contractor under the provisions of this act, and *provided, further,* that said Board of Supervisors shall have power to remove such commissioners, or any of them, for cause; but before said commissioners shall enter upon the duties of their office, or be qualified to act, they shall each execute a separate bond to said county, with good and sufficient sureties, in the penal sum of twenty thousand dollars, conditioned that they will faithfully, honestly and promptly discharge all their duties, collectively and severally, as such commissioners, under the provisions of this act, and that they will render to the Board of Supervisors of said county, full, true and accurate accounts of all their acts and doings as such commissioners, at any time when required by said Board of Supervisors, and filed in the office of the Clerk of said Board.

Compensation.

SEC. 6. At the time of electing said commissioners, said Board of Supervisors shall designate one of these as chairman of said commissioners, and the other two as associates, and shall fix the compensation of each: *Provided, however,* that said compensation shall not exceed the sum of two dollars per day for each of the associate commissioners, and three dollars per day for the chairman, and no allowance shall be made to said commissioners, or either of them, except for the actual time they, or either of them, shall be employed as herein described; and their accounts for services, when rendered to the Board of Supervisors, shall specify the number of days employed, and before being allowed by said Board of Supervisors, shall be verified by the affidavit of the commissioners in whose favor the account may be.

Powers of Commissioners.

SEC. 7. The said commissioners, or a majority of them, shall enter into and sign all contracts in their official name in behalf of the county for said buildings, and shall audit all claims against the county for work done or materials furnished for said buildings ; and all such contracts or adjustment of claims shall be binding on the county : *Provided, however*, such liability shall not exceed the amount hereby authorized to be raised by the issue of said county bonds, and shall alone be payable out of the funds so raised ; and when any contract shall have been entered into by said commissioners, such contract shall be filed in the office of the Clerk of said Board of Supervisors, and shall be open to the inspection of all parties interested ; and when an account shall have been audited by said commissioners, the chairman shall draw his check on the County Treasurer for the amount, payable to the order of the individual in whose favor the account may be, and it shall be the duty of the County Treasurer to pay the same, on presentation at his office, from the fund raised under the provisions of this act, and from no other.

Sec. 8. The commissioners shall keep a record of all their acts and doings, which records shall be open to the inspection of all parties interested, and they shall not be interested, directly or indirectly, in any contract in which the county is a party ; and in case of a violation of any of the provisions of this section by said commissioners, or either of them, the commissioner or commissioners so offending, shall forfeit his or their office, and all compensation for services rendered, and all contracts entered into in violation of this section, shall be null and void.

Sec. 9. It shall be the duty of the commissioners to cause plans, with estimates of the cost of such buildings, constructed of brick or stone, or part brick and part stone, on each separate plan, to be made, and to recommend, in writing, to the Board of Supervisors, at any annual or special meeting, that plan, and the materials which they may regard most advantageous to the county.

Site of building, &c.

SEC. 10. The said Board of Supervisors, at a meeting called for that purpose, shall designate the site for said county buildings, and shall adopt a plan of the same, and designate the materials of which said buildings shall be constructed, and the commissioners shall cause such plan, with full specifications of the work, to be made and filed in the office of the Clerk of said Board, and shall give four weeks notice in all the daily and weekly newspapers published in said county, of the time and place, when and where, they will receive proposals from contractors to furnish the materials, and to do the work according to the adopted plan and specifications; and they shall let the work by contract to the lowest responsible bidder, or to the bidder whose proposition is most advantageous to the county: *Provided, however,* such contract shall be subject to the approval of said county Board of Supervisors, at any meeting thereof; and it shall be the duty of the chairman of said commissioners, to oversee the work of building, causing all to be done according to contract, and in a good, substantial and workmanlike manner.

Shall make annual report.

SEC. 11. The aforesaid commissioners and the County Treasurer, shall severally make an annual and detailed report to the Board of Supervisors, at their meeting in January in each year, or if they have no meeting in January, then at their first meeting next thereafter; and they shall also report in detail, as often as the Board of Supervisors may require, showing in their several reports a true and accurate account of the amount of bonds negotiated, the amount of money received for the same, the amount of money expended on the work, and the amount of money in the treasury applicable to the same, and any other information pertaining to their several offices which the board may require.

Vacancy.

SEC. 12. In case of the death, resignation, inability, or forfeiture of office, under the eighth section of this act, of the commissioners, or either of them, elected as provided herein, the Board of Supervisors may, at any meeting called for that purpose, elect a commissioner to fill such vacancy, in the same manner as herein before provided for the election of commissioners; and a commissioner or commissioners thus elected to fill a vacancy, shall be subject to all the requirements and liabilities named in this act.

SEC. 13. It shall be the duty of said Board of Supervisors to provide for the payment of the interest, and the ultimate payment of the principal of any county bonds which shall be issued under this act, and for that purpose, said Board of Supervisors is hereby authorized and empowered to assess and collect annually a special tax on the real and personal property of said county, sufficient to pay the annual interest on said bonds, in the same manner as other taxes are now levied and collected by law; which special tax shall be payable in money only, and shall not be paid out by the County Treasurer for any other purpose than the payment of the interest on said bonds; and the good faith of said County of Milwaukee shall stand pledged for the punctual payment of the interest, and the ultimate payment, at maturity, of all county bonds issued under the provisions of this act. Payment of interest.

SEC. 14. This act shall take effect, and be in force, from and after the 10th day of April, in the year 1854.

Approved, March 25, 1854.

AN ACT

To Incorporate the Milwaukee Hydraulic Company.

The People of the State of Wisconsin, represented in Senate and Assembly, do enact as follows:

SECTION 1. Charles E. Jenkins, James Ludington, Joseph W. Haskins, William P. Young, Duncan C. Reed, Asahel Finch, Junior, and James H. Rogers, and such other persons as shall associate with them for that purpose, are hereby made and constituted a body corporate and politic, by the Body corporate.

name and style of the Milwaukee Hydraulic Company, with perpetual succession, and by that name and style shall be capable in law of taking, purchasing, holding, leasing and conveying estates and property, both real and personal, so far as the same may be necessary, for the purpose hereinafter mentioned, and no further; and in their corporate name may sue and be sued; may have a common seal, which they may alter or renew at pleasnre; may contract and be contracted with, and may have and exercise all the powers, rights, privileges and immunities, which are or may be necessary to carry into effect the purposes and objects of this act, as the same are hereafter set forth.

Capital stock

SEC. 2. The capital stock of said company shall not exceed four hundred thousand dollars, to be divided into shares of one hundred dollars each, and transferable in such manner as shall be prescribed in the by-laws of said company.

Election of officers.

SEC. 3. Charles E. Jenkins, James Ludington, Joseph W. Haskins, William P. Young, Duncan C. Reed, Asahel Finch, Jr., and James H. Rogers, shall be the first Directors of said company, and at their first meeting they may elect one of their number to be President; they may also elect such other officers as they may deem essential or necessary for the management of the company; and a majority of the said Directors shall constitute a quorum for the transaction of business; and said first meeting shall be held at such time and place as a majority of said Directors may agree upon, such agreement, however, to be in writing, and signed by them respectively.

May receive subscriptions to capital stock.

SEC. 4. The Directors of the said company may receive subscriptions to the capital of said company, at such times and in such manner and under such regulations as they may adopt for that purpose; and may commence business whenever one thousand shares of the capital stock shall have been subscribed.

SEC. 5. To continue the succession of President and Directors, five Directors shall be chosen by the stockholders annually ; and each share of stock shall entitle the holder thereof to one vote ; and the vote thereon may be cast by the holder in person or by proxy. The first election may be held at such time and place as the Directors shall have designated, by giving public notice thereof in one of the daily newspapers printed and published in the City of Milwaukee, for at least ten days prior thereto ; and the persons thus chosen shall be directors of said company, and shall hold their office for one year, and until others are chosen in their stead ; the Board of Directors shall choose any one of their number President of the company, who shall hold his office one year, and until his successor is elected ; subsequently meetings for the election of Directors shall be held at such time in each year as shall be prescribed in the by-laws of said company, and notice thereof shall be given in such manner as may be provided in the by-laws ; no person shall be competent to act as a director who is not a stockholder ; and if any vacancy shall occur, by death, resignation or otherwise, in the office of President or Directors, such vacancy may be filled by the Directors of said company or a majority of them ; and they shall have power to make and establish such by-laws, rules, orders and regulations as may be necessary for the management of the affairs of said company, to make such covenants, contracts and agreements with any person or persons, co-partnership or body politic whatever, as the execution and management of the works hereinafter specified, or the convenience and interests of the company may require.

When and where election to be held.

SEE. 6. The said company shall have power, and exercise the right and privilege of building water works in the City of Milwaukee for supplying water to said city and its inhabitants, to be taken from Lake Michigan, and for making all excavations, and completing such other work as may

Powers of the company

be necessary to convey water in pipes through all the streets, alleys, highways and commons now in said city, or that may be added thereto ; also for crossing under any river or stream of water now or hereafter to be brought within the limits of said city, and shall have all such other powers incident to corporations as may be necessary to carry out the object of this act.

Elections can be held at any time, by giving ten days notice.

SEC. 7. If from any cause, an election for Directors shall not be held at the time fixed therefor, the same may be held at any other time, upon giving ten days notice, in manner as hereinbefore prescribed ; and this charter shall not be voided by reason of any irregularity or want of such election.

May borrow money.

SEC. 8. The said company are hereby authorized, in their corporate capacity, to borrow any sum or sums of money from any person or persons, corporation or body politic of any kind, and make and execute, in their corporate name, all necessary writings, notes, bonds, or other papers, and make, execute, and deliver such securities, by way of mortgages or otherwise, in amount and kind as may be deemed expedient by said company, for all purposes necessary in carrying out the objects of said company ; and the official acts of said company are hereby declared binding in law and equity upon said corporation, and all other parties to such contracts.

Persons injuring works, guilty of a misdemeanor

SEC. 9. If any person shall wilfully and knowingly break, injure or destroy, or cause to be done any act whatever, and thereby injure or destroy any building, machinery, pipes, or structures of any kind, or anything appertaining to the works of said company, or whereby the same may be stopped, obstructed, or injured, the person or persons so offending shall be deemed guilty of a misdemeanor, and being thereof convicted, shall be punished by fine or imprisonment, or either, at the discretion of the court; *and provided*, such criminal prosecution shall not in any way impair the right of action of said company for damages by a civil suit hereby authorized to be brought for any such damage, or injury as aforesaid, by and in the name of said company, in any court of competent jurisdiction.

SEC. 10. This act shall be in force from and after its passage, and shall be favorably construed to effect the purposes thereby intended; and the same is hereby declared to be a public act, and copies thereof, printed by authority of the State, shall be received as evidence thereof.

Approved April 1, 1854.

AN ACT

To amend an Act entitled "An Act to consolidate and amend the Act to incorporate the City of Milwaukee, and the several Acts amendatory thereof."

The People of the State of Wisconsin, represented in Senate and Assembly, do enact as follows:

Corporate limits extended.

SECTION 1. The corporate limits of the City of Milwaukee are hereby extended so as to include the whole of sections fifteen and sixteen and the south half of section seventeen, in township number seven, north of range twenty-two east, and of the additional territory so included, all of section fifteen, and so much of section sixteen as lies east of the Milwaukee river, shall constitute, and be a part of the first ward of said city, and all of said section sixteen lying west of the Milwaukee river, and the south half of section seventeen, shall constitute, and be a part of the second ward of said city; and the additional territory hereby included in the corporate limits of the City of Milwaukee shall be taxed in the same manner that other lands mentioned in section twenty-three of chapter eight of the act of which this is amendatory are taxed: *Provided, however,* that should any street or streets through said lands be ordered graded, and the side-walks thereon be constructed, then the expenses of constructing such street and side-walks shall be chargeable

Streets and side-walks, when ordered graded, to what chargeable. to the lands on either side fronting on such street, and shall be certified to, assessed and collected, and the collection thereof enforced by sale in the same manner as the expenses of constructing streets and side-walks in other parts of the city are now charged and collected by law.

Council to have power to vacate streets, alleys, &c. Sec. 2. The Common Council shall have power, and are hereby authorized to vacate, in whole or in part, such highways, streets, alleys and public walks within the corporate limits of the city, as, in their opinion, the public interest may require, or such as, in their opinion, are of no public utility: *Provided, however*, the necessity of vacating any such highway, street, alley or public walk, or any part thereof, shall first be established by a verdict of a jury, in the same manner as is provided for laying out public squares, grounds and streets, in chapter six of the act of which this is amendatory; all the provisions of said chapter, so far as the same are applicable hereto, are hereby adopted as a part of this act.

Necessity of to be agreed upon by jury

Aldermen authorized to construct bridge. Sec. 3. The Aldermen of the first ward of the City of Milwaukee are hereby authorized and empowered to construct a bridge across the Milwaukee river, from Johnston street, in the first ward, to the Humboldt Plank Road, in the second ward, and to defray the expenses of the first construction of said bridge or the re-building of the same at any time thereafter. It shall be the duty of the Common Council to levy a tax upon the taxable real estate, in the first ward, upon lots eighty-two, eighty-three, eighty-four, eighty-five, eighty-six, eighty-seven and eighty-eight, on the west side of the Milwaukee river, in section twenty-one, and upon the lots on the west side of the Milwaukee river, in section sixteen, in township number seven, north of range twenty-two east. The plan and specifications for said bridge to be made, and the work to be let by contract, in the same manner as other city work is now required to be done by law. And when said bridge shall be completed, it shall be under the

Expenses, how defrayed.

Work to be let to the lowest bidder

control of, and kept in repair by the city, in the same manner as the other bridges across the Milwaukee river in said city.

SEC. 4. This act shall take effect and be in force from and after its passage.

Passed, February 21, 1855.

AN ACT

To amend an Act entitled "An act to consolidate and amend the Act to incorporate the City of Milwaukee, and the several Acts amendatory thereof," approved February 20, 1852, and to prescribe the form and effect of Tax Deeds in said city.

The People of the State of Wisconsin, represented in Senate and Assembly, do enact as follows:

SECTION 1. Certificates of the sale of lands for non-payment of taxes or assessments and charges, hereafter to be issued by the Treasurer of the City of Milwaukee, under the act to which this act is amendatory, shall be in the following, or equivalent, form :

Form of tax certificates.

STATE OF WISCONSIN, }
MILWAUKEE CITY AND COUNTY, } ss.

I, ..., Treasurer of the City of Milwaukee, in said State, do hereby certify that on this............day of.................A. D. 18...., I sold at public auction, pursuant to law, (here describe the land sold,) unto.......................for the sum of.................dollars and................cents, being the amount due for city taxes, assessments and charges on said .... This certificate bears interest at the rate of twenty-five per cent. per annum, and if the land so sold is not redeemed according to law, the owner of this certificate will be entitled to a conveyance of so much of said land as shall remain unredeemed.

This certificate is transferable by endorsement.

....

City Treasurer.

Sec. 2. Deeds to be executed by the Treasurer of the City of Milwaukee, on account of sale of lands for taxes or assessments and charges, under the act to which this act is amendatory, shall be signed by the Treasurer of said City, sealed with the corporate seal of said city, and shall be in the following, or equivalent, form :

Form of tax deeds.

Whereas, A B has deposited in the office of the Treasurer of the City of Milwaukee, in the State of Wisconsin, (naming the number,) certificate, whereof he is the legal owner, issued by C D, who, at the date thereof, was Treasurer of said city, whereby it appears that the following described land, situated in said city, was sold on the.................. day of...................., A. D. 18...., for the non-payment of taxes, assessments and charges due thereon at the date of said sale at public auction, by the said C D, Treasurer as aforesaid, at his office in said city, to the person (or persons, or to the said city,) for and for the sum (or sums) hereinafter named, to wit : Lot...........in block............in the.............. ward of said city, for the sum of........................dollars and ....cents to A B ; lot.................in block..................in the................ward of said city, for the sum of..................... dollars and....................cents to E F ; lot....................block ....in the..................ward of said city, for the sum of.........................dollars and....................cents to the said City of Milwaukee, which sum (or several sums) was (or were) the amount of taxes, assessments and charges due, at the date of such sale, on the land or lands (respectively) aforesaid ; (or in case less than the whole land taxed was sold, naming the land taxed or assessed, for which tax or assessment the sale was made,) and whereas, it further appears that said land (or lands) is (or are) now unredeemed from such sale (excepting such portion as may have been redeemed) whereby the same has (or have) become forfeited, and according to law the owner of said certificate (or certificates) is entitled to a conveyance thereof.

Now, Therefore, know all men by these presents, that the said City of Milwaukee, and the State of Wisconsin, in consideration of the said sum, (or sums of money,) and of the premises, do give, grant and convey the land above described, and remaining unredeemed as aforesaid, together with the hereditaments and appurtenances, to the said A B, and to his heirs and assigns, to their sole use and benefit forever.

In testimony whereof, I, G H, the Treasurer of said city, have executed this deed, pursuant to and in virtue of the authority in me vested by law; and I have, in behalf of the said State and of the said city, hereunto subscribed my name officially, and caused to be affixed the seal of said city, on this................day of......................in the year eighteen hundred and......................, at Milwaukee aforesaid.

....

Treasurer of the City of Milwaukee.

Done in presence of
....
....

STATE OF WISCONSIN, } ss.
MILWAUKEE COUNTY. }

On this......................day of.......................A. D. 18.... before me, personally appeared the above named G H, and acknowledged that he, as Treasurer of the City of Milwaukee, in said state, executed the foregoing instrument as the deed of the said city and of the said state, for the uses and purposes therein set forth.

....

SEC. 3. Every deed made substantially according to the above, or an equivalent, form, and executed as above directed, shall be *prima facie* evidence of the regularity and correctness of all the proceedings upon which its validity may depend, and that the title to the lands which such deed purports to convey, is vested in the grantee therein named, his heirs or assigns, and no other proof of title shall be required of any person claiming title under such a deed, than the production of such deed, and (if he be not the grantee therein named,) of the proper evidence that he claims through such grantee.

Deed to be *prima facie* evidence of proceedings.

SEC. 4. No action shall be maintained for the recovery of any lands which such deed may purport to convey, by any person claiming adversely to such deed, after the expiration of three years from the date of recording such deed, except in cases where the taxes or assessments and charges for which such land is alleged to have been sold, shall have been paid, or the land redeemed, as provided by law, or where such land

Limitation of right of action.

was not subject to taxation: *Provided*, That this section shall not be construed to apply to actions brought by the holders of a title acquired through subsequent sales for the non-payment of taxes.

Not repealable by implication.

SEC. 5. No law hereafter enacted, shall be construed to repeal, modify or effect any of the provisions of this act, unless such purposes be expressly declared therein.

SEC. 6. All acts, and parts of acts, conflicting with the provisions of this act, are hereby repealed.

Approved, March 20, 1855.

AN ACT

To amend An Act to consolidate and amend the Act to incorporate the City of Milwaukee, and the several Acts amendatory thereof," approved February 20, 1852.

The People of the State of Wisconsin, represented in Senate and Assembly, do enact as follows:

Owners may redeem.

SECTION 1. In all cases, within the corporate limits of the City of Milwaukee, when any lot or tract of land, or any portion thereof, shall have been sold and forfeited by reason of the non-payment of the taxes thereon, the owner or any person interested therein, may redeem the same, at any time prior to the execution of a tax deed, by the Treasurer, to the purchaser, by such owner or person interested therein paying to the Treasurer the amount for which the same was sold, together with the interest at the rate of twenty-five per cent. per annum, and the legal charges thereon; and it shall be lawful for the City Treasurer to receive such redemption money, on the same being tendered to him at any time prior to the execution of the tax deed.

SEC. 2. In all cases, within the corporate limits of the City of Milwaukee, where the taxes on personal property shall not be paid prior to the passage of this act, the City

Treasurer may, and it shall be lawful for him to issue a new warrant, directed to the City Marshal, requiring and commanding him, within a certain time specified in such warrant, to proceed and collect such taxes on personal property as shall then remain unpaid; and the Marshal receiving such warrant, shall be subject to all liabilities, and shall have all the powers of levying, distraining and selling, that are given to the Treasurer, and shall be entitled to the same fees for collecting which the Treasurer would have, had the tax been collected by him, in the same manner, and as fully, as is provided in section ten of chapter eight of the act of which this is amendatory.

Treasurer may issue new warrant

SEC. 3. In all cases where the street commissioners of either of the wards of the City of Milwaukee shall have issued a certificate for work done on the street, side-walk, or alley, chargeable to lots or lands, according to the provisions of section ten of chapter seven of the act of which this is amendatory, and such lot or tract of land shall have been subdivided prior to the date of such certificate, then the work certified to in such certificate, shall be chargeable to that subdivision of such lot or tract of land which fronts on the street, side-walk or alley on which such work shall have been done according to law; and it shall be lawful for the City Treasurer, in collecting the special taxes assessed by reason of the issue of such certificate, as provided in section ten of chapter seven of the act herein before referred to, to collect the amount named in such certificate, from that subdivision of lot or tract of land which fronts on the street or alley named in such certificates, and on which said work was done according to law.

Work chargeable to lots.

SEC. 4. Whenever any nuisance, source of filth, or cause of sickness, shall be found on private property, or in the street or alley in front or rear of such property, the Common Council may order the owner or occupant thereof, at his own expense, to remove or abate the same within twenty-four

Council may order owner to abate nuisance.

hours from the date of the order, or within such other time as may be named in such order, and if the owner or occupant shall refuse or neglect so to do, within the time named in said order, then the street commissioners of the ward wherein said nuisance, source of filth, or cause of sickness shall be found, shall forthwith cause said nuisance, source of filth, or cause of sickness to be abated or removed, at the expense of the lot or tract of land in the front or rear of which, or upon which, such nuisance, source of filth, or cause of sickness may be found, and when the work of abating or removing such nuisance, source of filth, or cause of sickness, shall have been completed, the street commissioners of the proper ward shall give to the contractor or contractors, a certificate under their hands, stating therein the amount of work done by such contractor, the nature thereof, and the description of the lot or parcel of land upon which the same is chargeable, which certificate may be transferred by endorsement thereon, and if the amount thereof shall not be paid before the time of making out the annual assessment roll, the same shall be assessed upon the said lots or parcels of land respectively, and collected for the use and benefit of the holder of such certificate, in the same manner as other taxes on real estate are collected by virtue of the act of which this is amendatory.

Chargeable to lot.

Certificate may be given to contractor

SEC. 5. This act shall take effect and be in force from and after its passage.

Passed March 27, 1855.

AN ACT

Supplementary to an Act to amend an Act entitled "An Act to consolidate and amend the Act to incorporate the City of Milwaukee, and the several Acts amendatory thereof," approved February 21, 1855.

The People of the State of Wisconsin, represented in Senate and Assembly, do enact as follows:

SECTION 1. The third section of the act, of which this is amendatory, is hereby amended so as to read as follows:

"The Aldermen of the first ward of the City of Milwaukee are hereby authorized and empowered to construst a bridge across the Milwaukee river, from Johnston street, or any other street or point," in the first ward, to the Humbolt Plank Road in the second ward, "and also to construct a bridge across the canal in the second ward, where the Humbolt Plank Road crosses the said canal," and to defray the expenses of the construction of said bridge, or the re-building, maintaining and repairing the same, at any time thereafter it shall be the duty of the Common Council to levy a tax upon the taxable real estate of the first ward and upon lots number eighty-two to eighty-eight, inclusive, on the west side of the Milwaukee river, in section twenty-one, and upon the lots on the west side of the Milwaukee river, in section sixteen, in township number seven, north of range twenty-two east. The plan and specifications for said bridge, or either of them, to be made and the work to be let by contract, in the same manner as other city work is now required to be done by law, and when said bridge shall be completed, or either of them, they or it shall be under the control of the city, in the same manner as the other bridges across the Milwaukee river in said city.

Bridge across from First Ward to Humboldt Plank Road.

Where tax levied to defray expenses of constructing and maintaining.

Work let to the lowest bidder.

SEC. 2. This act shall take effect and be in force from and after its passage.

Approved, March 31, 1855.

AN ACT

To amend an Act entitled "An Act to consolidate and amend the Act to incorporate the City of Milwaukee, and the several Acts amendatory thereof."

The People of the State of Wisconsin, represented in Senate and Assembly, do enact as follows:

SECTION 1. The act entitled "An Act to consolidate and amend the Act to incorporate the City of Milwaukee, and the several Acts amendatory thereof," is hereby so amended as to make the expense of re-constructing, enlarging and extending of any sewer in said city, chargeable to the lots, in the same manner as the construction of any sewer by the act to which this is amendatory, is made chargeable to lots; and all certificates to the contractor or contractors, given by the street commissioners of any ward, for re-constructing, enlarging or extending any sewer in the ward for which they are street commissioners, shall be assessed upon such lots or parcels of lands respectively, and collected for the use and benefit of the holder of such certificates, as other taxes on real estate are collected, by virtue of the act to which this is amendatory.

Tax chargeable to lots for enlarging and extending.

How assessed and collected.

SEC. 2. This act shall take effect and be in force from and after its passage.

Approved March 31, 1855.

AN ACT

To authorize the Common Council of the City of Milwaukee to levy a Special Tax on the taxable property of the Fifth Ward of said City, for Ward purposes.

The People of the State of Wisconsin, represented in Senate and Assembly, do enact as follows:

Common Council may levy special tax.

SECTION 1. The Common Council of the City of Milwaukee may, at any time of levying other city taxes for the year eighteen hundred and fifty-five, increase the amount to be raised for ward purposes in and for the fifth ward of the City of Milwaukee; such increased amount shall not exceed eight mills on the dollar upon all taxable property in said ward, such tax to be collected at the same time and in the same manner as other city taxes are collected.

SEC. 2. This act shall be in force from and after its passage.

Approved, March 29, 1855.

AN ACT

To authorize the Common Council of the City of Milwaukee to levy a Special Tax in the Second Ward, for ward purposes.

The People of the State of Wisconsin, represented in Senate and Assembly, do enact as follows:

SECTION 1. The Common Council of the City of Milwaukee are hereby authorized and empowered, at the time of levying other city taxes for the year eighteen hundred and fifty-five, to levy a special tax upon all the taxable property in the second ward of said city, for ward purposes, not exceeding one per cent., in addition to the tax now authorized by law to be levied and collected in said ward, for ward purposes; which special tax shall be collected at the same time and in the same manner as other city taxes, and all laws now in force, in regard to levying and collecting taxes for ward purposes in the said second ward, shall apply to the said special tax hereby provided for, so far as the same are not inconsistent with the provisions of this act: *Provided*, That the provisions of this act shall not extend to, or include, lands in said second ward used for farming purposes; this proviso being intended to exclude from the provisions of this act all property over which have been extended the provisions of section twenty-three, of chapter eight, of "An Act to consolidate and amend the Act to incorporate the City of Milwaukee, and the several acts amendatory thereof," approved February 20, 1852.

Council may levy special tax.

Special tax in 2d ward.

SEC. 2. The said tax, when collected, shall be used, applied, and appropriated, in the same manner and for the same purposes as other taxes collected in said ward for ward purposes.

How applied

SEC. 3. This act shall take effect, and be in force, from and after its passage.

Approved, March 29, 1855.

L

AN ACT

To vacate the Plat of Finch's Addition in the Fourth Ward of the City of Milwaukee.

The People of the State of Wisconsin, represented in Senate and Assembly, do enact as follows:

Finch's addition vacated.

SECTION 1. The plat by which Finch's addition in the fourth ward of the City of Milwaukee is laid out into lots, blocks, streets and alleys, is hereby vacated and set aside: *Provided, however,* The written assent of all the owners, or persons interested therein, shall first be filed in the office of the Register of Deeds of Milwaukee county.

SEC. 2. This act shall take effect and be in force from and after its passage.

Approved, March 31, 1855.

AN ACT

To vacate the Plat of Block twenty-two in the Fifth Ward of the City of Milwaukee, and authorize the owners thereof to re-plat the same.

The People of the State of Wisconsin, represented in Senate and Assembly, do enact as follows:

Block 22 vacated.

SECTION 1. The plat or map of block numbered twenty-two, of Walker's Point, in the fifth ward of the City of Milwaukee, by which said block is laid off into lots, together with the alley in said block, is hereby vacated.

Authority to re-plat.

SEC. 2. The owners of the lots in said block are hereby authorized to re-plat said block into lots, so as to front the same upon Florida and Virginia street, with an alley of not less than twenty feet in width running through the centre, and cause a map of the same to be made and recorded in the office of the Register of Deeds of Milwaukee county.

SEC. 3. This act shall take effect from and after its passage.

Approved, March 19, 1855.

AN ACT

To vacate the Plat of Maitland Place in the City of Milwaukee.

The People of the State of Wisconsin, represented in Senate and Assembly, do enact as follows:

SECTION 1. The plat of ground, known as "Maitland Place," situated in the north-east quarter of section number thirty, township number seven, north of range number twenty-two east, being in the fourth ward of the City of Milwaukee, is hereby vacated. Maitland Place vacated.

SEC. 2. This act shall take effect from and after its passage.

Approved, March 12, 1855.

AN ACT

Relative to certain Tax Titles in the City of Milwaukee.

The People of the State of Wisconsin, represented in Senate and Assembly, do enact as follows:

SECTION 1. All tax certificates, commonly so called, issued by the Treasurer of the City of Milwaukee, prior to the year eighteen hundred fifty-three, on sales of lands situated in said city, for the non-payment of any taxes, assessments, or charges, are hereby declared to be assignable by delivery, after the endorsement of the same by the persons to whom such certificates have been bid in for the said city, and all assignments or transfer of such certificates heretofore made, or attempted to be made, by endorsement of the purchaser, or of the present or any former City Treasurer, in cases where the said certificates have been bid in for the said city, are hereby declared valid and effectual: *Provided*, the Treasurer shall not transfer such certificates for a less price than may be allowed by law or by the order of the Common Council of said city.

Certificates declared valid.

SEC. 2. After the expiration of three years from the date of any such certificates, or if any other time may have been fixed by law for the redemption of the lands described therein, then after the expiration of time so limited, the holder of such certificate is hereby declared to be entitled to a conveyance of so much of the land therein described as remains unredeemed from such sale, such conveyance shall be signed by the Treasurer of the said city, and sealed with the seal of the said city, and shall be substantially in the following, or an equivalent, form:

Form of conveyance.

To all to whom these presents shall come, Greeting:

WHEREAS, A B has deposited in the office of the Treasurer of the City of Milwaukee, in the State of Wisconsin, a certificcate, (or certificates) whereof he is the legal holder, issued by C D, who, at the date thereof, was Treasurer of said city, whereby it appears that the lands situated in said city, and hereinafter described, was, on the................day of ....A. D. eighteen hundred and................, sold at public auction in said city by the said C D, Treasurer as aforesaid, for the non-payment of taxes, including assessments and charges due on said lands at the date of such sale, to the person (or several persons) or to the said city, and to the person (or several persons) and for the sum (or several sums) hereinafter named, to wit: Lot..........in block.......... in the...........ward, to E F, for the sum of.......................... Lot..............in block................in the.............ward, for the sum of............................ Which sum (or several sums) was (or were) the amount of taxes, including the assessments and charges due on the said land (or lands) respectively, for city or state and county, or city, state and county purposes, at the date of such sale.

AND, WHEREAS, it appears that said lands are now unredeemed from such sale, excepting the portion of any redeemed, and have become forfeited, and the said A B is, by law, entitled to a conveyance thereof.

Now, THEREFORE, know all men by these presents, that the said City of Milwaukee, in consideration of the said sum (or sums) of money and of the premises, and in conformity to law, hath given, granted and conveyed, and hereby doth give, grant and convey the lands above described and remaining unredeemed as aforesaid, together with the hereditaments and appurtenances, to the said A B, and to his heirs and assigns, to their sole use and benefit forever.

IN TESTIMONY WHEREOF, I, G H, the Treasurer of said city, have executed the deed in virtue of the authority in me vested, and I have, in the name and behalf of the said city, hereunto subscribed my name officially, and have caused to be affixed hereto the seal of said city, at Milwaukee aforesaid, on this................day of........................A. D. eighteen hundred and....................

[L. S.] G............ H.............,
Treasurer of the City of Milwaukee.

Done in presence of
....
....

STATE OF WISCONSIN,
MILWAUKEE COUNTY.

On this....................day of..........................before me, personally appeared the above named G H, and acknowledged that he, as Treasurer of the City of Milwaukee, above named, executed the foregoing instrument for the use and purposes therein mentioned. ....

SEC. 3. Every deed made and executed substantially in the above, or equivalent, form, shall be *prima facia* evidence that all the proceedings necessary to the validity and effectual operation of such deed, have been had according to law, and shall also be *prima facia* evidence that the title to the lands which such deed may purport to convey, is vested in the grantee therein named, his heirs or assigns, from the date of such deed, and no other proof of the title shall be required of any person claiming title under such deed, than the production of such deed, and if he be not the grantee therein named, of the proper evidence that the claims through such grantee. Deeds to be evidence of validity.

SEC. 4. Every conveyance heretofore made and executed by the Treasurer of said city, substantially in form according to the provisions of sections three and five of an act entitled "an act to amend the several laws of the State relating to the sale of lands for taxes, and the manner of perfecting tax titles," approved, March 31, 1854, and purporting to be executed upon the deposit in his office of a certificate or certificates, of even date with each other, issued by any former Treasurer of the City of Milwaukee, shall have all the force and effect, in every respect, as is given by this act to deeds made and executed, as prescribed in section two of this act.

Sec. 5. No action shall be maintained for the recovery of lands which any deed hereafter made and executed, substantially according to the provisions of this act, or heretofore made and executed, as specified in the last preceding section, may purport to convey by any person or body corporate claiming adversely to such deed after the expiration of three years from the date of recording such deed, unless the taxes, assessments or charges for which said lands are alledged to have been sold, shall have been paid before such sale, or said lands redeemed according to law after such sale: *Provided*, That this section shall not be construed to be a bar to actions brought by any person deriving title under a sale for non-payment of taxes, assessments or charges made subsequently to the sale set forth in such deed.

Sec. 6. No law hereafter enacted, shall be construed to repeal, modify, or effect any of the provisions of this act, unless such purpose be expressly declared therein.

Sec. 7. This act shall be published immediately after its passage, and shall take effect from and after its publication.

Passed, March 29, 1855.

AN ACT

To authorize the City of Milwaukee to aid in the construction of Water Works in said City.

The People of the State of Wisconsin, represented in Senate and Assembly, do enact as follows:

SECTION 1. The Mayor and Common Council of the City of Milwaukee are hereby authorized to loan the credit of said city, by issuing its bonds to an amount not exceeding, in the aggregate, one hundred thousand dollars, to the Milwaukee Hydraulic Company, incorporated April first, eighteen hundred and fifty-four, for the purpose of supplying water to said city and its inhabitants from Lake Michigan. **Council may loan credit of city.**

SEC. 2. Said bonds shall be signed by the Mayor, and countersigned by the Clerk of said city, under the corporate seal thereof; and shall be in sums of one thousand dollars each, for a time not less than ten nor more than twenty years, and shall bear interest at a rate not exceeding seven per cent. per annum, payable semi-annually. **Bonds to be issued.**

SEC. 3. Before the issue or delivery of said bonds, or any portion thereof, the said Milwaukee Hydraulic Company shall execute and deliver to the said city, for the benefit thereof, the bond of the said company, executed under the authority of its Board of Directors, signed by their President, and countersigned by their Secretary, under the corporate seal of said company, in the penal sum of two hundred thousand dollars, with the conditions and covenants that the said company shall punctually pay and discharge the principal and interest moneys of each and every of said bonds, and shall fully indemnify and save harmless the said city against all payments, liabilities, issues, damages and expenses which it may incur or sustain in consequence of the delivery and issue of said bonds. **Company to execute bond to city.**

Company to issue mortgage to city. SEC. 4. To secure the performance of the covenants and conditions of such bonds, said company shall, at the same time, execute and deliver to said city, in due form of law, a mortgage of the property of said company, as well that thereafter to be acquired as that already in possession, including real estate, fixture, machinery, water pipes and reservoirs, and shall give such further and additional security as the Common Council may require, which other and additional security said Common Council may, from time to time, in its descretion, surrender or discharge in whole or in part.

SEC. 5. Said bonds shall not be issued nor delivered except by virtue of an ordinance to be duly passed by a vote of a majority of the Aldermen of said city at a regular meeting of the Common Council.

Condition of bonds to be issued. SEC. 6. No bonds shall be issued under the provisions of this act to an amount greater than ten thousand dollars at any one time, and they shall be issued under the following conditions: When the said Hydraulic Company, by affidavit of their President and Secretary, shall show to the said Common Council that they have actually expended in the construction of said water works the sum of twenty thousand dollars, the said Common Council may, upon the said company giving the security required by this act, issue ten thousand dollar of city bonds to said company, and when the said company shall, in like manner, show that they have expended the sum of forty thousand dollars, the said Common Council may issue to said company ten thousand dollars more of the city bonds and so on till the one hundred thousand dollars of bonds of the said city shall be issued to said company, it being the meaning and intention of this section that the Common Council shall at no time issue bonds to an amount greater than one-half of the sum of money actually expended by said Milwaukee Hydraulic Company.

No bonds to be issued until voted on. SEC. 7. No bonds shall be issued in pursuance of this act, until a majority of the legal voters of said City of Milwaukee, voting upon said question, shall vote in favor of the same, at an election which shall be called by the Common Council of said city for that purpose, to be held at the usual places of holding elections in the several wards of said city. At such elections, those voting in favor of the loan shall vote a ballot with the words, "For the Water Works Loan," inscribed thereon, and those voting against shall vote a ballot with the words, "Against the Water Works Loan," inscribed thereon. Thirty days previous notice of said election shall be given in at least four newspapers printed in said city, and the act shall be published in connection therewith. Said election shall be conducted, and returns thereof made and canvassed, in the same manner as at the general elections in said city.

SEC. 8. This act shall take effect and be in force from and after its passage.

Passed, March 31, 1855.

AN ACT

To authorize the establishment of a House of Refuge, for juvenile and other delinquents, in the County of Milwaukee.

The People of the State of Wisconsin, represented in Senate and Assembly, do enact as follows:

SECTION 1. The Board of Supervisors of the county of Milwaukee shall be, and they are hereby authorized, to cause to be erected at such place within the limits of said county as shall be designated, in the manner hereinafter mentioned, a suitable building or buildings, to be called "The House of Refuge of Milwaukee County," to be used for the safe keeping, reformation and employment of vagrants, disorderly persons, and all prisoners under sentence or conviction, (except in those cases of conviction for a felony, in which the party convicted shall be sentenced to be punished by death or imprisonment in the State Prison,) who shall be sentenced

Supervisors may erect house of refuge.

Who may be confined.

to confinement at hard labor or to solitary imprisonment, by any court held in said County of Milwaukee, or who may be authorized to be confined therein by any of the provisions of this act.

Special meeting, how called.

SEC. 2. The Clerk of said Board of Supervisors, on receiving a written request to that effect from any five members of the said Board, shall immediately call a special meeting of such Board, which shall, when called, be a legal meeting of such Board for all lawful purposes, as well as for the purposes of proceeding under this act. Such special meeting shall be called by the Clerk, by sending by mail to each of the members of said Board, a written notice of the time and place of such meeting, at least six days before the day of such meeting, and publishing a copy of such notice, at least six days before such meeting, in two public newspapers in said county ; but no such meeting shall be informal or illegal on account of any defect in such notice or the publication thereof, if four-fifths of the members of such Board shall attend such meeting. The said Board at such meeting, or at the next annual meeting of such Board, shall appoint three commissioners who, or a majority of them, after taking the constitutional oath of office, shall, without unnecessary delay, select a proper site for the location of said building or buildings, with proper grounds, to be attached thereto, and make a conditional contract therefor, subject to the approval and confirmation of the said Board, and report such location and contract, together with a detailed plan for the construction, management and dicipline of said house of refuge, and the improvements of such grounds, and the erection of the necessary out-buildings, and also, an estimate of the expenses of the land for the site, and the improvements thereof, and of the construction of the said building or buildings and outbuildings, to the Board of Supervisors at the next annual meeting. In case of a vacancy in the said Board of Commissioners by death, resignation, removal from said county,

Four-fifths of members to be present.

To select site

To estimate the expense.

refusal or neglect to serve, or otherwise, such vacancy shall be filled by an appointment by the Judge of the Circuit Court of said County of Milwaukee. The said commissioners shall receive for their services, such sum as the Board of Supervisors shall allow, not exceeding three dollars for each day while actually engaged in the discharge of their duties, and such expenses as shall be actually incurred by them, in obtaining the necessary plans, estimates and information, preparatory to the report to be made by them as aforesaid; such several sums to be paid by the said Board of Supervisors, and the amount thereof added to the sum to be raised by tax as hereinafter mentioned.

Vacancy, how filled.

How much to receive for services.

Expenses to be paid by board of supervisors.

SEC. 3. Upon such report being made, the said Board of Supervisors shall examine the same and determine thereupon, and may alter, modify, reduce or increase the site, plan or expenses of construction of said building or buildings and out-buildings, as specified in such report, in such manner and to such extent as to them shall seem fit, expedient or necessary, and shall then determine whether they will authorize said commissioners to procure a site for such house of refuge and erect the same. The said commissioners, whenever they shall be empowered so to do, by the said Board of Supervisors, shall purchase or procure the lands necessary for said house of refuge according to the directions and determination of such board, and shall thereupon proceed to construct the same, at such place and on such plan, in all respects, as the said Board of Snpervisors shall, in manner aforesaid, have approved and directed; but before the said commissioners, or either of them, shall enter upon the construction of said house of refuge, or be entitled to draw or receive any moneys for any of the purposes mentioned in this act, they shall severally file, in the office of the County Treasurer of said county, a bond to the said County of Milwaukee, executed by themselves severally, with two sufficient sureties to be approved by said County Treasurer, in the penal sum of

To examine report.

Bonds to be filed.

thirty thousand dollars, and conditioned for the full and faithful performance of their duties as such commissioners, and the accounting to said Board of Supervisors at such annual meeting, and oftener if required by them, for all moneys received by them as such commisioners. If any such bond shall be forfeited, the same shall be prosecuted under the direction of said Board of Supervisors, and all sums recovered, for the breach of the condition thereof, applied to the erection, completion and furnishing of said house of refuge.

To be under the control of supervisors.

SEC. 4. The management of said house of refuge, when completed, shall be under the control and direction of the said Board of Supervisors, through such commissioners and officers as they may appoint for such purpose; and such Board of Supervisors is hereby authorized to establish and adopt, from time to time, at any annual meeting of said board, such rules for the regulation and management of said house of refuge, and the support, employment and dicipline of the persons confined therein, and to appoint such commissioners and other officers to take charge thereof, and prescribe their compensation and duties, and require from them such bonds and securities as to them may seem proper, expedient and fit, and generally to make all such by-laws, rules and regulations in relation to the government and management thereof, as they shall deem expedient, but the person who shall be appointed principal keeper of such house of refuge, shall hold his office for the term of two years, unless sooner removed by said board for incompetency, improper conduct or other causes, to be particularly assigned in writing, and entered on the minutes of said board with the ayes and noes upon the adoption of the resolution for such removal. No such by-law shall be finally adopted by said Board of Supervisors, on the same day on which the same shall be first presented to said board for consideration, nor until the same

Keeper to hold his office 2 years.

shall have been considered and reported upon by a select committee appointed for that purpose.

Supervisors authorized to borrow money.

SEC. 5. The said Board of Supervisors are hereby authorized to borrow, from time to time, on the credit of the County of Milwaukee, such sum or sums of money as shall be necessary to defray all the expenses of procuring the site and completing the erection of said house of refuge, and suitable out-houses, yard and appurtenances, and of procuring the necessary furniture and fixtures, and other things in and about the same; and the said Board is hereby authorized and required to levy and collect a sum sufficient to repay the principal sum so borrowed, in not less than ten nor more than twenty equal annual installments, and also the interest that shall become due on the same, which shall be levied and collected on and from the taxable property in the County of Milwaukee, in the same manner as other county charges are levied and collected; and the said Board or the County Treasurer, under their direction, shall, from time to time, pay such drafts as may be drawn by said commissioners, or a majority of them, for the cost of said site, and the erection of the said house of refuge, not exceeding the amount at which such cost may have been fixed by said Board, in case said Board of Supervisors shall have fixed the same. The County Treasurer of said county, under the direction of said Board of Supervisors, may execute to the person or persons from whom such moneys may be borrowed, such bond or bonds for the re-payment thereof as may be necessary or proper, which bonds shall be binding upon said County of Milwaukee, and shall draw interest at the rate of seven per centum per annum.

County treasurer to pay drafts.

Accounts to be audited by board of supervisors.

SEC. 6. The expenses of maintaining said house of refuge, over and above all receipts for the labor of persons confined therein, and for the support of prisoners therein whose support is not chargeable to said County of Milwaukee, shall be audited and paid by the said Board of Supervisors yearly, at their annual meeting, and shall be raised, levied and collected as part of the ordinary expenses of said County of Milwaukee.

Supervisors to make determents.

SEC. 7. Whenever the said house of refuge shall, in the opinion of said commissioners, or a majority of them, be so far completed as to insure the safe confinement and employment therein of all persons intended to be confined therein, they shall make triplicate determinations thereof, under their hands and seals, one of which they shall file in the office of the Clerk of the Circuit Court of said county ; one other they shall file with the Police Justice of the City of Milwaukee, and the other they shall cause to be published in the several newspapers published in the County of Milwaukee.

Prisoners to be transferred to house of refuge.

SEC. 8. The Circuit Court, in and for said County of Milwaukee, at the first term thereof, after the filing of the said determination, shall, by an order to be entered in its minutes, upon the motion of the District Attorney of Milwaukee County, direct all persons then confined in the jail of said county, and who, by the terms of this act, are authorized to be confined in said house of refuge, to be transferred to said house of refuge, and there to be confined until the term for which they were sentenced to be confined in said jail shall have expired ; and in said order shall be inserted the said determination at length, the names of the said persons respectively, the offence or cause for which they were committed, the court by which they were committed, the day of commitment, and the day on which their sentences will severally expire.

Copies of order to be made.

SEC. 9. The Clerk of the Circuit Court shall cause two copies of said order to be made, and to be attested by his hand and the seal of said court, which he shall deliver to the Sheriff of Milwaukee County ; and said Sheriff shall forthwith transfer the persons named in said order to said house of refuge,

Keeper to give receipt for prisoners

and shall deliver said persons, with one copy of said order, to the principal keeper of said house of refuge, and take his receipt therefor; thenceforward the persons named in said order shall be detained and held to labor in said house of refuge, for the same term of time they would have been required to remain in said jail, if this act had not been passed; and the said Sheriff shall, from that time, be discharged from all liability on account of said persons.

Justices and others may sentence persons to house of refuge.

SEC. 10. After the said determination shall be published as hereinbefore prescribed, every court, justice, magistrate or other officer, in the County of Milwaukee, shall be authorized by law to commit or sentence any person to the county jail of Milwaukee County as a vagrant, disorderly person or common prostitute, or by virtue of a final sentence for any offence, or upon a final conviction in any case, (except for contempt), may sentence such person to be confined in said house of refuge for such time as such person might have been sentenced to be confined in the county jail, if this act had not been passed; and in addition to any sentence now authorized by law to be pronounced in such case, may sentence such person to be confined at hard labor or to solitary confinement, in whole or in any part, or in part to each at the discretion of such court [or] officer.

Prisoners to be employed

SEC. 11. The officers having charge of said house of refuge shall, under the direction of the Board of Supervisors of said County of Milwaukee, place all such persons as shall be confined therein, at such employment or employments as shall be deemed fit and proper, and most conducive to the interests of said County of Milwaukee, and it shall be the duty of such officers to cause all male children, under the age of eighteen years, and all female children, under the age of sixteen years, who shall be legally committed to the said house of refuge, to be instructed during their minority in such branches of useful knowledge as shall be suitable to their years and capacities; and they shall have power, in their discretion, to bind out the said children, with their consent, and the con-

Male children, of what age to be received. Female ditto

Power to bind out children.

sent of their parents, if living, if not living, then with the consent of their guardians, as apprentices or servants, during their minority, to such persons, and at such places to learn such proper trades or employment as, in their judgment, will tend most to the reformation and amendment, and the future benefit and advantage of such children.

Sec. 12. All and singular the clauses and provisions contained in chapter eighty-one of the Revised Statutes, entitled "Of Masters and Apprentices," shall apply to the apprentices and servants, and the persons to whom they shall be bound, under and by virtue of this act, and every minor so bound, and the officers binding him and his master, shall be subject to all the provisions of said chapter.

May contract to receive prisoners for other counties.

Sec. 13. After the said house of refuge shall be completed, the Board of Supervisors of the said County of Milwaukee may contract with the Board of Supervisors of any other county, upon such terms as may be agreed upon by said Board, to receive into said house of refuge any person that may be sentenced therein by any court, justice or other officer of any such other county, for such offences as such court, justice or other officer, may, by law, have a right to sentence to confinement in the jail of the county in which such person may be sentenced; and any officer to whom the process of commitment in such case may be delivered for execution, shall, by virtue of such process, convey such person to the said house of refuge, and deliver him or her to the principal keeper thereof; and such keeper shall detain such person upon such sentence, and shall treat such person in the same manner as if he or she had been sentenced to like imprisonment therein by any court, justice or other officer in the County of Milwaukee. After such contract shall be made by the Board of Supervisors of the County of Milwaukee, with the Board of Supervisors of any other county, and so long as the same shall remain in force, the courts, justices and other officers of such other county shall have the same power, jurisdiction and authority to sentence and commit persons to such house of refuge, as is or shall be possessed or rightfully exercised by the courts, justices or other officers of the County of Milwaukee.

SEC. 14. The County Judge of Milwaukee County, the Police Justice of the City of Milwaukee, and the District Attorney of said County of Milwaukee, or any two of them, may, in their discretion, make such order for the employment upon said house of refuge, while the same is in course of construction, of such persons, as may, for the time being, be confined in the jail of Milwaukee County, upon final sentence of summary conviction or as disorderly persons or vagrants, as they may deem beneficial to the County of Milwaukee, and such order shall be in writing, and signed by such officers, and shall be carried into effect by the Sheriff of said county.

Vagrants to be confined.

SEC. 15. The County Judge, District Attorney and Sheriff of Milwaukee County, and the Mayor and Police Justice of the City of Milwaukee, shall constiute a Board of Visitors, whose duty it shall be to examine into and investigate the affairs of such house of refuge, on the first Monday of August in each year; and such Board of Visitors shall make a report, in writing, to the Board of Supervisors of the County of Milwaukee, at their regular annual meeting in each year, setting forth the condition of house of refuge, and suggesting such alterations and improvments in the management, dicipline and government of the same, as seems fit and proper, and most conductive to the punishment and reformation of the prisoners therein confined, and to the interests of said County of Milwaukee.

Board of visitors

SEC. 16. This act shall take effect immediately.

Approved, March 30, 1855.

AN ACT

To amend an Act entitled "An Act to Incorporate the City of Milwaukee, and the several Acts amendatory thereof," approved, February 20, 1852.

The People of the State of Wisconsin, represented in Senate and Assembly, do enact as follows :

Division ef second ward.

SECTION 1. All the territory now included in the second ward of the City of Milwaukee, which lies south of the centre of Vliet street and the Madison road, in said city, shall hereafter constitute and be the second ward of the City of Milwaukee, and all the territory now included in the second ward of the City of Milwaukee which lies north of the centre of Vliet street and the Madison road, in said city, shall constitute and be the sixth ward of the City of Milwaukee.

Division of first ward.

SEC. 2. All the territory, now included in the first ward of the City of Milwaukee, which lies north of the centre of Division street, in said city, shall hereafer constitute and be the first ward of the City of Milwaukee, and all the territory, now included in the first ward of the City of Milwaukee, which lies south of the centre of Division street, in said city, shall constitute and be the seventh ward of the City of Milwaukee.

Council to appoint inspectors.

SEC. 3. It shall be the duty of the Common Council to appoint three Inspectors of Election in each of the said wards, at the next city election, and to designate the place for holding the same, and there shall be elected at the said election, in the second and seventh wards, one Alderman for each ward, who shall hold his office for two years, and two Aldermen for each ward who shall hold their office for one year ; and there shall be elected at said election, in the first and sixth wards, one Alderman for each ward, who shall hold his office for two years, and one Alderman for each ward

Officers to be elected.

who shall hold his office for one year; and the Alderman elected for two years in the first and second wards, at the last city election, shall be Alderman for the wards respectively wherein they reside for the remainder of their term of office; and annually thereafter, there shall be elected one Alderman in each of the aforesaid first, second, sixth and seventh wards, who shall hold his office for two years, and one who shall hold his office for one year, and the said wards shall have all the rights and privileges as now provided by law for the wards of the City of Milwaukee, and shall elect all the officers prescribed by law to be elected in such wards.

Comptroller to apportion indebtedness

SEC. 4. It shall be the duty of the Comptroller of the City of Milwaukee, to apportion the amount of city indebtedness, now charged to the first ward of the City of Milwaukee, between the first and seventh wards, hereby created, in proportion to their respective equalized assessment roll, for the year 1855, and to credit to the said first ward such amount as will be charged to the seventh ward; and it shall be the duty of the said Comptroller, in the same manner, to apportion the amount of city indebtedness, now charged to the second ward, between the said second and sixth wards, hereby created, in proportion to their respective equalized assessment rolls, for the year 1855, and to credit to the said second ward the amount to be charged to the sixth ward.

Property to belong jointly.

SEC. 5. All property, real or personal, which, prior to the passage of this act, belonged to the first ward of the City of Milwaukee, shall hereafter belong, jointly, to the first and seventh wards of said city; and all property, real or personal, which, prior to the passage of this act, belonging to the second ward of the City of Milwaukee, shall thereafter belong, jointly, to the second and sixth wards of said city.

Improvement on public square to be determined by resolution.

SEC. 6. Whenever any improvement is to be made in front of or upon the public square, situated on the west side of Fifth street, and between Poplar and Vliet streets, such improvements to be made, shall first be determined by resolution, adopted by a majority of the Aldermen of the second and sixth wards of the City of Milwaukee, which resolution shall be recorded in the record of the Street Commissioners of said wards, and the expense of such improvements shall be paid from the joint funds of said wards, in proportion to their equalized assessment roll for the year in which such improvement shall be made.

Election, how conducted.

Sec. 7. The first section of chapter two of the act of which this is amendatory, is hereby so amended as to read as follows :—"The annual election for ward and city officers shall be held on the first Tuesday in April of each year, at such place in each ward as the Common Council shall designate, and the polls shall be kept open from nine o'clock in the forenoon till five o'clock in the afternoon ; and ten days previous notice shall be given by the Common Council of the time and place of holding such election, and of the city and ward officers to be elected."

Officers to hold their office till successors be elected.

Sec. 8. The seventeenth section of chapter two of the act of which this is amendatory, is hereby so amended as to read as follows :—"All the city and ward officers, now in office, shall hold their respective offices until their successors are elected or appointed under this act, and the term of every officer, elected under this law, shall commence on the second Tuesday in April of the year for which he is elected, and shall, unless herein otherwise provided, continue for one year, and until his successor is elected and qualified."

Sec. 9. This act shall take effect and be in force from and after its passage.

Approved, February 21, 1856.

AN ACT

To amend the Act to consolidate and amend the Act to Incorporate the City of Milwaukee, and the several Acts amendatory thereof, approved February 20, 1852.

The People of the State of Wisconsin, represented in Senate and Assembly, do enact as follows:

Council to have power to lay out squares, &c.

SECTION 1. The first section of chapter six of the act of which this is amendatory, is hereby so amended, as to be and read as follows :—"The Common Council shall have power to lay out squares, grounds, streets and alleys, and to widen the same, as follows: whenever ten or more freeholders, residing in any ward, shall, by petition, represent to the Common Council that it is necessary to take certain lands within the ward where such petitioners may reside, for public use, for the purpose of laying out public square, grounds and streets or alleys, or the enlarging or widening the same, the courses and distances, metes and bounds of the land proposed to be taken, together with the names and residences of the owners of such premises, if the same shall be known to the petitioners, to be set forth in such petition, the Common Council shall thereupon cause notice of such application to be given to the occupant or occupants of such lands, if any there be, by publishing notice of such application in the official papers for four weeks, at least once in each week."

Names of owners to be given.

Jurors, how appointed.

SEC. 2. The second section of chapter six of the act of which this is amendatory, is hereby so amended as to be and read as follows :—"Such notice shall state, that on a certain day therein to be named," but not before, "the expiration of such publication, application will be made to the Judge of the Circuit or County Court of Milwaukee County, for the appointment of twelve jurors to view said premises, and to determine whether it will be necessary to take the same for the purposes specified in said petition," at which time and place, any person interested in the lands proposed to be taken, may appear before said judge and make objections to the appointment of any juror proposed to be appointed by said judge, stating the grounds of objection.

Jurors to give notice.

SEC. 3. The fifth section of chapter six of the act of which this is amendatory, is hereby so amended, as to be and read as follows :—"The said jurors, at such time as they may agree upon, of which, at least three days notice shall be given, by publication in the official papers, shall proceed in a body to view the premises to be taken, or, the necessity of taking the same, said jury, or any one of their number, may apply to the judge appointing said jury, to summon such witnesses as they may desire, to appear before said jury and testify as to the facts in the case, and said jury shall hear such testimony as may be offered by any party interested, which testimony shall be reduced to writing by one of the jurors, and either of the jurors shall be authorized to administer the necessary oaths to witnesses."

Jurors to view premises.

SEC. 4. The seventh section of chapter six of the act of which this is amendatory, is hereby so amended, as to be and read as follows :—"Should the jurors report that it is necessary to take such premises, the Common Council may enter an order among their proceedings, confirming the whole of said report, or any part thereof; and, in case the Common Council shall confirm said report, or any part thereof, they shall direct the same jurors, within one month thereafter, or such further time as may be deemed proper, to again view said premises at such time as they may agree upon, of which, at least three days notice shall be given, by publication in the official paper, for the purpose of ascertaining and determining the amount of damages to be paid to the owner or owners of the property proposed to be taken, and also what lands or premises will be benefitted by such taking, and said jury may obtain the testimony of witnesses as to the facts in the case, in the same manner as provided in section three of this act, and shall hear such testimony as may be offered by any party interested, which testimony shall be reduced to writing by one of the jurors, and said jury shall determine and assess, and return such damages and benefits to the Common Council, by filing the same with the City Clerk, within the time limited." Jury to receive testimony.

SEC. 5. Add to section fourteen of chapter six of the act of which this is amendatory, as follows:—"And the award of said jury when so made as aforesaid, and confirmed by resolution adopted by the Common Council, shall be conclusive and final as to all parties interested, and from which there shall be no appeal." Report, when confirmed, to be final.

SEC. 6. Section twenty-one of chapter six of the act of which this is amendatory, is hereby repealed and declared null and void.

SEC. 7. All the directions hereby given in this act, or in the provisions of chapter six of the act of which this is amendatory, shall be deemed only directory, and no error, irregularity or informality in any of the proceedings under the provisions of this act, or the provisions of said chapter six of the act of which this is amendatory, not affecting substantial justice, shall in any way affect the validity of the proceedings.

SEC. 8. All the proceedings of the Common Council heretofore had, in laying out streets and alleys, are hereby confirmed, and all the streets and alleys heretofore laid out and opened by the Common Council, except such as have been legally vacated, are hereby declared public highways.

SEC. 9. The twenty-third section of chapter eight of the act of which this is amendatory, and all similar provisions embraced in any act, by which any lots or tracts of land, within the corporate limits of the City of Milwaukee, are exempt from taxes and assessment, are hereby repealed, provided, nothing herein contained shall be so construed as to Acts exempting certain property from taxation repealed repeal any of the provisions of chapter fifteen of the Revised Statutes of this state.

Council may dismiss officers.

SEC. 10. The Common Council shall have power to dismiss any officer appointed by said council under the provisions of section eight of chapter three of the act of which this is amendatory, at any time when, in the judgment of the Common Council, the services of such officer or appointee are no longer needed.

SEC. 11. The tenth section of the amendatory act, approved, February 18, 1853, amending the act of which this is amendatory, and fixing the salaries of the several officers of the City of Milwaukee, is hereby repealed.

Council may regulate piers, &c. constructing of.

SEC. 12. The twenty-second subdivision of section three of chapter four of the act of which this is amendatory, is hereby so amended as to be and read as follows:—"To regulate the construction of piers and wharves extending into Lake Michigan, within the limits of said city, and to prescribe and control the prices to be charged for pierage or wharfage thereon, and to regulate, prescribe and control the prices to be charged for dockage and storage within the city."

SEC. 13. Section six of chapter seven of the act of which this is amendatory, is hereby amended, by adding thereto, as follows:—"And if said work be not done within the time limited in such contract, or in case no time is named in such contract, then, in a reasonable length of time for completing the same, the said commissioner may re-let such work without further notice."

SEC. 14. This act shall take effect and be in force from and after its passage.

Approved, March 18, 1856.

AN ACT

To amend an Act entitled "An Act to consolidate and amend the Act to Incorporate the City of Milwaukee, and the several Acts amendatory thereof," approved, February 20, 1852, and to enlarge the boundary of said City.

The People of the State of Wisconsin, represented in Senate and Assembly, do enact as follows:

SECTION 1. The corporate limits of the City of Milwaukee are hereby enlarged, so as to include the north half of sections four, five and six, in town six, north of range twenty-two east, and also so much space as lies south of the present boundary line of said city, and north of the east and west quarter section line of said section, continued due east to the eastern boundary line of the state, in Lake Michigan; which quarter section line, so continued, shall be the southern boundary line of said city. The territory hereby added to said city, shall constitute a part of the fifth ward thereof, and shall be subject to the law, regulations and ordinances governing the said ward and the said city.

Ward limits extended.

SEC. 2. This act shall take effect and be in force from and after its passage.

Approved, March 18, 1856.

AN ACT

To authorize the several Wards in the City of Milwaukee to purchase grounds for Market and Public Squares.

The People of the State of Wisconsin, represented in Senate and Assembly, do enact as follows:

SECTION 1. Whenever twenty-five or more freeholders, residents of any ward in the City of Milwaukee, shall, by

Petition to be signed by 25 freeholders.

petition, represent to the Common Council of said city, that it is necessary to take certain lots or lands within the ward where such petitioners reside, for the purpose of a Market or Public Square, or for enlarging the same, setting forth in such petition the particular lots or lands which they desire to be taken for such purpose, together with the names of the owners of such lots or lands, if the same shall be known to the petitioners, the Common Council may thereupon order an election to be held in such ward, by giving at least two weeks notice of said election, by publishing the same, together with a copy of the petition, in the official papers of the city; such election shall be held at the usual place of holding elections in such ward, and shall be conducted and the votes returned and canvassed in the same manner as at city elections. The votes at such election shall be by ballot, on which shall be written or printed, the words, "For the Market Square," or "For the Public Square," as the case may be, or "Against the Market Square," or "Against the Public Square," as the case may be; and if a majority of the whole number of votes cast at such election in the ward shall be "For the Market Square," or "For the Public Square," or for both, according as may be set forth in the petition, then the lots or lands, named in the petition, may be purchased for such purpose by the ward, as hereinafter provided and not otherwise.

Ballots to read.

Aldermen may bargain

SEC. 2. If a majority of the whole number of votes cast at the election, called for the purpose, and in the manner provided in the foregoing section, shall be in favor of the proposition set forth in the petition, then the Aldermen of such ward may bargain with and purchase of the owner or owners, the lots or lands specified in the petition, on such terms as they may agree upon; and to pay for the same, they are hereby authorized and empowered to issue, for and in the name of such ward, the bonds of the wards to an amount not exceeding, in the aggregate, one hundred thousand dollars, for both Market and Public Squares in such ward, bearing interest at a rate not exceeding ten per cent., and being for a length of time not exceeding thirty years, and both principal and interest payable at such place or places as may be determined by the Aldermen of the ward; said bonds shall be signed by a majority of the Aldermen of such ward, and countersigned by the City Comptroller, and the bonds, or the proceeds thereof, shall be applied to the purchase of the lots or lands specified in the said petition, and for the improvement of the same, and for the erection of a Market House, and such other building as the wants of the ward may require, on the Public Square. Bonds, when payable.

SEC. 3. All purchases, made by virtue of this act, shall be in the name and for the use of the ward making such purchase, and the land so purchased, and the improvements that may be made thereon, shall be exempt from taxation, and the Aldermen of such ward, acting in behalf of the ward, shall have control of the grounds so purchased, and the improvements that may be made thereon, and may lease, rent and regulate the same, from year to year, and all moneys received by them, from the income thereof, shall be paid over by them to the City Treasurer, for the use and benefit of such ward; and the Mayor and Common Council of the City of Milwaukee may, by ordinance, provide for regulating the sale of meats, provisions and vegetables, and confine the selling thereof within such limits as they may deem proper. Exempt from taxation. Aldermen may lease.

SEC. 4. To pay the annual interest on any bonds issued by any ward, under the provisions of this act, or the principal of the same, when it shall become due, the Mayor and Common Council of the City of Milwaukee shall cause to be levied a special tax upon all the taxable real and personal property in such ward, which special tax shall be collected at the same time and in the same manner that other city taxes are collected by law, and when so collected, the same shall not be appropriated or used for any other purpose what- Interest, how paid.

ever than for paying the interest and principal of the bonds authorized to be issued by this act. After the expiration of ten years from the date of the bonds issued by any ward, under the provisions of this act, the Mayor and Common Council may, if they deem best, include in the special tax, levied annually to pay the interest on the bonds so issued by any ward, a sufficient additional amount, to pay thereafter in each year five per cent. of the principal of the bonds so issued by such ward.

Plans and specifications to be filed in city comptroller's office.

SEC. 5. Before proceeding to improve the grounds, or to erect a Market House or other buildings on a Market Square, purchased under this act, the Aldermen of the ward shall cause a plan and specification of the same to be drawn, and a copy thereof to be deposited in the office of the City Comptroller, and all contracts for buildings and improvements shall be let to the lowest responsible bidder, provided that no such contract shall be let until ten days previous notice shall be given, by publication in the official papers of the city, of the time and place of receiving proposals for such work, and of letting the same, and all contracts for buildings and improvements to be made on the real estate, purchased by any ward under this act, shall be signed by a majority of the Aldermen of such ward, and countersigned by the City Comptroller.

SEC. 6. If the Aldermen of any ward shall not be able to agree with the owner or owners of the lots or lands proposed to be taken, and purchase the same in the manner provided in the second section of this act, and shall so represent in a memorial to the Common Council, the Common Council may thereupon cause notice to be given to the occupant or occupants, if any there be, of such lots or lands, by publishing the same in the official papers of the city for four weeks, at least once in each week, that on a certain day therein to be named, not prior to the expiration of the time specified herein, that such notice shall be published, application will

To be published.

be made to the Judge of the Circuit or County Court of Milwaukee County, for the appointment of twelve jurors, to view said lots or lands, and determine the value of the same, at which time and place, any person interested in the land proposed to be taken may appear before said judge, and make objection to the appointment of any juror proposed to be appointed by said judge, stating the ground of his or her objection.

Judge to appoint Jury.

SEC. 7. Upon the presentation of such application, and upon proof of the publication of the notice hereinbefore required, the said judge shall thereupon appoint twelve reputable freeholders, residents of the city, but not residents of the ward in which such premises may lie, nor interested in the result of such application. The said judge shall thereupon issue his precept, directed to said jurors, requiring them, within thirty days, to view said premises, to be specified in said precept, and to determine and make return, under their hands, to the Common Council, what, in their judgment, is the true cash value of each and every lot or parcel of land to be taken for the purpose specified in such application.

Jurors to view premises.

SEC. 8. If any of the persons so appointed shall be disqualified from acting, or shall refuse to act, the judge shall appoint others in their places, and a memorandum of such substitution shall be endorsed on the precept.

Judge to fill vacancy.

SEC. 9. The said jurors, at such time as they may agree upon, of which at least one week's notice shall be given in the official papers, shall proceed in a body to view the premises in question, and shall hear such testimony as may be offered by any party interested, which testimony shall be reduced to writing by one of the jurors, and either of the jurors shall be authorized to administer the necessary oaths to witnesses, and for the purpose of better enabling said jury to determine the real value of the property to be taken, they, or any of them, may request the judge appointing said jury, to summon such witnesses as said jury may desire, to ap-

Notice to be given.

To hear testimony.

Witness to be summoned.

pear before them and testify to the facts in the case, touching the value of the property so taken.

Report to be returned to Common Council.

SEC. 10. After viewing the premises, and hearing such testimony as may be offered, the jurors shall make a report of their proceedings, which shall be signed by them respectively, and which shall state what, in their judgment, is the true cash value of each and every lot and parcel of land to be taken for the purpose specified in the precept, which said report, testimony and precept, shall be returned to the Common Council within the time limited therein.

Jurors to estimate value of buildings.

SEC. 11. If there should be any building or buildings standing in whole or in part upon the land to be so taken, the jurors, before proceeding to make their appraisement of the lots or lands, shall first estimate and determine the whole value of such building or buildings to the owners, aside from the value of the land, and the injury to him by having such building taken from him ; and, secondly, the value of such building to him to remove.

Length of notice to be given.

SEC. 12. At least twenty days notice of such determination shall be given to all persons interested, by publication in the official papers of the city, such notice shall specify the building or buildings, and the award of the jurors. It shall also require the parties interested to appear by a day therein named, or give notice to the Common Council of their election, either to accept the award of the jurors and allow such building to be taken with the land appropriated, or of their intention to remove such building at the value to remove, set thereon by the jurors ; and if the owner or owners shall agree to remove such building, he or they shall have such time for that purpose as the Common Council may allow.

Council may direct sale of buildings.

SEC. 13. If the owner refuse to take the building at its valuation to remove, or fail to give notice of his election in the matter as aforesaid, within the time prescribed, the Common Council shall have power to direct the sale of such building, at public auction, for cash, giving ten days' notice of such sale, in the official papers, and the proceeds of such sale shall be paid to the owner, or reserved in the City Treasury, to be paid to such owner when called for by him.

Testimony to be reduced to writing.

SEC. 14. The said jurors, within the time limited, shall view and examine the premises proposed to be taken, and after hearing such testimony as may be offered by any parties interested, and which shall be reduced to writing by one of the jurors, they shall proceed to make their appraisement and determine the value of the real estate proposed to be taken, which shall be awarded to the owners respectively; and in the appraised value of the land, the jurors shall include the value of the building or buildings (if the same shall be the property of the owner of such land), as estimated or valued by them as aforesaid, less the proceeds of the sale thereof, or if taken by the owner, at the value to remove, in such case they shall only include the difference between such value, and the whole estimated value of such building or buildings.

Lands subject to lease, &c.

SEC. 15. If the lands or buildings belong to different persons, or if the land be subject to lease, judgment or mortgage, or if there be any estate in it less than an estate in fee, the value of such interests to such persons may be awarded to them respectively by the jurors.

Award to be signed by jurors.

SEC. 16. Having determined the value of the real estate and buildings, if any, to be taken, and awarded the same to the proper owner or parties interested therein, such determination or award shall be signed by such jurors, and returned, together with the testimony taken, to the Common Council within the time limited in their order of appointment.

Deposit to be made if owner is unknown.

SEC. 17. The land required to be taken for the purposes mentioned in this act, shall be appropriated by the Aldermen of the proper ward, till the appraisement, or value awarded therefor to the owner thereof, shall be paid, or tendered by the Aldermen of such ward, to the owner or his agent, or in case the said owner or agent cannot be found, or is unknown, deposited to his or their credit in the City Treasury, and then, and not before, such lands may be taken and appropriated by the Aldermen of such ward, for the purposes required, and the same shall thereafter be subject to all the laws and ordinances of the city, in the same manner as streets, alleys and public grounds heretofore opened or laid out.

Contracts to cease when land is taken

SEC. 18. Where the whole of any lot or piece of land or any part thereof, or other premises under lease or other contract, shall be taken, by virtue of this act, all the covenants, contracts or agreements between landlords and tenants or any other contracting parties touching the same or any part thereof, shall, upon the confirmation of such report of said jurors, by the Common Council, respectively cease and be absolutely discharged.

SEC. 19. Whenever only a part of a lot or tract of land or other premises, so under lease or other contract, shall be taken for any of the purposes aforesaid, all the covenants, contracts or agreements respecting the same, upon the confirmation of such report by the Council, shall be absolutely discharged as to the part thereof so taken, but shall remain valid as to the residue thereof; and the rents, considerations and payments reserved, payable and to be paid for in respect to the same, shall be so proportioned so that the part thereof justly and equitably payable for such residue thereof, and no more, shall be paid, or recoverable for, in respect to the same.

Payment for land to be made within one year.

SEC. 20. The appraisement or valuation of the lot or lands, or other premises, shall be paid or tendered or deposited, as herein required, within one year from the confirmation of such appraisement and report, and if not so paid, tendered or deposited, all the proceedings in any such case shall be void.

SEC. 21. When any known owner of lands or tenements affected by any proceedings under this act, shall be an infant, or labor under legal disability, the Judge of the Circuit

Court of Milwaukee County, or in his absence, the judge of any court of record in said county, may, upon the application of the Aldermen of the proper ward, or such party, or his next friend, appoint a guardian for such party, and all notices, required by this act, shall be served upon such guardian. Guardian to be appointed in certain cases.

SEC. 22. Any person whose property is taken, may, within ten days from the return of the jurors to the Common Council, appeal from said appraisement or valuation to the Circuit Court of Milwaukee County, where such appeal shall be tried by the court and jury, as in ordinary cases, and in case the award of such court and jury shall not exceed the amount of the appraisement, then the party making the appeal shall pay all the costs of such appeal. The Aldermen of the ward shall have the same right of appeal. Appeals, how made.

SEC. 23. Whenever any Market or Public Square shall be laid out or enlarged, under the provisions of this act, the Aldermen of the proper ward shall cause an accurate survey and profile thereof to be made, and filed in the office of City Surveyor. Survey and profile to be made.

SEC. 24. All the expenses incurred, under the provisions of this act, in taking any lot or lands or other premises, shall be paid by the ward taking the same for the purposes specified, and in no case shall the city, or the other wards, be liable for any portion of the principal or the interest of the bonds issued by such ward, or the expenses incurred in taking the lots or lands or other premises by such ward, under this act. Ward to pay expenses.

SEC. 25. Any two wards in said city, may, by joint resolution of the Aldermen of such ward, unite and purchase, and improve for the joint use and benefit of such wards, a Market or Public Square, under the provisions of this act, in which case the amount of bonds which such wards may issue, for such joint purpose, may be increased to one hundred and fifty thousand dollars in the aggregate for the two wards, Joint improvements, how made.

N

and shall be apportioned between such wards in the ratio of the equalized assessment roll of such wards, in the year when such purchase and improvement shall be made by such wards, and such wards may issue their bonds separately, in the same ratio, for such purpose, and be subject to all the liabilities and requirements which any one ward would be in the purchase and improvement of a Market or Public Square, under this act, and all such property, when purchased and improved by any two wards jointly, shall be owned and held by such wards for their joint use and benefit.

Proceedings to be recorded.

SEC. 26. All proceedings under this act, by the Aldermen of any ward, shall be entered at length in the records of such ward, and in the case of any two wards acting jointly, as hereinbefore provided, then all the proceedings of such wards shall be entered at length in the records of both such wards.

SEC. 27. This act shall take effect and be in force from and after its passage.

Approved, March 19, 1856.

AN ACT

To authorize the Common Council of the City of Milwaukee to levy a Special Tax for Ward purposes.

The People of the State of Wisconsin, represented in Senate and Assembly, do enact as follows:

Council may levy special Tax.

SECTION 1. The Mayor and Common Council of the City of Milwaukee, are hereby authorized and empowered, at the time of levying other taxes for the year eighteen hundred and fifty-six, to levy a special tax on all taxable property in the several wards of said city, for ward purposes, not exceeding one per cent. in addition to the tax now authorized by law to be levied and collected in said wards for ward purposes; which special tax shall be collected at the same time and in the same manner as other city taxes, and all laws now in force, in regard to levying and collecting taxes for ward purposes in said city, shall apply to the said special tax hereby authorized to be levied and collected : *Provided*, This act shall not apply to the third ward.

How appropriated.

SEC. 2. The special tax hereby authorized to be levied and collected in each ward of the City of Milwaukee, shall, when collected, be used, applied and appropriated in the same manner and for the same purpose, as other taxes collected in such ward for ward purposes.

SEC. 3. This act shall take effect and be in force from and after its passage.

Approved, March 19, 1856.

AN ACT

Relating to the Settlement of Accounts between certain Wards in the City of Milwaukee.

The People of the State of Wisconsin, represented in Senate and Assembly, do enact as follows :

Comptroller to apportion between wards.

SECTION 1. It shall be, and is hereby made, the duty of the City Comptroller, of the City of Milwaukee, in case the expenditures for work done, or materials furnished for ward improvements by the Aldermen of the first or second wards in said city, prior to the passage of the act dividing said wards, shall exceed the amount of the respective ward fund for such ward, applicable for ward purposes, for the fiscal year ending April 1, 1856, to apportion such excess, if any, between the several wards, formed by the division of said wards, in the ratio of the equalized assessment rolls of said wards for the year 1855, and to charge to the proper wards respectively, the just apportionment so made.

SEC. 2. This act shall take effect and be in force from and after its passage.

Approved, March 29, 1856.

AN ACT

To make Street Commissioners Certificates in the City of Milwaukee a lien upon Lots or Lands against which they may issue.

The People of the State of Wisconsin, represented in Senate and Assembly, do enact as follows:

Certificates to be a lien on lots, &c.

SECTION 1. All certificates issued, or that may hereafter be issued, by the Aldermen of any ward of the City of Milwaukee, or a majority of them, as Street Commissioners for the purposes and under and in pursuance of any of the provisions of chap. 7 of the act, entitled "an act to consolidate and amend the act to incorporate the City of Milwaukee, and the several acts amendatory thereof," approved February 20, A. D. 1852, shall be lien upon the lots or parcel of land against which the said certificates shall respectively be chargeable, from and after the time when said certificates shall be countersigned by the City Comptoller, and said certificates shall draw interest at the rate of twenty-five per cent. per annum, upon the amount named in the same, from the time when such lots or lands shall be sold by the City Treasurer, as required by law, for and on account of such certificate liens; which said certificates may be transferred by endorsement thereon of the name of the person or persons, to whom the same may by issued, and such transfer shall in no way effect or impair the lien, given by this act, but shall transfer, to the assignee, all the rights of the assignor.

May be transferred by endorsement.

Holders may redeem.

SEC. 2. The holder of any Street Commissioners certificate may pay or redeem any taxes or assessments, assessed subsequent to the date of the certificate lien as provided by this act, and all such taxes, together with the interest thereon, at the rate of twenty-five per cent. per annum, shall be paid by the person seeking to discharge or redeem any lots or parcel of land from the lien given by this act, to the Treasurer of the City of Milwaukee, or to the proper officer of the city or county, authorized to receive money for the redemption of lands from taxes, for the benefit of the holder of said certificate as aforesaid, before said lot or parcel of land shall be discharged or redeemed from said certificate lien aforesaid.

Holder may file bill in chancery or other court.

SEC. 3. The holder of any street commissioner's certificate, which shall become a lien by virtue of this act, at any time after the expiration of three years from the time when such certificate shall have been countersigned by the City Comptroller, in case the same shall not have been paid or redeemed, and in case there is no subsequent certificate of tax sale of such land unredeemed and not owned by such holder, and also in case all taxes assessed on such lots or parcel of land, subsequent to the date of said lien, have been paid to the proper officer, may file his bill in chancery in the Circuit Court of the County of Milwaukee, or in any other court having equity jurisdiction in said county to enforce the lien given by this act, to cause such lot or parcel of land subject to such lien to be held under a decree of the court, for the satisfaction of such lien. The owner, and all persons having any interest in such lot or parcel of land, shall be made parties to the proceedings, and served with process; which process, and the service thereof, as well upon resident as non-resident defendant, shall conform to, and all proceedings in the case shall be conducted according to the law regulating the proceedings in courts of chancery, and according to the rules and practice of such court in the foreclosure of mortgages. The court shall allow the complainants lien, together with all the taxes which may have been paid by him, or by any person for him, or by any former holder of said certificate lien, with the interest thereon, as hereinafter provided, subsequent to the date of said lien aforesaid. And the street commissioner's certificate, duly countersigned by the City Comptroller, shall be *prima facie* evidence of the amount of such lien, as well also as of the validity and legality thereof,

How suit to be conducted

Certificate to be evidence of lien.

and of all the facts stated in such certificate; and the receipts of the proper officers authorized to receive taxes, shall also be evidence of the amount of taxes paid or redeemed by the complainant, or by any person for him, or by any former holder of said certificate lien. The court, upon ascertaining of such lien aforesaid, and also the amount of taxes paid by complainant, or for his benefit, shall enter up a decree against the lot or parcel of land for the amount of such lien and taxes, and the interest thereon, at the rate of twenty-five per cent. per annum as hereinbefore provided, together with the cost of suit and sale, and also that the lot or parcel of land, or so much or such part thereof as will be sufficient to satisfy the amount of such decree, be sold to satisfy and discharge the same; which decree of the court shall be carried into effect, as near as may be, in the same manner as decrees for the foreclosure of mortgages, and the complainant may become the purchaser at the sale; such decree shall forever bar and preclude persons, parties to said suit, from setting up any claim, right or title to the premises mentioned therein, and cut off all right and equity of redemption therein. If the lot or parcel of land should be sold for more than the amount of such decree against it and costs, the excess shall be paid into court by the Sheriff, or officer making the sale, for the benefit of those entitled to it, and subject to the order of the court. The officer making the sale, shall make, execute, acknowledge and deliver to the purchaser, or his or her assigns, a good and sufficient deed of the lot or parcel of land so sold; which deed shall be executed and acknowledged, as deeds for the conveyance of real estate are required to be executed and acknowledged by the laws of the state, and such deed, so executed and acknowledged, shall vest the title of the premises named therein in fee simple, indefeasibly in the grantee thereof, his or her heirs and assigns forever. The Sheriff, or officer making the sale, after the execution and delivery of the deed aforesaid, shall make report of his pro-

Receipt to be evidence of lien.

Sheriff to make deed.

Sheriff to make report to court.

ceedings to the court, and upon the coming in and filing of such report, the court shall make an order confirming such sale, and all the proceedings therein.

Minors, idiots and non-residents, not served with process, may petition

SEC. 4. Any minor, insane person or idiot, married woman, or any non-resident, upon whom process has not been personally served, having any interest in any such lot or parcel of land, so, as aforsesaid, sold under the provision of this act, may, in his or her own name, or by a next friend or guardian, within one year from the day of such sale, file a petition, under oath, setting forth such fact of his or her minority, insanity or idiocy or coverture, and in the case of a non-resident, the fact of having no personal service of process or notice of suit, and may have a rehearing upon the merits of the case: *Provided*, That in no case any decree of foreclosure be opened or set aside until all taxes and the interest thereon actually paid or redeemed on said premises by the purchaser, together with the purchase money for which said premises may have been sold, and the interest thereon, at the rate of twenty-five per cent. per annum, have been paid or tendered by the petitioner to said purchaser or his assigns.

Bill to be supported by the oath of complainant.

SEC. 5. In bills of foreclosure to enforce the lien, under this act, it shall not be necessary to a valid decree that the name of the owners be correctly set forth, if the premises are described with reasonable certainty. The bill shall be supported by the oath of the complainant, or of some person having a knowledge of the facts alledged; it shall set forth the names of the persons interested, if known, and who are proper defendants to the suit, and if unknown, that the complainant, on diligent enquiry, could not ascertain their names; and it shall also set forth the certificate upon which the suit is brought, and the amount of the lien claimed, with the interest thereon, and also the amount of taxes which have been paid or redeemed on the premises by the holder of the certificate, subsequent to the date of the lien, and that the complainant prays the sale of the premises to satisfy the lien, taxes and interest.

SEC. 6. Nothing in this act shall be construed as repealing any of the provisions of an act entitled "an act to consolidate and amend the act to incorporate the City of Milwaukee, and the several acts amendatory thereof," but this act shall be construed as additional to the remedy already existing for the collection and enforcement of taxes and assessments for city improvements, made by order of the street commissioners of the several wards of the City of Milwaukee.

SEC. 7. This act shall take effect and be in force from and after its passage.

Approved, March 29, 1856.

AN ACT

To regulate the platting of lots and lands in the City of Milwaukee.

The People of the State of Wisconsin, represented in Senate and Assembly, do enact as follows :

Streets and alleys to correspond with other streets and alleys.

SECTION 1. Every individual, or company of individuals, or body corporate, owning a lot or tract of land within the corporate limits of the City of Milwaukee, who may desire to subdivide or plat such lot or tract of land into city lots, shall, in platting the same, cause the streets and alleys in such plat to correspond in width and general direction with the streets and alleys through the lots and blocks in said city adjacent to such lot, to submit the same to the Common Council of said city for approval, and if said plat shall be approved by the Common Council, it shall be lawful for the party or parties making such plat to record the same in the manner prescribed in the Revised Statutes of this state concerning town plats ; but except such plat shall be approved by resolution adopted by said Common Council, a copy of

To submit plat to the Common Council.

Owners to record the plat.

which, duly certified by the City Clerk, shall be affixed to said plat, it shall not be lawful for the Register of Deeds of Milwaukee County to receive such plat for record, and the person or persons neglecting or refusing to comply with the requirements of this act, shall forfeit and pay a sum not less than one hundred dollars, nor more than one thousand dollars; and the Register of Deeds who shall record such plat without such resolution of the Common Council thereto attached, approving the same, shall forfeit and pay a sum not less than fifty dollars nor more than one hundred dollars.

Certified resolution from city clerk to accompany plat.

Penalty for neglect.

Sec. 2. All forfeitures and liabilities which may be incurred and arise under and by virtue of this act, shall be prosecuted for and recovered in the name of the City of Milwaukee, and paid into the City Treasury for the use and benefit of said city.

Forfeitures, how prosecuted, and when collected, to be paid into treasury

Sec. 3. This act shall take effect and be in force from and after its passage.

Approved, March 18, 1856.

AN ACT

To amend an Act to amend "An Act authorizing the City of Milwaukee to loan its credit in aid of certain Rail Roads and the acts amendatory thereof," approved, March 31, 1854.

The People of the State of Wisconsin, represented in Senate and Assembly, do enact as follows:

Section 1. The first section of the act of which this is amendatory, is hereby so amended that the last proviso in said section shall read and be as follows, to wit: "And provided, that the aggregate amount of bonds which shall be issued under said acts shall not exceed two millions of dollars."

Sec. 2. This act shall take effect and be in force from and after its passage.

Approved, March 18, 1856.

AN ACT

Relating to the dockets and papers of Justices of the Peace in the First and Seventh Wards of the City of Milwaukee.

The People of the State of Wisconsin, represented in Senate and Assembly, do enact as follows:

Dockets of first ward to remain in seventh ward.

SECTION 1. The dockets and other papers in suits, required by law to be kept by Justices of the Peace, heretofore belonging to the first ward of the City of Milwaukee, shall hereafter belong to and remain in the present seventh ward of said city, and be kept by the justice of said seventh ward; and the justice of the present first ward of said city, when elected, shall begin a new docket, as though said ward was newly organized.

SEC. 2. This act shall take effect and be in force from and after its passage.

Approved, March 18, 1856.

AN ACT

To authorize the City of Milwaukee to issue bonds to the Milwaukee and Watertown Rail Road Company.

The People of the State of Wisconsin, represented in Senate and Assembly, do enact as follows:

Council may issue bonds to Mil. & W. R. R. Co.

SECTION 1. The Mayor and Common Council of the City of Milwaukee, are hereby authorized and empowered to issue and deliver the bonds of said city to the Milwaukee and Watertown Rail Road Company, to aid further in the construction of that portion of their rail road from the City of Watertown to the Village of Columbus, Columbia County, to an amount not exceeding thirty-five thousand dollars: *Provided, however,* That no such bonds shall be delivered to said company till they shall have fully complied with all the requirements and given all the security which have been or may hereafter be required of said company by the Common Council: *and provided further*, that the aggregate amount of city bonds which may be legally issued by the City of Milwaukee to said company shall not exceed two hundred thousand dollars.

SEC. 2. This act shall take effect and be in force from and after its passage.

Approved, March 29, 1856.

AN ACT

Relating to Common Schools in the City of Milwaukee.

The People of the State of Wisconsin, represented in Senate and Assembly, do enact as follows:

SECTION 1. The Mayor and Common Council of the City of Milwaukee, are hereby authorized and empowered to purchase suitable grounds in the second and seventh wards of said city, and to erect thereon such school houses as they may deem proper, and to pay for such grounds and buildings, and to make such repairs and additions to the school houses now constructed in the several wards of said city, the Mayor and Common Council are hereby authorized and empowered to issue the bonds of said city in such denominations, bearing a rate of interest not exceeding seven per cent. per annum, payable semi-annually, and both principal and interest payable at such time and place as may be determined by ordinance of the Common Council, or they may levy an annual tax, not exceeding one-half of one per cent., on all taxable property in said city, to make the above improvements, which tax, if levied, shall be levied and collected and the collection thereof enforced by law in the same manner as

Common Council empowered to buy school house sites.

May issue bonds.

May levy annual tax

How collected.

other city taxes, or the Common Council may, in their discretion, make such improvements, partly by the issue of bonds and partly by tax, as hererein provided.

Council to levy tax to pay interest.

SEC. 2. The Common Council of the City of Milwaukee shall annually levy a tax upon all the taxable property in said city, sufficient to pay the interest on all the city bonds which may be issued under this act, and shall also provide in the same manner for the payment of the principal of all such bonds, which tax shall be levied and collected in the same manner as other city taxes are levied and collected by law.

How levied and collected

Power to fix by ordinance boundaries of districts.

SEC. 3. The Common Council shall have power to fix by ordinance the boundaries of all common school districts in said city, and to district the city as they may deem best calculated to promote the interests of the schools; and to defray the expenses of the common schools in said city, the Common Council shall annually levy and collect a sufficient tax, upon all the taxable property of the city, in the same manner as other city taxes are levied and collected by law, and the limitation as to the annual amount of per cent. of tax to be raised for school purposes in the County of Milwaukee shall not hereafter apply to the City of Milwaukee, but the Common Council shall have power to raise by tax such amount annually as may be necessary to pay the annual expenses of such schools.

Tax to be levied to support public schools.

SEC. 4. This act shall take effect and be in force from and after its passage.

Approved, March 19, 1856.

AN ACT

To Incorporate the Fifth Ward Gas Light Company of the City of Milwaukee.

The People of the State of Wisconsin, represented in Senate and Assembly, do enact as follows:

SECTION 1. Jasper Humphrey, John Roesbeck, Stoddard H. Martin, Andrew Mitchell, Hiram Merrill, J. Sherwood and William A. Hawkins, and such other persons as may hereafter be associated with them as stockholders, their successors and assigns, are hereby created a body corporate and politic, by the name of the Fifth Ward Gas Light Company of the City of Milwaukee, with perpetual succession, and by that name, shall have all the privileges, franchises and immunities incidental to a corporation; they shall be capable in law of contracting and being contracted with, suing and being sued, defending and being defended, in all courts and places, they shall be capable in law of purchasing, holding, selling, leasing and conveying estate, real or personal or mixed, so far as the same may be necessary and proper for the construction, extension, management and usefulness of the works of said company, and for the good government of the same, may have a common seal and alter the same at pleasure.

Who to constitute first directors.

Name of corporation.

SEC. 2. The capital stock of said company shall be one hundred thousand dollars, in shares of fifty dollars each. The affairs of said company shall be managed by a Board of five Directors, who shall be chosen by ballot, and each share of the stock shall be entitled to one vote, to be delivered in person or by proxy, duly authorized; and for the purpose of electing the first directors, the persons named in the preceding section, or a majority of them, shall give ten days notice, in two newspapers, printed in the City of Milwaukee,

Capital of company.

Five directors to be elected.

of the time and place, by them appointed, for the subscribers or stockholders to meet, for the purpose of electing directors; shall appoint one of their number President, and annually thereafter, on the first Monday in April, the stockholders shall meet for electing directors as aforesaid; *Provided*, that none but stockholders shall be elected directors.

To choose president and secretary. When election to be held.

Majority to constitute a quorum.

SEC. 3. A majority of said board shall constitute a quorom for the transaction of business; they shall have the power to appoint a Secretary and Treasurer and such other officers and agents as may be deemed necessary to make and prescribe such by-laws, order, and regulations respecting the management, control and disposition of the stock, property and affairs of said company, as they may deem proper, not inconsistent with the constitution and laws of the United States or of this state, to make such covenants, contracts and agreements with any person or persons, co-partnership or body politic, whatsoever, as the execution and management of the works and convenience and interests of the company may require.

To make by-laws.

To manufacture for 25 years.

SEC. 4. The said company shall have power and full authority for twenty-five years from the passage of this act, to manufacture, make and sell gas, to be made from any and all the substances, or a combination thereof, from which inflammable gas is obtained, for the purpose of lighting the fifth ward of the City of Milwaukee, or the streets thereof, or any building, manufactories, public places, or houses therein contained, and to erect all necessary works and apparatus, and to lay pipe for the purpose of conducting the gas in any of the streets, avenues, commons, lanes or alleys in said ward of the City of Milwaukee: *Provided*, That no permanent injury shall be done to any street, highway, lanes or alleys in said ward.

To erect necessary buildings. To lay pipe.

SEC. 5. If from any cause an election for directors shall not be held at the time specified therefor, the corporation for that reason shall not be dissolved, but it shall be lawful on any other day to hold an election for directors, as shall be provided for in the by-laws of said corporation, and until such election, the directors of the preceding year shall continue to act, and their doings shall be binding upon said corporation until their successors shall be elected.

Penalty for injuring or obstructing pipes or structures.

SEC. 6. If any person shall wilfully do, or cause to be done, any acts whatsoever to injure any machine, pipe or structure whatsoever, or anything appertaining to the works of said corporation, whereby the same may be stopped, obstructed or injured, the person or persons so offending shall be considered guilty of a misdemeanor, and being thereof convicted, shall be punished by a fine not exceeding three hundred dollars or by imprisonment not exceeding two years, or both: *Provided*, Such criminal prosecution shall not in any wise impair the right of said company from damages by a civil suit hereby authorized to be brought for any such injury as aforesaid, by and in the name of said corporation, in any court of the state having competent jurisdiction of the same.

Power to borrow money, &c.

SEC. 7. The said corporation are hereby authorized and fully empowered in their corporare capacity, to borrow any sum or sums of money from any person or persons, corporations or body politic of any kind, and make and execute in their corporate name all necessary writings, notes, bonds or other papers, and make and execute and deliver such securities in amount and kind as may be deemed expedient by said corporation for all purposes in carrying out the objects of this company, and the official acts of said company are hereby declared binding in law and equity upon said corporation, and upon all others, parties to such contract.

SEC. 8. All acts or parts of acts relating to gas lights of the City of Milwaukeee, are hereby repealed so far as relates to the fifth ward of the aforesaid city.

SEC. 9. This act shall be favorably construed to effect the purposes hereby intended, and the same is hereby declar-

Copy of act evidence in courts.

ed a public act, and copies thereof printed by authority of the state, shall be sufficient evidence thereof in all courts.

SEC. 10. This act shall take effect and be in force from and after its passage.

Approved, March 6, 1856.

ORDINANCES

OF THE

CITY OF MILWAUKEE.

o

ORDINANCES

RELATING TO STREETS, ALLEYS, SIDEWALKS, DOCK LINES, MARKET AND PUBLIC SQUARES.

AN ORDINANCE

To vacate an Alley in Block seventy-eight, in the First Ward.

Be it ordained by the Mayor and Aldermen of the City of Milwaukee, in Common Council assembled :

SECTION 1. That the alley at present established through the southerly portion of block number seventy-eight, in said ward, is hereby vacated, except the southerly 60 feet thereof. Alley vacated.

SEC. 2. It shall be the duty of the Marshal to summon some twelve freeholders, citizens, not directly interested in said block, who are hereby directed, being first duly sworn for that purpose, to assess the benefits, and appraise the damages to owners of the respective lots fronting on said alleys, if there be any benefits or damages, and make return, under their hands and seals, to the Common Council before the first day of March, 1847.

Passed, February 8, 1847.

AN ORDINANCE

To vacate the foot of Park Street, and lay out and establish a new street in lieu thereof.

Be it ordained by the Mayor and Aldermen of the City of Milwaukee, in Common Council assembled :

SECTION 1. That so much of Park street, in the Fifth Ward of the City of Milwaukee, as lies between South Water Park street, part of, vacated.

street and the Milwaukee river, is hereby vacated, and a new street shall be and is hereby laid out and established in lieu thereof, which shall be a continuation of said Park street in a right line to the Milwaukee river.

Surveyor to lay out new street.

SEC. 2. It shall be the duty of the Surveyor of the fifth ward to lay out and establish said street by metes and bounds, and return to the Common Council on or before the 25th instant, a plot of the same, showing the position and location of the street vacated, and the street hereby established, and the quantity of ground taken from lot one, in block sixty-seven, and the quantity of ground added to lot nine, in block sixty-six.

Benefits and damages.

SEC. 3. It shall be the duty of the City Marshal to summon twelve good and lawful freeholders, not directly interested, to assemble on or before the first day of April next, who, being first duly sworn, shall view the premises, and take the same into consideration, as well the benefits as the injury which shall accrue or may have accrued by vacating said street and laying the same anew, and shall estimate and assess the damage which any property shall have sustained by reason of the same, and shall moreover estimate the amount which other property will be benefitted thereby, and report the same to the Common Council, under their hands or seals, on or before the tenth day of April next.

Passed, March 18, 1847.

AN ORDINANCE

To vacate certain Streets and Alleys.

Be it ordained by the Mayor and Aldermen of the City of Milwaukee, in Common Council assembled :

Streets and alleys vacated.

SECTION 1. That all that portion of Knapp, Ogden, Lyon, Pleasant, Kewaunee and Brady streets, lying within the south-east quarter of section number twenty-one, of township number seven, north of range number twenty-two east, in the first ward of the City of Milwaukee, in Spencer's addition, and all of Hamilton, Massena, Monroe, Manestee, Pere, Marquette, St. Lawrence and Sauk streets, lying north of Division street, and also all the alleys passing through Blocks numbers one, two, three, seven, eight, nine, thirteen, fourteen, fifteen and twenty, in said addition be, and the same are hereby vacated, and all the right, claim, or interest, which the City of Milwaukee may have or be entitled to in the said streets and alleys as public highways, is hereby relinquished to the owner or owners of the land or lots in said streets contained.

Passed, June 17, 1847.

AN ORDINANCE

To vacate an Alley in the Fourth Ward.

Be it ordained by ehe Mayor and Aldermen of the City of Milwaukee, in Common Council assembled :

SECTION 1. That so much of the alley as runs east and west between lots eight and nine in block eighty-two in the fourth ward of the City of Milwaukee, Wisconsin Territory, be and the same is hereby vacated and declared closed up, and no longer for public purposes.

Alley vacated in block eighty-two.

Passed, October 13, 1847.

AN ORDINANCE

To lay out an Alley through Block 125, in the First Ward.

Be it ordained by the Mayor and Aldermen of the City of Milwaukee, in Common Council assembled :

SECTION 1. That there shall be laid out and established an alley fourteen feet in width, running at equal distance

Alley in block 125, First Ward.

from and upon a mean parallel to the north and south sides of block 125, in the first ward of the City of Milwaukee, and the same shall be a public highway in said city.

SEC. 2. It shall be the duty of the Marshal to summon some twelve freeholders, citizens, not directly interested in said block, who are hereby directed, being first duly sworn for that purpose, to assess the benefits, and appraise the damages to the owners of the respective lots fronting on said alley, if there be any benefits or damages, and make return under their hands and seals to the Common Council, before the first day of May, 1848.

Passed, March 23, 1848.

AN ORDINANCE

To change the location of an Alley in the First Ward.

Be it ordained by the Mayor and Aldermen of the City of Milwaukee, in Common Council assembled:

Alley in block 56, First Ward.

SECTION 1. That the location of the alley in the south half of block 56 in the first ward, be, and the same is hereby changed so that the west line thereof shall be as follows, to wit: Commencing at a point in the south line of lot six, in said block, one hundred and fourteen feet westwardly from Market street, and running thence northwardly parallel to Market street sixty feet, to the north line of said lot six; thence in a direct course to the north-east corner of lot eight, in said block 56.

Passed, March 23, 1848.

AN ORDINANCE

To change the location of an Alley in Block 78, in the Fourth Ward.

Be it ordained by the Mayor and Aldermen of the City of Milwaukee, in Common Council assembled:

SECTION 1. That the location of the alley running east and west in the east half of block 78, in the fourth ward, be, and the same is hereby changed, so as to run along the south end of lots one, two and three, instead of between lots eight and nine. **Alley in block 78, 4th Ward.**

SEC. 2. The ground for the alley so changed shall be taken off from the north side of lot eight, twenty feet wide, in exchange for the old alley of the same dimensions, viz: 20 by 150 feet.

Passed, March 30, 1848.

AN ORDINANCE

To lay out and establish certain Streets and Alleys therein mentioned.

Be it ordained by the Mayor and Aldermen of the City of Milwaukee, in Common Council assembled:

SECTION 1. There shall be laid out and established the following streets and alleys in the third ward, viz: all and singular the streets and alleys, and according to the courses, widths and dimensions laid down and platted on the map of partition, made by authority of the Court of Chancery for Milwaukee County, in the year 1846, at its June term, of the lots one and two of fractional section thirty-three in said ward, to wit: a street eighty feet wide, commencing in Water street, near to Douseman's warehouse, and running thence in a south-easterly direction, parallel to and corresponding with the bend of the river, and terminating at Cen-

Erie street, laying out of, and of other streets.

tre street, to be called Erie street; also a street one hundred feet wide, commencing at the foot of Main street, and running in a right line with said street, and as a continuance of the same, in a southerly direction to an intersection with Erie street; also a street eighty feet wide, commencing at the south termination of Milwaukee street, and running southwardly as a continuation of the same to an intersection with Erie street; also a street eighty feet wide, commencing at the south termination of Jefferson street, running southerly as a continuation of the same, to an intersection with Erie street; also a street eighty feet wide, commencing at the south termination of Jackson street, and running southerly as a continuation of the same, to an intersection with

Juneau st.

Erie street; also a street eighty feet wide, running easterly on the south side of blocks No. 156, 157, 158, 159 and 160, parallel to Menomonee street, from Erie street to the Lake,

Polk st.

to be called Juneau street; also a street eighty feet wide, running parallel to said Juneau street on the south side of blocks 161, 162 and 163, from Erie street to the Lake, to be

Oregon st.

called Polk street; also a street eighty feet wide, running parallel to said Polk street, on the south side of blocks 168, 169 and 170, from Erie street to the Lake, to be called Ore-

Pier st.

gon street; also a street eighty feet wide on the south side of block 172, running from Erie street to the Lake, to be called

Centre st.

Pier street; also a street —— feet wide at the Milwaukee river, and 300 feet wide at the Lake, running from the river to the Lake, to be called Centre street; also a street eighty feet wide in continuation of Beach street, southerly parallel to the Lake shore, to an intersection with Pier street; also a

Harbor st.

street sixty-six feet wide, commencing at Centre street, and running southerly and parallel to the Lake shore, and terminating in the river near its mouth, to be called Harbor street;

Mahnawauk st.

also a street sixty-six feet wide, running in direction from north-westerly to south-easterly, from the northern part of the island, in fraction two, to the southerly part of said fraction, to be called Mahnawauk street; also a street a hundred feet wide at right angles, from Erie street to the river, to be called the foot of Main street; also a street eighty feet wide at right angles from Erie street to the river, to be called the foot of Milwaukee street; also a street seventy-two feet wide from the river to the Lake, on the south side of blocks 175 and 176, to be called Rose street; also a street seventy-two feet wide, parallel to said Rose street, from the river to the Lake, on the south side of blocks 177 and 178, to be called Nauvoo street; also a street eighty feet wide at right angles, from Erie street to the river, to be called the foot of Jefferson street; also a street eighty feet wide at right angles, from Erie street to the river, to be called the foot of Jackson street; also a street seventy-two feet wide, parallel to said Nauvoo street, from the river to the Lake, on the south side of blocks 179 and 180, to be called Cooper street; also a street seventy-two feet wide, parallel to said Cooper street, from the river to the Lake, on the south side of blocks 181, 182 and 189, to be called Lynn street; also a street seventy-two feet wide, parallel to said Lynn street from the river to the Lake, on the south side of blocks 183 and 184, to be called Henry street; also a street seventy-two feet wide, running from north-easterly to south-easterly, on the south side of blocks 193 and 192 across the island aforesaid, to be called Nauvoo street; also a street seventy-two feet wide, running parallel to last mentioned street, and on the south sides of blocks 191 and 194, to be called Cooper street; also a street —— feet wide from Mahnawauk street, next and parallel to the north pier of the harbor to Lake Michigan, to be called Abert street, in perpetual remembrance of his ill-advised location of the harbor; also there shall be an alley fourteen feet wide, through the middle, from the northern to the southern side of each, the following numbered blocks, viz: blocks numbered one hundred and fifteen, now known as block one hundred and fifty-eight;

Rose st.

Cooper st.

Lynn st.

Henry st.

Nauvoo st.

Cooper st.

Abert st.

one hundred and sixteen, now known as one hundred and fifty-seven; also from the north to the east side of the blocks numbers one hundred and fifty-six and one hundred and sixty-four.

Chestnut st., continuation of.

SEC. 2. There shall be laid out and established the following streets in the second and fourth wards, viz: A street eighty feet wide, in continuation of Chesnut street, to the west line of the north-west quarter of section twenty-nine, to be called Chesnut street; also a street eighty feet wide, in continuation of Prairie street to Sixth street, and a further continuation of said street, seventy feet wide, to the center line, running north and south through said quarter section, to be called Prairie street; also a street eighty feet wide, in continuation of Tamarack street to Sixth street, and a further continuation of said street seventy feet wide to the center line of said quarter section, to be called Tamarack street; also a street, eighty feet wide, in continuation of Cedar street to Sixth street, and a further continuation of said street seventy feet wide, to the center line of said quarter section, to be called Cedar street; also a street eighty feet wide, in continuation of Wells street to Sixth street, and a further continuation of said street, seventy feet wide, to the center line of said quarter section, to be called Wells street; also a street eighty feet wide in continuation of Spring street, to the west line of said quarter section, and in further continuation of said street, seventy feet wide, running at an angle of south sixty degrees west, until the center line of said street shall fall upon the south line of said quarter section, and thence in further continuation of said street, due west, seventy feet wide, to the west line of the city limits, to be called Spring street; also a street seventy feet wide, in continuation of Sixth street, from Chesnut street to Spring street; also a street seventy feet wide, in continuation of Seventh street, from Chesnut street to Spring street; also a street seventy feet wide, in continuation of Eighth street, from Ches-

Prairie st. continued.

Tamarack st. continued.

Cedar st. continued.

Wells st. continued.

Spring st. continued.

6th, 7th, 8th and 9th sts. continued.

nut to Spring; also a street seventy feet wide, in continuation of Ninth street, from Chesnut to Spring street; also there shall be an alley, twenty feet wide, running north and south through the middle of each of the following blocks, viz: blocks numbered forty-four, forty-five, fifty-three, sixty-three, and there shall also be an alley, twenty feet wide, running east and west through the middle of each of the following blocks, viz: blocks numbered forty-four, forty-five, fifty-three, sixty-three, and one hundred and sixty-five; and there shall be two alleys, fifteen feet wide, each running east and west through each of the following blocks, (one of said alleys to be on the north side of lots seven and eight, and the other to be along the south line of lots nine and ten in each of said blocks,) viz: blocks one hundred and fifty-nine, one hundred and sixty, one hundred and sixty-one, one hundred and sixty-two, one hundred and sixty-three, one hundred and sixty-four, one hundred and sixty-six, one hundred and sixty-seven, one hundred and sixty-eight, one hundred and sixty-nine, one hundred and seventy, one hundred and seventy-one, one hundred and seventy-two, one hundred and seventy-three, and one hundred and seventy-four.

Alley in blocks 44, 45, 53, 63 & 165, 4th Ward.

SEC. 3. There shall be laid out and established the following streets in the second ward, viz: a street twenty-five feet wide, running east and west from Third street to the Milwaukee river, along the south side of the north line of Sherman's Addition, and of lots number two and three of section twenty-one, to be called North street.

North st.

SEC. 4. There shall be laid out and established the following streets in the first ward, viz: If not already laid out and established, Division street from Milwaukee river to the Lake shall be widened, so as to be eighty feet wide, that is to say, to be forty feet wide on each side of the line of sections twenty and twenty-nine and twenty-one and twenty-eight; also the following described streets as the same are delineated in the several partition plats, and to the extent

Certain sts. in 1st Ward regulated and extended.

hereinafter prescribed, of the following described tracts of land as the same have heretofore been partitioned by the District or Court of Chancery of Milwaukee County, to wit: the south-east fraction of section twenty, and the east and west halves of the south-west quarter of section twenty-one, in said ward, to wit: Knapp street, eighty feet wide, from the Milwaukee river to the center line of section twenty-one; Ogden and Lyon streets, each eighty feet wide, extending from River street to the center line of section twenty-one, forty feet in width, being south half of Pleasant street, to the center line of section twenty-one; River street to be continued from where it intersects Division street, eighty feet wide, due north one block, thence along parallel to the river to Pleasant street; East Water, Market, Milwaukee and Main streets to be continued due north from where they severally intersect Division street, until they intersect River street, the three first named to be 80, 4, 10 feet wide, and Main street 100, 5, 10 wide; Jefferson, Jackson, Van Buren, Cass and Marshal streets to be continued from where they severally intersect Division street, due north to Pleasant street, to be each 80, 4, 10 feet in width, and Astor street to be continued in like manner and width to the north boundary of the south-west quarter of section numbered twenty-one.

South Water and other streets in 5th Ward, regulated.

SEC. 5. The following alterations shall be made in South Water street, in the fifth ward, viz.:—The north side of said street, commencing at the south-west corner of lot three, in block one, in Walker's Point, Milwaukee, and running thence in a south-easterly direction, so as to strike the line between sections thirty-two and thirty-three, at a point thirty feet distant from the south-east corner of block fifty-three, as laid out by the proprietors of fraction three in section thirty-three, as at present laid out, thence continuing in a south-easterly direction, so as to terminate in the north line of said street, at the south-west corner of lot five, in block fifty-four, as now laid out in said fraction, and so much of said street as lies in section thirty-two, shall be fifty-nine feet wide, and so much of said street as lies in section thirty-three, shall be eighty feet wide; also, a street shall be laid from said Water street to the river, running in a north-easterly direction, so that the southerly side of said street shall pass through the south-west corner of lot one, in block fifty-four, as now laid out, and said street shall be sixty feet wide, in which will be included nearly all of said lot one, and-one third part of the present street between said Water street and the river, and the residue of said street, as laid by said proprietors, is hereby declared to be vacated, and so much of said street as is hereby vacated shall be added to block fifty-three in the fraction aforesaid.

Streets declared public highways.

SEC. 6. All the streets and alleys mentioned in the foregoing section of this ordinance, are hereby declared to be public highways, and as such, are hereby placed under the jurisdiction of the inspectors of streets in the several wards in which the same are situated, for the purpose of being open and worked, and kept in repair for the public use and convenience; and in order to ascertain what damages may be sustained and benefits received by owners of property, by reason of the opening and improving said streets and alleys, some twelve of the following persons shall be summoned by the Marshal to consider and report the damages and benefits so received in consequence of opening the said streets and alleys in the third ward, viz.:—N. P. Donaldson, Dagget, L. J. Farwell, John Furlong, Richard Hackett, Edward Hussey, Levi Hubbell, L. J. Higby, G. P. Hewitt, Jas. B. Martin, Andrew McCormick, D. Newhall, Fred. Wardner, J. D. Weston, John White, P. N. Bonesteel, J. S. Baker, R. G. Owens; and some twelve of the following named persons shall be summoned by the Marshal to consider and report the damages and benefits so received in consequence of opening the said streets and alleys in the second and fourth wards, viz: Hans Crocker, D. A. J. Upham, John Thomssen,

Juries to assess damages

Lindsey Ward, Wm. A. Prentiss, E. Eldred, James Kneeland, John Davis, Cyrus D. Davis, C. C. Comstock, A. J. Langworthy, John A. Messenger, G. F. Gruenhagen, James H. Rogers, Joel Kneeland, Caleb Harrison, Charles A. Tuttle, D. Merrill, James Magone, J. B. Zander and Wm. A. Hawkins ; and some twelve of the following named persons shall be summoned by the Marshal to consider and report the damages and benefits so received in consequence of opening North street in the second ward, viz : I. A. Lapham, C. W. Schwartz, J. A. Phelps, John Heustis, H. Niedeman, R. Gunyen, M. McKenna, S. Griffiths, B. Church, J. F. Greunhagan, D. Knabb, O. Hubbard, T. D. Butler, H. Mc Connell, R. Jennings, R. D. Jennings, J. B. Selby, H. Lieber and C. Werner; and some twelve of the following named persons shall be summoned by the Marshal to consider and report the damage and benefits so received in consequence of opening the said streets in the first ward, viz : Daniel Wells, jr., Wm. Paine, Victor Schulte, Francis Randall, Wm. Youlin, J. B. Martin, Lawrence Robbins, E. Eldred, H. Williams, John F. Smith, Fred. Wardner, Robert Caswell, H. W. Higgins, George Giesman, James H. Smith, Fred'k A. Luning, John Ryecraft, George Barber, John Thompson, M. Stein, Peter Jenssen, G. F. Fowler.

Sec. 7. It shall be the duty of the Marshal to summon twelve of each class of the foregoing named freeholders, not directly interested, to assemble on or before the first day of September next, on the several tracts (hereinbefore assigned to each of said classes) over which said streets and alleys are laid, and each of said classes of twelve freeholders shall constitute a board of assessment to examine said premises, and after being duly sworn for that purpose, shall enquire into, and take the same into consideration, as well the benefit as the injury which may accrue, and estimate and assess the damage, which would be sustained by reason of the laying out, opening and extension of said streets and alleys, and shall moreover estimate the amount which other property will be benefitted thereby, all of which shall be returned to the Common Council under their hands and seals, on or before the first day of October next.

Passed, August 10, 1856.

AN ORDINANCE

Granting the right of way to certain Plank Road Companies.

Be it ordained by the Mayor and Aldermen of the City of Milwaukee, in Common Council assembled:

Right of way to M. W. & M. Plank Road Co.

SECTION 1. That the right of way be, and the same is hereby granted to the Madison, Watertown and Milwaukee Plank Road Company, and they are hereby authorized to construct a single or double track of plank along the line heretofore located by the said company through 10th and Spring streets, and also along Chestnut street, in the second and fourth wards.

Right of way to Mil. & Janesville, & Mil. & Waterford P. R. Co

SEC. 2. That the right of way be, and the same is hereby granted to the Milwaukee and Janesville Plank Road Company, and to the Milwaukee and Waterford Plank Road Company over any street or streets in the third and fifth wards, to and from such eligible point or points in either of said wards as the said company or companies may respectively elect: *Provided*, That no toll-gate or gates shall be erected or kept within the corporate limits of the said city.

Passed, August 30, 1849.

AN ORDINANCE

For the extension of Virginia Street in the Fifth Ward of the City of Milwaukee.

Be it ordained by the Mayor and Aldermen of the City of Milwaukee, in Common Council assembled:

Virginia st. extended.

SECTION 1. That Virginia street, in the fifth ward, be laid out and extended from the middle of West Division street, west eleven (11) chains to angle post No. 1, thence south 41½, west nine (9) chains fifty (50) links, to angle post No. 2, thence south four (4) chains eighty-five (85) links, to east and west quarter section line at the middle of Brown street, as laid down in the annexed survey, made by John B. Vliet, said street to be seventy-five (75) feet wide, and shall be a public highway in the City of Milwaukee.

Sec. 2. It shall be the duty of the Marshal to summon twelve freeholders, citizens not directly interested along the route of said street, who are hereby directed, being first duly sworn for that purpose, to assess the benefit and appraise the damages to the owners of the respective lots fronting on said street, if there be any benefits or damages, and make return, under their hands and seals to the Common Council, before the 25th day of November instant.

Passed, November 8, 1849.

AN ORDINANCE

To vacate a certain Alley in the Fourth Ward of the City of Milwaukee.

Be it ordained by the Mayor and Aldermen of the City of Milwaukee, in Common Council assembled :

Alley in block 79, 4th Ward.

Section 1. That so much of the alley, in block seventy-nine, in the fourth ward, as runs south from Sycamore street, to the center of said block, is hereby vacated and closed from public purposes.

Passed, May 30, 1850.

AN ORDINANCE

For the extension of Oregon Street in the Fifth Ward.

Be it ordained by the Mayor and Aldermen of the City of Milwaukee, in Common Council assembled.

Oregon st. 5th Ward extended.

Section 1. That Oregon street, in the fifth ward of the city of Milwaukee, be extended as follows, to wit : commencing on the north and south quarter section line of section 32, township 7, range 22 east, at center of Oregon street, thence west seventy-nine links, to angle post No. 1, thence south forty-five and three-quarter degrees west, eleven chains and seventy-six links to angle post No. 2, thence south thirty-seven and one-quarter degrees, west ten chains and fourteen links to angle post No. 3, thence south eighty-three and three-quarter degrees, west twenty-four chains and twenty-two links to post No. 4, five chains and fourteen links north of quarter section post, in section line between sections thirty one and thirty-two.

Sec. 2. It shall be the duty of the Marshal to summon twelve freeholders, citizens not directly interested, along the route of said street, who are hereby directed, being first duly sworn for that purpose, to assess the benefits and appraise the damages to the owners of the respective lots fronting on said street, if there be any benefits or damages, and make return, under their hands and seals, to the Common Council before the 8th day of August instant.

Passed, August 1, 1850.

AN ORDINANCE

To lay out an Alley through Block 64, in the First Ward.

Be it ordained by the Mayor and Aldermen of the City of Milwaukee, in Common Council assembled :

Section 1. That there shall be laid out and established an alley fourteen feet in width, running at an equal distance from and upon a mean parallel to the east and west sides of block 64, in the first ward of the City of Milwaukee, and the same shall be a public highway in said city. Alley in block 64, 1st Ward.

Sec. 2. It shall be the duty of the Marshal to summon some twelve freeholders, citizens not directly interested in said block, who are hereby directed, being first duly sworn for that purpose, to assess the benefits and appraise the damages to the owners of the respective lots fronting on said alley, if their be any benefits or damages, and make return, under their hands and seals, to the Common Council before the first day of June next.

SEC. 3. An ordinance passed March 23d, 1848, to lay out an alley through block 64, is hereby repealed.

Passed, April 28, 1848.

AN ORDINANCE

To change the location of a certain Alley in Block 56, in the Fourth Ward.

Be it ordained by the Mayor and Aldermen of the City of Milwaukee, in Common Council assembled:

Alley in block 56, 4th Ward.

SECTION 1. That sections two and three of an ordinance, passed March 23d, 1848, entitled "an ordinance to change the location of certain alleys in the first and fourth wards," be, and the same are hereby repealed.

SEC. 2. In order to ascertain what damages may be sustained and benefits received by owners of property, by reason of opening said alley, some twelve of the following named persons, not directly interested, shall be summoned by the Marshal to consider and report to this Board, by the 20th day of May next, the damages and benefits so sustained and received, in consequence of opening said alley, viz: Joel Hood, John Plankinton, L. P. Crary, Benj. Bagnall, J. T. Sinclair, J. E. Cameron, H. Birchard, Daniel Nieman, H. Bosworth, John Mitchell, F. Hansel, Cornelius Lorton, John Beaversdorf, S. L. Rood, A. McFadyen, P. B. Hill and J. L. Shearman. The jury so summoned, shall assemble on the ground affected by the opening of said alley, on or before the 10th day of May next, and shall constitute a board of assessment to examine said premises, and after being duly sworn for that purpose, shall estimate and assess the damages which will be sustained, and the benefits accruing to the property interested, all which shall be returned to the Common Council, as above.

Passed, May 4, 1848.

AN ORDINANCE

To lay out anew, and to correct certain streets in Sherman's Addition.

WHERAS, it is evident that Sherman's Addition has been laid out with the intention to make the streets running north and south correspond with the same streets in the Second Ward; and, whereas, by mistake in laying out said addition, or in correcting the plat of said addition, Fifth street is made ten feet wider than it is south of said addition, and therefore a break of ten feet is made at the south line of said addition in Fifth street, and in the other streets running north, south and east of said Fifth street; therefore,

Be it ordained by the Mayor and Aldermen of the City of Milwaukee, in Common Council assembled:

SECTION. 1. Fifth street, in Sherman's addition, shall be established to be seventy feet wide, so as to correspond with the same street south of the east and west quarter of section line, and the side of all other streets running north and south, in said Sherman's addition, shall be in prolongation of the sides of the corresponding streets, south of the east and west quarter section line of section twenty, town seven, north range twenty-two east. **Fifth and other streets corrected.**

SEC. 2. It shall be the duty of the Marshal to summon twelve freeholders, citizens not directly interested in or near Sherman's addition, who are hereby directed, being first duly sworn for the purpose, to assess the benefits and appraise the damages caused by said change in said streets, to the owners of lots in said Sherman's addition, and shall moreover estimate the amount which other property will be benefitted thereby.

Passed, September 12, 1850.

AN ORDINANCE

To lay out and establish certain Streets in the Second Ward.

Be it ordained by the Mayor and Aldermen of the City of Milwaukee, in Common Council assembled:

SECTION 1. The following streets shall be laid out and established in the Second Ward of this city:

Chesnut street continued.

1st. A new street in continuation of Chesnut street, commencing 70 feet wide at Seventh street, running thence due west along and on the south side of the section line between sections 20 and 29 to the west line of said section, thence south 63° 20'' west to a point 698 feet south of the north-west corner of the east half of the north-east quarter of section 30.

Prairie street continued.

2d. A new street in continuation of Prairie street, commencing 70 feet wide at the intersection of the center line of Prairie street with the east side of the west half of the north-west quarter of section 29, and running thence west parallel with the north section line of section 29, to the west side of said section 29, this line is to be the center of the new street, the width of which shall be 70 feet.

Tamarack street continued.

3d. A new street in continuation of Tamarack street, commencing at a point 20 feet north of the point of intersection of the east side of the west half of the north-west quarter of section 29, with the south line of the north 30 acres of the said west half of the north-west quarter of section 29, running thence west parallel with said south line of 30 acres to the intersection with the Milwaukee and Watertown Plank Road, this line is to be the center of the new street, the width of which shall be 70 feet.

4th. A new street in continuation of Ninth street, commencing at the intersection of the south line of the north 30 acres of the west half of the north-west quarter of section 29, with Ninth street, running thence north to the north line of section 29, the width of said street to be the same as the width of Ninth street, south of said south line of the north 30 acres of the west half of the north-west quarter of section 29, and the sides of said new street to be a straight line in prolongation of the sides of Ninth street, south of said new street. Ninth street continued.

5th. A new street in continuation of Tenth street, commencing at the intersection of the south line of the north 30 acres of the west half of the north-west quarter of section 29, with Tenth street, running thence north to the north line of section 29, the width of said street to be the same as the width of Tenth street, south of said south line of the north 30 acres of the west half of the north-west quarter of section 29, and the sides of said new street to be a straight line in prolongation of the sides of Tenth street. Tenth street continued.

Sec. 2. It shall be the duty of the Marshal to summon twelve freeholders, citizens not directly interested in or near said new streets, who are hereby directed, being first duly sworn for the purpose, to assess the benefits and appraise the damages, caused by laying out of said streets, to the owners of lots fronting on said streets, and shall moreover estimate the amount which other property will be benefitted thereby.

Passed, December 5, 1850.

AN ORDINANCE

To open and extend Brown and Virginia Streets in the Fifth Ward.

Be it ordained by the Mayor and Aldermen of the City of Milwaukee, in Common Council assembled.

Section 1. That Brown street, in the Fifth Ward, be, and is hereby extended or prolonged in a direct line from its Brown street extended.

present northern termination, to the Menomonee river, at a width of seventy-six feet, and that Virginia street, in said ward, be, and the same is hereby prolonged or extended, in a direct line from its present western termination, to the Menomonee river aforesaid, at a width of seventy-five feet.

Virginia St. extended.

SEC. 2. That it shall be the duty of the Marshal to summon twelve freeholders, citizens not directly interested along the route of said streets, who are hereby directed, being first duly sworn for the purpose, to assess the damages and appraise the benefits to the owner or owners of the property in said street, if there be any benefits or damages, and make due return, under their hands and seals, to the Common Council, on or before the 24th day of February instant.

Passed, February 21, 1851.

AN ORDINANCE

Permanently regulating ard establishing the grade of certain streets, widening a portion of Spring Street, in the Fourth Ward of the City of Milwaukee.

Be it ordained by the Mayor and Aldermen of the City of Milwaukee, in Common Council assembled :

Spring street and Ninth st. —grade altered.

SECTION 1. That the grade of Spring street, commencing at the junction of Eighth street and running west, and the grade of Ninth street, from Spring street to the north line of Wells street, as represented by the profile thereof, now on file in the office of the Clerk of the Common Council, be, and the same are hereby adopted and established by the Mayor and Aldermen of the City of Milwaukee, as the permanent and fixed grade of said streets. The grade of Tenth street, from Spring to Cedar street, is established in accordance with the grade of the plank road thereon.

Spring st.,— a part of, widened.

SEC. 2. So much of Spring street as lies east of the section line, between sections twenty-nine and thirty, extending therefrom to the alley in block one hundred and seventy-five, in the fourth ward of the City of Milwaukee, is hereby widened seventy-three feet, and from said alley to Eighth street, forty feet on the south side thereof, according to and as represented on the profile thereof, now on file in the office of the City Clerk, the necessity thereof being first established by the verdict of a jury of twelve freeholders, not residents of the ward, who shall be summoned for that purpose by the Marshal of said city, at any time after the passage of this ordinance, and upon the determination of said jury of the necessity of taking said strip of seventy-three feet in width as aforesaid, and from said alley to Eighth street forty feet wide as aforesaid, for public use, the said portion of said street, so widened, shall be and remain permanently fixed and established.

SEC. 3. Clybourn street, in the fourth ward of the City of Milwaukee, is hereby extended from the east line of the west half of the south-west quarter of section twenty-nine, town seven, range twenty-two, to the west line of said quarter section, to be of the same width as now laid out on the recorded plat of said street, and the grade of said street, as laid out and represented by the profile, now on file in the office of the City Clerk, shall be, and the same is hereby adopted and established by the Mayor and Aldermen of the City of Milwaukee, as the permanent and fixed grade of said street. Clybourn street extended.

SEC. 4. A new street, to be called Ninth street, commencing on Spring street and running on the line between lots three and four and lots one and four and lots seven and one, in the west half of the south-west quarter of section twenty-nine aforesaid, and extending from Spring street to the rail road, is hereby laid out and to be opened sixty feet in width, taking thirty feet each side of said line. Ninth street extended.

SEC. 5. A new street, to be called Clermont street, commencing on Spring street and running on the line between Clermont st.

lots seven and eight and seven and nine, in the said quarter section, and extending from Spring street to the rail road, in the fourth ward, is hereby laid out, and to be opened sixty feet wide, taking thirty feet each side of said line.

SEC. 6. The said streets mentioned in the third fourth and fifth sections of this ordinance, to be opened and extended whenever the necessity thereof shall first be established by the verdict of a jury, as provided in section two of this ordinance.

Sidewalks in certain St's regulated.

SEC. 7. The width of the side-walk on each side of the streets hereinafter mentioned, shall be established as follows, to wit: on Spring street, from Eighth street to the section line, between sections twenty-nine and thirty, twenty feet, on Tenth street, from Spring street to Cedar street, fifteen feet, on Ninth street, from Spring street to Cedar street, fifteen feet, and the grade of the side-walks on either side of said streets shall conform, as far as practicable, to the grade of the streets running parallel with the same.

SEC. 8. It is hereby made the duty of the Local Committee of the fourth ward, to cause to be recorded in the office of the Register of Deeds of Mllwaukee County, an accurate copy of the profile of the grade and width of the streets herein adopted, properly certified to, and in case of the loss or destruction of said profiles of the grades of said streets, now on file with the City Clerk, said profile, so recorded in the office of the Register of Deeds in and for the County of Milwaukee, shall be evidence in all courts and places, of the permanent and established grades of said streets.

Grade not to be altered

SEC. 9. And it is further ordained, that in case any person or persons shall, at any time after this ordinance is in force and effect, purchase any real estate or erect, remove or alter any building or buildings, or make any improvements on any lot or parts of lots, or in case any person or persons have heretofore purchased any lots or parts of lots fronting on said streets, the grade whereof is hereby established, or on either of them, or erected, moved or altered any building, or made any improvements on any lot, lots, or parts of lots fronting on either of said streets above mentioned, the faith of the City of Milwaukee is hereby fully pledged that the grade of either of the said streets shall not be changed or altered, to the injury of any person or persons, without the fourth ward of the City of Milwaukee first making good all damages which may accrue thereby to any such person or persons.

SEC. 10. So much of section six of the ordinance mentioned and referred to in the previous section of this ordinance, as conflicts with the provisions of this ordinance, so far only as the same relates to the alteration of the grade of that portion of Spring street mentioned in the first section of this ordinance, is hereby repealed.

Passed, March 8, 1851.

AN ORDINANCE

Establishing the grades of side-walks on the west side of the Market Square, in Block one, in the First Ward of the City of Milwaukee.

Be it ordained by the Mayor and Aldermen of the City of Milwaukee, in Common Council assembled :

Sidewalks on Market Square—Grade established.

SECTION 1. That the grade of the side-walks on the west side of Market Square, between Mason and Oneida streets, on block one, in the first ward, shall be established as follows, to wit: the inside of the walk, beginning at the under side of the water table at the south-east corner of Prentiss' block, shall descend in a straight line, touching the upper side of the water table at the south-east corner of Nunnemacher's block, to the south side of Oneida street; the curb grade shall be on a line five inches lower than the grade of the inside of the walk.

SEC. 2. That all ordinances, resolutions, or other proceedings of the Common Council, contravening the provisions of this ordinance, be, and the same are hereby repealed and recinded.

Passed, November 14, 1851.

AN ORDINANCE

To vacate a Street in the Fourth Ward of the City of Milwaukee.

Be it ordained by the Mayor and Aldermen of the City of Milwaukee, in Common Council assembled :

Ninth street vacated.

SECTION 1. That a new street, called Ninth street, running north and south through the west half of south-west quarter of section 29, town 7, range 22 east, situated in the fourth ward of the City of Milwaukee, be, and the same is hereby vacated and closed up.

Passed, December 26, 1851.

AN ORDINANCE

To alter and correct Tamarack street, between Eighth and Ninth streets.

The Mayor and Common Council of the City of Milwaukee, do ordain as follows :

Tamarack street altered.

SECTION 1. A straight line beginning at the intersection of the centre line of Eighth street and Tamarack street, and running thence to a point, being ten feet south of the intersection of the east line of the west half of the north-west quarter of section twenty-nine with the center of the continuation of Tamarack street, shall be the center of a new street, the width of which shall be seventy feet.

SEC. 2. It shall be the duty of the City Surveyor to lay out and establish said street by metes and bounds, and return to the Common Council, on or before the 12th instant, a plat of the same, showing the position and location of the street hereby established, and quantity of ground taken from lots 16, 15, 14, 13, 12 and 11, in block 162.

SEC. 3. It shall be the duty of the street commissioners of the second ward to apply to the Judge of the Circuit or County Court of Milwaukee County, for the appointment of twelve respectable freeholders, residents of the city, but not of the second ward, as Jurors, who, being first duly sworn, shall, within one month after their appointment, view the premises and proceed in all respects in the manner prescribed for the assessment of damages and benefits in cases of laying out streets by "an act to consolidate and amend the act to incorporate the City of Milwaukee, and the several acts amendatory thereof," and return such assessment to the Common Council.

Passed, May 6, 1852.

AN ORDINANCE

To establish the Dock Line between Wisconsin and Chicago streets in the Third Ward.

The Mayor and Common Council of the City of Milwaukee, do ordain as follows:

SECTION 1. That the dock line be, and the same is hereby established between Wisconsin and Chicago streets, in the third ward, as follows, to wit: beginning at a point on the south side of Wisconsin street, one hundred and thirteen and a half feet west from East Water street, and running thence to the south side of Michigan street, at a point eighty-five feet from East Water street, thence to the north side of Huron street, one hundred and twenty-five feet from East Water street, thence to the north side of Detroit street, one hundred and ninety feet from East Water street, thence to the south side of Detroit street, one hundred and eighty feet from East

Establishing dock line between Wisconsin & Chicago streets, in 3d Ward.

Water street, thence to the south side of Buffalo street, one hundred and thirty-eight feet from East Water street, thence to the south line of Chicago street, one hundred and eighty feet from East Water street, the said distances from East Water street to be measured along the line of the cross streets.

SEC. 2. All ordinances or regulations in any manner conflicting with the foregoing provisions, are hereby repealed.

Passed, December 30, 1852.

AN ORDINANCE

Permanently to establish the grade of certain streets in the First Ward of the City of Milwaukee.

Be it ordained by the Mayor and Aldermen of the City of Milwaukee, in Common Council assembled :

Establishing the grades of certain streets in 1st Ward.

SECTION 1. The grade or heights of the several streets hereinafter mentioned, situated in the first ward of the City of Milwaukee, is hereby fixed and permanently established, as follows, the heights or elevation to be above the base which has been generally adopted in grading streets, which base was the level of the Milwaukee river as it was in the month of March, in the year eighteen hundred and thirty-six, and from a stone set in the centre of East Water and Wisconsin streets, which stone or monument is assumed to be eleven and one half feet above the surface of the Milwaukee river, as it was at the time above mentioned :

WISCONSIN STREET.

Wisconsin street.

At the middle of	East Water st. twelve ft.	12 ft.
" "	Main st. twenty-five ft.	25 ft.
" "	Milwaukee st. thirty-four ft.	34 ft.
" "	Jefferson st. thirty-eight ft.	38 ft.
" "	Jackson st. forty ft.	40 ft.

At the middle of Van Buren st. thirty-six ft.	36 ft.	
" " Cass st. thirty-two ft.	32 ft.	
" " Marshall st. twenty-eight ft.	28 ft.	
" " Lake st. twenty-seven ft.	27 ft.	

MASON STREET. Mason St.

At the middle of East Water street, fifteen ft.	15 ft.	
" " Main st. twenty-eight ft.	28 ft.	
" " Milwaukee st. forty-one ft. and 50-100	41 50-100 ft.	
" " Jefferson st. forty-seven ft. and 50-100	47 50-100 ft.	
" " Jackson st. fifty-one ft.	51 ft.	
" " Van Buren st. forty-nine ft.	49 ft.	
" " Cass st. forty-seven ft.	47 ft.	
" " Marshall st. forty-five ft.	45 ft.	
" " Lake st. forty-four ft.	44 ft.	

ONEIDA STREET. Oneida St.

At the middle of River st. five ft.	5 ft.	
" " East Water st. nine ft.	9 ft.	
" " Market st. ten 50-100 ft.	10 50-100 ft.	
" " Main st. thirty-one ft.	31 ft.	
" " Milwaukee st. forty-one 50-100 ft	41 50-100 ft.	
" " Jefferson st. fifty ft.	50 ft.	
" " Jackson st. fifty-three ft.	53 ft.	
" " Van Buren st. fifty-six ft.	56 ft.	
" " Cass st. sixty ft.	60 ft.	
" " Marshall st. sixty-four ft.	64 ft.	
" " Astor st. sixty-one 50-100 ft.	61 50-100 ft.	
" " Lake st. sixty-one ft.	61 ft.	

BIDDLE STREET. Biddle street

At the middle of River st. five ft.	5 ft.	
" " East Water st. six 50-100 ft.	6 50-100 ft.	
" " Market st. ten 50-100 ft.	10 50-100 ft.	
" " Main st. thirty-four ft.	34 ft.	
" " Milwaukee st. forty-one 50-100ft.	41 50-100 ft.	

At the middle of Jefferson st. fifty-one 50-100 ft.		51 50-100 ft.
"	" Jackson st. fifty-seven 50-100 ft.	57 50-100 ft.
"	" Van Buren st. sixty-three 50-100 ft	63 50-100 ft.
"	" Cass st. sixty-six ft.	66 ft.
"	" Marshal st. sixty-eight ft.	68 ft.
"	" Astor st. seventy ft.	70 ft.
"	" Lake st. sixty-nine 50-100 ft.	69 50-100 ft.

Martin street

MARTIN STREET.

At the middle of River st. five ft.		5 ft.
"	" East Water st. six ft.	6 ft.
"	" Market st. ten 50-100 ft.	10 50-100 ft.
"	" Main st. thirty-four ft.	34 ft.
"	" Milwaukee st. forty-three ft.	43 ft.
"	" Jefferson st. fifty-two 50-100 ft.	52 50-100 ft.
"	" Jackson st. sixty-one ft.	61 ft.
"	" Van Buren st. seventy 50-100 ft.	70 50-100 ft.
"	" Cass st. seventy-seven 50-100 ft.	77 50-100 ft.
"	" Marshall st. eighty-one ft.	81 ft.
"	" Astor st. eighty-one ft.	81 ft.
"	" Unnamed st. eighty-one ft.	81 ft.
"	" Lake st. seventy-nine ft.	79 ft.

Johnson street.

JOHNSON STREET.

At the middle of River st. five ft.		5 ft.
"	" East Water st. six ft.	6 ft.
"	" Market st. ten 50-100 ft.	10 50-100 ft.
"	" Main st. thirty-four ft.	34 ft.
"	" Milwaukee st. forty-eight ft.	48 ft.

Division street.

DIVISION STREET.

At the middle of River st. five ft.		5 ft.
"	" East Water st. six ft.	6 ft.
"	" Market st. nine 25-100 ft.	9 25-100 ft.
"	" Main st. thirty-two ft.	32 ft.
"	" Milwaukee st. fifty-three ft.	53 ft.
"	" Jefferson st. fifty-seven ft.	57 ft.

At the middle of Jackson st. sixty-two ft.	62 ft.
" " Van Buren st. eighty ft.	80 ft.
" " Cass st. eighty-nine ft.	89 ft.
" " Marshall st. ninety-six ft.	96 ft.
" " Astor st. ninety-four ft.	94 ft.
" " An unnamed st. ninety-one ft.	91 ft.
" " Prospect st. eighty-eight 50-100 ft.	88 50-100 ft.
" " Lake st. eighty-six 50-100 ft.	86 50-100 ft.
At the Bluff, eighty-five ft.	85 ft.

KNAPP STREET.

Knapp street.

At the middle of River st. five ft.	5 ft.
" " East Water st. six ft.	6 ft.
" " Market st. eight ft.	8 ft.
" " Main st. twenty-seven ft.	27 ft.
" " Milwaukee st. fifty-nine 50-100 ft.	59 50-100 ft.
" " Jefferson st. sixty-seven ft.	67 ft.
" " Jackson st. sixty-seven ft.	67 ft.
At a point half way between Jackson and Van Buren streets, seventy-one ft.	71 ft.
At the middle of Van Buren st. eighty ft.	80 ft.
" " Cass st. eighty-two 50-100 ft.	82 50-100 ft.
" " Marshall st. ninety ft.	90 ft.
" " Astor st. eighty-eight 50-100 ft.	88 50-100 ft.
At the west line of Rogers' Addition, eighty-eight 50-100 ft.	88 50-100 ft.

OGDEN STREET.

Ogden street.

At the middle of East Water st. six ft.	6 ft.
" " Market st. six 75-100 ft.	6 75-100 ft.
" " Main st. fourteen ft.	14 ft.
" " Milwaukee st. fifty ft.	50 ft.
" " Jefferson st. sixty-four 50-100 ft.	64 50-100 ft.
" " Jackson st. sixty-six 50-100 ft.	66 50-100 ft.
" " Van Buren st. sixty-eight ft.	68 ft.
" " Cass st. seventy-nine ft.	79 ft.

At the middle of Marshall st. eighty-four ft.	84 ft.
" " Astor st. eighty-four ft.	84 ft.
At the west of Rogers' Addition, seventy-five ft.	75 ft.

Lyon street.

LYON STREET.

At the middle of North Water st. six ft.	6 ft.
" " Milwaukee st. seventeen ft.	17 ft.
" " Jefferson st. forty-six ft.	46 ft.
" " Jackson st. fifty-six ft.	56 ft.
" " Van Buren st. sixty-eight ft.	68 ft.
" " Marshall st. seventy ft.	70 ft.
" " Astor st. seventy-five 50-100 ft.	75 50-100 ft.
At the west line of Rogers' Addition, eighty-seven ft.	87 ft.

Pleasant street.

PLEASANT STREET.

At the middle of North Water st. six ft.	6 ft.
" " Jefferson st. twenty-two ft.	22 ft.
" " Jackson st. forty ft.	40 ft.
" " Van Buren st. fifty-one 50-100 ft.	51 50-100 ft.
" " Cass st. sixty-three ft.	63 ft.
" " Marshall st. sixty-six 50-100 ft.	66 50-100 ft.
" " Astor st. seventy ft.	70 ft.
At the west line of Rogers' Addition, eighty ft.	80 ft.

River street.

RIVER STREET.

At the middle of Oneida street, five feet,	5 ft.
" " Biddle street, five feet,	5 ft.
" " Martin street, five feet,	5 ft.
" " Johnson street, five feet,	5 ft.
" " Division street, five feet,	5 ft.
" " Knapp street, five feet,	5 ft.

East Water street.

EAST WATER STREET.

At the middle of Wisconsin st. twelve ft.	12 ft.
" " Mason st. fifteen ft.	15 ft.
" " Oneida st. nine ft.	9 ft.
" " Biddle st. six 50-100 ft.	6 50-100 ft.

At the middle of Martin st. six ft.	6 ft.
" " Johnson st. six ft.	6 ft.
" " Division st. six ft.	6 ft.
" " Knapp st. six ft.	6 ft.

NORTH WATER STREET. North Water street.

At the middle of Ogden st. six ft.	6 ft.
" " Lyon st. six ft.	6 ft.
" " Pleasant st. six ft.	6 ft.

MARKET STREET. Market st.

At the middle of Mason st. fifteen ft.	15 ft.
" " Oneida st. ten 50-100 ft.	10 50-100 ft.
" " Biddle st. ten 50-100 ft.	10 50-100 ft.
" " Martin st. ten 50-100 ft.	10 50-100 ft.
" " Johnson st. ten 50-100 ft.	10 50-100 ft.
" " Division st. nine 25-100 ft.	9 25-100 ft.
" " Knapp st. eight ft.	8 ft.
" " Ogden st. six 75-100 ft.	6 75-100 ft.
" " North Water st. six ft.	6 ft.

MAIN STREET. Main st.

At the middle of Wisconsin st. twenty-five ft.	25 ft.
" " Mason st. twenty-eight ft.	28 ft.
" " Oneida st. thirty-one ft.	31 ft.
" " Biddle st. thirty-four ft.	34 ft.
" " Martin st. thirty-four ft.	34 ft.
" " Johnson st. thirty-four ft.	34 ft.
" " Division st. thirty-two ft.	32 ft.
" " Knapp st. twenty-seven ft.	27 ft.
" " Ogden st. fourteen ft.	14 ft.
" " North Water st. six ft.	6 ft.

MILWAUKEE STREET. Milwaukee street.

At the middle of Wisconsin st. thirty-four ft.	34 ft.
At a point 240 ft. north of the north side of Wisconsin st. 41 50-100 ft.	41 50-100 ft.

At the middle of Mason st. forty-one 50-100 ft. 41 50-100 ft.
" " Oneida st. forty-one 50-100 ft. 41 50-100 ft.
" " Biddle st. forty-one 50-100 ft. 41 50-100 ft.
" " Martin st. forty-three 50-100 ft. 43 50-100 ft.
" " Johnson st. forty-eight ft. 48 ft.
" " Division st. fifty-three ft. 53 ft.
" " Knapp st. fifty-nine ft. 59 ft.
At a point half way between Knapp and Ogden sts. fifty-eight ft. 58 ft.
At the middle of Ogden st. fifty ft. 50 ft.
" " Lyon st. seventeen ft. 17 ft.
" " North Water st. six ft. 6 ft.

Jefferson st.

JEFFERSON STREET.

At the middle of Wisconsin st. thirty-eight ft. 38 ft.
" " Mason st. forty-seven 50-100 ft. 47 50-100 ft.
" " Oneida st. fifty ft. 50 ft.
" " Biddle st. fifty-one 50-100 ft. 51 50-100 ft.
" " Martin st. fifty-two 50-100 ft. 52 50-100 ft.
" " Division st. fifty-seven 50-100 ft. 57 50-100 ft.
" " Knapp st. sixty-seven 50-100 ft. 67 50-100 ft.
At a point half way between Knapp and Ogden sts. sixty-seven 50-100 ft. 67 50-100 ft.
At the middle of Ogden st. sixty-four 50-100 ft. 64 50-100 ft.
At a point half way between Ogden and Lyon sts. fifty-eight ft. 58 ft.
At the middle of Lyon st. forty-six ft. 46 ft.
At a point half way between Lyon and Pleasant sts. thirty-one 50-100 ft. 31 50-100 ft.
At the middle of Pleasant st. twenty-two ft. 22 ft.

Jackson st.

JACKSON STREET.

At the middle of Wisconsin st. forty-two ft. 42 ft.
" " Mason st. fifty-one ft. 51 ft.
" " Oneida st. fifty-three ft. 53 ft.
" " Biddle st. fifty-seven 50-100 ft. 57 50-100 ft.

At the middle of Martin st. sixty-one ft.	61 ft.
" " Division st. sixty-two ft.	62 ft.
" " Knapp st. sixty-seven ft.	67 ft.
" " Ogden st. sixty-six ft.	66 ft.
" " Lyon st. fifty-six ft.	56 ft.
At a point half way between Lyon and Pleasant sts. 50 50-100 ft.	50 50-100 ft.
At the middle of Pleasant st. forty ft.	40 ft.

VAN BUREN STREET.

Van Buren street.

At the middle of Wisconsin st. thirty-six ft.	36 ft.
" " Mason st. forty-nine ft.	49 ft.
" " Oneida st. fifty-six ft.	56 ft.
" " Biddle st. sixty-three ft.	63 ft.
" " Martin st. seventy 50-100 ft.	70 50-100 ft.
At a point 300 ft. north of the north side of Martin st. 78 ft.	78 ft.
At the middle of Division st. eighty ft.	80 ft.
" " Knapp st. eighty ft.	80 ft.
" " Ogden st. sixty-eight ft.	68 ft.
" " Lyon st. sixty-eight ft.	68 ft.
" " Pleasant st. fifty-one 50-100 ft.	51 50-100 ft.

CASS STREET.

Cass st.

At the middle of Wisconsin st. thirty-two ft.	32 ft.
" " Mason st. forty-seven ft.	47 ft.
" " Oneida st. sixty ft.	60 ft.
" " Biddle st. sixty-six ft.	66 ft.
" " Martin st. seventy-seven 50-100 ft.	77 50-100 ft.
At a point 300 ft. north of north side of Martin st. eighty-six 50-100 ft.	86 50-100 ft.
At the middle of Division st. eighty-nine ft.	89 ft.
" " Knapp st. eighty-two 50-100 ft.	82 50-100 ft.
At a point half way between Knapp and Ogden sts. seventy-nine ft.	79 ft.
At the middle of Ogden st. seventy-nine ft.	79 ft.

At the middle of Lyon st. sixty-eight ft.	68 ft.
" " Pleasant st. sixty-three ft.	63 ft.
At a point half way between Ogden and Lyon sts. seventy-nine ft.	79 ft.

Marshall st.

MARSHALL STREET.

At the middle of Wisconsin st. twenty-eight ft.	28 ft.
" " Mason st. forty-five ft.	45 ft.
" " Oneida st. sixty-four ft.	64 ft.
" " Biddle st. sixty-eight ft.	68 ft.
At a point half way between Biddle and Martin sts. seventy-two ft.	72 ft.
At the middle of Martin st. eighty-one ft.	81 ft.
At a point 300 ft. north of the north side of Martin st. ninety-two ft.	92 ft.
At the middle of Division st. ninety-six ft.	96 ft.
" " Knapp st. ninety ft.	90 ft.
" " Ogden st. eighty-four ft.	84 ft.
" " Lyon st. seventy ft.	70 ft.
" " Pleasant st. sixty-six 50-100 ft.	66 50-100 ft.

Astor st.

ASTOR SREET.

At the middle of Oneida street, sixty-one 50-100 ft.	61 50-100 ft
At a point half way between Oneida and Biddle sts. sixty-seven 50-100 ft.	67 50-100 ft.
At the middle of Biddle st. seventy ft.	70 ft.
At a point half way between Biddle and Martin sts. seventy-four ft.	74 ft.
At the middle of Martin st. eighty-one ft.	81 ft.
At a point 300 ft. north of the north side of Martin st. eighty-nine ft.	89 ft.
At the middle of Division st. ninety-four ft.	94 ft.
At a point half way between Division and Knapp sts. ninety-two ft.	92 ft.
At the middle of Knapp st. eighty-eight 50-100 ft.	88 50-100 f

At the middle of Ogden st. eighty-four ft.	84 ft.
" " Lyon st. seventy-five 50-100 ft.	75 50-100 ft.
" " Pleasant st. seventy ft.	70 ft.

AN UNNAMED STREET BETWEEN ASTOR AND LAKE STREETS. Unnamed st.

At the middle of Martin st. eighty-one ft.	81 ft.
" " Division st. ninety-one ft.	91 ft.

LAKE STREET Lake st.

At the middle of Wisconsin st. twenty-seven ft.	27 ft.
" " Mason st. forty-four ft.	44 ft.
" " Oneida st. sixty-one ft.	61 ft.
" " Biddle st. sixty-nine 50-100	69 50-100 ft.
" " Martin st. seventy-nine ft.	79 ft.
" " Division st. eighty-six 50-100 ft.	86 50-100 ft.

PROSPECT STREET. Prospect st.

At the middle of Division st. eighty-eight 50-100 ft.	88 50-100 ft.
At a point 560 ft. north of the middle of Division st. 82 50-100 ft.	82 50-100 ft.
At a point 925 ft. north of the middle of Division st. ninety-one 50-100 ft.	91 50-100 ft.
" " 1170 ft. north of the middle of Division st. sixty-eight ft.	68 ft.
" " 1410 ft. do. do.	69 ft.
" " 1770 ft. do. do.	77 ft.
" " 2500 ft. do. do.	71 50-100 ft.
" " 2940 ft. do. do.	71 50-100 ft.
At the half section line, seventy-three ft.	73 ft.

Grade of Sidewalks.

SEC. 2. The grade or elevation of the sidewalks on the sides of the streets named in the first section of this ordinance, shall conform, as far as practicable, to the grades of streets running parallel with the same, and the grade of alleys, running through the blocks bounded by said streets, shall, in all cases, conform to the grade of the respective streets in which such alleys may terminate.

SEC. 3. All ordinances contravening the provisions of this ordinance are hereby repealed.

Passed, 24th February, 1853.

AN ORDINANCE

Permanently to establish the grade of a part of North Water street, in the First Ward.

The Mayor and Common Council of the City of Milwaukee, do ordain as follows:

Establishing grade of North Water street in 1st ward.

SECTION 1. The grade or height of North Water street, in the first ward of the City of Milwaukee, at the points hereinafter mentioned, is hereby fixed and permanently established, as follows: the heights or elevations to be above the base, which has been generally adopted in grading streets, which base was the level of the Milwaukee river, as it was in the month of March, in the year eighteen hundred and thirty-six:

At the middle of Pleasant st. eight ft. 8 ft.

At a point 685 ft. north of the north side of Pleasant st. twelve ft. 12 ft.

At the south side of Brady st. twenty-nine ft. 29 ft.

At the middle of Henry st. thirty-five ft. 35 ft.

At the center of Persons st. thirty-seven ft. 37 ft.

At the intersection of Hunter and Hamilton sts. thirty-five ft. 35 ft.

At the center of Berry st. twenty-eight ft. 28 ft.

" " Kenzie st. twenty-three ft. 23 ft.

At the east end of the Milwaukee and Humboldt Plank Road Company's bridge across Milwaukee river, seven 50-100 ft. 7 50-100 ft.

SEC. 2. The grades or elevation of side-walks on each side of North Water street, within the limits above mentioned, and the grade of all Alleys running into said street, shall conform to the grade above mentioned, as nearly as practicable.

SEC. 3. All Ordinances contravening the provisions of this ordinance, are hereby repealed.

Passed, March 3, 1853.

AN ORDINANCE

Permanently establishing the grade in certain streets, therein described, in the Third Ward of the City of Milwaukee.

The Mayor and Common Council of the City of Milwaukee, do ordain as follows :

SECTION 1. The grade or elevations of the several streets hereinafter mentioned, in the third ward of the City of Milwaukee, is hereby determined and permanently established, as follows : assuming as a base, the level of the Milwaukee river as it was in March, (1836) one thousand eight hundred and thirty-six, which base is determined by a stone monument set in the center of the intersections of East Water and Wisconsin streets, and marks eleven and one half feet above the aforesaid level of the river. Establishing the grade of certain sts., in 3d ward.

WISCONSIN STREET. Wisconsin st.

At the middle of East Water st. twelve ft.			12 ft.
"	"	Main st. twenty-five ft.	25 ft.
"	"	Milwaukee st. thirty-four ft.	34 ft.
"	"	Jefferson st. thirty-eight ft.	38 ft.
"	"	Jackson st. forty ft.	40 ft.
"	"	Van Buren st. thirty-six ft.	36 ft.
"	"	Cass st. thirty-two ft.	32 ft.
"	"	Marshal st. twenty-eight ft.	28 ft.
"	"	Lake st. twenty-seven ft.	27 ft.

MICHIGAN STREET.

Michigan st.

At the middle of East Water st. nine 50-100 ft.			9 50-100 ft.
"	"	Main st. fourteen ft.	14 ft.
"	"	Milwaukee st. sixteen ft.	16 ft.
"	"	Jefferson st. eighteen ft.	18 ft.
"	"	Jackson st. twenty ft.	20 ft.
"	"	Van Buren st. eighteen ft.	18 ft.
"	"	Cass st. sixteen ft.	16 ft.
"	"	Lake st. fourteen 50-100 ft.	14 50-100 ft.

HURON STREET.

Huron st.

At the middle of East Water st. seven ft.			7 ft.
"	"	Main st. eight ft.	8 ft.
"	"	Milwaukee st. nine ft.	9 ft.
"	"	Jefferson st. ten ft.	10 ft.
"	"	Jackson st. nine ft.	9 ft.
"	"	Van Buren st. eight ft.	8 ft.
"	"	Cass st. seven ft.	7 ft.
"	"	Beach st. six 50-100 ft.	6 50-100 ft.

DETROIT STREET.

Detroit st.

At the middle of East Water st. six ft.			6 ft.
"	"	Main st. seven ft.	7 ft.
"	"	Milwaukee st. eight ft.	8 ft.
"	"	Jefferson st. nine ft.	9 ft.
"	"	Jackson st. eight ft.	8 ft.
"	"	Van Buren st. seven ft.	7 ft.
"	"	Beach st. six ft.	6 ft.

BUFFALO STREET.

Buffalo st.

At the middle of East Water st. five ft.			5 ft.
"	"	Main st. six ft.	6 ft.
"	"	Milwaukee st. seven ft.	7 ft.
"	"	Jefferson st. eight ft.	8 ft.
"	"	Jackson st. seven ft.	7 ft.
"	"	Beach st. five 50-100 ft.	5 50-100 ft.

CHICAGO STREET.

Chicago st.

At the middle of East Water st. five ft. 5 ft.
" " Main st. six ft. 6 ft.
" " Milwaukee st. seven ft. 7 ft.
" " Jefferson st. seven ft. 7 ft.
" " Jackson st. six ft. 6 ft.
" " Beach st. five ft. 5 ft.

MENOMONEE STREET.

Menomonee street.

At the middle of Erie st. five ft. 5 ft.
" " Main st. five ft. 5 ft.
" " Milwaukee st. six ft. 6 ft.
" " Jefferson st. seven ft. 7 ft.
" " Jackson st. six ft. 6 ft.

JUNEAU STREET.

Juneau st.

At the middle of Erie st. five ft. 5 ft.
" " Milwaukee st. five ft. 5 ft.
" " Jefferson st. six ft. 6 ft.
" " Jackson st. six ft. 6 ft.
" " Beach st. five ft. 5 ft.

POLK STREET.

Polk st.

At the middle of Erie st. five ft. 5 ft.
" " Jefferson st. five ft. 5 ft.
" " Jackson st. six ft. 6 ft.
" " Beach st. five ft. 5 ft.

OREGON STREET.

Oregon st.

At the Middle of Erie st. five ft. 5 ft.
" " Jackson st. five ft. 5 ft.
" " Beach st. five ft. 5 ft.

EAST WATER STREET.

East Water street.

At the middle of Erie st. five ft. 5 ft.
" " Chicago st. five ft. 5 ft.
" " Buffalo st. five ft. 5 ft.
" " Detroit st. six ft. 6 ft.

At the middle of Huron st. seven ft.	7 ft.
" " Michigan st. nine 50-100 ft.	9 50-100
" " Wisconsin st. twelve ft.	12 ft.

Main st.

MAIN STREET.

At the middle of Erie st. five ft.	5 ft.
" " Menomonee st. five ft.	5 ft.
" " Chicago st. six ft.	6 ft.
" " Buffalo st. six ft.	6 ft.
" " Detroit st. seven ft.	7 ft.
" " Huron st. eight ft.	8 ft.
" " Michigan st. fourteen ft.	14 ft.
" " Wisconsin st. twenty-five ft.	25 ft.

Milwaukee street.

MILWAUKEE STREET.

At the middle of Erie st. five ft.	5 ft.
" " Juneau st. five ft.	5 ft.
" " Menomonee st. six ft.	6 ft.
" " Chicago st. seven ft.	7 ft.
" " Buffalo st. seven ft.	7 ft.
" " Detroit st. eight ft.	8 ft.
" " Huron st. nine ft.	9 ft.
" " Michigan st. sixteen ft.	16 ft.
" " Wisconsin st. thirty-four ft.	34 ft.

Jefferson st.

JEFFERSON STREET.

At the middle of Erie st. five ft.	5 ft.
" " Polk st. five ft.	5 ft.
" " Juneau st. six ft.	6 ft.
" " Menomonee st. seven ft.	7 ft.
" " Chicago st. seven ft.	7 ft.
" " Buffalo st. eight ft.	8 ft.
" " Detroit st. nine ft.	9 ft.
" " Huron st. ten ft.	10 ft.
" " Michigan st. eighteen ft.	18 ft.
" " Wisconsin st. thirty-eight ft.	38 ft.

JACKSON STREET. — Jackson st.

At the middle of Erie st. five ft.	5 ft.
" " Oregon st. five ft.	5 ft.
" " Polk st. six ft.	6 ft.
" " Juneau st. six ft.	6 ft.
" " Menomonee st. six ft.	6 ft.
" " Chicago st. six ft.	6 ft.
" " Buffalo st. seven ft.	7 ft.
" " Detroit st. eight ft.	8 ft.
" " Huron st. nine ft.	9 ft.
" " Michigan st. twenty ft.	20 ft.
" " Wisconsin st. forty ft.	40 ft.

VAN BUREN STREET. — Van Buren street.

At the middle of Detroit st. seven ft.	7 ft.
" " Huron st. eight ft.	8 ft.
" " Michigan st. eighteen ft.	18 ft.
" " Wisconsin st. thirty-six ft.	36 ft.

PIER STREET. — Pier st.

At the middle of Erie st. five ft.	5 ft.
" " Beach st. five ft.	5 ft.

CENTER STREET, — Center st.

And all streets south of it, in the third ward, to be five ft. 5 ft.

ERIE STREET. — Erie st.

At the middle of Center st. five ft.	5 ft.
" " Pier st. five ft.	5 ft.
" " Jackson st. five ft.	5 ft.
" " Oregon st. five ft.	5 ft.
" " Jefferson st. five ft.	5 ft.
" " Polk st. five ft.	5 ft.
" " Milwaukee st. five ft.	5 ft.
" " Juneau st. five ft.	5 ft.
" " Main st. five ft.	5 ft.
" " Menomonee st. five ft.	5 ft.
" " East Water st. five ft.	5 ft.

Cass st.

CASS STREET.

At the middle of Huron st. seven ft.	7 ft.
" " Michigan st. sixteen ft.	16 ft.
" " Wisconsin st. thirty-two ft.	32 ft.

Beach st.

BEACH STREET.

At the middle of Pier st. five ft.	5 ft.
" " Oregon st. five ft.	5 ft.
" " Polk st. five ft.	5 ft.
" " Juneau st. five ft.	5 ft.
" " Chicago st. five ft.	5 ft.
" " Buffalo st. five 50-100 ft.	5 50-100 ft.
" " Detroit st. six ft.	6 ft.
" " Michigan st. six 50-100 ft.	6 50-100 ft.

Lake st.

LAKE STREET.

At the middle of Huron st. fourteen 50-100 ft.	14 50-100 ft.
" " Wisconsin st. twenty-seven ft.	27 ft.

SEC. 2. The grade or elevation of the sidewalks on the streets named in the first section of this ordinance, shall conform, so far as practicable, to the grades of the several streets running parallel with the same; and the grade of alleys running through blocks bounded by said streets, shall, in all cases, conform to the grades of the respective streets in which such alleys may terminate.

SEC. 3. All ordinances contravening the provisions of this ordinance are hereby repealed.

Passed, March 3d, 1853.

AN ORDINANCE

Permanently to establish the grade of certain streets in the Fourth Ward of the City of Milwaukee.

The Mayor and Common Council of the City of Milwaukee, do ordain as follows:

Establishing grades of certain sts. in 4th ward.

SECTION 1. The grade or elevation of the several streets, hereinafter mentioned, situated in the fourth ward of the City of Milwaukee is hereby fixed and permanently established, as follows: the height or elevation to be above the base, which has been generally adopted in grading streets, which base was the level of Milwaukee river as it was in the month of March, in the year eighteen hundred and thirty-six, (1836) these heights or elevations are obtained by using the water table of the Congregational Church, on Spring street, as a bench, which is seven 68-100 feet above the water in the Milwaukee river, at the time above referred :

Menomonee street.

MENOMONEE STREET.

At the middle of Water st. five ft.	5 ft.
" " Second st. five ft.	5 ft.
" " Third st. five ft.	5 ft.
" " Fourth st. five ft.	5 ft.
" " Fifth st. five ft.	5 ft.
" " Seventh st. five ft.	5 ft.
" " Eighth st. five ft.	5 ft.
" " Ninth st. five ft.	5 ft.

Fowler st.

FOWLER STREET.

At the middle of Water st. five ft.	5 ft.
" " Second st. six ft.	6 ft.
" " Third st. seven ft.	7 ft.
" " Fourth st. eight ft.	8 ft.
" " Fifth st. ten ft.	10 ft.
" " Sixth st. ten ft.	10 ft.

Hinman st.

HINMAN STREET.

At the middle of Sixth st. ten ft.	10 ft.
" " Seventh st. eight ft.	8 ft.
" " Eighth st. six ft.	6 ft.
" " Ninth st. six ft.	6 ft.

Hill st.

HILL STREET.

At the middle of Clybourn st. twenty-seven 25-100 ft.	27 25-100 ft.
" " Sixth st. thirty-eight ft.	38 ft.

At the middle of Seventh st. thirty-one ft.	31 ft.
" " Eighth st. thirty-three ft.	33 ft.

Clybourn st.

CLYBOURN STREET.

At the middle of Water st. five ft.	5 ft.
" " Second st. six ft.	6 ft.
" " Third st. seven ft.	7 ft.
" " Fourth st. eight ft.	8 ft.
" " Fifth st. fourteen ft.	14 ft.
" " Sixth st. forty ft.	40 ft.
" " Seventh st. forty-two ft.	42 ft.
At the alley between Seventh and Eighth sts. forty-three ft.	43 ft.
At the middle of Eighth st. forty-two ft.	42 ft.
At a point on a line with the west of Blocks eighty-one and one hundred and thirty-two, thirty-two ft.	32 ft.

Sycamore st.

SYCAMORE STREET.

At the middle of Water st. five ft.	5 ft.
" " Second st. six ft.	6 ft.
" " Third st. seven ft.	7 ft.
" " Fourth st. nine ft.	9 ft.
" " Fifth st. seventeen ft.	17 ft.
" " Sixth st. forty-four ft.	44 ft.
" " Seventh st. forty-five ft.	45 ft.
" " Eighth st. fifty-eight ft.	58 ft.
At the termination of said st. fifty-eight ft.	58 ft.

Spring st.

SPRING STREET.

At the middle of Water st. five ft.	5 ft.
" " Second st. six 50-100 ft.	6 50-100 ft.
" " Third st. eight ft.	8 ft.
" " Fourth st. ten ft.	10 ft.
" " Fifth st. twenty ft.	20 ft.
" " Sixth st. thirty-one ft.	31 ft.
" " Seventh st. N. side, forty-one ft.	41 ft.

At the middle of Seventh st. S. side, forty-one 50-100 ft.	41 50-100 ft.
At a point on a line parallel with the east line of Eighth st., south of Spring, fifty-three ft.	53 ft.
At the middle of Ninth st. fifty-five ft	55 ft.
" " Tenth street fifty-seven ft.	57 ft.
At the section line between sec. 29 & 30 sixty-one 50-100 ft.	61 50-100 ft.

WELLS STREET. Wells st.

At the middle of Water st. five ft.	5 ft.
" " Second st. five 50-100 ft.	5 50-100 ft.
" " Third st. six 50-100 ft.	6 50-100 ft.
" " Fourth st. seven 50-100 ft.	7 50-100 ft.
" " Fifth st. nine ft.	9 ft.
" " Sixth st. eleven ft.	11 ft.
" " Seventh st. fifteen ft.	15 ft.
" " Eighth st. thirty ft.	30 ft.
" " Ninth st. fifty-six 50-100 ft.	56 50-100 ft.
" " Tenth st. sixty-four ft.	64 ft.

CEDAR STREET. Cedar st.

At the middle of Water st. five ft.	5 ft.
" " Third st. five 50-100 ft.	5 50-100 ft.
" " Fourth st. six 50-100 ft.	6 50-100 ft.
" " Fifth st. seven 50-100 ft.	7 50-100 ft.
" " Sixth st. nine ft.	9 ft.
" " Seventh st. thirteen ft.	13 ft.
" " Eighth st. twenty-five ft.	25 ft.
" " Ninth st. fifty-eight ft.	58 ft.
" " Tenth st. seventy-two ft.	72 ft.

WATER STREET. Water st.

At the middle of Menomonee st. five ft.	5 ft.
" " Fowler st. five ft.	5 ft.
" " Clybourn st. five ft.	5 ft.
" " Sycamore st. five ft.	5 ft.

	At the middle of Spring st. five ft.	5 ft.
	" " Wells st. five ft.	5 ft.
	" " Cedar st. five ft.	5 ft.
Second st.	SECOND STREET.	
	At the middle of Menomonee st. five ft.	5 ft.
	" " Fowler st. six ft.	6 ft.
	" " Clybourn st. six ft.	6 ft.
	" " Sycamore st. six ft.	6 ft.
	" " Spring st. six 50-100 ft.	6 50-100 ft.
	" " Wells st. five 50-100 ft.	5 50-100 ft.
	" " Water st. five ft.	5 ft.
Third st.	THIRD STREET.	
	At the middle of Menomonee st. five ft.	5 ft.
	" " Fowler st. seven ft.	7 ft.
	" " Clybourn st. seven ft.	7 ft.
	" " Sycamore st. seven ft.	7 ft.
	" " Spring st. eight ft.	8 ft.
	" " Wells st. six 50-100 ft.	6 50-100 ft.
	" " Cedar st. six 50-100 ft.	6 50-100 ft.
Fourth st.	FOURTH STREET.	
	At the middle of Menomonee st. five ft.	5 ft.
	" " Fowler st. eight ft.	8 ft.
	" " Clybourn st. eight ft.	8 ft.
	" " Sycamore st. nine ft.	9 ft.
	" " Spring st. ten ft.	10 ft.
	" " Wells st. seven 50-100 ft.	7 50-100 ft.
	" " Cedar st. six 50-100 ft.	6 50-100 ft.
Fifth st.	FIFTH STREET.	
	At the middle of Menomonee st. five ft.	5 ft.
	" " Fowler st. ten ft.	10 ft.
	" " Clybourn st. fourteen ft.	14 ft.
	" " Sycamore st. seventeen ft.	17 ft.
	" " Spring st. twenty ft.	20 ft.
	" " Wells st. nine ft.	9 ft.
	" " Cedar st. seven 50-100 ft.	7 50-100 ft.

SIXTH STREET. Sixth st.

At the middle of Fowler st. ten ft. 10 ft.
" " Hill st. thirty-eight ft. 38 ft.
" " Clybourn S. st. forty ft. 40 ft.
" " Sycamore st. forty-four ft. 44 ft.
" " Spring st. thirty-one ft. 31 ft.
" " Wells st. eleven ft. 11 ft.
" " Cedar st. nine ft. 9 ft.

SEVENTH STREET. Seventh st.

At the middle of Menomonee st. five ft. 5 ft.
" " Hinman st. eight ft. 8 ft.
" " Hill st. thirty-one ft. 31 ft.
" " Clybourn st. forty-two ft. 42 ft.
" " Sycamore st. fifty-five ft. 55 ft.
" " Spring st. S. forty-one 50-100 ft. 41 50-100 ft.
" " Spring st. N. forty-one ft. 41 ft.
" " Wells st. fifteen ft. 15 ft.
" " Cedar st. thirteen ft. 13 ft.

EIGHTH STREET. Eighth st.

At the middle of Menomonee st. five ft. 5 ft.
" " Hinman st. six ft. 6 ft.
" " Hill st. twenty-three ft. 23 ft.
" " Clybourn st. forty-two ft. 42 ft.
" " Sycamore st. fifty-eight ft. 58 ft.
" " Spring st. S. fifty-three ft. 53 ft.
" " Spring st. N. fifty-two ft. 52 ft.
" " Wells st. thirty ft. 30 ft.
" " Cedar st. fifty-eight ft. 58 ft.

NINTH STREET. Ninth st.

At the middle of Menomonee st. five ft. 5 ft.
" " Hinman st. six ft. 6 ft.
" " Spring st. fifty-five ft. 55 ft.
" " Wells st. fifty-six 50-100 ft. 56 50-100 ft.
" " Cedar st. fifty-eight ft. 58 ft.

Tenth st.

TENTH STREET.

At the middle of Spring st. fifty-seven ft. 57 ft.
" " Wells st. sixty-four ft. 64 ft.
" " Cedar st. seventy-two ft. 72 ft.

Spring st.

SPRING STREET.

At the quarter post in the east line of section 30, sixty-one 50-100 ft. 61 50-100 ft.
At 300 ft. west of said quarter post, sixty-three 50-100 ft. 63 50-100 ft.
At 1700 ft. west of the last-named point, ninety ft. 90 ft.
At 900 ft. west of the last-named point, one hundred and twenty-five ft. 125 ft.
At 1250 ft. west of the last-named point, one hundred and thirty-three ft. 133 ft.
At 1120 ft. west of the last-named point, one hundred and nine ft. 109 ft.
The last-named point being at the quarter section post, in the west line of said section, thirty ft. 30 ft.

Grade of side-walks.

Sec. 2. The grades or elevation of the side-walks on the sides of the streets named in the first section of this ordinance, shall conform, as far as practicable, to the grades of streets running parallel with the same; and the grade of alleys running through the blocks bounded by said streets, shall, in all cases, conform to the grade of the respective streets in which such alleys may terminate.

Sec. 3. All ordinances contravening the provisions of this ordinance are hereby repealed.

Passed, April 14, 1853.

AN ORDINANCE

Permanently establishing the grade of certain streets in the Fifth Ward of the City of Milwaukee.

The Mayor and Common Council of the City of Milwaukee, do ordain as follows:

SECTION 1. The grade or elevation of the several streets hereinafter mentioned, in the fifth ward of the City of Milwaukee, are hereby determined and permanently established, assuming as a base the Milwaukee river, as it was in March, A. D. 1836, which base is determined by the water table of the brick building on lot sixteen, block six, on the corner of South Water and River streets, which is assumed to be five 4-10 feet above said Milwaukee river. **Establishing grades of certain sts. in 5th Ward.**

WATER STREET. **Water st.**

At the middle of		Grove or Marshal st. four ft.	4 ft.
"	"	Hanover st. four ft.	4 ft.
"	"	Reed or Kent st. four ft.	4 ft.
"	"	River or Clinton st. four ft.	4 ft.
"	"	Barclay st. four ft.	4 ft.
"	"	Oregon st. four ft.	4 ft.
"	"	Florida st. four ft.	4 ft.
"	"	Virginia st. four ft.	4 ft.
"	"	Park st. four ft.	4 ft.
"	"	South Division st. four ft.	4 ft.
"	"	Elizabeth st. four ft.	4 ft.
"	"	Walker st. four ft.	4 ft.
"	"	Mineral st. four ft.	4 ft.

BARCLAY STREET. **Barclay st.**

At the middle of		Water st. four ft.	4 ft.
"	"	Lake st. five ft.	5 ft.
"	"	Oregon st. five ft.	5 ft.

At the middle of		Florida st. five ft.	5 ft.
"	"	Virginia st. five ft.	5 ft.
"	"	Park st. five ft.	5 ft.
"	"	South Division st. five ft.	5 ft.
"	"	Elizabeth st. five ft.	5 ft.
"	"	Walker st. five ft.	5 ft.
"	"	Mineral st. five ft.	5 ft.
"	"	Washington st. five ft.	5 ft.
"	"	Main st. five ft.	5 ft.
"	"	Madison st. five ft.	5 ft.
"	"	Rail Road st. five ft.	5 ft.

River or Clinton st.

RIVER OR CLINTON STREET.

At the middle of		Water st. four ft.	4 ft.
"	"	Lake st. five ft.	5 ft.
"	"	Oregon st. five ft.	5 ft.
"	"	Florida st. five ft.	5 ft.
"	"	Virginia st. five ft.	5 ft.
"	"	Park st. five ft.	5 ft.
"	"	South Division st. six ft.	6 ft.
"	"	Elizabeth st. six ft.	6 ft.
"	"	Walker st. six ft.	6 ft.
"	"	Mineral st. six ft.	6 ft.
"	"	Washington st. six ft.	6 ft.
"	"	Main st. six ft.	6 ft.
"	"	Madison st. six ft.	6 ft.
"	"	Railroad st. six ft.	6 ft.

Reed or Kent st.

REED OR KENT STREET.

At the middle of		Water st. four ft.	4 ft.
"	"	Lake st. five ft.	5 ft.
"	"	Oregon st. six ft.	6 ft.
"	"	Florida st. six ft.	6 ft.
"	"	Virginia st. six ft.	6 ft.
"	"	Park st. six ft.	6 ft.
"	"	South Division st. six ft.	6 ft.

At the middle of Elizabeth st. eight ft.	8 ft.
" " Walker st. nine 72-100 ft.	9 72-100 ft.
" " Mineral st. eleven 5-100 ft.	11 5-100 ft.
" " Washington st. thirteen 5-100 ft.	13 5-100 ft.
" " Main st. fifteen 25-100 ft.	15 25-100 ft.
" " Madison st. seventeen 13-100 ft.	17 13-100 ft.
" " Railroad st. nineteen ft.	19 ft.

HANOVER OR DUANE STREET.

Hanover or Duane st.

At the nort line of ward four ft.	4 ft.
At the middle of Water st. four ft.	4 ft.
" " Lake st. five ft.	5 ft.
" " Oregon st. six ft.	6 ft.
" " Florida st. twenty ft.	20 ft.
" " Virginia st. twenty ft.	20 ft.
" " Park st. twenty ft.	20 ft.
" " South Division st. twenty-two ft.	22 ft.
" " Elizabeth st. twenty-eight ft	28 ft.
" " Walker st. twenty-five 4-100 ft.	25 4-100 ft.
" " Mineral st. thirteen ft.	13 ft.
" " Washington st. fifteen ft.	15 ft.
" " Main st. twenty-eight 75-100 ft.	28 75-100 ft.
" " Madison st. thirty 25-100 ft.	30 25-100 ft.
" " Railroad st. thirty-one 75-100 ft.	31 75-100 ft.

GREENBUSH OR ABERT STREET.

Greenbush or Abert st.

At the south side of Oregon street, six ft.	6 ft.
At the north side of Florida st. twenty-two ft.	22 ft.
Half way to Virginia st. twenty-five ft.	25 ft.
At the center of Virginia st. twenty-four ft.	24 ft.
" " Park st. twenty-six ft.	26 ft.
" " South Division st. twenty-four ft.	24 ft.
" " Elizabeth st. thirty ft.	30 ft.
" " Walker st. twenty-eight ft.	28 ft.
" " Mineral st. fourteen ft.	14 ft.
" " Washington st. fifteen ft.	15 ft.

At the center of Main st. thirty-two 68-100 ft.	32 68-100 ft.
" " Madison st. fifty 36-100 ft.	50 36-100 ft.
" " Railroad st. forty-four 55-100 ft.	44 55-100 ft.

Grove or Marshall st.

GROVE OR MARSHALL STREET.

At the south side of Oregon st. six ft.	6 ft.
At the north side of Florida st. twenty-four ft.	24 ft.
At the center of Virginia st. twenty-six ft.	26 ft.
" " Park st. twenty-three 50-100 ft.	23 50-100 ft.
" " South Division st. twenty-three ft.	23 ft.
" " Elizabeth st. twenty-two 50-100ft.	22 50-100 ft.
" " Walker st. twenty- two ft.	22 ft.
" " Mineral st. seventeen 37-100 ft.	17 37-100 ft.
" " Washington st. twenty-two ft.	22 ft.
" " Main st. 36 50-100 ft.	36 50-100 ft.
" " Madison st. fifty-one ft.	51 ft.
" " Railroad st. fifty-seven 33-100 ft.	57 33-100 ft.

West Division or Chicago st.

WEST DIVISION OR CHICAGO STREET.

At the south side of Oregon st. six ft.	6 ft.
At the north side of Florida st. twenty-four ft.	24 ft.
At the center of Virginia st. twenty-eight ft.	28 ft.
" " Park st. twenty-three 12-100 ft.	23 12-100 ft.
" " South Division st. twenty-two 30-100 ft.	22 30-100 ft.
" " Elizabeth st. twenty-one 48-100 ft.	21 48-100 ft.
" " Walker st. twenty 66-100 ft.	20 66-100 ft.
" " Mineral st. twenty 74-100 ft.	20 74-100 ft.
" " Washington st. forty ft.	40 ft.
" " Main st. forty-two ft.	42 ft.
" " Madison st. forty-seven ft.	47 ft.
Half way to Railroad st. forty-nine 50-100 ft.	49 50-100 ft.
At North side of Railroad st. sixty ft.	60 ft.

Lake st.

LAKE STREET.

At the center of Water st. four ft.	4 ft.
" " Barclay st. five ft.	5 ft.

At the center of River or Clinton st. five ft.	5 ft.
" " Reed or Kent st. five ft.	5 ft.
" " Hanover or Duane st. five ft.	5 ft.

FLORIDA STREET. Florida st.

At the center of Water st. four ft.	4 ft.
At the section line, four ft.	4 ft.
At the center of Barclay st. five ft.	5 ft.
" " River or Clinton st. 5 ft.	5 ft.
West side of Reed or Kent st. six ft.	6 ft.
" " Hanover or Duane st. twenty ft.	20 ft.
At the center of Greenbush or Abert st. twenty-two ft.	22 ft.
" " Grove or Marshall st. twenty-four ft.	24 ft.
" " West Division or Chicago st. twenty-four ft.	24 ft.

VIRGINIA STREET. Virginia st.

At the center of Water st. four ft.	4 ft.
" " Main st. four ft.	4 ft.
" " Section-line st. five ft.	5 ft.
" " Barclay st. five ft.	5 ft.
" " River or Clinton st. five ft.	5 ft.
" " Reed or Kent st. six ft.	6 ft.
At the west side of Reed or Kent st. six ft.	6 ft.
At the east side of Hanover or Duane st. twenty ft.	20 ft.
At the center of Greenbush or Abert st. twenty-four ft.	24 ft.
" " Grove or Marshal st. twenty-six ft.	26 ft.
" " West Division or Chicago st. twenty-eight ft.	28 ft.

PARK STREET. Park st.

At the center of Water st. four ft.	4 ft.
" " Barclay st. five ft.	5 ft.

At the center of River or Clinton st. six ft. 6 ft.
" " Reed or Kent st. six ft. 6 ft.
At the west side of Reed or Kent st. six ft. 6 ft.
At the east side of Hanover or Duane sts. twenty ft. 20 ft.
At the center of Greenbush or Abert st. twenty-six ft. 26 ft.
" " Grove or Marshall st. twenty-three 50-100 ft. 23 50-100 ft.
" " West Division or Chicago st. twenty-three 12-100 ft. 23 12-100 ft.

South Division st.

SOUTH DIVISION STREET.

At the center of Water st. four ft. 4 ft.
" " Barclay st. five ft. 5 ft.
" " River or Clinton st. six ft. 6 ft.
" " Reed or Kent st. six ft. 6 ft.
At the west side of Reed or Kent st. six ft. 6 ft.
At the east side of Hanover or Duane st. twenty-two ft. 22 ft.
At the center of Greenbush or Abert st. twenty-four ft. 24 ft.
" " Grove or Marshall st. twenty-three ft. 23 ft.
" " West Division or Chicago st. twenty-two ft. 22 ft.

Elizabeth st.

ELIZABETH STREET.

At the center of Water st. four st. 4 ft.
" " Barclay st. six ft. 6 ft.
" " River or Clinton st. six ft. 6 ft.
" " Reed or Kent st. seven 86-100 ft. 7 86-100 ft.
At the west side of Reed or Kent st. seven 86-100 ft. 7 86-100 ft.
" " Hanover or Duane st. twenty-eight ft. 28 ft.

At the center of Greenbush or Abert st. thirty ft. 30 ft.
" " Grove or Marshall st. twenty-two 50-100 ft. 22 50-100 ft.
" " West Division or Chicago st. twenty-one 48-100 ft. 21 48-100 ft.
" " Baulding st. twenty-nine 70-100 ft. 29 70-100 ft.
" " Sanderson st. fifty-one 40-100 ft. 51 40-100 ft.
" " Jones st. fifty-eight ft. 58 ft.
" " Section-line st. fifty-eight ft. 58 ft.

WALKER STREET.

Walker st.

At the center of Water st. four ft. 4 ft.
" " Barclay st. five ft. 5 ft.
" " River or Clinton st. six ft. 6 ft.
" " Reed or Kent st. nine 72-100 ft. 9 72-100 ft.
At the west side of Reed or Kent st. nine 72-100 ft. 9 72-100 ft.
At the east side of Hanover or Duane st. twenty-five 40-100 ft. 25 40-100 ft.
At the center of Greenbush or Abert st. twenty-eight ft. 28 ft.
" " Grove or Marshall st. twenty-two ft. 22 ft.
" " West Division or Chicago st. twenty ft. 20 ft.

MINERAL STREET.

Mineral st.

At the center of Water st. four ft. 4 ft.
" " Section-line st. four ft. 4 ft.
" " Barclay st. five ft. 5 ft.
" " River or Clinton st. six ft. 6 ft.
" " Reed or Kent st. eleven 57-100 ft. 11 57-100 ft.
" " Hanover or Duane st. thirteen ft. 13 ft.
" " Greenbush or Abert st. sixteen ft. 16 ft.

At the center of Grove or Marshall st. seventeen 57-100 ft. 17 57-100 ft.
" " West Division st. twenty 74-100 ft. 20 74-100 ft.

Washington street.

WASHINGTON STREET.

At the center of Water st. four ft. 4 ft.
" " Section-line st. four ft. 4 ft.
" " Barclay st. five ft. 5 ft.
" " Clinton or River st. six ft. 6 ft.
" " Reed or Kent st. thirteen 42-100 ft. 13 42-100 ft.
" " Hanover or Duane st. fifteen ft. 15 ft.
" " Greenbush or Abert st. fifteen ft. 15 ft.
" " Grove or Marshall st. twenty-two ft. 22 ft.
" " West Division st. forty ft. 40 ft.

Main st.

MAIN STREET.

At the center of Clinton or River st. six ft. 6 ft.
" " Reed or Kent st. fifteen 27-100 ft. 15 27-100 ft.
" " Hanover or Duane st. twenty-eight 75-100 ft. 28 75-100 ft.
" " Greenbush or Abert st. thirty-two 68-100 ft. 32 68-100 ft.
" " Grove or Marshall st. thirty-six 50-100 ft. 36 50-100 ft.
" " West Division or Chicago st. forty-two ft. 42 ft.

Madison st.

MADISON STREET.

At the center of Clinton or River st. six ft. 6 ft.
" " Reed or Kent st. seventeen 13-100 ft. 17 13-100 ft.
" " Hanover or Duane st. twenty 25-100 ft. 20 25-100 ft.
" " Greenbush or Abert st. thirty 36-100 ft. 30 36-100 ft.

At the center of Grove or Marshall st. fifty-one ft. 51 ft.

" " West Division st. forty-seven ft. 47 ft.

RAILROAD STREET. Railroad st.

At the center of Clinton or River st. six ft. 6 ft.

" " Reed or Kent st. nineteen ft. 19 ft.

" " Hanover or Duane st. thirty-one 77-100 ft. 31 77-100 ft.

" " Greenbush or Abert st. forty-four 55-100 ft. 44 55-100 ft.

" " Grove or Marshall st. fifty-seven 33-100 ft. 57 33-100 ft.

Half way to West Division or Chicago st. sixty-three 72-100 ft. 63 72-100 ft.

At the center of West Division or Chicago st. sixty ft. 60 ft.

SEC. 2. The grade or elevation of the side-walks on the streets named in the first section of this ordinance, shall conform, as far as practicable, to the grades of the several streets running parallel with the same; and the grade of all alleys running through the blocks bounded by said streets, shall, in all cases, conform to the grades of the respective streets in which such alleys may terminate. Grade of side-walks.

SEC. 3. All ordinances contravening the provisions of this ordinance are hereby repealed.

Passed, April 14, 1853.

AN ORDINANCE

To establish a Dock Line on the west side of Milwaukee River.

The Mayor and Common Council of the City of Milwaukee, do ordain as follows:

SECTION 1. That the dock line on the west side of the Milwaukee river, between the line dividing the Fourth and Fifth wards and the north-east corner of block one hundred Establishing dock line on west side of Milwaukee river.

and fifty-eight, in the Fourth ward, shall be, and hereby is established, as follows, to wit: commencing at the northeast corner of block one hundred and fifty-eight (158), in the Fourth ward, at a point one hundred and forty-two feet east from Reed street, and running parallel with said street to the line dividing the Fourth and Fifth wards to a point, the same distance from said Reed street.

Passed, May 5, 1853.

AN ORDINANCE

To designate the name of a certain street or highway.

The Mayor and Common Council of the City of Milwaukee, do ordain as follows:

Naming a certain st.

SECTION 1. Hereafter all that part of what is now called the Port Washington road, which lies within the city limits, and between the south line of section numbered fifteen, in township numbered seven, north of range numbered twenty-two east, and an east and west line drawn through the center of said section, shall be known, called and designated as Michigan avenue.

Passed, May 5, 1853.

AN ORDINANCE

Changing the names of certain streets in the Fifth Ward of the City of Milwaukee.

The Mayor and Common Council of the City of Milwaukee, do ordain as follows:

Changing the names of certain sts.

SECTION 1. The names of the several north and south streets, running from the north and south lines of the Fifth ward, are hereby so changed that the street known as Water and Barclay shall be known and called Barclay street. The street known as Clinton and River street shall be known and called Clinton street. The street known as Kent and Reed street shall be known and called Reed street. The street known as Hanover and Duane street shall be known and called Hanover street. The street known as Greenbush and Abert street shall be known and called Greenbush street. The street known as Grove and Marshall street shall be known and called Grove street. The street known as West Division and Chicago street shall be known and called Monroe street.

SEC. 2. The names of the several east and west streets, running from the east line of the Fifth ward westwardly, are hereby so changed that the street known as South Division street shall be known and called Pierce street. The street known as Washington and Center street shall be known and called Washington street. The street known as Beaubien and Main street shall be known and called Scott street. The street known as Crockett and Madison street shall be known and called Madison street.

SEC. 3. All ordinances contravening the provisions of this ordinance are hereby repealed.

Passed, May 5, 1853.

AN ORDINANCE

Permanently establishing the grade of a part of Prospect Street.

The Mayor and Common Council of the City of Milwaukee, do ordain as follows :

SECTION 1. The grade or elevation of Prospect street, at the points hereinafter mentioned, is hereby permanently established, as follows : Establishing grade of Prospect st.

At a point where Prospect st. intersects the north line of Rogers' addition, seventy-four feet, 74 ft.

At a point 423 feet north of the above-mentioned point, eighty-two feet, 82 ft.

At a point 200 feet north of the last-mentioned point, eighty-four feet, 84 ft.

At a point 150 feet north of said last-mentioned point, eighty-two feet, 82 ft.

At a point 486 feet farther north than the last-mentioned point, sixty-six 50-100 feet, 66 50-100 ft.

SEC. 2. The said elevations are to be calculated from the surface of the Milwaukee river, as it was in the month of March, in the year eighteen hundred and thirty-six; and the grade of the alleys running into and the side-walks on said street shall conform to the grade hereby established as nearly as practicable.

Passed, May 19, 1853.

AN ORDINANCE

To amend "An Ordinance permanently to establish the grade of certain streets in the First Ward of the City of Milwaukee.

The Mayor and Common Council of the City of Milwaukee, do ordain as follows:

Establishing grade of certain sts. in First Ward.

SECTION 1. The fifth line of the nineteenth paragraph of an ordinance permanently to establish the grade of certain streets in the first ward in the City of Milwaukee, passed the 24th day of February, A. D. 1853, is hereby amended so as to read as follows: At the middle of Martin street, at the crossing of Jefferson street, fifty and fifty-hundreths feet, this alteration in said grade being made on the written application and request of the owners of property fronting on both sides of Jefferson street, between Biddle and Martin streets.

Passed, May 16, 1853.

AN ORDINANCE

Prescribing the manner of letting a contract for the filling of the Bayou, in the First Ward of the City of Milwaukee.

The Mayor and Common Council of the City of Milwaukee, do ordain as follows :

SECTION 1. It is hereby made the duty of the Aldermen of the first ward, in the City of Milwaukee, at such times as they may deem most expedient, to cause the bayou in said ward to be filled with earth or gravel, to the grade established for River street, such work to be done by contract, on a letting to the lowest responsible bidder, on notice to be published as hereinafter provided. Bayou in First Ward to be filled.

SEC. 2. The notice required to be given, as provided in the preceding section, shall be headed : "Notice for proposals for filling the bayou in the first ward," shall be signed by the Aldermen of said ward, and shall be published for ten successive days in the official papers of the city, previous to the letting of such contract. Form of notice.

SEC. 3. The City Surveyor is hereby required to make an estimate, and report to the Common Council the amount of filling required opposite each lot abutting on or extending to said bayou, within twenty days from the first publication of this ordinance. City Surveyor to make an estimate.

Passed, June 16, 1853.

AN ORDINANCE

Permanently to establish the grade of Clermont Street, in the Fourth Ward of the City of Milwaukee.

The Mayor and Common Council of the City of Milwaukee, do ordain as follows :

SECTION 1. The grade or elevation of Clermont street, in the fourth ward of the City of Milwaukee, is hereby fixed Establishing grade of Clermont st. in 4th Ward.

and permanently established, as follows: The height or elevation to be above the base, which has been generally adopted in grading streets, which base was the level of the Milwaukee river, as it was in the month of March, in the year eighteen hundred and thirty-six (1836), making use of the water table of the Congregational Church, at the corner of Spring and Second streets, which is seven 68-100 feet above said base.

At the south side of Spring st. fifty-nine ft. 59 ft.

At a point 350 feet south of the south side of Spring st. fifty-two ft. 52 ft.

At a point 550 feet further south thirty-two 50-100 ft. 32 50-100 ft.

At a point 400 feet further south eighteen 39-100 ft. 18 39-100 ft.

At the north rail of the Milwaukee and Missippi Rail Road six ft. 6 ft.

Sec. 2. The grade or elevation of the side-walks on the sides of said street shall conform, as nearly as practicable, to the grade of said street.

Passed, October 6, 1853.

AN ORDINANCE

Permanently to establish the grade of certain streets, in the Second Ward of the City of Milwaukee.

The Mayor and Common Council of the City of Milwaukee, do ordain as follows:

Establishing grade of certain streets in 2d Ward.

Section 1. The grade and elevation of the several streets hereinafter mentioned, situated in the second ward of the City of Milwaukee, is hereby fixed and permanently established as follows: The height or elevation to be above the level of the Milwaukee river, as it was in the month of March, in the year 1836.

THIRD STREET. Third st.

At the middle of Cedar st. five 50-100 ft.	5 50-100 ft.
" " Tamarack st. five 50-100 ft.	5 50-100 ft.
" " Prairie st. five 50-100 ft.	5 50-100 ft.
" " Chesnut st. nine 50-100 ft.	9 50-100 ft.
" " Poplar st. eleven ft.	11 ft.
" " Vliet st. thirteen ft.	13 ft.
At 300 feet north of center of Vliet st. seventeen ft.	17 ft.
At the middle of Cherry st. twenty-five ft.	25 ft.
" " Court st. thirty-seven ft.	37 ft.
" " Galena st. forty-seven ft.	47 ft.
" " Walnut st. sixty-two ft.	62 ft.
" " Sherman st. eighty ft.	80 ft.
" " Beers st. ninety-three ft.	93 ft.
" " Harman st. one hundred and two feet.	102 ft.
" " Lloyd st. one hundred and two ft.	102 ft.
" " Beaubien st. one hundred and two feet	102 ft.
" " North st. one hundred and eight feet	108 ft.

WATER STREET. Water st.

At the middle of Cedar st. five ft.	5 ft.
" " Third st. five 50-100 ft.	5 50-100 ft.

FOURTH STREET. Fourth st.

At the middle of Cedar st. six 50-100 ft.	6 50-100 ft.
" " Tamarack st. six ft.	6 ft.
" " Prairie st. six 50-100 ft.	6 50-100 ft.
" " Chesnut st. eleven 50-100 ft.	11 50-100 ft.
" " Poplar st. ten 50-100 ft.	10 50-100 ft.
" " Vliet st. fourteen ft.	14 ft.
At the south side of alley, nineteen 90-100 ft.	19 90-100 ft.

At the north side of alley, twenty-one 30-100 feet 21 30-100 ft.
At 50 feet north of alley, twenty-five 64-100 ft. 25 64-100 ft.
At 100 feet north of alley, thirty 80-100 ft. 30 80-100 ft.
At 150 feet north of alley, thirty-six ft. 36 ft.
At the south side of Cherry st. forty-one 20-100 ft. 41 20-100 ft.
At the middle of Cherry st. forty-five 35-100 ft. 45 35-100 ft.
At the north side of Cherry st. forty-nine 50-100 ft. 49 50-100 ft.
At 50 feet north of Cherry st. fifty-four 70-100 ft. 54 70-100 ft.
At 100 feet north of Cherry st. fifty-nine 90-100 ft. 59 90-100 ft.
At 150 feet north of Cherry street, sixty-four 90-100 ft. 64 90-100 ft.
At south side of alley, sixty-nine 17-100 ft. 69 17-100 ft.
At north side of alley, seventy 80-100 ft. 70 80-100 ft.
At the middle of Court st. seventy-one 56-100 ft. 71 56-100 ft.
50 feet north of alley, seventy-three 35-100 ft. 73 35-100 ft.
100 feet north of alley, seventy-four 90-100 ft. 74 90-100 ft.
150 feet north of alley, seventy-five 43-100 ft. 75 43-100 ft.
South side of Galena st. seventy-five 76-100 ft. 75 76-100 ft.
At the middle of Galena st. seventy-six ft. 76 ft.
" " Walnut st. seventy-eight 50-100 ft. 78 50-100 ft.
" " Sherman st. eighty-one ft. 81 ft.
" " Beers st. ninety-seven ft. 97 ft.
" " Harman st. one hundred and four ft. 104 ft.
" " Lloyd st. one hundred and six ft. 106 ft.
" " Beaubien st. one hundred and five 50-100 ft. 105 50-100 ft.
" " North st. one hundred and ten ft. 110 ft.

FIFTH STREET. Fifth st.

At the middle of	Cedar st. seven 50-100 ft.	7 50-100 ft.
"	"	Tamarack st. seven ft.	7 ft.
"	"	Prairie st. seven 50-100 ft.	7 50-100 ft.
"	"	Chesnut st. thirteen 50-100 ft.	13 50-100 ft.
"	"	Poplar st. eleven 50-100 ft.	11 50-100 ft.
"	"	Vliet st. fifteen 50-100 ft.	15 50-100 ft.
"	"	Cherry st. thirty ft.	30 ft.
"	"	Galena st. seventy-eight ft.	78 ft.
"	"	Walnut st. eighty ft.	80 ft.
"	"	Sherman st. eighty-six ft.	86 ft.
"	"	Beers st. ninety-three ft.	93 ft.
"	"	Harman st. one hundred and two ft.	102 ft.
"	"	Beaubien st. one hundred and seven ft.	107 ft.
"	"	North st. one hundred and ten ft.	110 ft.

SIXTH STREET. Sixth st.

At the middle of	Cedar st. nine ft.	9 ft.
"	"	Tamarack st. eight ft.	8 ft.
"	"	Prairie st. nine ft.	9 ft.
"	"	Chesnut st. twenty-four ft.	24 ft.
"	"	Poplar st. thirteen 50-100 ft.	13 50-100 ft.
"	"	Vliet st. seventeen ft.	17 ft.
"	"	Cherry st. thirty ft.	30 ft.
"	"	Galena st. eighty ft.	80 ft.
"	"	Walnut st. eighty-two ft.	82 ft.

SEVENTH STREET. Seventh st.

At the middle of	Cedar st. thirteen ft.	13 ft.
"		Tamarack st. nine ft.	9 ft.
"	"	Prairie st. ten 50-100 ft.	10 50-100 ft.
"	"	Chesnut st. forty-one ft.	41 ft.
"	"	Poplar st. thirty-eight ft.	38 ft.
"	"	Vliet st. thirty-eight ft.	38 ft.

At the middle of Cherry st. fifty-six ft.	56 ft.
" " Galena st. eighty ft.	80 ft.
" " Walnut st. eighty-four ft.	84 ft.

Eighth st.

EIGHTH STREET.

At the middle of Cedar st. twenty-five ft.	25 ft.
" " Tamarac st. twenty-five ft.	25 ft.
" " Prarie st. thirty ft.	30 ft.
" " Chesnut st. fifty-four ft.	54 ft.
" " Poplar st. sixty-three ft.	63 ft.
" " Winnebago st. sixty-six ft. (upper,)	66 ft.
" " Vliet st. sixty ft.	60 ft.
" " Mill st. eighty ft. (w. upper,)	80 ft.
" " Mill st. seventy-five 50-100 ft. (e. lower)	75 50-100 ft.
" " Galena st. eighty ft.	80 ft.
" " Walnut st eighty-six ft.	86 ft.

Ninth st.

NINTH STREET.

At the middle of Cedar st. fifty-eight ft.	58 ft.
" " Tamarack st. fifty-four ft.	54 ft.
" " Prairie st. sixty-four ft.	64 ft.
" " Chesnut st. sixty-nine ft.	69 ft.
" " Winnebago st. eighty-six ft. (w. upper,)	86 ft.
" " Vliet st. eighty ft.	80 ft.
" " Mill st. eighty-seven ft. (w. upper,)	87 ft.
" " Mill st. eighty-three ft. (e. lower,)	83 ft.
" " Galena st. eighty-two ft.	82 ft.
" " Walnut st. eighty-eight ft.	88 ft.

Tenth st.

TENTH STREET.

At the middle of Cedar st. seventy-two ft.	72 ft.
" " Tamarack st. seventy ft.	70 ft.
" " Prairie st. eighty ft.	80 ft.

At the middle of		Chesnut st. eighty-four ft.	84 ft.
"	"	Poplar st. ninety ft.	90 ft.
"	"	Winnebago st. ninety-three 50-100 ft.	93 50-100 ft.
"	"	Mill st. eighty-nine ft.	89 ft.
"	"	Galena st. ninety-three ft.	93 ft.
"	"	Walnut st. ninety ft.	90 ft.

ELEVENTH STREET. Eleventh st.

At the middle of		Chesnut st. ninety-five ft.	95 ft.
"	"	Poplar st. eighty-seven ft.	87 ft.
"	"	Vliet st. ninety-nine ft.	99 ft.
"	"	Cherry st. ninety-three ft.	93 ft.
"	"	Galena st. ninety-eight ft.	98 ft.
"	"	Walnut st. ninety-two ft.	92 ft.

TWELFTH STREET. Twelfth st.

At the middle of		Chesnnt st. ninety-nine ft.	99 ft.
"	"	Poplar st. ninety-one ft.	91 ft.
"	"	Vliet st. one hundred and four ft.	104 ft.
"	"	Cherry st. one hundred and eight ft.	108 ft.
"	"	Galena st. one hundred and four ft.	104 ft.
"	"	Walnut st. one hundred and three ft.	103 ft.

THIRTEENTH STREET. Thirteenth st

At the middle of		Chesnut st. one hundred and two ft.	102 ft.
"	"	Poplar st. ninety-three ft.	93 ft.
"	"	Vliet st. one hundred and three ft.	103 ft.
"	"	Cherry st. one hundred and twelve ft.	112 ft.
"	"	Galena st. one hundred and eight ft.	108 ft.
"	"	Walnut st. one hundred ft.	100 ft.

Fourteenth st.

FOURTEENTH STREET.

At the middle of Poplar st. ninety-five ft. 95 ft.
" " Vliet st. one hundred and two ft. 102 ft.
" " Cherry st. one hundred and eight ft. 108 ft.
" " Galena st. one hundred and six ft. 106 ft.
" " Walnut st. one hundred and two ft. 102 ft.

Fifteenth st.

FIFTEENTH STREET.

At the middle of Vliet st. one hundred and one ft. 101 ft.
" " Cherry st. one hundred and six ft. 106 ft.
" " Galena st. one hundred and four ft. 104 ft.
" " Walnut st. one hundred and four ft. 104 ft.

Sixteenth st.

SIXTEENTH STREET.

At the middle of Vliet st. one hundred ft. 100 ft.
" " Cherry st. one hundred and six ft. 106 ft.
" " Galena st. one hundred and two ft. 102 ft.
" " Walnut st. one hundred and four ft. 104 ft.

Cedar st.

CEDAR STREET.

At the middle of Water st. five ft. 5 ft.
" " Third st. five 50-100 ft. 5 50-100 ft.
" " Fourth st. six 50-100 ft. 6 50-100 ft.
" " Fifth st. seven 50-100 ft. 7 50-100 ft.
" " Sixth st. nine ft. 9 ft.
" " Seventh st. thirteen ft. 13 ft.
" " Eighth st. twenty-five ft. 25 ft.

At the middle of Ninth st. fifty-eight ft.	58 ft.
" " Tenth st. seventy-two ft.	72 ft.

TAMARACK STREET. Tamarack st

At the middle of Third st. five 50-100 ft.	5 50-100 ft.
" " Fourth st. six ft.	6 ft.
" " Fifth st. seven ft.	7 ft.
" " Sixth st. eight ft.	8 ft.
" " Seventh st. nine ft.	9 ft.
At 185 ft. west of center of Seventh st. eleven 50-100 ft.	11 50-100 ft.
At the east side of Eighth st. twenty-four ft.	24 ft.
At the west side of Eighth st. twenty-six ft.	26 ft.
At the east side of Ninth st. fifty-three ft.	53 ft.
At the west side of Ninth st. fifty-five ft.	55 ft.
At the middle of Tenth st. seventy ft.	70 ft.

PRAIRIE STREET. Prairie st.

At the middle of Third st. five 50-100 ft.	5 50-100 ft.
" " Fourth st. six 50-100 ft.	6 50-100 ft.
" " Fifth st. seven 50-100 ft.	7 50-100 ft.
" " Sixth st. nine ft.	9 ft.
" " Seventh st. ten 50-100 ft.	10 50-100 ft.
At the east side of Eighth st. twenty-nine ft.	29 ft.
At the middle of Eighth st. thirty ft.	30 ft.
At the west side of Eighth st. thirty-one ft.	31 ft.
At the east side of Ninth st. sixty-three ft.	63 ft.
At the middle of Ninth st. sixty-four ft.	64 ft.
At the west side of Ninth st. sixty-five ft.	65 ft.
At the middle of Tenth st. eighty ft.	80 ft.

CHESNUT STREET. Chesnut st.

At the middle of Third st. nine 50-100 ft.	9 50-100 ft.
" " Fourth st. eleven 50-100 ft.	11 50-100 ft.
" " Fifth st. thirteen 50-100 ft.	13 50-100 ft.
" " Sixth st. twenty-four ft.	24 ft.
" " Seventh st. forty-one ft.	41 ft.

At the middle of Eighth st. fifty-four ft.	54 ft.
" " Ninth st. sixty-nine ft.	69 ft.
" " Tenth st. eighty-four ft.	84 ft.
" " Eleventh st. ninety-five ft.	95 ft.
" " Twelfth st. ninety-nine ft.	99 ft.
" " Thirteenth st. one hundred and two ft.	102 ft.

Poplar st.

POPLAR STREET.

At the middle of Third st. eleven ft.	11 ft.
" " Fourth st. ten 50-100 ft.	10 50-100 ft.
" " Fifth st. eleven 50-100 ft.	11 50-100 ft.
" " Sixth st. thirteen 50-100 ft.	13 50-100 ft.
" " Seventh st. thirty-eight ft.	38 ft.
" " Eighth st. sixty-three ft.	63 ft.
" " Tenth st. ninety ft.	90 ft.
" " Eleventh st. eighty-seven ft.	87 ft.
" " Twelfth st. ninety-one ft.	91 ft.
" " Thirteenth st. ninety-three ft.	93 ft.
" " Fourteenth st. ninety-five ft.	95 ft.

Winnebago st.

WINNEBAGO STREET.

At the middle of Seventh st. forty-one ft.	41 ft.
" " Eighth st. sixty-six ft. (w. upper)	66 ft.
" " Ninth st. eighty-six ft. (w. upper)	86 ft.
At 150 ft. north-west of centre of Ninth st. ninety-two 75-100 ft.	92 75-100 ft.
At the middle of Tenth st. ninety-three 50-100 ft.	93 50-100 ft.
" " Eleventh st. ninety-nine ft.	99 ft.

Vliet st.

VLIET STREET.

At the middle of Third st. thirteen ft.	13 ft.
" " Fourth st. fourteen ft.	14 ft.
" " Fifth st. fifteen 50-100 ft.	15 50-100 ft.
" " Sixth st. seventeen ft.	17 ft.

At the middle of Seventh st. thirty-eight ft. 38 ft.
" " Eighth st. sixty ft. 60 ft.
" " Ninth st. eighty ft. 80 ft.
" " Eleventh st. ninety-nine ft. 99 ft.
" " Twelfth st. one hundred and four ft. 104 ft.
" " Thirteenth st. one hundred and three ft. 103 ft.
" " Fourteenth st. one hundred and two ft. 102 ft.
" " Fifteenth st. one hundred and one ft. 101 ft.
" " Sixteenth st. one hundred ft. 100 ft.

MILL STREET.

Mill st.

At the middle of Seventh st. eighty ft. 80 ft.
" " an alley, but lots 3 & 4, block 104 seventy-four ft. 74 ft.
" " Eighth st. seventy-five 50-100 ft. (e. lower) 75 50-100 ft.
" " Eighth st. eighty ft. (w. upper) 80 ft.
" " Ninth st. eighty-three ft.(e. lower) 83 ft.
" " Ninth st. eighty-seven ft. (w. upper) 87 ft.
" " Tenth st. eighty-nine ft. 89 ft.
" " alley between lots 7 and 8, block 113, ninety-one ft. 91 ft.
" " Eleventh st. ninety-nine ft. 99 ft.

CHERRY STREET.

Cherry st.

At the middle of Third st. twenty-five ft. 25 ft.
" " Fourth st. forty-five 35-100 ft. 45 35-100 ft.
" " Fifth st. thirty ft. 30 ft.
" " Sixth st. thirty ft. 30 ft.
" " Eighth st. seventy-four ft. 74 ft.
" " Twelfth st. one hundred and eight ft. 108 ft.

At the middle of Thirteenth st. one hundred and twelve ft. 112 ft.
" " Fourteenth st. one hundred and eight ft. 108 ft.
" " Fifteenth st. one hundred and six ft. 106 ft.
" " Sixteenth st. one hundred and six ft. 106 ft.

Court st.

COURT STREET.

At the middle of Third st. thirty-seven ft. 37 ft.
" " Fourth st. seventy-one 56-100 ft. 71 56-100 ft.

Galena st.

GALENA STREET.

At the middle of Third st. forty-seven ft. 47 ft.
" " Fourth st. seventy-six ft. 76 ft.
" " Fifth st. seventy-eight ft. 78 ft.
" " Sixth st. eighty ft. 80 ft.
" " Seventh st. eighty ft. 80 ft.
" " Eighth st. eighty ft. 80 ft.
" " Ninth st. eighty-two ft. 82 ft.
" " Tenth st. ninety-three ft. 93 ft.
" " Eleventh st. ninety-eight ft. 98 ft.
" " Twelfth st. one hundred and four ft. 104 ft.
" " Thirteenth st. one hundred and eight ft. 108 ft.
" " Fourteenth st. one hundred and six ft. 106 ft.
" " Fifteenth st. one hundred and four ft. 104 ft.
" " Sixteenth st. one hundred and two ft. 102 ft.

Walnut st.

WALNUT STREET.

At the middle of Third st. sixty-two ft. 62 ft.
" " Fourth st. seventy-eight 50-100 ft. 78 50-100 ft.

At the middle of Fifth st. eighty ft. 80 ft.
" " Sixth st. eighty-two ft. 82 ft.
" " Seventh st. eighty-four ft. 84 ft.
" " Eighth st. eighty-six ft. 86 ft.
" " Ninth st. eighty-eight ft. 88 ft.
" " Tenth st. ninety ft. 90 ft.
" " Eleventh st. ninety-two ft. 92 ft.
" " Twelfth st. one hundred and three ft. 103 ft.
" " Alley between Twelfth and Thirteenth sts. ninety-eight ft. 98 ft.
" " Thirteenth st. one hundred ft. 100 ft.
" " Fourteenth st. one hundred and two ft. 102 ft.
" " Fifteenth st. one hundred and four ft. 104 ft.
" " Sixteenth st. one hundred and four ft. 104 ft.

SHERMAN STREET.

Sherman st.

At the middle of Third st. eighty ft. 80 ft.
" " Fourth st. eighty-one ft. 81 ft.
" " Fifth st. eighty-six ft. 86 ft.

BEERS STREET.

Beers st.

At the middle of Third st. ninety-three ft. 93 ft.
" " Fourth st. ninety-seven ft. 97 ft.
" " The alley between Fourth and Fifth sts. ninety-nine ft. 99 ft.
" " Ffth st. ninety-three ft. 93 ft.

HARMAN STREET.

Harman st.

At the middle of Third st. one hundred and two ft. 102 ft.
" " Alley between Third and Fourth sts. one hundred and six ft. 106 ft.

At the middle of Fourth st. one hundred and four ft. 104 ft.
" " Fifth st. one hundred and two ft. 102 ft.

Lloyd st.

LLOYD STREET.

At the middle of Third st. one hundred and two ft. 102 ft.
" " Alley between Third and Fourth sts. one hundred and three ft. 103 ft.
" " Fourth st. one hundred and six ft. 106 ft.
" " Fifth st. one hundred and six ft. 106 ft.

Beaubien st.

BEAUBIEN STREET.

At the middle of Third st. one hundred and two ft. 102 ft.
" " Alley between Third and Fourth sts. one hundred and six ft. 106 ft.
" " Fourth st. one hundred 50-100 ft. 100 50-100 ft.
" " Alley between Fourth and Fifth sts. one hundred and eight ft. 108 ft.
" " Ffth st. one hundred and seven ft. 107 ft.

North st.

NORTH STREET.

At the middle of Third st. one hundred and eight ft. 108 ft.
" " Alley between Third and Fourth sts. one hundred and fifteen ft. 115 ft.
" " Fourth st. one hundred and ten ft. 110 ft.
" " Fifth st. one hundred and ten ft. 110 ft.

Grade of side-walks.

SEC. 2. The grades or elevations of the side-walks on the sides of the streets named in the first section of this ordinance, shall conform, as far as practicable, to the grades of the streets on which they are laid out; and the grades of alleys running through the blocks bounded by the said streets shall conform to the grade of the respective streets in which such alleys may terminate ; provided that the decision of the City Engineer shall be final as to the grades of said side-walks and alleys.

Passed, July 14, 1853.

AN ORDINANCE

To establish the grade of Michigan Avenue, in the First Ward.

The Mayor and Common Council of the City of Milwaukee, do ordain as follows :

Establishing the grade of Michigan avenue in 1st Ward.

SECTION 1. The grade or elevation of Michigan avenue, in the First ward, is hereby established as follows :

At the south-western end of said avenue, ninety-six ft. 96 ft.

At a point 750 ft. northerly on said avenue, ninety ft. 90 ft.

Thence on a level for two hundred and fifty ft.

At a point 300 feet further, ninety-six ft. 96 ft.

At a point 350 feet further, one hundred ft. 100 ft.

At a point 200 feet further, one hundred and two ft. 102 ft.

At a point 250 feet further, one hundred and three ft. 103 ft.

At a point 490 feet further, ninety-nine ft. 99 ft.

At a point 1000 feet further, ninety-three 50-100 ft. 93 50-100 ft.

Thence on a level two hundred feet further.

At a point 133 feet further, ninety-six 50-100 ft. 96 50-100 ft.

SEC. 2. The elevation above-mentioned shall be calculated from the level of Milwaukee river, as it was in the month of March, A. D. 1836.

Passed, September 8, 1853.

AN ORDINANCE

To amend an Ordinance permanently to establish the grade of certain streets in the Second Ward of the City of Milwaukee, passed July 14, 1853.

The Mayor and Common Council of the City of Milwaukee, do ordain as follows :

Establishing grade of Walnut st.

SECTION 1. The grade or elevation of Walnut street, in the second ward of the City of Milwaukee, is hereby changed and is established as follows : the height or elevation of said street to be calculated from the level of the Milwaukee river, as it was in the month of March, in the year eighteen hundred and thirty-six.

At the middle of		Fifth st. eighty-nine ft.	89 ft.
"	"	Sixth st. eighty-nine ft.	89 ft.
"	"	Seventh st. eighty-nine ft.	89 ft.
"	"	Eighth st. eighty-nine ft.	89 ft.
"	"	Ninth st. eighty-nine ft.	89 ft.
"	"	Tenth st. eighty-nine ft.	89 ft.
"	"	Eleventh st. ninety-one ft.	91 ft.
"	"	Twelfth st. one hundred and two ft.	102 ft.

SEC. 2. The change or elevation of the grade as above mentioned, is made on the written application of John T. Perkins, and thirty-nine others, owners of property on and in the vicinity of Walnut street.

Former ordinance repealed.

SEC. 3. All ordinances heretofore passed, contravening the provisions of this ordinance, are hereby repealed.

Passed, October 6, 1853.

AN ORDINANCE

To alter and establish the grade of Hanover, Greenbush, Pierce, Elizabeth, Walker, Florida, Virginia and Park Streets, in the Ffth Ward of the City of Milwaukee.

Be it ordained by the Mayor and Aldermen of the City of Milwaukee, in Common Council assembled :

Grade of Reed st. established.

SECTION 1. The grade of Reed street shall be as follows :

At the middle of		Pierce street,	6 ft.
"	"	Elizabeth street,	8 ft.
"	"	Walker street,	10 ft.
"	"	Mineral street,	11 ft.
"	"	Oregon street, its present grade.	
"	"	Florida street, " "	
"	"	Virginia street, " "	
"	"	Park street, " "	

Hanover st.

The grade of Hanover street shall be as follows, to wit :

At the center of		Pierce street,	20 ft.
"	"	Elizabeth street,	20 ft.
"	"	Walker street,	20 ft.
"	"	Mineral street,	13 ft.
"	"	Oregon street,	6 ft.
"	"	Florida street,	17 ft.
"	"	Virginia street,	20 ft.
"	"	Park street,	20 ft.

Greenbush st

The grade of Greenbush street shall be as follows, to wit :

At the center of		Pierce street,	22 ft.
"	"	Elizabeth street,	21 25-100 ft.
"	"	Walker street,	21 ft.
"	"	Mineral street,	14 ft.
"	"	Oregon street, present grade.	
"	"	Florida street,	22 ft.
"	"	Virginia street,	24 ft.
"	"	Park street,	20 ft.

Green st. The grade of Green street shall be as follows, to wit:

At the center of	Pierce street,	23 ft.
" "	Elizabeth street,	22 50-100 ft.
" "	Walker street,	22 ft.
" "	Mineral street,	17 37-100 ft.
" "	Oregon street, present grade.	
" "	Florida street,	24 ft.
" "	Virginia street,	26 ft.
" "	Park street,	23 50-100 ft.

Pierce st. The grade of Pierce street shall be as follows, to wit:

At the center of	Hanover street,	20 ft.
" "	Reed street,	6 ft.
" "	Greenbush street,	22 ft.
" "	Grove street,	23 ft.

Elizabeth st. The grade of Elizabeth street shall be as follows, to wit:

At the center of	Reed street,	8 ft.
" "	Hanover street,	20 ft.
" "	Greenbush street,	21 25-100 ft.
" "	Grove street,	22 50-100 ft.

Walker st. The grade of Walker street shall be as follows, to wit:

At the center of	Reed street,	10 ft.
" "	Hanover street,	20 ft.
" "	Greenbush street,	21 ft.
" "	Grove street,	22 ft.

Mineral st. The grade of Mineral street shall be as follows, to wit:

At the center of	Reed street,	11 ft.
" "	Hanover street,	13 ft.
" "	Greenbush street,	14 ft.
" "	Grove street,	17 37-100 ft.

Oregon st. The grade of Oregon street shall be as follows, to wit:

At the center of Reed, Greenbush and Grove, at the present grade.

" " Hanover street, 6 ft.

Florida st. The grade of Florida street shall be as follows, to wit:

At the center of Reed street, present grade.

At the center of Hanover street, 17 ft.
" " Greenbush street, 22 ft.
" " Grove street, 24 ft.

The grade of Virginia street shall be as follows, to wit: Virginia st

At the center of Reed street, present grade.
" " Hanover street, 20 ft.
" " Greenbush street, 24 ft.
" " Grove street, 26 ft.

The grade of Park street shall be as follows, to wit: Park st.

At the center of Reed street, present grade.
" " Hanover street, 20 ft.
" " Greenbush street, 20 ft.
" " Grove street, 23 50-100 ft.

Passed, December 28, 1854.

AN ORDINANCE

To amend an Ordinance permanently to establish the grade of certain streets in the First Ward of the City of Milwaukee.

The Mayor and Common Council of the City of Milwaukee, do ordain as follows:

SECTION 1. The ninth line of the second paragraph of "An ordinance permanently to establish the grade of certain streets in the first ward of the City of Milwaukee," passed the 24th day of February, A. D. 1853, is hereby so amended as to read as follows: At a point in the center of Mason street, 120 feet east of the center of Marshall street, 43 1-100 feet. At the center of Lake street, 40 27-100 feet, and at a point in the center of Mason street, 300 feet east of the center of Marshall street, 39 56-100 feet. This alteration in said grade being made on the written application and request of the owners of the property fronting on both sides of Mason street, between Marshall street and the Lake. Gra ed o app of o pr

Passed, June 15, 1854.

T

AN ORDINANCE

To establish the grade of Spring Street, from Water Street to the end of the Bridge, in the Fourth Ward.

Be it ordained by the Mayor and Aldermen of the City of Milwaukee, in Common Council assembled:

Establishing grade of a part of Spring st.

SECTION 1. That the grade of Spring street, in the fourth ward of the City of Milwaukee, from Water street to the end of the Bridge, be established, as follows:

At the center of Water st.	5 ft.
At the east side of Water st.	5 ft.
At a point 80 ft. from the east side of Water st.	5 50-100 ft.
At the end of the Bridge,	6 82-100 ft.

Passed, June 20, 1854.

AN ORDINANCE

To permanently establish the grade of Seventh Street, from Walnut Street to Beers Street.

Be it ordained by the Mayor and Aldermen of the City of Milwaukee, in Common Council assembled:

Establishing grade of a part of Seventh st.

SECTION 1. That the grade of Seventh street, commencing at the center of Walnut street, thence running north to the south line of prolongation of Beers street, as represented by the profile thereof, be, and the same is hereby adopted permanently, as follows:

At the center of Walnut street,	89 ft.
" " Sherman street,	91 ft.
At the south line of prolongation of Beers st.	93 ft.

Passed, July 13, 1854.

AN ORDINANCE

To permanently establish the grade of Fourth Street, in the Fourth Ward, from Spring Street to Sycamore Street.

Be it ordained by the Mayor and Aldermen of the City of Milwaukee, in Common Council assembled:

SECTION 1. The grade of Fourth street, commencing at the south side of Spring street, and running south to the center of Sycamore street, as represented by the profile thereof made by the City Engineer, and signed by him, dated July 27, 1854, and on file in the office of the Clerk of the City, be, and the same is hereby adopted permanently, as follows: Establishing grade of a part of Fourth st.

At the south side of Spring st.	9 51-100 ft.
At the north side of Sycamore st.	8 40-100 ft.

Being one foot lower than the present grade.

Passed, July 27, 1854.

AN ORDINANCE

To establish a Dock Line on the East side of the Milwaukee River, between Wisconsin and Lyon streets.

The Mayor and Common Council of the City of Milwaukee, do ordain as follows:

SECTION 1. That the dock line on the east side of the Milwaukee river, between Wisconsin street and Lyon street, in the first ward of the City of Milwaukee, shall be, and hereby is, established as follows, to wit: commencing on the north side of Wisconsin street, at a point one hundred and twenty-three feet from East Water street, and running thence to a point on the south side of Oneida street, one hundred and sixteen feet, from the alley in block one, in the first Dock line established on east side of Milwaukee river, First ward.

ward, thence along the south line of Oneida street, one hundred and seventy feet, thence to its intersection with the extension of the north boundary line of lot one, in block forty-seven, at a point one hundred and thirty-four feet from River street; thence to its intersection with the northerly boundary line of lot one, in block forty-eight, produced to a point one hundred and sixteen feet from the north-east corner of said last-mentioned lot; thence to its intersection with the division line between lots nine and ten, in block forty-nine, produced to a point one hundred and twenty feet from River street; thence to its intersection with the southerly boundary of block fifty, at a point one hundred feet from said River street; thence parallel with and one hundred feet from River street, to the south side of Division street; thence to the north side of Division street, at a point one hundred and ten feet from River street; thence parallel with and one hundred and ten feet from River street, to the line between lots three and four, in block one hundred and fifty-four; thence to the north side of Knapp street, at a point one hundred feet from River street; thence to the line between lots one and two, in block one hundred and forty-seven, at a point one hundred feet from River street; thence to the south line of lot eighteen, in block one hundred and forty-four, at a point one hundred feet from East Water streer; thence parallel with and one hundred feet from East Water street, to Lyon street.

Sec. 2. All ordinances, acts and proceedings of the Common Council, conflicting with the provisions of this ordinance, are hereby repealed.

Passed, March 14, 1854.

AN ORDINANCE

To amend an Ordinance, entitled " An Ordinance to alter and establish the grade of Hanover, Greenbush, Pierce, Elizabeth, Walker, Florida, Virginia and Park streets, in the Fifth Ward of the City of Milwaukee," passed, December 28, 1854.

Be it ordained by the Mayor and Common Council of the City of Milwaukee :

To alter and establish grade of Hanover, Greenbush, Pierce, Elizabeth, Walker, Florida, Virginia and Park streets.

Grade of Greenbush and Elizabeth streets.

SECTION 1. Section one of an ordinance, entitled " an ordinance to alter and establish the grade of Hannover, Greenbush, Pierce, Elizabeth, Walker, Florida, Virginia, and Park streets, in the fifth ward of the City of Milwaukee," is hereby amended as follows : The grade of Greenbush street, at the center of Park street, shall be twenty-three feet ; the grade of Greenbuh street, at the center of Elizabeth street, shall be twenty-four feet ; the grade of Park street, at the centre of Greenbush street, shall be twenty-three feet ; the grade of Elizabeth street, at the centre of Greenbush street, shall be twenty-four feet.

Elevation of grade of Hanover, Greenbush, Pierce, Elizabeth, Walker, Florida, Virginia and Park streets.

SEC. 2. The grade or elevation of the several streets mentioned in this ordinance, and the ordinance to which this ordinance is amedatory, is hereby determined and permanently established, assuming, as a base, the Milwaukee river, as it was in March, A. D. 1836, which base is determined by the water fall of the brick building on lot 16, block 6, on the corner of South Water, River and Clinton streets, which is taken to be five and 4-10 feet above the level of said river.

Repealing clause.

SEC. 3. All ordinances or parts of ordinances contravening the provisions of this ordinance is hereby repealed.

Passed, March 3, 1855.

AN ORDINANCE

To permanently establish the grade of North Water Street, from Pleasant to Racine streets, in the First Ward of the City of Milwaukee.

The Mayor and Common Council of the City of Milwaukee, do ordain as follows :

Grade of North Water street.

SECTION 1. The grade of North Water street, commencing at the middle of Pleasant street, running thence to the middle of Racine street, is hereby permanently established, as follows :

At the middle of	Pleasant st. eight ft.	8 ft. A
" "	the north end of Jefferson st. twelve ft.	12 ft. "
At the south side	of Brady st. twenty-nine ft.	29 ft. "
At the middle of	Henry st. thirty-five ft.	35 ft. "
" "	Pearson st. thirty-seven ft.	37 ft. "
" "	Hamilton st. thirty-five ft.	35 ft. "
" "	Berry st. twenty-nine ft.	29 ft. "
" "	Kenzie st. twenty-seven ft.	27 ft. "
At the angle of	North Water st. twenty-three ft.	23 ft. "
At the middle of	Racine st. twenty ft.	20 ft. "

Passed, May 14, 1855.

AN ORDINANCE

To establish a Dock Line in the Fourth Ward, south of the Menomonee River.

The Mayor and Common Council of the City of Milwaukee, do ordain as follows :

n SECTION 1. The dock line on the west side of the Milwaukee river, between the line dividing the fourth and fifth wards, shall be, and is hereby permanently established as follows, to wit: commencing at the north-east corner of block one hundred and fifty-eight, in the fourth ward, at a point one hundred and forty feet east from Reed street, and running parallel with said street, to the line dividing the fourth and fifth wards, to a point the same distance from said Reed street. **Dock line established.**

Passed, June 8, 1855.

AN ORDINANCE

To designate the name of a Street or Highway through Block one, in the First Ward.

The Mayor and Common Council of the City of Milwaukee, do ordain as follows :

SECTION 1. Hereafter the alley through block one, in the first ward, shall not be regarded an alley, but shall be known, called and designated as "Front Street." **Alley to be called Front street.**

Passed, September 3, 1855.

AN ORDINANCE

Permanently to establish the grade of certain streets in the Second Ward of the City of Milwaukee.

The Mayor and Common Council of the City of Milwaukee, do ordain as follows :

SECTION 1. The grade and elevation of the several streets hereinafter mentioned, situated in the second ward of the City of Milwaukee, is hereby fixed and permanently established as follows, the height or elevation to be above the level of the Milwaukee river, as it was in the month of March, in the year 1836 : **Establishing grade of sts. in 2d Ward.**

FOND DU LAC PLANK ROAD.

At the middle of Seventh street, 92 92-100 feet A, thence with a uniform ascent of 0.44 to each 100 feet, to the north line of the north-east quarter of section nineteen. (Corporation line.)

SECOND STREET.

At the middle of Cherry street, eighteen feet above said level of the river, above described.

At the middle	of	Galena st.	24 ft.	above said	level.
"	"	Walnut st.	30	"	"
"	"	Sherman st.	76	"	"
"	"	Beers st.	92	"	"
"	"	Harman st.	94	"	"
"	"	Lloyd st.	97	"	"
"	"	Beaubien st.	100	"	"
"	"	North st.	102	"	"

GREEN BAY STREET.

At the middle	of	Galena st.	23 ft.	above said	level.
"	"	Walnut st.	29	"	"
"	"	Sherman st.	72	"	"
"	"	Beers st.	90	"	"
"	"	Harman st.	92½	"	"
"	"	Lloyd st.	95	"	"
"	"	Beaubien st.	95	"	"
"	"	North st.	92	"	"

SHORT STREET.

At the middle	of	Walnut st.	28 ft.	above said	level.
"	"	Sherman st.	56	"	"
"	"	Beers st.	84	"	"
"	"	Harman st.	91	"	"
"	"	Lloyd st.	91	"	"
"	"	Beaubien st.	91	"	"
"	"	North st.	88	"	"

HUBBARD STREET.

At the	middle of	Sherman st.	46 ft.	above	said level.
"	"	Beers st.	55	"	"
"	"	Harman st.	64	"	"
"	"	Lloyd st.	72	"	"
"	"	Beaubien st.	80	"	"
"	"	North st.	86	"	"

Grade of side walks to conform with streets.

SEC. 2. The grade or elevation of the side-walks, on the sides of the streets named in the first section of this ordinance, shall conform, as far as practicable, to the grades of said streets and those streets running parallel with the same ; and the grade of alleys running through the blocks bounded by said streets, shall, in all cases, conform to the grade of the respective streets in which such alleys may terminate.

SEC. 3. All ordinances contravening the provisions of this ordinance, are hereby repealed.

Passed, October 1, 1855.

AN ORDINANCE

For the extension of Clybourn and Hill Streets, in the Fourth Ward of the City of Milwaukee.

The Mayor and Common Council of the City of Milwaukee, do ordain as follows :

Extension of Clybourn st.

SECTION 1. Clybourn street is hereby extended from its present terminus, at the east line of the west half of the south-west quarter of section No. 29, town 7, north of range 22 east, west to the east line of Clermont street, being 982 feet long and 80 feet wide, and running parallel with the south line of Spring street.

Extension of Hill st.

SEC. 2. Hill street is hereby extended from its present terminus, on the east line of the west half of the south-west quarter of section No. 29, town 7, north of range 22 east, west on a line parallel with the south line of Spring street

982 feet, to the east line of Clermont street, to be 80 feet wide, said lands taken for said extensions having been conveyed by James Kneeland and wife to the City of Milwaukee, by deed bearing date the 14th day of September, A. D. 1855, for that purpose.

Passed, October 1, 1855.

AN ORDINANCE

Permanently to establish the grade of North Water Street, in the First Ward, from Kenzie Street to the center of Racine Street.

The Mayor and Common Council of the City of Milwaukee, do ordain as follows :

Grade of North Water st. established.

SECTION 1. The grade or height of North Water street, in the first ward of the City of Milwaukee, at the points hereinafter mentioned, is hereby fixed and permanently established, as follows : The height or elevations to be above the base generally adopted in grading streets, which base was the level of the Milwaukee river, as it was in the month of March, in the year eighteen hundred and thirty-six, at the point of intersection of the center of North Water street and a straight line drawn from the south-west corner of water lot 10, to the north-west corner of lot 3, in block 2, all in Hubbard and Pearsons' addition, twenty-three (23) feet, at the center of Johnsons' street, twenty-four (24) feet, at the center of Racine street, twenty-six (26) feet.

Grade of side-walk to conform with street.

SEC. 2. The grades or elevations of the side-walks on each side of North Water street, within the limits above mentioned, and the grade of all alleys running into said street, shall conform to the grade above mentioned, as nearly as practicable.

Passed, November 12, 1855.

AN ORDINANCE

To establish the grade of Seventh Street, in the Second Ward, frcm Beers Street to the section line.

The Mayor and Common Council of the City of Milwuukee, do ordain as follows :

Section 1. The grade of Seventh street, in the second ward, from Beers street to the section line, is hereby established, as follows: Grade of streess in 2d Ward established.

At the center of Beers st. ninety-three ft. 93 ft.

" " Harman st. ninety-seven 25-100 ft. 97 25-100 ft.

" " Lloyd st. one hundred and one 50-100 ft. 101 50-100 ft.

" " Beaubien st. one hundred and five 75-100 ft. 105 75-100 ft.

" " Section-line st. one hundred and ten ft. 110 ft.

Passed, December 17, 1855.

AN ORDINANCE

To amend an Ordinance permanently to establish the grade of certain streets, in the First Ward of the City of Milwaukee, passed February 24, 1853.

The Mayor and Common Council of the City of Milwaukee, do ordain as follows :

Section 1. So much of section one of the ordinance entitled "An ordinance permanently to establish the grade of certain streets, in the first ward of the City of Milwaukee," passed February 24, 1853, as relates to Prospect street, is hereby so amended as to read as follows : Grade of streets in 1st Ward established.

At the middle of Division st. eighty-eight 50-100 ft. 88 50-100 ft.

At a point 560 ft. north of the middle of Division st. seventy-seven 30-100 ft.	77 30-100 ft.
At a point 925 ft. north of the middle of Division st. seventy ft.	70 ft.
At a point 1048 ft. north of the middle of Division st. sixty-seven 50-100 ft.	67 50-100 ft.
At a point 1170 ft. north of the middle of Division st. sixty-eight ft.	68 ft.
At a point 1410 ft. north of the middle of Division st. sixty-nine ft.	69 ft
At a point 1770 ft. north of the middle of Division st. seventy-seven ft.	77 ft.
At a point 2500 ft. north of the middle of Division st. seventy-one 50-100 ft.	71 50-100 ft.
At a point 2940 ft. north of the middle of Division st. seventy-one 50-100 ft.	71 51-100 ft.
At the half section line, seventy-three ft.	73 ft.

This amendment or alteration in the grade of Prospect street is made on the written application and request of the owners of property fronting on both sides of said Prospect street, said request or petition being on file in the office of the City Clerk.

Passed, January 5, 1856.

AN ORDINANCE

To permanently establish the Dock Line of the Milwaukee River, on the West side of said river, from the Menomonee River to the south side of Spring Street, in the Fourth Ward of the City of Milwaukee.

The Mayor and Common Council of the City of Milwaukee, do ordain as follows:

Dock line. SECTION 1. That the dock line of the Milwaukee river, between the Menomonee river and the south line of Spring street, in the fourth ward, be, and the same is hereby established, as follows: The distance from the east side of West Water street to the dock line, to be as follows: At the Menomonee river, 277 feet at the south side of Fowler street, 127½ feet at the north side of Fowler street, 137 feet at the north side of Clybourn street, 197 feet thence, in a direct line, to the south side of the alley, in block 72, to a point 170 74-100 feet from the east line of West Water street, thence to the south side of Spring street to a point 150 feet from the east line of West Water street. Said dock line to run direct from the points above named at angle points.

Line established.

SEC. 2. All ordinances, in any manner conflicting with the foregoing provisions, are hereby repealed.

Passed, February 9, 1856.

AN ORDINANCE

To alter and permanently establish the grade of Elizabeth Street, and to permanently establish the grade of certain other streets, in the Fifth Ward of the City of Milwaukee.

The Mayor and Common Council of the City of Milwaukee, do ordain as follows:

SECTION 1. The grade or elevation of the several streets hereinafter mentioned, in the fifth ward of the City of Milwaukee, are hereby determined and permanently established, assuming, as a base, the Milwaukee river, as it was in March, A. D. 1836, which base is determined by the water table of the brick building on lot 16, block 6, on the corner of South Water street and River street, which is assumed to be five 4-10 feet above Milwaukee river, (said alteration of grade being petitioned for by owners of lots fronting on said Elizabeth street.)

Grade of streets in 5th Ward.

ELIZABETH STREET.

At the middle of Monroe		st.	21 48-100	ft. above	said base.
"	"	Gedding st.	25 59-100	"	"
"	"	Baulding st.	29 70-100	"	"
"	"	Brown st.	35 40-100	"	"
"	"	Sanderson st.	43 10-100	"	"
"	"	Cook st.	46 80-100	"	"
"	"	Jones st.	52 50-100	"	"
At the section line,			52 50-100	"	"

WALKER STREET.

At the middle of Monroe		st.	20 66-100	ft. above	said base.
"	"	Gedding st.	26	"	"
"	"	Baulding st.	31	"	"
"	"	Brown st.	34	"	"
"	"	Sanderson st.	42	"	"
"	"	Cook st.	50	"	"
"	"	Jones st.	54 50-100	"	"
At the section line,			56 50-100	"	"

MINERAL STREET.

At the middle of Monroe		st.	20 74-100	ft. above	said base.
"	"	Gedding st.	23 50-100	"	"
"	"	Baulding st.	27 50-100	"	"
"	"	Brown st.	33	"	"
"	"	Sanderson st.	38 50-100	"	"
"	"	Cook st.	44	"	"
"	"	Jones st.	52	"	"
At the section line,			57	"	"

WASHINGTON STREET.

At the middle of Monroe		st.	23	ft. above	said base.
"	"	Gedding st.	24	"	"
"	"	Baulding st.	26	"	"
"	"	Brown st.	30	"	"
"	"	Sanderson st.	33	"	"
"	"	Cook st.	42	"	"

At the middle of Jones st. 46 ft. above said base.
At the section line, 50 " "

SCOTT STREET.

At the middle of Monroe st. 42 ft. above said base.
" " Gedding st. 39 " "
" " Baulding st. 36 " "
" " Brown st. $36\frac{1}{3}$ " "
" " Sanderson st. $34\frac{2}{3}$ " "
" " Cook st. 37 " "
" " Jones st. 40 " "
At the section line, 42 " "

MADISON STREET.

At the middle of Monroe st. 47 ft. above said base.
" " Gedding st. $44\frac{1}{4}$ " "
" " Baulding st. $41\frac{1}{2}$ " "
" " Brown st. $38\frac{3}{4}$ " "
" " Sanderson st. 38 " "
" " Cook st. $41\frac{1}{2}$ " "
" " Jones st. 47 " "
At the section line, $52\frac{1}{2}$ " "

RAIL ROAD STREET.

At the middle of Monroe st. 55 ft. above said base.
" " Gedding st. 52 " "
" " Baulding st. 52 " "
" " Brown st. 46 " "
" " Sanderson st. 40 " "
" " Cook st. $43\frac{1}{3}$ " "
" " Jones st. $46\frac{2}{3}$ " "
At the section line, 50 " "

MONROE STREET.

At the middle of Railroad st. 55 ft. above said base.
" " Madison st. 47 " "
" " Scott st. 42 " "
" " Washington st. 23 " "

At the middlee of		Mineral st.	20 74-100	ft. above	said base.
"	"	Walker st.	20 66-100	"	"
"	"	Elizabeth st.	21 48-100	"	"

GEDDING STREET.

At the middle of		Railroad st.	52	ft. above	said base.
"	"	Madison st.	44¼	"	"
"	"	Scott st.	39	"	"
"	"	Washington st.	24	"	"
"	"	Mineral st.	23 50-100	"	"
"	"	Walker st.	26	"	"
"	"	Elizabeth st.	25 59-100	"	"

BAULDING STREET.

At the middle of		Railroad st.	52	ft. above	said base.
"	"	Madison st.	41½	"	"
"	"	Scott st.	36	"	"
"	"	Washington st.	26	"	"
"	"	Mineral st.	27½	"	"
"	"	Walker st.	31	"	"
"	"	Elizabeth st.	29 70-100	"	"

BROWN STREET.

At the middle of		Railroad st.	46	ft. above	said base.
"	"	Madison st.	38¾	"	"
"	"	Scott st.	36⅓	"	"
"	"	Washington st.	30	"	"
"	"	Mineral st.	33	"	"
"	"	Walker st.	34	"	"
"	"	Elizabeth st.	35 40-100	"	"

SANDERLON STREET.

At the middle of		Railroad st.	40	ft. above	said base.
"	"	Madison st.	38	"	"
"	"	Scott st.	34⅔	"	"
"	"	Washington st.	33	"	"
"	"	Mineral st.	38½	"	"
"	"	Walker st.	42	"	"
"	"	Elizabeth st.	43 10-100	"	"

COOK STREET.

At the middle	of	Railroad st.	$43\frac{1}{3}$	ft. above	said	base.
"	"	Madison st.	$41\frac{1}{2}$		"	"
"	"	Scott st.	37		"	"
"	"	Washington st.	42		"	"
"	"	Mineral st.	44		"	"
"	"	Walker st.	50		"	"
"	"	Elizabeth st.	46 80-100		"	"

JONES STREET.

At the middle	of	Railroad st.	$46\frac{2}{3}$	ft. above	said	base.
"	"	Madison st.	47		"	"
"	"	Scott st.	40		"	"
"	"	Washington st.	46		"	"
"	"	Mineral st.	52		"	"
"	"	Walker st.	$54\frac{1}{2}$		"	"
"	"	Elizabeth st.	$52\frac{1}{2}$		"	"

SECTION LINE, WEST OF JONES STREET.

At the middle	of	Railroad st.	50	ft. above	said	base.
"	"	Madison st.	$52\frac{1}{2}$		"	"
"	"	Scott st.	42		"	"
"	"	Washington st.	50		"	"
"	"	Mineral st.	57		"	"
"	"	Walker st.	$56\frac{1}{2}$		"	"
"	"	Elizabeth st.	$52\frac{1}{2}$		"	"

Grade of side-walk.

SEC. 2. The grade or elevation of the side-walks on the streets named in the first section of this ordinance, shall conform, as far as practicable, to the grades of the several streets running parallel with the same ; and the grade of the alley running through the blocks bounded by said streets, shall, in all cases, conform to the grades of the respective streets in which such alleys may terminate.

SEC. 3. All ordinances contravening the provisions of this ordinance, are hereby repealed.

Passed, March 8, 1856.

AN ORDINANCE

Relating to certain privileges and exemptions, granted to Daniel Newhall.

The Mayor and Common Council of the City of Milwaukee, do ordain as follows :

Privilege granted to set posts in side-walks.

SECTION 1. Permission is hereby granted to Daniel Newhall, and he is hereby authorized to set the four iron posts which support the balcony to his hotel, about to be constructed on the corner of Main and Michigan streets, in the third ward, six feet out on the side-walk on Main street, as shown in the plan of said building, also to change the grade of the side-walk on Main street, in front of said hotel building, from 4½ feet, including in 180 feet as now established, to 3½ feet in the same distance ; also, to construct arched vaults under the side-walks on Main street, in front of said building ; also, to construct a brick or stone sewer, not less than four feet in diameter, from Main street, through the center of Michigan street, to the Milwaukee river ; also, to land all materials for such building, which he may desire, at the foot of Michigan street from the river.

Privilege to build sewer.

Exempt from taxes.

SEC. 2. In view of the great public benefit which the construction of said hotel will be to our city, and to encourage its early completion, said hotel property is hereby exempted from all city and ward taxes and assessments for the years 1856 and 1857 : *Provided,* Said building shall be completed within eighteen months from the first day of May, A. D. 1856.

Passed, March 22, 1856.

AN ORDINANCE

To change the names of certain streets in the First Ward of the City of Milwaukee.

The Mayor and Common Council of the City of Milwaukee, do ordain as follows:

SECTION 1. The names of the several north and south streets, running from the south line of Brady street, or the east and west half section line, through section twenty-one to the Milwaukee river, in the first ward of the City of Milwaukee, are hereby changed, and Henry street shall hereafter be known as the continuation of, and called, Van Buren street; Hunter street shall hereafter be known as the continuation of, and called, Cass street; Kenzie street shall hereafter be known as the continuation of, and called, Marshall street, and Johnson street shall hereafter be known as the continuation of, and called, Astor street. Names of streets in 1st ward changed.

SEC. 2. Elizabeth street, in the first ward of the City of Milwaukee, shall hererereafter be known as, and be called, Franklin street.

SEC. 3. The streets between blocks 197 and 198, in Rogers' addition, in the first ward of the City of Milwaukee, shall hereafter be known as, and called, Doty street.

Passed, May 26, 1856.

AN ORDINANCE

To amend the several ordinances relating to the grade of Walnut Street.

The Mayor and Common Council of the City of Milwaukee, do ordain as follows:

SECTION 1. On petition of Peter Harong, Reenharat, Barnes and others, the grade and elevation of Walnut street, Grade of Walnut st. in 6th ward.

in the sixth ward of the City of Milwaukee, is hereby changed, and is hereby fixed and permanently established, as follows : the height of said street above the usual base or level of the Milwaukee river, as it was in March, in the year one thousand eight hundred and thirty-six, to be as follows :

At the middle of	Fifth st.	eighty-seven ft.	87 ft.
" "	Sixth st.	eighty-eight ft.	88 ft.
" "	Seventh st.	eighty-nine ft.	89 ft.
" "	Eighth st.	ninety ft.	90 ft.
" "	Ninth st.	ninety-one ft.	91 ft.
" "	Tenth st.	ninety-two ft.	92 ft.
" "	Eleventh st.	ninety-three ft.	93 ft.
" "	Twelfth st.	ninety-nine ft.	99 ft.
" "	Thirteenth st.	one hundred ft.	100 ft.

SEC. 2. The grade and elevation of the side-walks on the sides of Walnut street, and of all alleys terminating in the same, shall conform to the grade of the said street as near as possible.

SEC. 3. The provisions of any ordinance heretofore passed, which may conflict with this ordinance, are hereby repealed.

Passed, May 26, 1856.

AN ORDINANCE

To establish the permanent grade of certain streets, in the First Ward of the City of Milwaukee.

The Mayor and Common Council of the City of Milwaukee, do ordain as follows :

SECTION 1. The grade or height of the several streets hereafter mentioned, situated in the first ward of the City of Milwaukee, is hereby fixed and permanently established, as follows : the height or elevations to be above the base which has been generally adopted in grading streets, which base was the level of the Milwaukee river, as it was in the month of March, in the year eighteen hundred and thirty-six, and from a stone set in the center of East Water and Wisconsin street, which stone or monument is assumed to be eleven and one-half feet above the surface of the Milwaukee river, as it was at the time above mentioned.

JACKSON STREET.

Grade of Jackson st.

At the north line of Pleasant st. forty ft. 40 ft.

At a point 404 ft. north from Pleasant st., at the line between lots 32 and 33, in block B, and between lots 8 and 9, in block E, fifty ft. 50 ft.

VAN BUREN STREET.

Van Buren st.

At the north line of Pleasant st. fifty-one 50-100 ft. 51 50-100 ft.

At a point four hundred and four ft. north from Pleasant st., at the line between lots 12 and 13, in block B, and 12 and 13, in block A, sixty-one 50-100 ft. 61 50-100 ft.

At the south line of Brady st. forty-five 50-100 ft. 45 50-100 ft.

CASS STREET.

Cass st.

At the middle of Pleasant st. sixty-three ft. 63 ft.

At a point opposite the middle of Kewaunee st. fifty-six ft. 56 ft.

At the south side of Brady st. forty-seven ft. 47 ft.

At the middle of Pierson st. forty-two ft. 42 ft.

MARSHALL STREET.

Marshall st.

At the middle of Pleasant st. sixty-six 50-100 ft. 66 50-100 ft.

" " Kewaukee st. sixty-two 50-100 ft. 62 50-100 ft.

At the south side of Brady st. fifty-eight ft. 58 ft.

At the middle of Pierson st. fifty-five 25-100 ft. 55 25-100 ft.

" " Hamilton st. fifty-two 50-100 ft. 52 50-100 ft.

" " Berry st. thirty-eight ft. 38 ft.

Astor st.

ASTOR STREET.

At the middle of Pleasant st. seventy ft.	70 ft.
" " Kewaunee st. sixty-eight 50-100 ft.	68 50-100 ft.
At the south side of Brady st. sixty-seven ft.	67 ft.
At the middle of Pierson st. sixty-six ft.	66 ft.
" " Hamilton st. sixty-five ft.	65 ft.
" " Berry st. sixty-four ft.	64 ft.

Racine st.

RACINE STREET.

At the middle of Knapp st. eighty-eight 50-100 ft.	88 50-100 ft.
" " Ogden st. seventy-seven ft.	77 ft.
" " Lyon st. eighty-seven ft.	87 ft.
" " Pleasant st. eighty ft.	80 ft.
" " Kewaunee st. sixty-eight ft.	68 ft.
At the south side of Brady st. sixty-six ft.	66 ft.
At the middle of Pierson st. sixty-five ft.	65 ft.
" " Hamilton st. sixty-two ft.	62 ft.
" " Berry st. thirty-nine ft.	39 ft.

Franklin st.

FRANKLIN STREET.

Opposite the middle of Knapp st. eighty-three ft.	83 ft.
" " Ogden st. seventy-five ft.	75 ft.
" " Lyon st. sixty-nine ft.	69 ft.
" " Pleasant st. sixty-four ft.	64 ft.
" " Kewaunee st. fifty-nine ft.	59 ft.
" " south line of Brady st., (section line,) forty-eight ft.	48 ft.

Kewaunee st

KEWAUNEE STREET.

At the middle of Marshall st. sixty-two 50-100 ft.	62 50-100 ft.
" " Astor st. sixty-eight 50-100 ft.	68 50-100 ft.
" " Racine st. sixty-eight ft.	68 ft.
" " Franklin st. fifty-nine ft.	59 ft.

SOUTH SIDE OF BRADY STREET. — South side of Brady st.

At the middle of Van Buren st. forty-five 50-100 ft.	45 50-100 ft.
" " Cass st. forty-seven ft.	47 ft.
" " Marshall st. fifty-eight ft.	58 ft.
" " Astor st. sixty-seven ft.	67 ft.
" " Racine st. sixty-six ft.	66 ft.
" " Franklin st. forty-eight ft.	48 ft.

PIERSON STREET. — Pierson st.

At the middle of Cass st. forty-two ft.	42 ft.
" " Marshall st. fifty-five 25-100 ft.	55 25-100 ft.
" " Astor st. sixty-six ft.	66 ft.
" " Racine st. sixty-five ft.	65 ft.

HAMILTON STREET. — Hamilton st.

At the middle of Marshall st. fifty-two 50-100 ft.	52 50-100 ft.
" " Astor st. sixty-five ft.	65 ft.
" " Racine st. fifty-two ft.	52 ft.

BERRY STREET. — Berry st.

At the middle of Marshall st. thirty-eight ft.	38 ft.
" " Astor st. sixty-four ft.	64 ft.
" " Racine st. thirty-nine ft.	39 ft.

Side-walks and alleys.

SEC. 2. The grade or elevation of the side-walks on the sides of the streets named in the first section of this ordinance, shall conform, as far as practicable, to the grades of streets running parallel with the same ; and the grade of alleys running through the blocks bounded by said streets, shall, in all cases, conform to the grade of the respective streets in which such alleys may terminate.

SEC. 3. All ordinances contravening the provisions of this ordinance, are hereby repealed.

Passed, May 26, 1856.

AN ORDINANCE

To amend an Ordinance, passed, March 8, 1856, entitled "An Ordinance to amend an Ordinance permanently establishing the grade of certain streets, in the Fifth Ward of the City of Milwaukee," passed, April 19, 1853.

The Mayor and Common Council of the City of Milwaukee, do ordain as follows :

Grade of streets in 5th ward.

SECTION 1. The grade or elevation of Elizabeth street, and the several streets enumerated below, where they cross said Elizabeth street, in the fifth ward of the City of Milwaukee, are hereby determined and established at the number of feet, below specified, above the base established for calculating grades in said fifth ward, as follows :

Elizabeth st.

ELIZABETH STREET.

At the	center of	Boulding st. thirty-two ft.	32 ft.
"	"	Brown st. thirty-eight ft.	38 ft.
"	"	Sanderson st. forty-seven ft.	47 ft.
"	"	Cook st. fifty-two ft.	52 ft.
"	"	Jones st. fifty-five ft.	55 ft.
"	"	Section-line st. fifty-four ft.	54 ft.

SEC. 2. The grade or elevation of the side-walks, on the streets named above, shall conform, as far as practicable, to the grade of the streets running parallel with the same ; and the grade of all alleys running through the blocks bounded by said streets, shall, in all cases, conform to the grades of the respective streets in which such alleys may terminate.

SEC. 3. All ordinances contravening the provisions of this ordinance, are hereby repealed.

Passed, June 23, 1856.

AN ORDINANCE

Authorizing the improvement of the Public Square, and Alley adjoining the same, in the Second Ward of Milwaukee.

The Mayor and Common Council of the City of Milwaukee, do ordain as follows:

SECTION 1. More than twenty-five freeholders, residents of the second ward of the City of Milwaukee, having, by a petition, represented to the Common Council, that it is necessary for the health and convenience of the inhabitants of said ward to have the Public Squares, being the east half of blocks 36 and 165, in said ward, and the alleys adjoining, filled to the established grade, and otherwise improved; authority, therefore, is hereby given to the Aldermen of said second ward to fill, to the established grade, and otherwise improve said premises or any part thereof, in accordance with, and according to the provisions of an act of the Legislature, entitled "an act to authorize the several wards, in the City of Milwaukee, to purchase grounds for Market and Public Squares," approved, March 19, 1856. Public Square to be improved.

SEC. 2. For the purpose of making the above-mentioned improvements, the Aldermen of said ward are hereby authorized, for and in the name of said ward, to issue bonds, not exceeding in amount the sum of ten thousand dollars, on such terms, for such time, and drawing such interest, as to them shall seem advisable, but to be issued in accordance with and within the restrictions imposed by said act of the Legislature. May issue city bonds.

SEC. 3. The Aldermen of said ward shall cause an accurate estimate to be made by the City Engineer, of the amount of earth necessary to fill the said Square and alley, and also an estimate of the other improvements necessary, and filed in his office, and a copy thereof filed in the office of the City Comptroller. Estimate to be made.

To be recorded on ward record. SEC. 4. All the proceedings of said Aldermen, under this ordinance and said act of the Legislature, shall be entered at length in the records of said ward, and they shall make out a certified list of the bonds so issued, specifying the amount, the rate of interest they draw, and the time when the interest and principal thereon becomes due, which shall be filed with the City Comptroller and entered of record in his office.

To be voted on. SEC. 5. This ordinance shall not be in force until submitted to the legal voters of the second ward of the City of Milwaukee, at an election to be held for that purpose, at the time hereinafter provided, and adopted by a majority of the whole number of votes given at such election.

When and where election held. SEC. 6. An election shall be held on the first Wednesday in June next, A. D. 1856, between the hours of two and six o'clock in the afternoon of said day, at the usual place in said ward for holding elections, for the purpose of the adoption or rejection of this ordinance, and such election shall be conducted and the votes canvassed and returned in the same manner and by the same officers as at other city elections.

Ballots to read. SEC. 7. On the ballots which shall be received by the inspectors at said election, shall be either written or printed the words, "For the improvement of Public Square," or the words, "Against the improvement of the Public Square."

Returns, how made. SEC. 8. At the next regular or special meeting of the Common Council, after the returns of the election from said ward are made to the City Clerk, the Common Council shall proceed to canvass said returns, and if it is found that a majority of all the votes taken are in favor of said improvement, it shall be the duty of the Mayor to make proclamation thereof in the official papers of the City, and this ordinance shall be in force from and after its first publication, subsequent to the date of such proclamation.

Clerk to publish notice and petition. SEC. 9. It is hereby made the duty of the City Clerk, to cause a certified copy of the petition, on file in his office, for this improvement, together with a notice of the time and place of holding the election specified in this ordinance, to be published in the official papers of this city three several times, one of which publications shall be made in each of said newspapers at least fifteen days previous to the time of holding said elections.

Passed, May 12, 1856.

AN ORDINANCE

Authorizing the purchasing, improving and establishing a Public Square in the Seventh Ward of the City of Milwaukee.

The Mayor and Common Council of the City of Milwaukee, do ordain as follows:

SECTION 1. More than twenty-five freeholders, residents of the seventh ward of the City of Milwaukee, having, by petition, represented to the Common Council that it is necessary to take for a Public Square in said ward, the following premises, viz: lots No. one, five, six and seven (1, 5, 6 and 7), in block No. seventy-one (71), in said ward, authority therefore is hereby given to the Aldermen of said seventh ward to purchase said premises of the owner or owners thereof, or to take the same in accordance with, and according to the provisions of an act of the Legislature, entitled "an act to authorize the several wards in the City of Milwaukee, to purchase grounds for Market and Public Squares," approved, March 19th, 1856. Public Square, 7th ward.

SEC. 2. The premises described in the foregoing section are hereby set off and established as a Public Square in said seventh ward, to be under the control of the Aldermen of said ward, and to be kept and regulated for the public use.

SEC. 3. For the purpose of purchasing and improving said Public Square, the Aldermen of said ward are hereby authorized, for, and in the name of said Ward, to issue bonds Bonds to be issued.

in accordance with the provisions of an act, entitled "an act to authorize the several wards, in the City of Milwaukee, to purchase grounds for Market and Public Squares," approved, March 19, 1856, upon such terms, for such time, and drawing such interest, as to them shall seem desirable, but to be issued in accordance with, and within the restrictions imposed by said act of the Legislature.

Profile to be filed.

SEC. 4. The Aldermen of said ward shall cause an accurate survey and profile, or map of said Public Square, to be made by the City Surveyor and filed in his office; and before proceeding to improve the same, they shall cause a plan and specifications of such improvement to be drawn, and a copy thereof to be deposited in the office of the City Comptroller.

Proceedings to be recorded.

SEC. 5. All the proceedings of said Aldermen, under this ordinance and said act of the Legislature, shall be entered at length in the records of said ward, and they shall make out a certified list of all the bonds so issued, specifying the amount, the rate of interest they draw, and the time when the interest and principal thereon becomes due, which shall be filed with the City Comptroller, and entered of record in his office.

Submitted to voters.

SEC. 6. This ordinance shall not be in force until submitted to the legal voters of the seventh ward of the City of Milwaukee, at an election held for that purpose, at the time hereinafter provided, and adopted by a majority of the whole number of votes given at such election.

Time of election.

SEC. 7. An election shall be held on Thursday, the 26th day of June, A. D. 1856, between the hours of two and six o'clock, in the afternoon of said day, at the usual place in said ward for holding elections, for the purpose of the adoption or rejection of this ordinance, and such election shall be conducted, and the votes canvassed and returned, in the same manner and by the same officers, as at other city elections.

SEC. 8. On the ballots which shall be received by the inspectors, at said election, shall be either written or printed, the words, "For the Public Square," or the words, "Against the Public Square."

Votes canvassed.

SEC. 9. At the next regular or special meeting of the Common Council, after the returns of the election from said ward are made to the City Clerk, the Common Council shall proceed to canvass said returns, and if it is found that a majority of the whole votes taken are in favor of said Public Square, it shall be the duty of the Mayor to make proclamation thereof in the official papers of the city, and this ordinance shall be in force from and after its first publication, subsequent to the date of such proclamation.

Proclamation of Mayor.

SEC. 10. It is hereby made the duty of the City Clerk to cause a certified copy of the petition on file in his office, for this Public Square, together with a notice of the time and place of holding the election, specified in this ordinance, to be published in the official papers of this city three several times, one of which publications shall be made in each of said newspapers at least fifteen days previous to the time of holding said election.

Passed, June 9, 1856.

AN ORDINANCE

Authorizing the purchasing, improveing, and establishing a Market Square in the Seventh Ward of the City of Milwaukee.

The Mayor and Common Council of the City of Milwuukee, do ordain as follows:

Market Square in 7th ward.

SECTION 1. More than twenty-five freeholders, residents of the seventh ward of the City of Milwaukee, having, by petition, represented to the Common Council that it is necessary, in addition to the property already owned by said seventh ward, to take for a Market Square lots Nos. one, two, three and four (1, 2, 3 and 4), in block No. fifty-five (55), in said ward; authority, therefore, is hereby given to the Aldermen of said seventh ward to purchase said premises, or any part thereof, of the owner or owners thereof, with whom they can agree for such purchase, or to take the same or any portion thereof, which they may be unable to purchase in accordance with and according to the provisions of an act of the Legislature, entitled "an act to authorize the several wards in the City of Milwaukee to purchase grounds for Market and Public Squares," approved, March 19th, 1856.

SEC. 2. The premises described in the foregoing section, in addition to the lots already owned by the said seventh ward adjoining the same, are hereby set off and established as a Market Square in said seventh ward, to be under the control of the Aldermen of said ward, and to be kept and regulated for the public use, and hereafter to be called and known by the name of the Seventh Ward Market Square.

Bonds issued

SEC. 3. For the purpose of purchasing and improving said Market Square, the Aldermen of said ward are hereby authorized, for and in the name of said ward, to issue bonds in accordance with the provisions of an act, entitled "an act to authorize the several wards in the City of Milwaukee to purchase grounds for Market and Public Squares," approved, March 19th, 1856, upon such terms, for such time, and drawing such interest, as to them shall seem advisable, but to be issued in accordance with and within the restrictions imposed by said act of the Legislature.

Profile filed.

SEC. 4. The Aldermen of said ward shall cause an accurate survey and profile or map of said Market Square to be made by the City Surveyor, and filed in his office, and before proceeding to improve the same, they shall cause a plan and specifications of such improvement to be drawn, and a copy thereof deposited in the office of the City Comptroller.

SEC. 5. All the proceedings of said Aldermen, under this ordinance and said act of the Legislature, shall be entered at length in the records of said ward, and they shall make out a certified list of all the bonds so issued, specifying the amount, the rate of interest they draw, and the time when the principal and interest thereon becomes due, which shall be filed with the City Comptroller, and entered of record in his office. Proceedings to be recorded.

SEC. 6. This ordinance shall not be in force until submitted to the legal voters of the seventh ward of the City of Milwaukee, at an election to be held for that purpose, at the time hereinafter provided, and adopted by a majority of the whole number of votes given at such election. Submitted to voters.

SEC. 7. An election shall be held on Thursday, the 26th day of June, A. D. 1856, between the hours of two and six o'clock, in the afternoon of said day, at the usual place in said ward for holding elections, for the purpose of the adoption or rejection of this ordinance, and such election shall be conducted, and the votes canvassed and returned, in the same manner and by the same officers as at other city elections. Time of election.

SEC. 8. On the ballots which shall be received by the inspectors at said election, shall be either written or printed the words, "For the Market Square," or the words "Against the Market Square.

SEC. 9. At the next regular or special meeting of the Common Council, after the returns of the election from said ward are made to the City Clerk, the Common Council shall proceed to canvass said returns, and if it is found that a majority of all the votes taken are in favor of said Market Square, it shall be the duty of the Mayor to make proclamation thereof in the official papers of the city, and this ordinance shall be in force from and after its first publication, subsequent to the date of such proclamation. Votes canvassed. Proclamation of Mayor.

SEC. 10. It is hereby made the duty of the City Clerk tc cause a certified copy of the petition, on file in his office, for this Market Square, together with a notice of the time and place of holding the election specified in this ordinance, to be published in the official papers of this city three several times, one of which publications shall be made in each of said newspapers at least fifteen days previous to the time of holding said election.

Passed, June 9, 1856.

AN ORDINANCE

To amend the several Ordinances relating to the grade on Poplar Street.

The Mayor and Common Council of the City of Milwaukee, do ordain as follows :

SECTION 1. It appearing, by the report of the Aldermen of the second ward, that the grade, as now established on Poplar street, does not permit the water to run off : in order to effect this object, the grade on said Poplar street is hereby changed, and is hereby fixed and permanently established, as follows : The height or elevation of said street, above the usual base or level of the Milwaukee river, as it was in March, in the year one thousand eight hundred and thirty-six, to be as follows : at the middle of Eleventh street eighty-nine, and at the middle of Tenth street, eighty-seven.

Grade of Poplar st. 2d ward.

SEC. 2. The grades and elevations of the side-walks, on the sides of Poplar street, and of all alleys terminating in the same, shall conform to the grade of said street, as near as practicable.

SEC. 3. The provisions of any ordinances heretofore passed, which may conflict with this ordinance, are hereby repealed.

Passed, June 16, 1856.

AN ORDINANCE

Permanently to establish the grade of certain streets, in the Fourth Ward of the City of Milwaukee.

The Mayor and Common Council of the City of Milwaukee, do ordain as follows :

SECTION 1. The grade or elevation of the several streets, hereinafter mentioned, situated in the fourth ward of the City of Milwaukee, is hereby fixed and permanently established, as follows : The height or elevation to be above the base, which has been generally adopted in establishing grades in said ward, which base was the Milwaukee river, as it was in the month of March, in the year 1836 ; the height or elevation is obtained by using the water table of the Congregational Church, on Spring street, as a bench, which is seven 68-100 feet above the water in the Milwaukee river, at the time above referred. Grade of streets in 4th ward.

CLYBOURN STREET. Clybourn st.

At a point 325 ft. west of block 81 and 132,	15 ft.
" " 370 ft. farther west,	16 ft.
At the center of Clermont st.	25 ft.

HILL STREET. Hill st.

At the west side of blocks 137 and 132,	10 ft.
At a point 325 ft. west of blocks 137 and 132	6 ft.
" " 370 ft. farther west,	6 ft.
At the center of Clermont st.	10 ft.

CLERMONT STREET. Clermont st.

At the center of Clybourn st.	25 ft.
" " Hill st.	10 ft.
" " a street on the north side of the Railroad,	6 ft.
A st. between block 195 and the Railroad, at the center of Clermont st.	6 ft.

V

At the west line of section 29, 6 ft.
A st. known as the Kilbourn road, at the intersection with st. south of block 195, 6 ft.
At a point 400 ft. south-west in center of said st. 5 ft.
At the south line of the fourth ward, 5 ft.

Passed, July 21, 1856.

AN ORDINANCE

To amend an Ordinance permanently to establish the grade of certain streets, in the First Ward of the City of Milwaukee, passed, February 24, 1853.

The Mayor and Common Council of the City of Milwaukee, do ordain as follows:

Grade of streets in 1st ward.

SECTION 1. The first section of an ordinance, entitled "an ordinance permanently to establish the grade of certain streets in the first ward of the City of Milwaukee," passed February 24, 1853, is hereby amended, and the height or elevation of Milwaukee street, at the points hereinafter named, is hereby permanently fixed and established, as follows, to wit: At the middle of Knapp street, fifty-six feet (56 feet); at the middle of Ogden street, forty-four feet (44 feet.) The grade of said Milwaukee street to slope out from the gutter on the south side of Knapp street, within sixty feet south from the south line of said Knapp street, and to run a straight grade of uniform descent from the middle of Knapp street to the middle of Ogden street. Also, from the middle of Ogden street to the middle of Lyon street.

Milwaukee st

SEC. 2. The height or elevation of Knapp street, at the middle of Jefferson street, is hereby permanently fixed and established at sixty-six feet (66 feet), and the grade of Jefferson street to slope out from the gutter on the south side of Knapp street, within sixty feet south from the south line of said Knapp street, and from the gutter on the north side of Knapp street to a point half way between Knapp and Ogden streets.

SEC. 3. The grade of Knapp street is hereby fixed and determined, and shall run a straight grade of uniform descent from the middle of Jackson street to the middle of Jefferson street, and from the middle of Jefferson street to the middle of Milwaukee street, and from the middle of Milwaukee street to the middle of Main street.

SEC. 4. The grade of Ogden street is hereby fixed and determined, and shall run a straight grade of uniform descent from the middle of Jefferson street to the middle of Milwaukee street, and from the middle of Milwaukee street to the middle of Main street. Ogden st.

SEC. 5. In consideration of the passage of this ordinance, and the fixing of the points of elevation, in the streets named in the foregoing sections, it is distinctly understood and agreed, by all parties interested, and by the Common Council, that no change shall ever be made hereafter in the grade of the above-named streets, at the points named in this ordinance.

SEC. 6. All ordinances and parts of ordinances fixing the grade of the several streets named in this ordinance, and conflicting with the heights or elevations fixed and established by this ordinance, are hereby repealed so far as relates to the points of grade named in this ordinance, but in no other respect whatever.

Passed, August 1, 1856.

AN ORDINANCE

Permanently to establish the grade of certain streets in the Second and Fourth Wards of the City of Milwaukee.

The Mayor and Common Council of the City of Milwaukee, do ordain as follows:

Grade of streets in 2d & 4th wards.

SECTION 1. The grade or elevation of the several streets hereinafter mentioned, situated in the second and fourth wards of the City of Milwaukee, is hereby fixed and permanently established, as follows: The height or elevation to be above the base, which has been generally adopted in grading streets, which base was the level of the Milwaukee River, as it was in the month of March, in the year 1836. These heights or elevations are obtained by using the water-table of the Congregational Church on Spring street as a bench, which is 7 and 68-100 feet above the water in the Milwaukee river at the time above referred to.

Tenth st.

TENTH STREET.

At the middle of	Prairie street,	76 50-100 ft.
" "	Poplar st.	87 ft.
" "	Chesnut st.	84 ft.
" "	Tamarack st.	70 ft.
" "	Cedar st.	69 ft.
" "	Wells st.	63 ft.
" "	Spring st.	57 ft.

Eleventh st.

ELEVENTH STREET

At the middle of	Chesnut st.	95 ft.
" "	Prairie st.	85 ft.
" "	Tamarack st.	77 ft.
" "	Cedar st.	72 ft.
" "	Wells st.	64 ft.
" "	Spring st.	58 75-100 ft.

TWELFTH STREET. Twelfth st.

At the middle of		Chesnut st.	99 ft.
"	"	Prairie st.	91 ft.
"	"	Tamarack st.	84 ft.
"	"	Cedar st.	75 ft.
"	"	Wells st.	66 ft.
"	"	Spring st.	60 50-100 ft.

PRAIRIE STREET. Prairie st.

At the middle of		Ninth st.	64 ft. A.
"	"	Tenth st.	76½ ft. "
"	"	Eleventh st.	85 ft. "
"	"	Twelfth st.	81 ft. "
At the section line between sections 29 and 30			94 ft. "

TAMARACK STREET. Tamarack st

At the middle of		Ninth st.	54 ft. A.
"	"	Tenth st.	70 ft. "
"	"	Eleventh st.	77 ft. "
"	"	Twelfth st.	84 ft. "
At a line between sections 29 and 30			87 ft. "

CEDAR STREET. Cedar st.

At the middle of		Ninth st.	58 ft. A.
"	"	Tenth st.	69 ft. "
"	"	Eleventh st.	72 ft. "
"	"	Twelfth st.	75 ft. "
At the line between sections 29 and 30			77 ft. "

WELLS STREET. Wells st.

At the middle of		Ninth st.	56 ft. A.
"	"	Tenth st.	63 ft. "
"	"	Eleventh st.	64 ft. "
"	"	Twelfth st.	66 ft. "
At the line between sections 29 and 30			67 ft. "

SEC. 2. The grades or elevations of the side walks onthe sides of the streets named in the first section of this ordinance, shall conform, as far as practicable, to the grades of

streets running parallel with the same; and the grade of alleys running through the blocks bounded by said streets, shall, in all cases, conform to the grade of the respective streets in which such alleys may terminate.

Sec. 3. All ordinances contravening the provisions of this ordinance, are hereby repealed.

Passed, September 13, 1856.

AN ORDINANCE

Authorizing the purchasing, improving, and establishing a Market Square in the Third Ward of the City of Milwaukee.

The Mayor and Common Council of the City of Milwaukee, do ordain as follows:

Market Square in 3d ward.

Section 1. More than twenty-five freeholders, residents of the third ward of the City of Milwaukee, having, by petition, represented to the Common Council that it is necessary to take, for a Market Square, all of block forty-five (45), in said ward; authority, therefore, is hereby given to the Aldermen of said third ward to purchase said premises, or any part thereof, of the owner or owners thereof, with whom

Lots taken.

they can agree for such purchase, or to take the same or any portion thereof, which they may be unable to purchase in accordance with and according to the provisions of an act of the Legislature, entitled "an act to authorize the several wards in the City of Milwaukee to purchase grounds for Market and Public Squares," approved, March 19th, 1856.

Sec. 2. The premises described in the foregoing section are hereby set off and established as a Market Square in said third ward, to be under the control of the Aldermen of said ward, and to be kept and regulated for the public use, and hereafter to be called and known by and under the name of Third Ward Market Square.

SEC. 3. For the purpose of purchasing and improving said Market Square, the Aldermen of said ward are hereby authorized, for and in the name of said ward, to issue bonds not exceeding in amount the sum of fifty thousand dollars, on such terms, for such time, and drawing such interest, as to them shall seem advisable, but to be issued in accordance with and within the restrictions imposed by said act of the Legislature. Bonds issued

SEC. 4. The Aldermen of said ward shall cause an accurate survey and profile or map of said Market Square to be made by the City Surveyor, and filed in his office, and before proceeding to improve the same, they shall cause a plan and specifications of such improvement to be drawn, and a copy thereof deposited in the office of the City Comptroller. Plan and profile to be made.

SEC. 5. All the proceedings of said Aldermen, under this ordinance, and said act of the Legislature, shall be entered at length in the records of said ward, and they shall make out a certified list of all the bonds so issued, specifying the amount, the rate of interest they draw, and the time when the interest and principal thereon becomes due, which shall be filed with the City Comptroller, and entered on record in his office. Proceedings recorded.

SEC. 6. This ordinance shall not be in force until submitted to the legal voters of the third ward of the City of Milwaukee, at an election to be held for that purpose, at the time hereinafter provided, and adopted by a majority of the whole number of votes given at such election.

SEC. 7. An election shall be held on Saturday, October 4th, A. D. 1856, between the hours of two and seven o'clock, in the afternoon of said day, at the usual place in said ward for holding elections, for the purpose of the adoption or rejection of this ordinance, and such election shall be conducted, and the votes canvassed and returned, in the same manner and by the same officers as at other city elections. Election held.

SEC. 8. On the ballots which shall be received by the inspectors at said election, shall be either written or printed the words, "For the Market Square," or the words "Against the Market Square."

Proclamation of Mayor.

SEC. 9. At the next regular or special meeting of the Common Council, after the returns of the election from said ward are made to the City Clerk, the Common Council shall proceed to canvass said returns, and if it is found that a majority of all the votes taken are in favor of said Market Square, it shall be the duty of the Mayor to make proclamation thereof in the official papers of the city, and this ordinance shall be in force from and after its first publication, subsequent to the date of such proclamation.

Notice of election.

SEC. 10. It is hereby made the duty of the City Clerk to cause a certified copy of the petition, on file in his office, for this Market Square, together with a notice of the time and place of holding the election specified in this ordinance, to be published in the official papers of this city, three several times, one of which publications shall be made in each of said newspapers at least fifteen days previous to the time of holding said election.

Passed, September 13, 1856.

ORDINANCES

PROVIDING FOR ISSUING BONDS TO AID RAIL ROADS, AND FOR OTHER PURPOSES.

AN ORDINANCE

To aid in the construction of a Rail Road from Milwaukee to the Mississippi River.

Be it ordained by the Mayor and Aldermen of the City of Milwaukee, in Common Council assembled :

Subscription of $100,000.

SECTION 1. That the Mayor be, and he is hereby authorized to subscribe, in behalf of this city, for stock in the Milwaukee and Waukesha Rail Road Company, to the amount of one hundred thousand dollars, on the terms and conditions hereinafter provided.

Tax levied.

SEC. 2. There shall be, and hereby is, levied and assessed annually, a tax on the real estate within the incorporated limits of this city, at the rate of one per centum on the assessed value of such property, to be called the Rail Road Tax.

SEC. 3. The payment on the stock subscribed shall be made to said company so fast, and only so fast, as money shall be received into the City Treasury from the proceeds of said tax.

SEC. 4. The City Treasurer is hereby authorized and required to pay such proceeds, from time to time, to the proper officer of the company, and for each one hundred dollars so paid, he shall take a separate assignable certificate for one share of stock.

Rail road tax receipt, form of.

SEC. 5. Upon the payment of any Rail Road Tax, the Treasurer shall deliver to the person making the payment, a receipt in the following form, to wit:

MILWAUKEE CITY RAIL ROAD TAX RECEIPT.

$............... No............

Received, Milwaukee,............................184.....of..............................
the sum of...............................and 100 Dollars, in full for the Rail Road Tax for the year eighteen hundred and..........................on the following named real estate in the City of Milwaukee. Upon the surrender of these receipts to the Common Council, to the amonnt of one hundred dollars, the holder or assignee will be entitled to one share of stock in the Milwaukee and Waukesha Rail Road Company.

PART OF LOT.	NO. OF LOT.	NO. OF BLOCK.	NO. OF WARD.	AMOUNT OF TAX.

Receipts to be registered and numbered.

SEC. 6. All such receipts shall be regularly numbered and recorded in a book to be kept for that purpose by the Treasurer, such record to show, in separate columns, the date, numbers and amount of the receipt, and the name of the person to whom it was issued.

Right to use certain alleys.

SEC. 7. Full right and authority is hereby granted, on part of the city, to the said rail road company, to construct and maintain a rail road along the alley in blocks one hundred and fifty-four, one hundred and fifty-three, and one hundred and fifty-two, in the fourth ward, and thence westwardly on such line as has been, or may hereafter be, located and determined upon by said company.

Proviso as to city subscription.

SEC. 8. The subscription, hereby authorized, shall not be binding on the city, until the amount of capital stock in said company, subscribed by individuals, shall be equal to two hundred thousand dollars, and the subscription, on the part of the city, shall not be called in or paid faster than individual subscriptions, and ten per cent. thereon actually paid.

Passed, July 19, 1849.

AN ORDINANCE

To provide for the payment of the installments coming due on the stock subscribed by the City of Milwaukee, in the Milwaukee and Mississippi Rail Road Company.

Whereas, the people of the State of Wisconsin, represented in Senate and Assembly, did, by an act, approved March 12, 1849, authorize the Common Council of the City of Milwaukee to subscribe, in behalf of said city, to the capital stock of the Milwaukee and Waukesha Rail Road Company, incorporated February 11th, 1847, to the amount of one hundred thousand dollars and upwards, and to borrow, on the faith of said city, such sum or sums as may be necessary in order to provide for the payment of the stock so subscribed, and, whereas, the said Common Council did, by an ordinance, passed July 19, 1849, authorize the Mayor to subscribe, in behalf of the city, for stock in said rail road company, to the amount of one hundred thousand dollars, by virtue whereof, the Mayor did subscribe for said stock, in behalf of the city, and, whereas, there is unpaid, and to become due, on said stock, the sum of eighty-four thousand dollars, therefore,

Be it ordained by the Mayor and Aldermen of the City of Milwaukee, in Common Council assembled :

Bonds to amount of $84,000 issued by city.

Section 1. That bonds be issued, on the faith of the city, by the Mayor and Clerk, to the amount of eighty-four thousand dollars, in such sums as will be desired by the Directors of the Milwaukee and Mississippi Rail Road Company, not exceeding, in the aggregate, the whole amount of the installments to become due on the stock subscribed by the city in said rail road company.

Sec. 2. Said bonds shall be payable ten years from their date, and the interest on them shall be payable annually at a rate not exceeding ten per cent. per annum.

M. & M. R. R. Co., guarantee the interest on the bonds.

SEC. 3. The offer of the Milwaukee and Mississippi Rail Road Company to assume and guarantee the payment of the interest on the bonds so issued, is hereby accepted, and the City of Milwaukee does hereby relinquish the dividends and profits that may accrue on the stock given in exchange for such bonds, so long as the interest on such bonds shall be paid by said company, or until said bonds become due and payable.

SEC. 4. The bonds issued by virtue of this ordinance, shall not be delivered to the rail road company until said company shall have given security to the city for the punctual payment of the interest on said bonds, and after said security shall have been accepted by the Common Council.

Passed, May 18, 1850.

AN ORDINANCE

To grant further aid in the construction of the Milwaukee and Mississippi Rail Road.

Be it ordained by the Mayor and Aldermen of the City of Milwaukee, in Common Council assembled:

Additional subscription of $150,000 in M. & M. R. R. Co.

SECTION 1. That the Mayor be, and he is hereby authorized to subscribe in behalf of the city, for stock in the Milwaukee and Mississippi Rail Road Company, in pursuance of the act of the Legislature, passed, March 12th, 1849, to the amount of one hundred and fifty thousand dollars, in addition to the subscription of one hundred thousand dollars, made in pursuance of an ordinance to aid in the construction of a rail road from Milwaukee to the Mississippi river, passed, July 19th, 1849, the same being (in the opinion of the Common Council) required by the interests of the City of Milwaukee.

Bonds authorized.

SEC. 2. In order to provide for the payment of the installments on the stock subscribed as aforesaid, a loan is hereby authorized to be made, on the faith of the city, for a sum of money not exceeding, in the aggregate, the whole amount of the installments to become due on such stock, and for the purpose of effecting such loan, and to secure the payment of the same, the bonds of the city shall be issued, by the Mayor and Clerk, to the amount of one hundred and fifty thousand dollars, in addition to bonds heretofore authorized to be issued for a loan with which to pay the former subscription of the city to the stock of said company, and said bonds hereby authorized, to be in sums of one thousand dollars each, payable ten years from the first day of July, 1850, with interest at the rate of ten per centum per annum, payable semi-annually in the City of New York, for which purpose coupons to be attached to said bonds.

Company guarantees payment of the interest on bonds.

SEC. 3. The proposition of the Milwaukee and Mississippi Rail Road Company, to assume and guarantee the payment of the interest on the bonds so issued, is hereby accepted, and the City of Milwaukee does hereby relinquish the dividends and profits that may accrue on the stock given in exchange for such bonds, so long as the interest on the said bonds shall be paid by said company, or until said bonds become due and payable, provided that such acceptance be on the condition, that said company shall furnish securities, satisfactory to the Common Council, for the said payment of interest, and also for the ultimate purchase of the stock to be issued to the city on such subscription, agreeably to the proposition of said company, this 17th day of June, 1850, submitted in the event that the city authorities should decide to sell the same at any time within ten years from the first day of July, 1850, and demand payment for the same of said company.

Former ordinance amended.

SEC. 4. The second section of the ordinance authorizing the issue of eighty-four thousand dollars of city bonds, in part of the former subscription of stock, passed, May 18th, 1850, be so amended that said bonds be issued uniformly with those authorized by this ordinance, viz : said bonds to be payable in ten years from the 1st day of July, 1850, with interest at the rate of ten per centum per annum, payable semi-annually in the City of New York, for which purpose coupons to be attached to said bonds, and the bonds heretofore executed in pursuance of the said ordinance, to be cancelled.

AN ORDINANCE

Authorizing an issue of City Bonds to the Green Bay, Milwaukee and Chicago Rail Road Company.

The Mayor and Common Council of the City of Milwaukee, do ordain as follows :

Authorizing an issue of bonds to the G. B., M. & Chicago R. R. Co.

SECTION 1. For the purpose of aiding in the construction of the Green Bay, Milwaukee and Chicago Rail Road, city bonds, to an amount not exceeding two hundred thousand dollars, may be issued and delivered to the Green Bay, Milwaukee and Chicago Rail Road Company, on the terms and conditions specified in "an act authorizing the City of Milwaukee to loan its credit in aid of certain rail roads," approved, April 2d, 1853, and on terms and conditions hereinafter provided.

Bonds to be made payable at Union Bank, City of New York.

SEC. 2. Every bond, issued under the authority contained in the preceding section, shall be made payable in twenty years from the date thereof, with interest, payable semi-annually, at the rate of seven per cent. per annum, and both principal and interest payable at the Union Bank of the City of New York, shall be signed by the Mayor and countersigned by the Clerk of the Common Council, under the corporate seal of the city.

Provisions to be complied with before issue of bond.

SEC. 3. No bonds shall be issued to said rail road company until all the provisions relating to the bonds and securities to be given and furnished to said city, as provided in the third, fourth, fifth and sixth sections of an act authorizing the City of Milwaukee to loan its credit in aid of certain rail roads, are fully complied with on the part of said company.

SEC. 4. This ordinance shall not be in force until submitted to the legal voters of the City of Milwaukee, at an election held for that purpose at the time hereinafter provided, and adopted by a majority of the whole number of votes given at such election. Adoption to be submitted to the legal voters of the city.

SEC. 5. An election shall be held on Tuesday, the seventeenth day of May, A. D. 1853, between the hours of two and six o'clock in the afternoon of said day, at the places in the several wards of the city where the last elections were held, for the purpose of the adoption or rejection of this ordinance, and such election shall be conducted, and the votes canvassed and returned in the same manner and by the same officers as at other city elections.

SEC. 6. On the ballots which shall be received by the inspectors of such elections, shall be either written or printed, the words, "For the Rail Road Ordinance," or the words, "Against the Rail Road Ordinance." Form of ballots.

SEC. 7. At the next meeting of the Common Council after the returns of such election from the several wards in the city are made to the City Clerk, the Common Council shall proceed to canvass such returns, and if it is found that a majority of the whole votes taken are in favor of this ordinance, it shall be the duty of the Mayor to make proclamation thereof in the official papers of the city, and the said ordinance shall be in force from and after its first publication, subsequent to the date of such proclamation. Vote to be canvassed.

SEC. 8. It is hereby made the duty of the City Clerk to cause a certified copy of this ordinance, together with a notice of the time and place of holding the election specified therein, to be published in all the city papers three several times, one of which publications shall be made in each of Notice to be given of election.

said newspapers at least two weeks previous to the time of holding such election.

Passed, April 30, 1853. Proclamation of the adoption by the legal voters, made May 19, 1853.

AN ORDINANCE

Authorizing an issue of City Bonds to the Milwaukee and Fond du Lac Rail Road Company.

The Mayor and Common Council of the City of Milwaukee, do ordain as follows :

City Bonds may be issued to M. & Fond du Lac R. R. Co.

SECTION 1. For the purpose of aiding in the construction of the Milwaukee and Fond du Lac Rail Road, city bonds to an amount not exceeding the sum of two hundred thousand dollars, may be issued and delivered to the Milwaukee and Fond du Lac Rail Road Company, on the terms and conditions specified in " an act authorizing the City of Milwaukee to loan its credit in aid of certain rail roads," approved, April 2d, 1853, and on the terms and conditions hereinafter provided.

Where payable.

SEC. 2. Every bond issued under the authority contained in the preceding section, shall be made payable in twenty years from the date thereof, with interest payable semi-annually, at the rate of seven per cent. per annum, and both principal and interest payable at the Union Bank of New York, in the City of New York, shall be signed by the Mayor and countersigned by the Clerk of the Common Council, under the corporate seal of the city.

Provisions to be complied with before issue of bonds.

SEC. 3. No bonds shall be issued to said rail road company until all the provisions relating to the bonds and securities to be given and furnished to said city, as provided in the 3d, 4th, 5th and 6th sections of an act authorizing the City of Milwaukee to loan its credit in aid of certain rail roads, are fully complied with on the part of said company.

SEC. 4. This ordinance shall not be in force until submitted to the legal voters of the City of Milwaukee, at an election held for that purpose at the time hereinafter provided, and adopted by a majority of the whole number of votes given at such election.

Adoption to be submitted to the legal voters of the city.

SEC. 5. An election shall be held on Tuesday, the seventh day of June, A. D. 1853, between the hours of two and six o'clock in the afternoon of said day, at the places in the several wards of the city where the last elections were held, for the purpose of the adoption or rejection of this ordinance, and such election shall be conducted, and the votes canvassed and returned, in the same manner and by the same officers as at other elections.

Time of holding election.

SEC. 6. On the ballots which shall be received by the inspectors of such election shall be either written or printed, the words, "For the Rail Road Ordinance," or the words, "Against the Rail Road Ordinance."

Form of ballots.

SEC. 7. At the next meeting of the Common Council, after the returns of such election from the several wards in the city are made to the City Clerk, the Common Council shall proceed to canvass such returns, and if it is found that a majority of the whole votes taken are in favor of this ordinance, it shall be the duty of the Mayor to make proclamation thereof in the official paper of the city, and the said ordinance shall be in force from and after its first publication, subsequent to the date of such proclamation.

Common Council to canvass votes.

SEC. 8. It is hereby made the duty of the City Clerk to cause a certified copy of the ordinance, together with a notice of the time and places of holding the election specified therein, to be published three several times in all the daily papers of the city, one of which publications shall be in each of said newspapers, at least two weeks previous to the time of holding such election.

Notice of election to be published.

Passed May 19th, 1853.

AN ORDINANCE

Authorizing an issue of City Bonds to the La Crosse and Milwaukee Rail Road Company.

The Mayor and Common Council of the City of Milwaukee, do ordain as follows:

City bonds may be issued to the La Crosse & M. R. R. Co.

SECTION 1. For the purpose of aiding in the construction of the La Crosse and Milwaukee Rail Road, city bonds, to an amount not exceeding two hundred thousand dollars, may be issued and delivered to the La Crosse and Milwaukee Rail Road Company, on the terms and conditions specified in "an act authorizing the City of Milwaukee to loan its credit in aid of certain rail roads," approved, April 2d, 1853, and on the terms and conditions hereinafter provided.

When and where payable.

SEC. 2. Every bond, issued under authority contained in the preceding section, shall be made payable in twenty years from the date thereof, with interest, payable semi-annually, at the rate of seven per cent. per annum, and both principal and interest payable at the Union Bank of New York, shall be signed by the Mayor and countersigned by the Clerk of the Common Council, under the corporate seal of the city.

Provisions to be complied with before issue of bonds.

SEC. 3. No bonds shall be issued to said rail road company until all the provisions relating to the bonds and securities to be given and furnished to said city, as provided in the third, fourth, fifth and sixth sections of an act authorizing the City of Milwaukee to loan its credit in aid of certain rail roads, are fully complied with on the part of said company.

Adoption to be submitted to the legal voters of the city.

SEC. 4. This ordinance shall not be in force until submitted to the legal voters of the City of Milwaukee, at an election held for that purpose at the time hereinafter provided, and adopted by a majority of the whole number of votes given at such election.

SEC. 5. An election shall be held on Thursday, the 23d day of June, 1853, between the hours of two and six o'clock in the afternoon of said day, at the places in the several wards of the city where the last elections were held, for the purpose of the adoption or rejection of this ordinance, and such election shall be conducted, and the votes canvassed in the same manner and by the same officers as at other city elections. When an election is to be held.

SEC. 6. On the ballots which shall be received by the inspectors of such elections, shall be either written or printed, the words, "For the Rail Road Ordinance," or the words, "Against the Rail Road Ordinance." Form of ballots.

SEC. 7. At the next meeting of the Common Council, after the returns of such election from the several wards in the city are made to the City Clerk, the Common Council shall proceed to canvass such returns, and if it is found that a majority of the whole number of votes taken are in favor of this ordinance, it shall be the duty of the Mayor to make proclamation thereof in the official papers of the city, and the said ordinance shall be in force from and after its first publication, subsequent to the date of such proclamation. Common Council to canvass votes.

SEC. 8. It is hereby made the duty of the City Clerk to cause a certified copy of this ordinance, together with a notice of the time and places of holding the election specified therein, to be published three several times in all the daily papers in the city, one of which publications shall be in the official newspapers at least two weeks previous to the time of holding such election. Notice of election to be published

Passed, June 2, 1853. Proclamation of the adoption by the legal voters, made June 23, 1853.

AN ORDINANCE

To authorize an issue of City Bonds to the Milwaukee, Fond du Lac and Green Bay Rail Road Company.

The Mayor and Common Council of the City of Milwaukee, do ordain as follows:

Authorizing an issue of bonds to M. F. du L. & G. B. R. R. Co.

SECTION 1. The Mayor of the City and the Clerk of this Board, are hereby authorized to execute and deliver to the Milwaukee, Fond du Lac and Green Bay Rail Road Company, city bonds to an amount not exceeding two hundred thousand dollars, in the manner and upon the conditions hereinafter mentioned.

Bonds to be issued in pursuance of law.

SEC. 2. Every bond issued shall be made and executed in pursuance of the provisions of section two of an ordinance entitled, "an ordinance authorizing an issue of city bonds to the Milwaukee and Fond du Lac Rail Road Company," passed, May 19th, 1853, and approved by a majority of the votes taken at an election held in the several wards of the city on the 7th day of June, in the year eighteen hundred and fifty-three.

Bonds may be issued at any time on certain conditions.

SEC. 3. Such bonds may be issued, from time to time, in amounts proportioned to the whole quantity of rail road iron to be sold and delivered to the City of Milwaukee, in the manner provided in a certain bond executed to the Treasurer of said city, on the first day of September, A. D. 1853, by the President and Secretary of said rail road company, in behalf of said company, and by the Directors thereof, and when the receipt of the City Comptroller therefor is presented and filed with the Clerk of this Board.

Passed, September 2, 1853.

AN ORDINANCE

To authorize an issue of City Bonds to the Milwaukee and Watertown Rail Road Company.

The Mayor and Common Council of the City of Milwaukee, do ordain as follows :

SECTION 1. The Mayor of the City, and the Clerk of this Board, are hereby authorized to execute and deliver to the Milwaukee & Watertown Rail Road Company, city bonds, to an amount not exceeding seventy-five thousand dollars, in the manner and upon the conditions hereinafter mentioned, said bonds to be used in the completion and equipment of the rail road now being constructed by said company from Milwaukee to Watertown, as mentioned in the proviso to "An ordinance authorizing an issue of city bonds to said Rail Road Company," passed, Oct. 6th, 1853.

Authority to issue bonds to the M. & W. R. R. Co.

SEC. 2. Every bond issued shall be made and executed in pursuance of the provisions of section two of "An ordinance authorizing an issue of city bonds to the Milwaukee & Watertown Rail Road Company" and approved by a majority of votes taken on an election held in the several wards of the City on the 24th of October, A. D. 1853.

Bonds to be issued according to law.

SEC. 3. Such bonds may be delivered by the Mayor and Clerk of this Board at any time after the securities from said rail road company, for the payment of the principal and interest on said bonds, shall have been submitted to and approved and accepted by this Board.

Bonds may be delivered upon certain conditions.

Passed, January 26, 1854.

AN ORDINANCE

To authorize the issue of City Bonds to the Green Bay, Milwaukee and Chicago Rail Road Company.

The Mayor and Common Council of the City of Milwaukee, do ordain as follows :

SECTION 1. The Mayor of the City and the Clerk of this Board, are hereby authorized to execute and deliver to the

Authority to issue bonds to the

G. B., M. & C. R. R. Co. Green Bay, Milwaukee and Chicago Rail Road Company, city bonds (at this time) to an amount not exceeding one hundred thousand dollars, in the manner and upon the conditions hereinafter mentioned. Said bonds to be issued in the completion and improvement of the rail road now being constructed by said company from the Illinois state line, and mentioned in the proviso to "An ordinance authorizing an issue of city bonds to said rail road company," passed April 30, 1853.

Bonds to be issued according to law. SEC. 2. Every bond issued shall be made and executed in pursuance of the provision of section two of "An ordinance authorizing an issue of city bonds to the Green Bay, Milwaukee and Chicago Rail Road Company," and approved by a majority of votes taken on an election held in the several wards in the city, on the 17th day of May, A. D. 1853.

Bonds may be delivered upon certain condiiions. SEC. 3. Such bonds may be delivered by the Mayor and Clerk of this Board at any time after the securities from said rail road company, for the payment of the principal and interest on said bonds, (executed in accordance with the requirements of the report of the special committee submitted and approved February 11th, 1854,) shall have been approved by a vote of the Common Council.

Passed, February 11, 1854.

AN ORDINANCE

To authorize an issue of City Bonds to the La Crosse and Milwaukee Rail Road Company.

The Mayor and Common Council of the City of Milwaukee, do ordain as follows:

Authority to issue bonds to the La C. & M. R.R. Co. SECTION 1. The Mayor of the City, and the Clerk of the Board, are hereby authorized to execute and deliver to the La Crosse and Milwaukee Rail Road, city bonds, to an amount not exceeding two hundred thousand dollars, in the manner and upon the conditions hereinafter mentioned, such bonds, or the proceeds thereof, to be used in the completion and equipment of the rail road now being constructed by said company, from the City of Milwaukee to the Town of La Crosse, in the State of Wisconsin.

SEC. 2. Every bond issued shall be made and executed in pursuance of the provisions of section two, of an ordinance authorizing an issue of city bonds to the La Crosse and Milwaukee Rail Road Company, and approved by a majority of the votes taken at an election held in the several wards of the city, on the 23d day of June, A. D. 1853.

Bonds to be issued according to law.

SEC. 3. Such bonds may be delivered by the Mayor and Clerk in amounts less, and not in the whole exceeding the sum herein authorized to be issued, at any time after the securities from said rail road company, for the payment of the principal and interest to accrue on said city bonds, shall have been first submitted to, approved and accepted by the Common Council.

Bonds may be delivered upon certain conditions.

Passed, February 11, 1854.

AN ORDINANCE

To amend an Ordinance to authorize an issue of City Bonds to the La Crosse and Milwaukee Rail Road Company, passed, June 2d, 1853.

The Mayor and Common Council of the City of Milwaukee, do ordain as follows.

SECTION 1. Section two of an ordinance, entitled, "an ordinance, to authorize an issue of city bonds to the La Crosse and Milwaukee Rail Road Company," passed, June 2d, 1853, is hereby amended, so as to authorize the Mayor and Clerk of the Common Council to make the principal and interest on all bonds issued to said rail road company, in pur-

Bonds made payable at the office of Duncan, Sherman & Co.

suance of said ordinance, payable at the office of Duncan, Sherman & Co., in the City of New York, instead of the Union Bank, in said City of New York.

Passed, February 16, 1854.

AN ORDINANCE

To amend an Ordinance to authorize an issue of City Bonds to the Milwaukee, Fond du Lac and Green Bay Rail Road Company, passed September 2d, 1853.

The Mayor and Common Council of the City of Milwaukee, do ordain as follows:

Bonds made payable at the office of Duncan, Sherman & Co.

SECTION 1. Section two of an ordinance, entitled "An ordinance to authorize an issue of city bonds to the Milwaukee, Fond du Lac and Green Bay Rail Road Company," passed September 2d, 1853, is hereby amended so as to authorize the Mayor and Clerk of the Common Council to make the principal and interest on all bonds issued to said rail road company, in pursuance of said ordinance, payable at the office of Duncan, Sherman and Company, in the City of New York, instead of the Union Bank, in said City of New York.

Passed, October 20, 1853.

AN ORDINANCE

Authorizing an issue of City Bonds to the Milwaukee and Watertown Rail Road Company.

The Mayor and Common Council of the City of Milwaukee, do ordain as follows:

Authortty to issue bonds to the M. & W. R. R. Co.

SECTION 1. For the purpose of aiding in the construction of the Milwaukee and Watertown Rail Road, city bonds may be issued and delivered to the Milwaukee and Watertown Rail Road Company to an amount not exceeding two hundred thousand dollars, on the terms and conditions specified in "an act authorizing the City of Milwaukee to loan its credit in aid of certain rail roads," approved April 2, 1853, and on the terms and conditions hereinafter mentioned, provided, that not more than seventy-five thousand dollars shall be issued to said company, to be used in the completion and equipment of the road from the City of Milwaukee to the City of Watertown, and the balance when necessary to be used in the construction and completion of said road between Watertown and Portage City, and beyond that point.

SEC. 2. Every bond issued under the authority contained in the preceding section, shall be made payable in twenty years from the date thereof, with interest, payable semi-annually, at the rate of seven per cent., and both principal and interest payable at the Union Bank of New York, in the City of New York; shall be signed by the Mayor, and countersigned by the Clerk of the Common Council, under the corporate seal of the city. Bonds, made payable at.

SEC. 3. No bonds shall be issued to the said rail road company until all the provisions relating to the bonds and securities, to be given and furnished to said city, as provided in the 3d, 4th, 5th and 6th sections of "an act authorizing the City of Milwaukee to loan its credit in aid of certain rail roads," are fully complied with on the part of said company. Bonds to be issued according to law.

SEC. 4. This ordinance shall not be in force until submitted to the legal voters of the City of Milwaukee, at an election held for that purpose at the time hereinafter provided, and adopted by a majority of the whole number of votes given at such election. Adoption to be submitted to the legal voters of the city.

SEC. 5. An election shall be held on Monday, the twenty-fourth day of October, 1853, between the hours of one and five o'clock in the afternoon of said day, at the places in the several wards where the last elections were held, or at such other places as may be provided by the Aldermen of the several wards, for the purpose of the adoption or rejection of Time of holding an election.

this ordinance, and such election shall be conducted, and the votes canvassed and returned in the same manner and by the same officers as other city elections.

Form of ballots.

SEC. 6. On the ballots which shall be received by the inspectors of such election, shall be either written or printed, the words, "For the Rail Road Ordinance," or the words, "Against the Rail Road Ordinance."

Common Council to canvass returns.

SEC. 7. At the next meeting of the Common Council, after the returns of such election from the several wards are made to the City Clerk, the Common Council shall proceed to canvass such returns, and if it is found that a majority of the whole votes taken are in favor of this ordinance, it shall be the duty of the Mayor to make proclamation thereof in the official papers of the city, and the said ordinance shall be in force from and after its first publication, subsequent to the date of such proclamation.

Passed, October 6, 1853. Proclamation of the adoption by the legal voters, made November 4, 1853.

AN ORDINANCE

To provide for opening the Harbor at the Straight Cut.

The Mayor and Common Council of the City of Milwaukee, do ordain as follows:

Bonds to be issued for opening the Harbor at the Straight Cut.

SECTION 1. For the purpose of providing funds to construct the Harbor, at the Straight Cut, it shall be the duty of the Mayor, and he is hereby authorized and empowered, to issue coupon bonds, (attested by the Clerk of this Board, under the seal of the city,) in the name of the City of Milwaukee, to the amount of fifty thousand dollars, payable in twenty years from the first day of July, 1854, with interest at the rate of seven per cent. per annum, payable semi-annually, at some bank or other place to be designated, in the City of New York, and the faith of the city is hereby irrevocably pledged for the payment of the interest punctually on said bonds, when due, and also for the payment of the principal of said bonds at maturity.

SEC. 2. A committee of three members of this Board shall be appointed, to be called the Harbor Committee, whose duty it shall be to proceed immediately with the City Surveyor and make such further surveys as they may deem necessary to exhibit fully the amount of work to be done at said Straight Cut, and make out a plan and specifications of said work, and report the same to this Board, on Thursday, the 23d day of the present month. Committee and Surveyor to make plans and specifications.

SEC. 3. It shall be the duty of the Harbor Committee to advertise immediately for proposals for the performance of the work of opening the Harbor at the Straight Cut, agreeably to the plan and specifications, which shall have been adopted by the Common Council, and submit all bids received for that purpose to this Board, on Thursday, the sixth day of April next, for the purpose of letting and contracting for the performance of said work. Duty of Committee.

Passed, March 18, 1854.

AN ORDINANCE

To authorize the issue of Bonds for Dredging the Milwaukee River, and to make said issue in common with the issue of Bonds for the construction of the Harbor.

The Mayor and Common Council of the City of Milwaukee, do ordain as follows :

SECTION 1. It is hereby made the duty of the Mayor to issue coupon bonds, in the corporate name of the City of Milwaukee, in pursuance of the authority for such purpose, granted by an act of the Legislature of the State of Wisconsin, entitled, "an act to amend an act entitled an act to consolidate and amend the act to incorporate the City of Mil- Mayor to issue bonds for dredging Milwaukee River.

waukee, and the several acts amendatory thereof," to the amount of fifty thousand dollars, payable in twenty years from the first day of July, in the present year, (1854), with interest at the rate of seven per centum per annum, payable semi-annually, and both principal and interest to be made payable at such place in the City of New York, as he may deem expedient; and the faith of the City of Milwaukee is hereby irrevocably pledged to pay the said principal and interest, when due, agreeably to the conditions of said bonds, for which purpose a tax shall be levied annually in pursuance of the provisions contained in the third section of said act.

When payable.

Tax levied for payment of interest.

SEC. 2. The bonds authorized shall be issued in one series, with the bonds authorized to be issued by an ordinance entitled, "an ordinance to provide for opening the Harbor at the Straight Cut," passed on the 18th day of March, 1854, amounting, in the aggregate, to one hundred thousand dollars, for the purpose of Harbor and River Improvements.

Passed, May 18, 1854.

AN ORDINANCE

Authorizing an issue of City Bonds to the Milwaukee and Mississippi Rail Road Company.

The Mayor and Common Council of the City of Milwaukee, do ordain as follows:

For what purpose bonds issued

SECTION 1. For the purpose of aiding in the construction of a line of rail road from Janesville to the Mississippi river, at or near Dubuque, on or near the line lately adopted by the Southern Wisconsin Rail Road Company, the capital of which company is now consolidated with the capital stock of the Milwaukee and Mississippi Rail Road Company, by an agreement bearing date the 8th day of June instant, city bonds, to an amount not exceeding three hundred thousand dollars, may be issued and delivered to the Milwaukee and Mississippi Rail Road Company, (that being the name of the consolidated company), on the terms and conditions specified in "an act authorizing the City of Milwaukee to loan its credit in aid of certain rail roads," approved, April 2, 1853, and also an act, amendatory thereto, approved, March 31, 1854, and on the terms and conditions hereinafter provided.

When payable, rate of interest, &c.

SEC. 2. Every bond, issued under the authority contained in the preceding section, shall be made payable in twenty years from the date thereof, with interest, payable semi-annually, at the rate of seven per cent. per annum, and both principal and interest, payable at the Union Bank of the City of New York, shall be signed by the Mayor and countersigned by the Clerk of the Common Council, under the corporate seal of the city.

Conditions to be complied with before bonds and issues.

SEC. 3. No bonds shall be issued to said rail road company until all the provisions relating to the bonds and securities to be given and furnished to said city, as provided in the aforesaid acts, are fully complied with on the part of said company, or until such securities shall be furnished to said city, as shall be satisfactory to the Common Council thereof, nor shall they be issued until said company shall execute a good and sufficient or satisfactory bond to the said city, with the condition that the avails or proceeds of said bonds shall be faithfully applied in the construction of a rail road, from some point in the City of Janesville, to the Mississippi river, and in accordance with the terms of consolidation hereinafter referred to, and for no other purpose.

Ordinance to to be submitted to legal voters.

SEC. 4. This ordinance shall not be in force until submitted to the legal voters of the City of Milwaukee, at an election held for that purpose, at the time hereinafter provided, and adopted by a majority of the whole number of votes given at such election.

Time of holding election, &c. &c.

SEC. 5. An election shall be held on Thursday, the 6th day of July next, A. D. 1854, between the hours of two and six o'clock in the afternoon of said day, at the places in the several wards of the city, where the last elections were held, for the purpose of the adoption or rejection of this ordinance, and such election shall be conducted, and the votes canvassed and returned in the same manner, and by the same officers as at other city elections.

Form of ballots.

SEC. 6. On the ballots which shall be received by the inspectors of such election, shall be either written or printed, the words, "For the Rail Road Ordinance," or the words, "Against the Rail Road Ordinance."

Votes to be canvassed and proclamation to be made.

SEC. 7. At the next regular or special meeting of the Common Council, after the returns of such election from the several wards in the City of Milwaukee are made to the City Clerk, the Common Council shall proceed to canvass such returns, and if it is found that a majority of the whole votes taken are in favor of this ordinance, it shall be the duty of the Mayor to make proclamation thereof in the official paper or papers of the city, and the said ordinance shall be in force from and after its first publication, subsequent to the date of such proclamation.

Clerk to give notice of time and place of holding election.

SEC. 8. It is hereby made the duty of the City Clerk to cause a certified copy of this ordinance, together with a notice of the time and place of holding the election specified therein, to be published in the official city papers three several times, one of which publications shall be made in each of said newspapers, at least fifteen days previous to the time of holding such election.

Passed, June 15, 1854. Proclamation of the adoption by the legal voters, made July 14, 1854.

AN ORDINANCE

Authorizing an issue of City Bonds to the Milwaukee and Horicon Rail Road Company.

The Mayor and Common Council of the City of Milwaukee, do ordain as follows :

SECTION 1. For the purpose of aiding in the construction of the Milwaukee and Horicon Rail Road, city bonds, to an amount not exceeding the sum of one hundred and sixty-six thousand dollars, may be issued and delivered to the Milwaukee and Horicon Rail Road Company, on the terms and conditions specified in "an act authorizing the City of Milwaukee to loan its credit, in aid of certain rail roads," approved, April 2, 1853, and also an act, amendatory thereto, approved, March 31, 1854, and on the terms and conditions hereinafter provided.

Issue of city bonds to M. & H. R. R. Co.

SEC. 2. Every bond, issued under the authority contained in the preceding section, shall be made payable in twenty years from the date thereof, with interest, payable semi-annually, at the rate of seven per cent. per annum, and both principal and interest payable at the Bank of the Republic, in the City of New York, shall be signed by the Mayor and countersigned by the Clerk of the Common Council, under the corporate seal of the city.

When and where payable.

SEC. 3. No bonds shall be issued to said rail road company until all the provisions relating to the bonds and securities to be given and furnished to said city, as provided in the aforesaid acts, are fully complied with on the part of said company, or until such securities shall be furnished to said city as shall be satisfactory to the Common Council thereof.

No bonds to be issued until security be accepted.

SEC. 4. This ordinance shall not be in force until submitted to the legal voters of the City of Milwaukee, at an election held for that purpose, at the time hereinafter provid-

Ordinance to be submitted to legal voters.

ed, and adopted by a majority of the whole number of votes given at such election.

When and where elections to be held.

SEC. 5. An election shall be held on Monday, the 25th day of June, A. D. 1855, between the hours of two and six o'clock in the afternoon of said day, at the places in the several wards of the city where the last elections were held, except in the third ward, in which said election shall be held at the Engine House of Fire Company, No. 6, for the purpose of the adoption or rejection of this ordinance, and such election shall be conducted, and the votes canvassed and returned in the same manner, and by the same officers, as at other city elections.

Ballots to designate for or against R. R. ordinance.

SEC. 6. On the ballots which shall be received by the inspectors of such election, shall be either written or printed, the words, "For the Rail Road Ordinance," or the words, "Against the Rail Road Ordinance."

Returns, when and how to be canvassed.

SEC. 7. At the next regular or special meeting of the Common Council, after the returns of such election from the several wards in the City of Milwaukee are made to the City Clerk, the Common Council shall proceed to canvass such returns, and if it is found that a majority of the whole votes taken are in favor of this ordinance, it shall be the duty of the Mayor to make proclamation thereof in the official paper or papers of this city, and the said ordinance shall be in force from and after its first publication, subsequent to the date of such proclamation.

Proclamation to be made.

Ordinance, when to be in force.

Clerk to cause a certified copy of ordinance and notice of election to be given.

SEC. 8. It is hereby made the duty of the City Clerk to cause a certified copy of this ordinance, together with a notice of the time and place of holding the election specified therein, to be published in the official city papers three several times, one of which publications shall be made in each of said newspapers at least two weeks previous to the time of holding such election.

Passed, June 8, 1855. Proclamation of the adoption by the legal voters, made June 25, 1855.

AN ORDINANCE

To authorize an issue of City Bonds to the Milwaukee and Horicon Rail Road Company.

The Mayor and Common Council of the City of Milwaukee, do ordain as follows:

Section 1. The Mayor of the City, and Clerk of this Board, are hereby authorized to execute and deliver to the Milwaukee and Horicon Rail Road Company, city bonds, to an amount not exceeding one hundred and sixty-six thousand dollars, in the manner and upon the conditions hereinafter mentioned; said bonds to be used in the completion and equipment of the rail road, now being constructed by said company, from Horicon to Berlin, in this state, as mentioned in the provisions of an ordinance, authorizing an issue of city bonds to said rail road company, passed, June 8th, 1855, and adopted, by a vote of the people, on the 25th of June, 1855. **Mayor and City Clerk to issue city bonds to M. & H. R. R. Co**

Sec. 2. Such bonds may be delivered by the Mayor and Clerk of this Board at any time after the securities from said rail road company, for the payment of the principal and interest on said bonds, are executed, in accordance with the requirements of the conditions of the report of the special committee, submitted and approved, June 28, 1855. **Bonds to be delivered when securities are approved.**

Passed, June 28, 1855.

AN ORDINANCE

To authorize an issue of City Bonds to the Milwaukee and Mississippi Rail Road Company.

The Mayor and Common Council of the City of Milwaukee, do ordain as follows:

Section 1. The Mayor of the City, and the Clerk of this Board, are hereby authorized to execute and deliver to the **City bonds to be issued to M. & M. R. R. Co.**

Milwaukee and Mississippi Rail Road Company, city bonds to an amount not exceeding three hundred thousand dollars, in the manner and upon the conditions hereinafter mentioned, for the purpose of aiding in the construction of a line of rail road from Janesville to the Mississippi river, at or near Dubuque, on or near the line lately adopted by the Southern Wisconsin Rail Road Company; the capital stock of said Southern Wisconsin Rail Road Company having been consolidated with the capital stock of the Milwaukee and Mississipppi Rail Road Company, by an agreement, bearing date of the 8th day of June, 1854. The name of the consolidated company being the "Milwaukee and Mississippi Rail Road Company;" said bonds to be used in the construction of said rail road, from Janesville to the Mississippi river, as mentioned in the provisions of an ordinance authorizing an issue of city bonds to said rail road company, passed, June 15, 1854.

Sec. 2. Every bond, issued to said company, shall be made and executed in pursuance of the provisions of section two of "an ordinance authorizing an issue of city bonds to the "Milwaukee and Mississippi Rail Road Company," approved by a majority of the votes taken at an election held in the several wards of the city, on the 6th day of July, A. D. 1854.

Bonds to be issued by Mayor and Clerk, &c., when report of committee complied with.

Sec. 3. Such bonds may be delivered to said rail road company, by the Mayor and Clerk of this Board, at any time after the securities from said company, for the payment of the principal and interest on said bonds, shall have been executed by said company and delivered to the city, in accordance with the conditions and resolutions contained in the report of the committee, to whom the subject of issuing city bonds to said company was referred, which report and resolutions have been adopted by this Board.

Passed, October 9, 1855.

AN ORDINANCE

To authorize an issue of City Bonds to the Milwaukee and Watertown Rail Road Company.

The Mayor and Common Council of the City of Milwaukee, do ordain as follows:

SECTION 1. The Mayor of the City and Clerk of this Board are hereby authorized to execute and deliver to the Milwaukee and Watertown Rail Road Company, city bonds, to an amount not exceeding ninety-five thousand dollars, in the manner and upon the conditions hereinafter mentioned, said bonds to be used in the completion and equipment of the rail road now being constructed by said company from Watertown to Columbus, as mentioned in the proviso to an ordinance authorizing an issue of city bonds to said rail road company, passed, October 6, 1853.

Amount of bonds to be issued.

SEC. 2. Every bond issued shall be made and executed in pursuance of the provisions of section two of an ordinance authorizing an issue of city bonds to the Milwaukee and Watertown Rail Road Company, approved by a majority of votes taken at an election held in the several wards of the city, on the 24th day of October, A. D. 1853.

How bonds made.

SEC. 3. Such bonds may be delivered to said company, by the Mayor and Clerk of this Board, at any time after the securities from said rail road company, for the payment of the principal and interest on said bonds, shall have been executed by said company, and delivered to the city, in accordance with the conditions and resolutions, contained in the report of committee, to whom the subject of issuing city bonds to the Milwaukee and Watertown Rail Road Company was referred, which report and resolutions have been adopted by this Board.

When delivered.

Passed, January 26, 1856.

AN ORDINANCE

To authorize an issue of City Bonds to the Fox River Valley Rail Road Company.

The Mayor and Common Council of the City of Milwaukee, do ordain as follows:

Bonds to be issued.

SECTION 1. For the purpose of aiding in the construction of the Fox River Valley Rail Road, city bonds may be issued and delivered to the Fox River Valley Rail Road Company, to an amount not exceeding fifty thousand dollars, on the terms and conditions specified in "an act authorizing the City of Milwaukee to loan its credit in aid of certain rail roads," approved, April 2, 1853, and the subsequent amendatory acts thereof, and on the terms and conditions hereinafter mentioned: *Provided,* no such bonds shall be issued to said Fox River Valley Rail Road Company till said company shall have executed and delivered to the City of Milwaukee a good and sufficient bond, to be approved by the Common Council, conditioned that said company will connect the said Fox River Valley Rail Road with the Milwaukee and Beloit Rail Road, at or near Prattsburg or Muskego Center, in Waukesha County, and use the track of the said Milwaukee and Beloit Rail Road from the point of junction to the City of Milwaukee, on such fair and equitable terms as may be agreed upon by and between said companies, or in case the companies cannot agree, then upon such terms as may be determined by three disinterested and competent commissioners to be appointed by the Common Council, or in place of such a bond of the company, a copy of an agreement to connect, duly executed by said companies, may be filed with the City Clerk.

Security to be given.

Commissioners to be appointed.

When payable.

SEC. 2. Every bond, issued under the authority contained in the preceding section, shall be made payable in twenty years from the date thereof, with interest, payable semi-annually, at the rate of seven per cent. per annum, and both principal and interest payable at the Union Bank of New York, in the City of New York, and shall be signed by the Mayor and countersigned by the Clerk of the Common Council, under the corporate seal of the city.

SEC. 3. No bonds shall be issued to said rail road company until all the provisions, relating to the bonds and securities, to be given and furnished to the City of Milwaukee, as provided in the acts referred to in the first section of this ordinance, are fully complied with on the part of said company, nor until such securities shall be furnished, to said city, as shall be satisfactory to the Common Council. Provisions to be complied with.

SEC. 4. This ordinance shall not be in force until submitted to the legal voters of the City of Milwaukee, at an election held for that purpose, at the time hereinafter provided, and adopted by a majority of the whole number of votes given at such election. To be voted on.

SEC. 5. An election shall be held on Monday, the sixteenth day of June, 1856, between the hours of three and seven o'clock in the afternoon of that day, at the places in the several wards where the last election was held, for the purpose of the adoption or rejection of this ordinance, and such election shall be conducted, and the votes canvassed and returned in the same manner and by the same officers as other city elections. When election held.

SEC. 6. On the ballots which shall be received by the inspectors of such election, shall be written or printed, the words, "For the Rail Road Ordinance," or the words, "Against the Rail Road Ordinance." Ballots read.

SEC. 7. At the next meeting of the Common Council, after the returns of such election from the several wards are made to the City Clerk, the Common Council shall proceed to canvass such returns, and if it is found that a majority of the whole number of votes taken are in favor of this ordi- Council to canvass votes.

Mayor to make proclamation.

nance, it shall be the duty of the Mayor to make proclamation thereof in the official papers of the city, and this ordinance shall be in force from and after its first publication, subsequent to the date of such proclamation.

Passed, May 5, 1856.

AN ORDINANCE

To authorize an issue of City Bonds to the Milwaukee and Beloit Rail Road Company.

The Mayor and Common Council of the City of Milwaukee, do ordain as follows :

Bonds to Beloit R. R. Co.

SECTION 1. For the purpose of aiding in the construction of the Milwaukee and Beloit Rail Road, city bonds may be issued and delivered to the Milwaukee and Beloit Rail Road Company, to an amount not exceeding one hundred and fifty thousand dollars, on the terms and conditions specified in "an act authorizing the City of Milwaukee to loan its credit in aid of certain rail roads," approved, April 2d, 1853, and the subsequent amendatory acts thereof, and on the terms and conditions hereinafter mentioned : *Provided*, no such bonds shall be issued to said Milwaukee and Beloit Rail Road Company till said company shall have executed and delivered to the City of Milwaukee a good and sufficient bond, to be approved by the Common Council, conditioned that said company will allow the Fox River Valley Rail Road Company to connect the Fox River Valley Rail Road with the Milwaukee and Beloit Rail Road, at or near Prattsburg or Muskego Center, in Waukesha County, and use the track of the Milwaukee and Beloit Rail Road, from the point of junction to the City of Milwaukee, on such fair and equitable terms as may be agreed upon by and between said companies, or in case the companies cannot agree, then upon such terms as may be determined by three disinterested and

Company to execute bond.

competent commissioners, to be appointed by the Common Council ; or in place of such a bond of company, a copy of an agreement to connect, duly executed by said companies, may be filed with the City Clerk.

SEC. 2. Every bond, issued under the authority contained in the preceding section, shall be made payable in twenty years from the date thereof, with interest, payable semi-annually, at the rate of seven per cent. per annum, and both principal and interest payable at the Union Bank of New York, in the City of New York, and shall be signed by the Mayor and countersigned by the Clerk of the Common Council, under the corporate seal of the city.

Bonds, where payable.

SEC. 3. No bonds shall be issued to said rail road company until all the provisions relating to the bonds and securities, to be given and furnished to the City of Milwaukee, as provided in the acts referred to in the first section of this ordinance, are fully complied with on the part of said company, nor until such securities shall be furnished to said city, as shall be satisfactory to the Common Council.

Securities to be given before bonds issued.

SEC. 4. This ordinance shall not be in force until submitted to the legal voters of the City of Milwaukee, at an election held for that purpose at the time hereinafter provided, and adopted by a majority of the whole number of votes given at such election.

Election to be held.

SEC. 5. An election shall be held on Monday, the twenty-sixth day of May, 1856, between the hours of three and seven o'clock in the afternoon of that day, at the places in the several wards where the last election was held, for the purpose of the adoption or rejection of this ordinance, and such election shall be conducted, and the votes canvassed and returned, in the same manner and by the same officers as other city elections.

Election, when held.

SEC. 6. On the ballots which shall be received by the inspectors of such election shall be written or printed,

Ballots to read.

the words, "For the Rail Road Ordinance," or the words, "Against the Rail Road Ordinance."

Council to canvass votes.

SEC. 7. At the next meeting of the Common Council, after the returns of such election from the several wards are made to the City Clerk, the Common Council shall proceed to canvass such returns, and if it is found that a majority of the whole number of votes taken are in favor of this ordinance, it shall be the duty of the Mayor to make proclamation thereof in the official papers of the city, and this ordinance shall be in force from and after its first publication, subsequent to the date of such proclamation.

Passed, May 5, 1856.

AN ORDINANCE

To authorize the Mayor and City Clerk to sign and issue City Bonds to the Milwaukee and Watertown Rail Road Company.

The Mayor and Common Council of the City of Milwaukee, do ordain as follows :

Additional issue of city bonds to M. &W.R. R. Co.

SECTION 1. The Mayor and City Clerk are hereby authorized and empowered to sign and issue to the Milwaukee and Watertown Rail Road Company, city bonds, to an amount not exceeding thirty thousand dollars. This amount, added to the amount of city bonds heretofore issued to said company, will make an aggregate amount issued to said company of two hundred thousand dollars, the full amount authorized by law to be issued to said company.

S c. 2. The bonds authorized to be signed and issued to said company, by this ordinance, to be for the same length of time, and at the same rate of interest, and payable at the same place, and to be delivered to said company upon the same conditions as the bonds issued to said company under the provisions of an ordinance passed January 26, 1856.

Passed, May 26, 1856.

AN ORDINANCE

To authorize an issue of City Bonds to the Milwaukee and Superior Rail Road Company.

The Mayor and Common Council of the City of Milwaukee, do ordain as follows :

SECTION 1. For the purpose of aiding in the construction of the Milwaukee and Superior Rail Road, city bonds may be issued and delivered to the Milwaukee and Superior Rail Road Company, to an amount not exceeding one hundred thousand dollars, on the terms and conditions specified in "an act authorizing the City of Milwaukee to loan its credit in aid of certain rail roads," approved, April 2d, 1853, and the subsequent amendatory acts thereof, and on the terms and conditions hereinafter mentioned: *Provided*, the bonds issued to said company, or the proceeds thereof, shall be expended in the construction of that part of said rail road between the City of Milwaukee and the City of Sheboygan. **Bonds issued to M. & S. R. R. Co.**

SEC. 2. Every bond, issued under the authority contained in the preceding section, shall be made payable in twenty years from the date thereof, with interest, payable semi-annually, at the rate of seven per cent. per annum, and both principal and interest payable at the Union Bank of New York, in the City of New York, shall be signed by the Mayor and countersigned by the Clerk of the Common Council, under the corporate seal of the city. **Interest payable in New York.**

SEC. 3. No bonds shall be issued to said rail road company till all the provisions relating to the bonds and securities to be given and furnished to said city, as provided in the act entitled "an act authorizing the City of Milwaukee to loan its credit in aid of certain rail roads," are fully complied with on the part of said company, and to the satisfaction of the Common Council. **Security given to the city.**

Submitted to the voters. SEC. 4. This ordinance shall not be in force until submitted to the legal voters of the City of Milwaukee, at an election held for that purpose at the time hereinafter provided, and adopted by a majority of the whole number of votes cast at such election.

Time of election. SEC. 5. An election shall be held on Monday, the 4th day of August, 1856, between the hours of three and seven o'clock in the afternoon of that day, at the places in the several wards of the city where the last elections were held, for the purpose of the adoption or rejection of this ordinance, and such election shall be conducted, and the votes canvassed and returned in the same manner and by the same officers as other city elections.

SEC. 6. On the ballots which shall be received by the inspectors of such election, shall be either written or printed, the words, "For the Rail Road Ordinance," or the words, "Against the Rail Road Ordinance."

Votes canvassed. SEC. 7. At the next meeting of the Common Council, after the returns of such election from the several wards in the city are made to the City Clerk, the Common Council shall proceed to canvass such returns, and if it be found that a majority of the whole number of votes taken are in favor of this ordinance, it shall be the duty of the Mayor to make proclamation thereof in the official papers of the city, and this ordinance shall be in force from and after its first publication, subsequent to the date of such proclamation.

Passed, June 16, 1856.

AN ORDINANCE

To authorize an issue of City Bonds to the Fox River Valley Rail Road Company.

The Mayor and Common Council of the City of Milwaukee, do ordain as follows.

SECTION 1. For the purpose of aiding in the construction of the Fox River Valley Rail Road, city bonds may be issued and delivered to the Fox River Valley Rail Road Company, to an amount not exceeding thirty-four thousand dollars, on the terms and conditions specified in "an act authorizing the City of Milwaukee to loan its credit in aid of certain rail roads," approved April 2, 1853, and the subsequent amendatory acts thereof, and on the terms and conditions hereinafter mentioned: *Provided,* no such bonds shall be issued to said Fox River Valley Rail Road Company till said company shall have executed and delivered to the City of Milwaukee, a good and sufficient bond, to be approved by the Common Council, conditioned that said company will connect the said Fox River Valey Rail Road with the Milwauwaukee and Beloit Rail Road, at or near Prattsburg or Muskego Center, in Waukesha county, and use the track of the said Milwaukee and Beloit Rail Road, from the point of junction to the City of Milwaukee, on such fair and equitable terms as may be agreed upon by and between said companies; or, in case the companies cannot agree, then upon such terms as may by determined, by three disinterested and competent commissioners, to be appointed by the Common Council; or, in place of such a bond of the company, a copy of an agreement to connect, duly executed by said companies, may be filed with the City Clerk. Bonds issued to Fox R. V. R. R. Co.

SEC. 2. Every bond, issued under the authority contained in the preceding section, shall be made payable in twen- Interest payable in New York.

ty years from the date thereof, with interest, payable semi-annually, at the rate of seven per cent. per annum, and both principal and interest payable at the Union Bank of New York, in the City of New York, and shall be signed by the Mayor, and countersigned by the Clerk of the Common Council, under the corporate seal of the city.

Security to be given.

SEC. 3. No bonds shall be issued to said rail road company until all the provisions relating to the bonds and securities, to be given and furnished to the city of Milwaukee, as provided in the acts referred to in the first section of this ordinance are fully complied with on the part of said company, nor until such securities shall be furnished to said city, as shall be satisfactory to the Common Council.

Submitted to voters.

SEC. 4. This ordinance shall not be in force until submitted to the legal voters of the City of Milwaukee, at an election held for that purpose at the time hereinafter provided, and adopted by a majority of the whole number of votes given at such election.

Time of election.

SEC. 5. An election shall be held on Monday, the twenty-fifth day of August, 1856, between the hours of three and seven o'clock in the afternoon of that day, at the places in the several wards where the last election was held, for the purpose of the adoption or rejection of this ordinance, and such election shall be conducted, and the votes canvassed and returned in the same manner and by the same officers as other city elections.

SEC. 6. On the ballots which shall be received by the inspectors of such election, shall be written or printed, the words, "For the Rail Road Ordinance," or the words, "Against the Rail Road Ordinance."

Votes canvassed.

SEC. 7. At the next meeting of the Common Council, after the returns of such election from the several wards are made to the City Clerk, the Common Council shall proceed to canvass such returns, and if it is found that a majority of the whole number of votes taken are in favor of this ordinance, it shall be the duty of the Mayor to make proclamation thereof in the official papers of the city, and this ordinance shall be in force from and after its first publication, subsequent to the date of such proclamation.

Passed, June 16, 1856.

AN ORDINANCE

To authorize an issue of City Bonds to the Milwaukee and Beloit Rail Road Company.

The Mayor and Common Council of the City of Milwaukee, do ordain as follows:

Bonds issued to M. & B. R. R. Co.

SECTION 1. For the purpose of aiding in the construction of the Milwaukee and Beloit Rail Road, city bonds may be issued and delivered to the Milwaukee and Beloit Rail Road Company, to an amount not exceeding one hundred thousand dollars, on the terms and conditions specified in "an act authorizing the City of Milwaukee to loan its credit in aid of certain rail roads," approved, April 2, 1853, and the subsequent amendatory acts thereof, and on the terms and conditions hereinafter mentioned: *Provided*, no such bonds shall be issued to said Milwaukee and Beloit Rail Road Company till said company shall have executed and delivered to the City of Milwaukee a good and sufficient bond, to be approved by the Common Council, conditioned that said company will allow the Fox River Valley Rail Road Company to connect the Fox River Valley Rail Road with the Milwaukee and Beloit Rail Road, at or near Prattsburgh or Muskego Center, in Waukesha County, and use the track of the Milwaukee and Beloit Rail Road, from the point of junction to the City of Milwaukee, on such fair and equitable terms as may be agreed upon by and between said companies; or, in case the companies cannot agree, then upon such terms as may be determined by three disinterested and competent commissioners, to be appointed by the Common Council ; or, in place of such a bond of the company, a copy of an agreement to connect, duly executed by said companies, may be filed with the City Clerk.

Interest payable in New York.

SEC. 2. Every bond, issued under the authority contained in the preceding section, shall be made payable in twenty years from the date thereof, with interest, payable semi-annually, at the rate of seven per cent. per annum, and both principal and interest payable at the Union Bank of New York, in the City of New York, and shall be signed by the Mayor and countersigned by the Clerk of the Common Council, under the corporate seal of the city.

Security to be given.

SEC. 3. No bonds shall be issued to said rail road company until all the provisions relating to the bonds and securities to be given and furnished to the city of Milwaukee, as provided in the acts referred to in the first section of this ordinance are fully complied with on the part of said company, nor until such securities shall be furnished to said city, as shall be satisfactory to the Common Council.

Submitted to voters.

SEC. 4. This ordinance shall not be in force until submitted to the legal voters of the City of Milwaukee, at an election held for that purpose, at the time hereinafter provided, and adopted by a majority of the whole number of votes given at such election.

Time of election.

SEC. 5. An election shall be held on Monday, the 14th day of July, 1856, between the hours of three and seven o'clock in the afternoon of that day, at the places in the several wards where the last election was held, for the purpose of the adoption or rejection of this ordinance, and such election shall be conducted, and the votes canvassed and returned in the same manner, and by the same officers as other city elections.

SEC. 6. On the ballots which shall be received by the inspectors of such election, shall be written or printed, the words, "For the Rail Road Ordinance," or the words, "Against the Rail Road Ordinance."

SEC. 7. At the next meeting of the Common Council, after the returns of such election from the several wards are made to the City Clerk, the Common Council shall proceed to canvass such returns, and if it is found that a majority of the whole number of the votes taken are in favor of this ordinance, it shall be the duty of the Mayor to make proclamation thereof in the official papers of the city, and this ordinance shall be in force from and after its first publication, subsequent to the date of such proclamation. **Canvass o votes.**

Passed, June 16, 1856.

AN ORDINANCE

To authorize an issue of City Bonds to purchase grounds in the Second and Seventh Wards, for School purposes.

The Mayor and Common Council of the City of Milwaukee, do ordain as follows :

SECTION 1. The Mayor and City Clerk are hereby authorized and directed to sign and execute eighteen thousand dollars, in city bonds of one thousand dollars each, payable in ten years from the date thereof, at the office of Messrs. Duncan, Sherman & Co., in New York City, with interest, semi-annually, at the rate of seven per cent. per annum, payable at the same place. Said bonds to be issued for the purpose of paying for grounds purchased for school purposes, in the second and seventh wards. **Bonds issued for school house grounds in 2d and 7th wards.**

SEC. 2. The City Clerk is hereby authorized and directed to deliver twelve of the city bonds named in the first section of this ordinance, to Otis B. Hopkins, in full payment to him for lots 8 and 9, in block 68, in the seventh ward, taking his receipt for the same, and a good and sufficient deed of said lots to the city from him.

SEC. 3. The City Clerk is hereby authorized and directed to deliver six of the city bonds, named in the first section of this ordinance, to Jas. B. Cross, Mayor, and take his receipt for the same.

SEC. 4. The Mayor of the city is hereby authorized and directed to negotiate and sell the six bonds named in the third section of this ordinance, and place the proceeds thereof in the City Treasury, and pay to Kneeland and Lewis forty-five hundred dollars, from such proceeds, in full payment for lots 16 and 17, in block 197, in the second ward, on delivery to the city of a good and sufficient deed of said lots 16 and 17, by said Kneeland and Lewis.

Passed, August 1, 1856.

AN ORDINANCE

To authorize an issue of City Bonds to make Repairs and Additions to the several Common School Houses in the City of Milwaukee.

The Mayor and Common Council of the City of Milwaukee, do ordain as follows :

City bonds authorized.

SECTION 1. The Mayor and City Clerk are hereby authorized and directed to sign and execute twenty-five thousand dollars, in Milwaukee city bonds of one thousand dollars each, payable in ten years from the date thereof, at the office of Messrs. Duncan, Sherman & Co., in New York City, with interest, semi-annually, at the rate of seven per cent. per annum, payable at the same place. Said bonds to be issued for the purpose of making additions to, and repairing the several Common School Houses in the City of Milwaukee.

SEC. 2. The City Clerk is hereby authorized and directed to deliver the city bonds, named in the first section of this ordinance, to Jas. B. Cross, Mayor, and take his receipt for the same.

SEC. 3. The Mayor of the city is hereby authorized and directed to negotiate and sell the city bonds, named in this ordinance, and place the proceeds thereof in the City Treaury, to be paid out by the Treasurer on city orders for work done under the contracts for the additions and repairs to the several Common School Houses in the City of Milwaukee.

Mayor to negotiate the sale.

SEC. 4. The Mayor may, in his discretion, instead of selling at once the city bonds, to be issued under the provisions of this ordinance, hypothecate them in whole or in part, and raise the money necessary to continue and complete the work named in this ordinance, and thereafter sell the bonds to replace such money, at such time and place as he may deem for the best interest of the city.

Authorized to hypothecate them.

Passed, August 18, 1856.

AN ORDINANCE

To create a Sinking Fund for the redemption of the general City indebtedness.

The Mayor and Common Council of the City of Milwaukee, do ordain as follows :

SECTION 1. On the first Monday of October, of the present year, and hereafter on the first Monday of August in each year, it shall be the duty of the City Comptroller to report to the Common Council the total amount of the then general city indebtedness, over and above any floating debt that is to be paid out of the taxes of the current year, and not to include any bonds issued to rail road or other companies for the final payment of which the city has taken security.

Comptroller to report City indebtedness.

SEC. 2. For the purpose of creating a sinking fund for the ultimate redemption of the said general city indebtedness, upon receiving said report from the Comptroller, it shall be the duty of the Common Council, each year, to levy a gen-

Tax of five per cent. to be levied.

eral city tax upon all the property in said city, subject to taxation, at a rate sufficient to raise a sum equal to five per cent. of the then said general city indebtedness, said tax to be collected in the same manner as other city taxes are collected, and if for any reason the whole of said sum should not be collected, any deficiency each year may be made up by appropriating and drawing the same from any other portion of the general city fund.

Bonds to contain a sinking fund clause.

SEC. 3. All general city bonds hereafter issued, either to take up present out-standing city bonds, or for any other purpose of general city indebtedness, shall contain a clause reciting in substance, that the City of Milwaukee has, by ordinance, created a permanent sinking fund, of five per cent. annually, of all the city indebtedness, and that said bond is issued in accordance with, and to receive the benefit of such sinking fund. All such bonds hereafter issued to be numbered, commencing with No. one, and so on in numerical order according to the date of their issue. City bonds heretofore issued are not to receive the benefit of this sinking fund until they are exchanged for bonds issued under this ordinance.

SEC. 4. All bonds issued under this ordinance to be $1,000 bonds, to be made payable twenty years from date, with seven per cent. interest per annum, interest payable semi-annually, which, together with the principal when due, is to be made payable in the City of New York.

Drawn Nos. to be paid.

SEC. 5. On the first Monday of February, in each year, the Mayor, City Comptroller and City Clerk shall meet in the Common Council Room of said city, and place in a box or wheel, numbers corresponding to the numbers of all the city bonds issued under this ordinance, and which are then out-standing and unpaid, one of whom shall then, after said box or wheel is well shaken, draw by lot sufficient numbers corresponding to numbers on said bonds, so that the amount of bonds, having the drawn numbers on them, may be equal, as near as may be, to five per cent. of the city indebtedness, as set forth in the last preceding report of the City Comptroller. The City Clerk shall then publish for one week in the official papers of the city, and in the "Journal of Commerce," one of the commercial papers of the City of New York, a notice of the result of said drawing, and the time when said bonds, whose numbers were drawn, will be redeemed and paid at the place at which they are made payable in New York, and also a notice to the holders of said bonds, to present the same for payment, as they will cease to draw interest at the expiration of sixty days from the time it has been advertised they would be paid.

Result of drawing to be published.

SEC. 6. From and after sixty days from the time any bonds, with drawn numbers, have been advertised as payable in New York, the interest on the same shall terminate, but the money placed for the redemption of the same shall remain on deposit at interest, in the name of the City Treasurer, for the use and benefit of the city.

Interest to cease, when.

Passed, August 29, 1856.

ORDINANCES

PROVIDING FOR THE ORGANIZATION AND REGULATION OF THE POLICE, FOR IMPOSING FINES AND PENALTIES, AND FOR MISCELLANEOUS PURPOSES.

RULES & REGULATIONS

For the Government of the Police of the City of Milwaukee.

Policemen to report all violation of ordinances.

SECTION 1. The Policemen shall obey the orders of the Chief of the Police, and shall report to the Chief of the Police all violations of the City Ordinances, and all suspicious persons, bawdy houses, pawn-broker's shops, gambling houses, and all places where idlers, tipplers, gamblers, and other disorderly and suspicious persons congregate. And it shall also be their duty to caution strangers and others against going into such places, and against pick-pockets, watch-stuffers, droppers, mock auctioneers, and all other suspicious persons, to render assistance to officers of Justice, to direct strangers the nearest way to their places of destination, and, when necessary, to cause them to be accompanied by one of the Police.

Conduct of Policemen.

SEC. 2. Each and every member of the Police, in his conduct and deportment, must be quiet, civil and orderly. In the performance of his duty he must maintain decorum and attention, command of temper, patience and discretion. He must at all times refrain from harsh, violent, coarse, profane or insolent language, and act with firmness and energy.

Penalty for intoxication and indecent condu

SEC. 3. Any person who shall be found intoxicated in the City of Milwaukee, or who shall be guilty of any indecent exposure of his or her person, or who shall make use of any vulgar or obscene language, or who shall make use of any loud, boisterous or insulting language, tending to excite a breach of the peace, or who shall be guilty of any other disorderly conduct in said City of Milwaukee, shall forfeit a penalty of not less than one nor more than twenty-five dollars.

Policemen to receive no reward.

SEC. 4. No Policeman shall accept or receive from any person while in custody, or after such person shall have been discharged, nor from any such person's friends, any gratuity, reward, or gift, directly or indirectly, or any article or thing as compensation for damages sustained in the discharge of his duty, (without a written permission from the Mayor.)

Policemen not to apply for warrant without permission.

SEC. 5. No member or Policeman will be permitted to apply for a warrant for an assault upon himself, without first reporting the case to the Chief of the Police, and obtaining from him, or from the Mayor, permission, in writing, to make application.

Offences not to be compounded.

SEC. 6. No Policeman must compound any offence committed against persons or property, or withdraw any complaint therefor, unless by the written consent of the Mayor or Chief of the Police.

SEC. 7. No member shall communicate to any person any information which may enable persons to escape from arrest or punishment, or enable them to dispose of or secrete any goods, or other valuable thing stolen or embezzled.

Orders to be kept secret.

SEC. 8. No Policeman shall communicate, except to such persons as directed by the Chief of the Police, any information respecting orders he may have received, or any regulations that may be made for the government of the Department.

Badge of office to be worn.

SEC. 9. The Chief of the Police, and Policemen when on duty, shall wear the insignia of their office on the outside of the outermost garment, over the left breast, conspicuously displaying the same so that the entire surface thereof may be seen, (except when caution may dictate that the same shall not be exposed.)

SEC. 10. No member of the Department shall be absent from duty, or leave the city without permission of the Chief of the Police. Not to be absent from duty without leave.

SEC. 11. All persons who shall be arrested during the time the Police Court shall be open, shall be taken immediately to the Police Court, and all persons who shall be arrested at any other time, shall be conveyed to the Station House, unless otherwise ordered by the Mayor or Chief of the Police, or unless it shall require a place of greater security, in which case he or she shall be immediately taken to jail. Persons arrested, where taken.

SEC. 12. Members of the Police must be civil and respectful to each other on all occasions.

SEC. 13. Members of the Department must not render any ussistance in civil cases, except to prevent an immediate breach of the peace, or to quell a disturbance actually commenced. When to assist in civil cases.

SEC. 14. The Chief of the Police and every Policeman shall be furnished with a copy of the ordinance and rules and regulations, which they must frequently peruse so that they may become perfectly acquainted with their several duties; they shall always have the same in their possession to refer to when in doubt of their authority for acting. To study the rules and regulations.

SEC. 15. Any officer or Policeman who shall wilfully maltreat, or use unnecessary violence toward a prisoner, or other person, shall, on complaint being made and the fact established, be immediately discharged. Not to maltreat prisoners.

SEC. 16. Where an offence has been committed, and the Mayor or Chief of the Police has cause to suspect that negligence is attributable to the Policeman on whose beat or district the offence has been committed, the Policeman will be required to show, by his own affidavit, or by the testimony of other persons, that the offence was not committed in conse- Neglect of Policemen, how punished.

quence of any neglect or inattention on his part; and, in case he or they fail to show that they were attending to their duties, strictly, and in accordance with the rules and regulations, they will be subject to suspension or dismissal from office.

Beggars to be arrested and removed

SEC. 17. The members of the Police Department are particularly enjoined to remove all beggars found begging in the streets, and, if on enquiry, they shall be found to be proper subjects for relief from the Poor Department, they are to take them to the Overseers of the Poor for relief. If they are found to be imposters, or vagrants, to take them before the Police Justice, to be dealt with according to law.

SEC. 18. Members of the Police Department, on resigning their office, or on removal from office, will surrender their book of regulations and insignia of office, and all other property belonging to the City that may be in their possession, to the Chief of the Police.

Chief of Police to report complaints.

SEC. 19. The Chief of the Police shall obey the rules and regulations prescribed by the Mayor and the Ordinances of the Common Council, and shall promptly report to the Mayor all complaints made to him against any member of the department.

To be present at fires and disturbances.

SEC. 20. He shall repair to the scenes of fires, riots and tumultuous assemblages, and take charge of the Police present, and use every exertion to save and protect property, disperse mobs, and arrest such persons as he may find engaged in disturbing the peace, or who may aid and abet others in doing so.

SEC. 21. He shall have power to direct any of the Police force to any place where their services may be deemed necessary.

Notice of commitment to be given to Police Justice.

SEC. 22. Wenever the Chief, or any Policeman, shall commit to prison any person charged with, or being suspected of, having committed any criminal offence, until examination shall be had before the Police Justice, he shall immediately give notice of such commitment to the Police Justice, specifying therein the name of the person committed, the name of the complainant, and of the officer who arrested the person committed, and the time of commitment, and also the charge made against such person, and shall follow the directions of the Police Justice in relation thereto.

Chief of Police to keep a record of all persons arrested.

SEC. 23. The Chief of Police shall keep in his office a book in which shall be entered the name of each Policeman, his number and his place of residence, specifying the ward and street, and the time of any removal from office, or the occuring of a vacancy, he shall also keep in his office a book, in which shall be entered the name, if known, and if not known, under an alias, of all persons arrested by any Policeman, with the date of the arrest and cause of arrest, with such other facts as he shall deem proper and necessary, and report the same at the end of each month to the Common Council.

SEC. 24. He shall also enter in said book an accurate account of the time each Policeman shall be on duty, and report the same to the Common Council at the end of each month.

Prisoners every morning to be taken before the Police Justice.

SEC. 25. The Chief of the Police shall, every morning, on the opening of the Police Court, cause the persons who may be detained at the Station House, the night previous, and all property which may have come into his possession during the night, to be conveyed to the Police Court, accompanied by the Policeman who made the arrest, and who may be a witness, and cause the witnesses to be summoned to testify in relation to the charges made, or to be made, against such persons.

Entries to be made of offences committed.

SEC. 26. The Chief of Police shall enter in a book, to be kept at the Station House, all information he may receive of offences committed, or of suspecious persons or plans, and the entries of offences committed, the hour, place and manner in which the offence was committed, the property stolen, enumerating the articles, the name and residence of the owner, (if known,) and the names of the Policemen on the beat at the time the offence was committed.

Officers may inspect the Police books.

SEC. 27. The Mayor, the District and City Attorney, or either of them, are authorized to inspect at all times, any or all the books directed to be kept by the Chief of the Police, but no person not herein named shall be permitted to examine any of said books without permission, in writing, from the Mayor or Chief of the Police, except that Policemen may be allowed to examine the book in which shall be entered the statement of offences committed, and of suspicious persons and places.

Policemen to prevent crimes.

SEC. 28. Every Policeman must examine and make himself perfectly acquainted with every part of his beat, and vigilantly watch every description of persons passing his way so as to acquire a faculty of observing, as well as detecting, offenders. He must also, to the utmost of his power, prevent the commission of assaults and batteries, and breaches of the peace, and other crimes about to be committed. He must, by his vigilance, render it extremely difficult for any one to commit crime on his beat. The absence of crime will be considered the best proof of the efficiency of the Police; and when, in any beat, offences frequently occur, there will be good reason to suppose there is negligence or want of ability on the part of the Police in charge of such district or beat.

Policemen to have exact knowledge of their beat.

SEC. 29. The Policemen in each ward will, and must, acquire such knowledge of the inhabitants within their beat, as to enable them at once to recognize them. He must inspect every part of his beat, in order that any person requiring assistance, may be enabled to find him. The regularity of inspection above enjoined shall not prevent his remaining at any particular place if his presence be required. He must, at all times, be enabled to furnish particular information as to the state of his beat, and if not, he must satisfy his superior that there is sufficient cause for such inability.

SEC. 30. The Policemen shall carefully examine, in the night time, all doors and low windows of dwelling houses and stores, to see that they are properly secured, also areas and area gates of the several houses in his beat. Thieves frequently conceal themselves in such places until the officers pass, and then commence operations. He must, if possible, fix in his mind such impressions as will enable him to recognize persons he frequently meets in the street at night, and endeavor to ascertain their names and residences, and communicate to his commanding officer all information regarding them. Policemen to make examinations in night time.

SEC. 31. He shall strictly watch the conduct of all persons of known bad character, and in such manner that it will be evident to such persons that they are watched, and that certain detection must follow the attempt to commit crime. He will note the time of the appearance of any person of known bad character in his beat, and the circumstances attending, and the premises that the person may enter, and report to the Chief of the Police. He will also report all receivers of stolen goods, or his suspicions that they are such. To watch bad characters.

SEC. 32. When any person charges another with crime, and insists that the person charged shall be taken in custody, the Policeman will take the accuser along with the accused, to the Police Court, or Station House, as the case may be, and deliver them to the person in charge of the Station House, and then return to his beat with as little delay as possible, and inspect his beat with great care, to see that no depredations have been committed during his absence. To take prisoner and accuser to Police Court.

SEC. 33. The Policemen shall carefully watch all disorderly houses or houses of ill fame, within his beat, and elsewhere, by whom they are frequented, and report his observations to the Chief of the Police. He shall arrest all and every person who shall be seen by him violating any ordinance of the city, or who shall be found in the street To arrest all persons violating ordinances, &c.

drunk, noisy, using boisterous and threatening or insulting language, tending to produce a quarrel or breach of the peace, all persons who shall be guilty of indecent conduct or of an indecent exposure of their person; all persons who shall be in the act of committing a felony or misdemeanor, or who shall be reasonably suspected of having committed any such act, and all and every person who, from his conduct, may reasonably be suspected of an intention to commit either of said acts, and all and every person found in any street, alley or secret place under such circumstances as to create a reasonable belief that such person is in such place for the purpose and with intent to commit a felony or misdemeanor; in these and similar cases Policemen must judge from all the circumstances of the case, what the intention of the party is. In some cases, no doubt can exist—as where the party is a notorious thief, or acting with those who are known to be thieves, or where the party is attempting to break into a house or examining the doors and windows, or endeavoring to take property secretly. If the intention of the party admits of a doubt, the Police will not act hastily, but will closely watch the suspected party, that he may discover the design, and shall detain such person or persons in the Station House, or deliver them to the jailor of the county to be kept over night or over the Sabbath, and until such person can be brought before some competent court or magistrate, to be dealt with according to law.

To arrest all persons suspected of crime.

SEC. 34. Policemen should never use their club except in the most urgent cases of necessity, or in self defence, and he shall give his name to all persons who may, in a respectful manner, enquire.

Not to walk together.

SEC. 35. Policemen must not walk together, or spend their time in talking together, where they meet on the confines of their beats, unless it is to communicate information appertaining to the department, such communication to be as brief as possible.

SEC. 36. The person arrested should be notified of the officers authority, and this will often prevent resistance, by taking away the prospect of justifying or extenuating it.

SEC. 37. If a Policeman finds his personal efforts insufficient to effect an arrest, or if he has reason to apprehend that resistance will be made, he ought to require all or as many persons present as he may deem necessary and think proper to assist him. (See sec. 7 of the Police Ordinance.) To require persons to assist.

SEC. 38. Policemen must recollect that in making arrests he is not justified in doing more than is *absolutely necessary* for the safe custody of the parties until he conveys them to the place of their destination. Persons under arrest must be dealt with properly in all cases. It is the duty of Policemen to keep persons safely, but he has no right to punish them, and he must not even use language to them calculated to provoke or offend them, for such conduct would create resistance by the party, and a hostile feeling among bystanders towards the Policemen. To use only such force as is necessary.

SEC. 39. A Policeman must be cautious never to interfere idly or unnecessarily, but when required to act he will do so with discretion, decision and boldness ; and he may arrest any one who shall oppose him in his duty, if he can prove some specific fact not otherwise.

SEC. 40. Policemen will be immediately discharged or dismissed from office, against whom any of the following charges shall be made and substantiated :—1st, Intoxication. 2d, Wilful disobedience of orders. 3d, Violent, coarse, or insolent language or behavior to a superior officer, or to a subordinate. 4th, Receiving money or other valuable thing contrary to law and the rules and regulations. 5th, Wilful disobedience of, or non-compliance with, the requirements of the ordinance establishing the Police, or the rules and regulations of the Police. For what offences Policemen will be discharged.

Policemen not to become bail. SEC. 41. The Chief of the Police and Policemen shall be incompetent bail for any person arrested, and shall in no case become bail for any person under arrest.

Adopted by the Common Council, October 22, 1855.

AN ORDINANCE

Establishing a Police in the City of Milwaukee.

The Mayor and Common Council of the City of Milwaukee, do ordain as follows :

To establish Police. SECTION 1. There shall be, and hereby is established a Police Department for the City of Milwaukee, which shall consist of one Chief of the Police, and not less than one nor exceeding five Policemen in each ward of said city.

Police, how appointed. SEC. 2. The Chief of the Police and the Policemen shall be appointed in the following manner :—The Mayor shall nominate and the Council appoint one Chief of the Police. The Mayor and the Chief of the Police, so appointed, shall nominate and the Council appoint not less than one nor exceeding five persons in each ward of the city, as Policemen. And the Chief of the Police shall be, and hereby is, authorized to employ such other assistants as he may deem necessary, not exceeding five in number at any time, to perform such special service as the Chief of the Police may require.

Police to enforce ordinances. SEC. 3. The several Policemen, so appointed as above, shall be in subordination to, and under, the control and direction of the Chief of the Police. It shall be the duty of the Chief of the Police to cause the public peace to be preserved and to see that all the laws and ordinances of the city are enforced, and whenever any violation thereof shall come to his knowledge, he shall cause the requisite complaint to be made, and see that the evidence is procured, for the successful prosecution of the offender or offenders. He shall obey, and cause those Policemen under him to obey, the police rules and regulations which may be prescribed by the Common Council, and in case of tumult, insurection or threatening thereof, to take charge, in person, of the Policemen, and direct them in the discharge of their respective duties. He shall cause to be made and kept, a record of his proceedings, which he may deem necessary, or as shall be directed by the Mayor. He shall be responsible for the efficiency and general good conduct of the department, and shall report, in writing, to the Mayor, all complaints made to him against any member thereof.

Chief to keep record.

SEC. 4. The Chief of the Police and the Policemen are respectively authorized and empowered, in a peaceable manner, (or if refused admittance after demand made), with force and arms, to enter into any house, store, shop, grocery or other place or building whatever or wheresoever in said city in which any person or persons may reasonably be suspected to be for unlawful purposes, and if any person or persons shall be found therein guilty of any crime or misdemeanor, or violation of any law or ordinance for the preservation of the peace and good order of the city, or who may reasonably be suspected thereof, or who shall be aiding and abetting such person or persons so found, said Police Officer or Policeman shall apprehend and keep in custody such person or persons, as in case of other arrests made by Police Officers, until they shall be discharged by due course of law.

Have power to enter premises.

SEC. 5. The Chief of the Police and the Policemen, respectively, shall have full power and authority, and it shall be their duty, to arrest all persons in the city found in the act of violating any law or ordinance of the city, or aiding or abetting in any such violation, and shall arrest all persons found under suspicious circumstances, and shall take all such persons in charge and confine them until reasonable time bring such person before the Police Justice to be dealt with according to law.

Duty to arrest all persons violating laws or ordinances.

Penalty for resisting Policemen.

SEC. 6. Whoever, in the city, shall resist any Police Officer, or member of the Police Department, in the discharge of his duty, or shall in any way interfere with, or hinder or prevent him from discharging his duty as such officer or member, and shall offer, or endeavor so to do, and whoever shall, in any manner, assist any person in custody of any Police Officer or member of the Police Department, to escape or attempt to escape from such custody, or shall rescue or attempt to rescue any person so in custody, shall forfeit a penalty not less than five nor more than one hundred dollars.

Assistance to be rendered when called for.

SEC. 7. It shall be the duty of all persons in the city, when called upon by any Police Officer or Policemen, to promptly aid and assist him in the execution of his duties. Whoever shall neglect or refuse to give such aid and assistance, shall forfeit a penalty of not exceeding one hundred dollars, in the discretion of the court or magistrate convicting. And if the person offending be a licensed hackman, cabman or drayman, or the driver of any hackney coach, cab, omnibus, dray or wagon, or other vehicle, the court or magistrate convicting, shall be authorized to give judgment that the license of the said person, or of the owner of such vehicle, be cancelled and revoked.

Penalty for refusing.

Hackmen, &c., to obey directions of Police.

SEC. 8. Hackmen, cabmen, omnibus drivers, draymen, porters, runners and other persons, when at or about any rail road depot or station, or steamboat or other vessel landing, or other public place in the city, shall obey the commands and directions of the Police Officer or Policemen, and the Marshal, Deputy Marshal and Constables of the city, who may be stationed or doing duty at or about such place, for the purpose of preserving order and enforcing the ordinances. Whoever shall refuse to obey the commands or directions of said officer or officers as aforesaid, shall forfeit a penalty of not exceeding twenty dollars.

Penalty for refusing.

Penalty of Policemen for neglect of duty.

SEC. 9. Any Police Officer or Policeman, who shall neglect or refuse to perform any duty required of him by the ordinance of the city, or the Police rules which may be made, or who shall, in the discharge of his duties as such officer, be guilty of any fraud, extortion, oppression, favoritism, partiality or wilful wrong or injustice, shall forfeit a penalty of not exceeding one hundred dollars for each offence.

Police department to be under control of Mayor.

SEC. 10. The Chief of the Police, and each and every of the Policemen, shall be subordinate to and subject to the direction and control of the Mayor at all times, and the Mayor shall have power to suspend the Chief of the Police or any Policeman from office, for cause, subject to an appeal to the Common Council from such suspension, and such person so suspended, shall not exercise any function or perform any duty of his office, and shall not be entitled to any pay during such suspension. The Common Council may remove or re-install such officer.

How vacancies to be filled.

SEC. 11. All vacancies which may occur in the Police department, shall, on the recommendation of the Mayor and Chief of the Police, be supplied by the appointment by the Common Council of such person so recommended.

Chief to hold office during the pleasure of Mayor.

SEC. 12. The Chief of the Police shall hold his office during the pleasure of the Mayor, and the Policemen during the pleasure of the Chief of the Police, unless removed as hereinbefore provided.

Salary of Chief of Police.

SEC. 13. The Chief of the Police shall receive an annual salary of eight hundred dollars, payable quarterly, and each Policeman shall receive the monthly pay of thirty dollars, payable at the end of each month; and in case of the employment by the Chief of the Police of an assistant or assistants, pursuant to the Police ordinance for special duty, he shall report the same to the Mayor, together with the amount of compensation agreed upon, subject to his approval, who shall certify such sum as shall be approved by him to the Common Council to be audited and allowed.

Salary of Policemen.

Passed, September 10, 1855.

AN ORDINANCE

To amend an Ordinance entitled, "An Ordinance establishing a Police in the City of Milwaukee," passed, September 10, 1855.

The Mayor and Common Council of the City of Milwaukee, do ordain as follows :

Salary of Chief of Police.

SECTION 1. Section 13 of an ordinance establishing a Police in the City of Milwaukee, passed, September 10th, 1855, is hereby amended so as to read as follows: The Chief of the Police shall receive an annual salary of one thousand dollars, payable quarterly, and each Policeman shall receive the monthly pay of forty dollars, payable at the end of each month, and in case of the employment by the Chief of the Police of any assistant or assistants, pursuant to the Police ordinance, for special duty, he shall report the same to the Mayor, together with the amount of compensation agreed upon, subject to his approval, who shall certify such sum as shall be approved by him to the Common Council to be audited and allowed.

Salary of Policemen and whom payable.

Passed, October 1, 1855.

AN ORDINANCE

Relating to Streets, Alleys and Side-walks, and to prevent the obstruction thereof.

The Mayor and Common Council of the City of Milwaukee, do ordain as follows :

No porch, stoop, &c. to extend on sidewalk more than 3 or 4 feet.

SECTION 1. No porch, gallery, stoop or platform shall be allowed to extend into or upon any side-walk more than three feet, where the side-walk is not more than twelve feet in width, nor exceeding four feet, where the side-walk is fifteen feet and upwards in width, and no railing on any side-walk shall in any case exceed three feet in width from the building; any violation hereof shall subject the offender to a penalty of five dollars, and to a like penalty for every day such violation shall continue after the first conviction. And *provided further*, That no cellar-doors, for mercantile or other establishments, used for receiving goods or other purposes, shall extend so as to occupy more than five feet of any side-walk, and the same are always to be kept shut and secure, when not open for immediate use, under a penalty in each case of five dollars for each and every offence.

Cellar doors not more than 5 feet.

SEC. 2. No bow window, or other window, shall extend into any side-walk more than twenty-four inches, nor shall any sign project from any store or other building, into or over any side-walk or street more than three feet, nor shall any cellar door rise or project above the surface of the side-walk more than one inch at the outer side, nor more than three inches near the store or other building, nor shall the hinges thereof, or any other thing connected therewith project or rise above the door, nor shall any staple, lock or other fastening be placed on the upper side thereof, under a penalty of five dollars for each offence to any person violating the provisions of this section, and to a like penalty for every day such violation shall continue, after a request or notice to remove the same by the Mayor, any Policeman, or an Alderman.

Windows not to project more than 24 in.

Signs not more than 3 feet.

SEC. 3. No sign or other posts, except awning posts, hereinafter provided, shall be erected or placed on or upon any side-walk or street, or other public way within the city limits, or if heretofore erected or placed, shall be permitted to remain on or upon any side-walk or street, or other public way, under a penalty of five dollars, and a like penalty for every day such post shall be allowed to remain after notice to the owner or occupant of the premises, from the Mayor, any Alderman or Policeman, to remove the same, but nothing herein contained shall prevent the erection of

Sign-posts not to be erected on sidewalk or street.

one, and not to exceed two posts in front of each building, for the purpose of hitching horses, every such posts so erected shall be not more than eight inches, nor less than six inches in diameter, and not to exceed four feet in height, and placed in a line within the outer edge of the side-walk.

Awnings how erected.

SEC. 4. All awnings hereafter erected shall be elevated at least eight feet, at the lowest part thereof, above the top of the side-walks, and shall not project over the side-walks to exceed three-fourths of the width thereof; they shall be supported without posts by iron brackets, or by an iron frame work attached firmly to the building, so as to leave the side-walk wholly unobstructed thereby; all awnings heretofore erected in a different manner, shall be removed in a reasonable time after notice, as hereinafter specified. If any person shall erect any awning contrary to the provisions hereof, or shall refuse or neglect forthwith to remove any awning or awning posts, after verbal or written notice to remove the same, to be given by the Mayor, any Alderman or Policeman, he shall be subjected to a penalty of five dollars for every offence, and to a further penalty of five dollars for every day he shall fail to comply with such notice, after a lapse of five days from the service thereof.

Goods not to be placed on sidewalk.

SEC. 5. No person shall place any goods or merchandize for sale or exhibition upon any side-walk, or suspend any goods over the same for sale or show, except as provided in the next section, or place or deposit thereon, cause or suffer the same to be done, any cask, barrel, wood, stove, or any other article whatsoever, under a penalty of three dollars for each offence, and a like penalty for each and every hour the same shall remain after the notice by the Mayor, either Alderman or Policeman, to remove the same.

How goods may be placed and received.

SEC. 6. It shall be lawful for any person to place, hang or set out for sale, any goods, wares or merchandize on or over the side-walk, in front of and within three feet of his store or buildings; it shall also be lawful for any person to place and leave for a period not exceeding one hour, on three feet of the outer edge of the side-walk in front of his store or building, any goods, wares, or merchandize, which he shall be in the act of receiving or delivering.

Horses not to be fastened so as to obstruct sidewalk

Sec. 7. No person shall at any time fasten any horse or horses in such a way that the horse, vehicle, reins or lines shall be an obstacle to the free use of the side-walk, or cross walk, under the penalty of one dollar for each offence, and the person in whose possession or use such horse or horses shall then be, shall be deemed the offender, unless he can prove to the contrary to the satisfaction of the magistrate before whom he shall be prosecuted.

Vehicle not to be drawn on sidewalk.

Sec. 8. No person or persons shall push or draw back any horse, wagon, cart, or other vehicle, on any side-walk, or use, ride or drive any horse, wagon, sled or sleigh thereon, unless it be in crossing the same to go into a yard or lot, when no other suitable crossing or means of access is provided, under a penalty of one dollar for each offence.

Signs, &c. not to project more than 3 feet.

Sec. 9. No owner or occupant of any dwelling house, store, or other building, shall fix, put up or erect, or suffer the same to remain fixed, put up or erected, any sign, show-bill, show-case, canvass, or other thing projecting from any building or hanging over the sidewalk more than three feet in front of and from the wall of such building, under a penalty of five dollars for each offence, and a like penalty of five dollars for every forty-eight hours the same shall remain after being requested to remove the same by the Mayor, any Alderman, or Policeman.

Crosswalks to be kept free.

Sec. 10. All cross walks in the city shall be kept and reserved free from any sleigh, wagon, carts or carriages, horses or other animals being placed or suffered to stand thereon, except so far as may be necessary in crossing the same; and the owner or driver of any sleigh, cart or carriage, or horse or other animal offending herein, shall forfeit and pay a penalty of three dollars.

Posts and obstructions to be removed.

SEC. 11. The Mayor, or any Policeman, is hereby authorized to cause any post or other obstruction, erected, placed or continued on or over any sidewalk, contrary to the provisions hereof, to be removed, after due notice has been given to remove the same, and a neglect to comply with such notice.

Written permission may be given for placing materials on streets and sidewalks.

SEC. 12. No person shall place, or cause to be placed, any stones, timber, lumber, plank, board, or other materials for building, in or upon any street, alley or public square, without a written permission from two of the Aldermen of the ward, in which said street, alley or public square is situated, under the penalty of two dollars for each and every twenty-four hours during which the articles or materials aforesaid shall be or remain in any such street, alley or public square, without permission as aforesaid, after notice to remove the same.

Aldermen to give permission for building materials.

SEC. 13. Any two of the Aldermen are authorized to grant any person permission in writing, to place and keep any building materials in any of the public streets, situated in the ward which said Aldermen represent, for a period of time, not exceeding four months; but such permission shall not authorize the obstructing of more tnan one-third of the sidewalk, and one-third of the carriage way of said street, opposite the lot on which an erection is to be made, by the person to whom such permission is granted, and such permission may be revoked at any time by the Common Council, and such materials shall, in no case, be so placed as to obstruct the free flow of water in the side gutters.

How such materials shall be removed.

SEC. 14. Every person to whom permission is granted, as aforesaid, shall cause all the timber, building materials, and rubbish arising therefrom, to be removed from the street, at the expiration of the time limited, as aforesaid, under the penalty of three dollars for every forty-eight hours the timber, materials, or rubbish aforesaid, shall be and remain in such street, after the expiration of the time limited in the permission granted as aforesaid; but no single recovery shall exceed the sum of twenty-six dollars.

Vehicles not to stand in street.

SEC. 15. No person shall suffer any carriage, wagon, cart, sleigh, or sled, without horses or other beasts of burden, to remain or stand in any street, alley, or public wharf, or dock, for more than two hours, under the penalty of one dollar for each offence.

Horses not to be fasten- to shade trees.

SEC. 16. No person shall, at any time, fasten any horse in such way that such horse, or the reins or other fastenings shall be an obstacle to the free use of any side or crosswalk, under the penalty of one dollar for each and every offence; nor shall any person fasten any horse to any ornamental or shade-tree, in any of the streets of this city, or to any box or case around such tree, without the consent of the owner of such tree, under the penalty of five dollars for each and every offence.

Not to drive fast.

SEC. 17. No person shall ride or drive any horse or horses in any street, alley or highway, in this city, faster than a moderate trot, nor over any crosswalk, faster than a walk, under a penalty of five dollars for each and every offence.

Firewood, how left.

SEC. 18. It shall be lawful for any person to place and leave in the street in front of his store or building, for a period not exceeding twenty-four hours, and at not less than two feet, nor more than seven from the curb, any fire wood, or other material for fuel.

Paved ways across side-walks.

SEC. 19. Persons owning or occupying any shop, yard, lot, stable, or other place, when in the pursuit of business, it is necessary to pass over the sidewalk with animals or carriages of any discription, shall pave said sidewalk neatly with stone, entirely across the same, and to a width sufficient, not more than eight feet, to prevent damage being done to the sidewalk, on each side of such passage, but not more than one such passage to be constructed in any fifty feet of sidewalk, and all such persons refusing or neglecting to comply with this provision shall forfeit and pay a fine of one dollar for every day that he shall so neglect to make such pavement, after being notified by the Mayor, or Aldermen, or any Policeman, to make the same.

Shade trees, how set out.

SEC. 20. All ornamental or shade trees hereafter placed, or set out in any street, shall be placed or set out within the outer lines of the sidewalk, and within two feet of the said outer line of the sidewalk of such street, and every person placing, or causing, or procuring to be placed, any tree contrary to the provisions of this section, shall forfeit the penalty of five dollars for each and every offence, and the further penalty of one dollar for each week such tree shall be suffered to remain, contrary to the provisions of this section.

Pavements, &c. not to be torn up.

SEC. 21. Any person who shall injure, or tear up, any pavement, side or crosswalk, drain, or sewer, or any part thereof, or who shall dig any hole, ditch, or drain, in any street, pavement, or sidewalk, without written permission from two of the Aldermen of the ward in which such street, pavement, or side or crosswalk shall be situated, or who shall hinder or obstruct the making or repairing any pavement, side or crosswalk, which is, or may be making under any law or resolution of the Common Council, or who shall hinder or obstruct any person employed by the Common Council, or Street Commissioners, or persons employed by them, in making or repairing any public improvement, or work ordered by the Common Council, or Street Commissioners, shall for each and every offence, forfeit the sum of ten dollars, and pay all damages which may be so done.

Drains and sewers not to be filled up.

SEC. 22. No person shall cast or throw, or cause to be cast or thrown, into any of the drains or sewers within the city, any filthy substance, or any substance calculated to cause any obstructions, nuisances or injury in or to the same, under a penalty of five dollars for each and every offence.

Permission from Aldermen to construct vaults, &c.

SEC. 23. No person shall construct, or cause to be constructed, or made, any sewer, vault, cistern or well in any of the streets of this city, without the permission of two of the Aldermen of the ward in which said streets are situated, under the penalty of twenty-five dollars for each and every offence.

SEC. 24. The person making, or having charge of such sewer, vault, cistern or well, shall, during the whole of every night, while such sewer, vault, cistern or well shall be opened, or uncovered, fence in the same, and cause a lighted lamp or lantern to be placed and kept so as to cast its light upon such vault, cistern, well or sewer; and every such owner, occupant or person making, or having in charge, such work, who shall neglect the provisions of this section, shall forfeit the penalty of twenty-five dollars for each and every offence. To be fenced and lighted.

SEC. 25. No person shall construct, or cause to be constructed or made, any drain or sewer, leading into any of the common sewers of the City of Milwaukee, without the written permission of the Aldermen of the ward in which the same is situated, under the penalty of ten dollars for each and every offence. Permission of Aldermen to construct sewers, &c.

SEC. 26. All vaults under sidewalks in this city, shall be constructed of brick or stone, and the outward side of the grating or opening into the street, shall be within one foot of the outside of the curb stone of the sidewalk, and all such vaults shall be completed, and the ground and sidewalks replaced over them, within two weeks after they are respectively commenced, and every person neglecting any of the provisions of this section, whether the owner or builder of such vault, shall forfeit the penalty of twenty-five dollars. Vaults under sidewalks, how constructed.

SEC. 27. Whenever permission is given to any person to lay any drain, sewer, gas pipe, or aqueduct, along or in any public street, or to dig, or take up any street, pavement or sidewalk, he shall cause the same to be done in such manner, within such time, as two of the Aldermen of the ward in which said pavement, street, or sidewalk is situated, shall direct; and shall cause the same to be re-built and re-laid in as substantial and permanent a manner as the same was be- Aldermen to direct.

fore, under the penalty of twenty-five dollars for each and every neglect, refusal or offence.

Snow, &c. to be removed.

SEC. 28. All persons shall, by ten o'clock every morning, remove all snow, ice and dirt from the sidewalks in front of the premises, owned or occupied by them, under the penalty of one dollar for each and every neglect.

Permission of Aldermen to remove buildings.

SEC. 29. No person shall remove, or cause, or permit to be removed, or shall aid or assist in removing any building into, along, or across any street, in the City of Milwaukee, without permission from the Street Commissioners of the ward, under the penalty of twenty-five dollars for each offence.

Not to remain longer than one day.

SEC. 30. No person, owner of any building, permitted to be removed into, along, or across any street, alley or public ground, nor the contractor for moving any building into, along, or across any street, alley or public ground in the City of Milwaukee, shall suffer or permit such building to remain in any such street, alley or public ground, for a longer time than one day, after notice from the Mayor, an Alderman, or the Chief of the Police, to remove the same, under the penalty of five dollars for each and every offence, to be sued for and recovered from the owner or contractor thereat, severally and respectively.

Vehicles, &c. not to remain in streets.

SEC. 31. It shall not be lawful for any owner or driver of any carriage, cart, dray, sled, omnibus, or other vehicle, to suffer the same to stand or remain in any street, side-walk, alley, wharf or dock, within the City of Milwaukee, so as to incumber the same, or prevent the free passage thereof, under the penalty of two dollars. Any such person, above named, who shall neglect or refuse to remove his or her carriage, cart, dray, sled, omnibus, or other vehicle, which shall be found so standing in any street, side-walk, alley, wharf or dock, as aforesaid, when requested or notified to remove the same by the Mayor, any Alderman or Policeman, shall forfeit a penalty of not less than five nor more than ten dollars ; nor shall the owner or driver of any vehicle above named, suffer his or her vehicle to stand or remain stationary in any street, alley, wharf or dock, within said city, for a longer period than ten minutes, unless actually engaged in receiving or discharging passengers or property, under the penalty of two dollars.

SEC. 32. No owner or occupant of any livery stable, wagon or blacksmith shop, or other place of business, shall suffer any wagon, cart, carriage, dray or other vehicle, whether left for safe keeping, repair or otherwise, to be or remain on the side-walk or alley, adjoining or fronting any such premises, nor on that half of the street adjoining and fronting the same, under a penalty of five dollars for each and every offence. Nor on side-walks.

SEC. 33. No person shall leave any horse or horses (except as provided in the next section,) in any street or alley, or other highway within this city, without being sufficiently secured by a halter, under the penalty of two dollars for each offence. Horses to be hitched.

SEC. 34. Every truckman or cartman, who drives a truck or cart within this city, shall have a strong chain attached to the body of his truck or cart, which shall be made fast to one of the wheels whenever the horse shall be left alone in any street or alley. Cartmen to have a strong chain.

SEC. 35. No person shall cut any tree or shrub in any of the streets or side-walks or public grounds in this city, without obtaining the written consent of the owner or of all the Aldermen of the ward in which such tree or shrub may be, under the penalty of ten dollars for every offence. Trees and shrubs not to be cut.

SEC. 36. An ordinance relating to streets and side-walks, passed, July 6th, 1846, and an ordinance to prevent obstructions to side-walks, passed, May 6th, 1852, and an ordinance to amend the first named ordinance, passed, November 12th, 1855, are hereby repealed.

Passed, August 18, 1856.

AN ORDINANCE

To prevent nuisances and disorderly practices in the City of Milwaukee.

The Mayor and Common Council of the City of Milwaukee, do ordain as follows:

Nauseous substances not to be put on streets or sidewalks.

SECTION 1. No person shall throw or leave, or suffer his or her servant, child or family to throw, place or leave any dead carcass, carrion, fish, entrails, or other nauseous and unwholsome substance or matter, on any street, side-walk, alley, or upon any lot or public grounds in this city, under a penalty of not less than two, nor more than twenty-five dollars for each and every offence.

SEC. 2. No person shall throw or deposite any dirty water, dirt, filth, straw or other rubbish in any street, side-walk or alley in this city, or upon any public ground of the same, under the penalty of one dollar for each and every offence.

Nor to be left on owner's lots.

SEC. 3. No owner or occupant of any tenement or lot in this city, shall permit any substance mentioned in the last two sections to be or remain upon said tenement or lot, or between the same and the center of the street adjoining, under the penalty of two dollars for each and every twenty-four hours during which the same shall remain or be thereon.

Tenements not to become nauseous.

SEC. 4. Any owner or occupant of any house or place, who shall suffer the same to become nauseous, or injurious to the health of the inhabitants of this city, shall forfeit the penalty of five dollars for each and every offence.

Houses may be ordered cleansed.

SEC. 5. It shall be lawful for the Mayor, any Alderman of the proper ward, Health Officer or any Policeman, to order the owner or occupant of any house or place to cleanse, remove or abate the same, as often as may be necessary for the health, comfort and convenience of the inhabitants of this city; and any person refusing or neglecting to obey such order, shall forfeit the penalty of five dollars for every twenty-four hours he shall neglect or refuse.

Contents of privy, when to be removed.

SEC. 6. No tub containing the contents of any vault, privy, or necessary-house within the limits of the city, shall be removed therefrom, except between the hours of eleven o'clock at night and four in the morning, under the penalty of not less than two, nor more than ten dollars.

Noise and riot.

SEC. 7. Any person who shall make or assist in making any riot, noise or disturbance in this city, or shall aid or countenance any disorderly assemblage, shall forfeit a penalty not exceeding fifty dollars for each offence.

Bathing in city limits.

SEC. 8. No person shall bathe or swim in the Menomonee or Milwaukee rivers, within the limits of this city, nor shall any person bathe or swim between the hours of seven o'clock in the morning and eight in the evening, in Lake Michigan or Milwaukee Harbor, within sight of any dwelling-house, public walk, pier or other place of business, within the limits of said city, under a penalty in each case of not less than two nor more than ten dollars for each and every offence: *Provided, however,* That suitable bathing places may be named and designated by the Common Council.

Vagrants, beggars, &c.

SEC. 9. Every person being a vagrant, mendicant, street-beggar, common prostitute or gambler, in this city, shall, upon conviction, forfeit a penalty of not less than one nor more than twenty-five dollars.

Holes in ice.

SEC. 10. No person shall cut any ice, or any holes in any river, canal, bayou, basin, or slip, within the bounds of this city, without first enclosing that portion of said ice intended to be cut with a suitable fence, under the penalty of not less than five, nor more than twenty five dollars.

Fast driving on bridges.

SEC. 11. It shall not be lawful for any person to ride or drive over any bridge in this city faster than a walk, under a penalty of not less than one, nor more than five dollars for each and every offence.

Offal on Lake bluffs, &c. SEC. 12. No drayman, cartman, or other person shall throw, place, or leave any dead animal, carrion, offal, or other offensive matter on the lake bluff or bank, or in the Milwaukee Harbor, or in any river or bayou within the limits of this city, under a penalty of not less than two, nor more than twenty-five dollars for each and every offence.

Pasting up bills, &c. SEC. 13. No person shall paste, or in any other manner post up, any written or printed bill, notice or advertisement, on any part of the outer walls of any brick or wood building within the limits of the City of Milwaukee, without first having obtained the consent of the owner thereof, under a penalty of not less than one, nor more than five dollars for each offence.

SEC. 14. "An ordinance to prevent nuisances in the City of Milwaukee," and "an ordinance to prevent gaming and other disorderly practices in the City of Milwaukee," passed, July 13th, 1846, "an ordinance to prevent the throwing of offensive matter on the lake bluff, or any other place in the city limits," passed, May 6th, 1852, and "an ordinance to prevent placing or putting post-bills or notices on buildings," passed, June 29th, 1852, are hereby repealed.

Passed, August 18, 1856.

AN ORDINANCE

To restrain Horses, Cattle, Sheep, Goats, Dogs, Mules, Jackasses, and other Animals and Fowls, from running at large.

The Mayor and Common Council of the City of Milwaukee, do ordain as follows.

Animals not to run at large. SECTION 1. No horses, cattle, milch cows, sheep, goats, swine, mules, jackasses, or other animals and fowls, shall hereafter run at large within the limits of the City of Milwaukee, and the owner, lessee, or any person who has the custody or charge of any such animals, and who shall suffer or permit the same to run at large, contrary to the provisions of this section, shall, on conviction thereof, be liable to a penalty of not less than two, or more than ten dollars for each and every offence.

SEC. 2. That every person residing in this city, and owning, or having in his or her possession any dog, and suffering the same to run at large at any season of the year, shall be liable to a penalty of two dollars, unless protected as hereinafter provided. Any person paying to the City Treasurer the sum of one dollar for every dog in his or her possession, shall, upon the presentation to the City Clerk of said Treasurer's receipt, be entitled to a license for such dog to run at large for one year, without any further protection, except between the 15th of June and the 15th of October in each year, provided such person, upon procuring the license as aforesaid, shall put upon the neck of such dog a metallic collar with the owner's name engraved thereon, and shall pay said Clerk fifty cents for making out such license.

Dogs not to run at large.

May be licensed.

SEC. 3. Between the 15th of June and the 15th of October, in each year, no person residing in this city, and owning or having in his or her possession any dog, shall suffer the same to run at large, without causing such dog or dogs to be securely muzzled so as to prevent them from biting, under a penalty of five dollars for each and every offence.

Muzzled, when.

SEC. 4. Any person causing a dog fight, or who shall be aiding and abetting the same, shall be liable to a penalty of not less than one, nor more than five dollars for each and every offence.

Dog fights.

SEC. 5. In order to carry out the provisions of this ordinance, and to provide for keeping and confining all animals and dogs running at large, contrary to its provisions, there shall be established, under the authority of the Common Council and at the expense of said city, a *Pound*, to be under the charge of the Chief of the Police, and to be kept by some person to be appointed and designated by him, and

Pound established.

until the Common Council shall provide and fit up a suitable establishment for this purpose, it shall be the duty of the Chief of the Police to provide, in his discretion, a temporary place for enforcing and carrying out this ordinance.

Dogs, when impounded.

SEC. 6. Any dogs found running at large in this city, and not licensed, or without a collar on their neck with the owner's name thereon, as hereinbefore provided, and any dogs running at large, between the 15th of June and the 15th of October, without being securely muzzled, it shall be the duty of the Police to seize and confine for forty-eight hours in said Pound, and if within that time any such dog is called for, to deliver the same to the owner, upon his paying the keeper of the Pound the sum of three dollars, and the license, if not paid. But all dogs not claimed after a detention of forty-eight hours are to be killed and destroyed by said Police.

Other animals to be impounded.

SEC. 7. It shall be the duty of the Chief of the Police and all Policemen under his direction, to secure and confine in said Pound all horses, cattle, milch cows, sheep, goats and swine found running at large within the limits of this city, the same to be safely kept and provided for, and to be delivered to any owner calling for the same, upon the payment by him to the keeper of the Pound of the sum of two dollars, together with the expense of subsistence for the length of time any such animal may have been impounded, to be estimated at a reasonable and fair rate.

Register to be kept.

SEC. 8. It shall be lawful for any person finding any of the above named animals running at large within the limits of the city, before specified, to drive them to the Pound, and it shall be the duty of the Pound-keeper thereupon to receive the same, and to pay the person delivering the same, the sum of twenty-five cents for each animal so impounded, and to enter the name of the person delivering the same, the date of impounding and the description of all the animals impounded, in a register to be kept by him for that purpose, which register shall be kept open for inspection to all persons applying therefor.

SEC. 9. Any impounded animal not released as above provided, within ten days from the impounding thereof, may be sold at public vendue, at the pound gate, after giving three days notice of such sale, with a description of the animal or animals to be sold, but no pound-keeper or Policeman shall be a purchaser at such sale. Animals sold when.

SEC. 10. The moneys received at any such sale, after deducting the amount of the release fee and expense of subsistence and sale, shall be paid to the owner of the animal sold when ascertained, and if not ascertained within thirty days, shall be paid over to the City Treasurer, and in the latter event, it shall be the duty of the pound-keeper to report the same to the City Clerk forthwith. Moneys, how paid.

SEC. 11. No person shall wilfully obstruct or prevent the apprehension or impounding of any animal running at large, contrary to this ordinance, under a penalty of not less than two nor more than ten dollars for each and every offence. Penalty for obstructing.

SEC. 12. An ordinance to restrain horses, cattle, sheep, goats and swine from running at large, passed, January 21st, 1847 ; an ordinance to license dogs, passed, July 13th, 1846, and the ordinances in amendment thereof, passed, June 22d, 1848, passed, June 9th, 1856, and passed, July 21st, 1856, are hereby repealed.

Passed, August 18, 1856.

AN ORDINANCE

Prescribing Fire Limits, and the construction of Buildings therein.

The Mayor and Common Council of the City of Milwaukee, do ordain as follows :

SECTION 1. All that part of the City of Milwaukee, embraced in the following limits, shall hereafter be known as the fire limits, to wit: Fire limits.

2d ward. In the second ward, all that portion of said ward, known and described as blocks thirty-two, thirty-three, thirty-nine, forty, forty-one, forty-two, forty-eight, forty-nine, and fifty, the east half of blocks thirty-four, forty-seven, and fifty-one, the south half of blocks thirty-seven and thirty-eight, and the north half of blocks forty-three and forty-four.

3d ward. In the third ward, all that portion of said ward known and described as blocks three, four, five, six, seven, eight, thirteen, thirty-one, thirty-two, thirty-three, thirty-five, thirty-six, thirty-seven, and one hundred and fifty-five, and also the west half of blocks fourteen and fifteen in said ward.

4th ward. In the fourth ward, blocks fifty-seven, fifty-eight, fifty-nine, seventy-one, and seventy-two.

5th ward. In the fifth ward, all that portion of said ward known and described as blocks two, six and seven, and lots one, two, three, four, five and six, in block five.

7th ward. In the seventh ward, all that portion of said ward known as blocks one, two, nine, ten, eleven, twelve, fifty-one, fifty-two, fifty-three, fifty-four, fifty-five, fifty-six, fifty-seven, and fifty-eight, and also the west half of blocks fifty-nine, sixty, sixty-one, and sixty-two.

Buildings in the fire limits how erected. SEC. 2. No building shall hereafter be erected within the fire limits (except as hereinafter excepted,) unless the same be constructed in conformity with the following provisions:

1. All outside and party walls shall be made of stone, brick, or other fire-proof material.

2. Outside and party walls, not exceeding twenty-four feet in height from the level of the side-walk to the under side of the roof joists, or rafters, (except for stores, mills, breweries, and warehouses), shall not be less than eight inches in thickness, if of brick, and not less than sixteen inches in thickness, if of stone. But stores, mills, breweries and warehouses, exceeding twenty-four feet in height, as aforesaid, shall not be less than twelve inches in thickness, if of brick, nor less than eighteen inches in thickness, if of stone.

3. All joists, beams and other timbers in outside and party walls, shall be separated at least four inches from each other with stone or brick laid in mortar, and all wooden lintels, or plate pieces, in front or rear walls, shall recede from the outside of the wall at least four inches, except that lintels of timber may be used in cornices covered with copper, tin, iron, or other fire-proof material, which recede four inches from the outside or front as aforesaid.

4. Roofs, cornices, and gutters, shall be covered on the outside surface with copper, tin, iron, or other fire proof material; and all buildings to be used for stores or warehouse purposes, which exceed twenty-four feet in height from the level of the side-walk to the under side of the rafters, shall have shutters to all outside doors and windows, made of iron, or covered with iron or other fire-proof material. But steeples, cupolas, spires of churches or other public buildings, which shall stand thirty feet apart from any other building, may be covered with boards or shingles.

5. There shall not be more than thirty feet space between the party or outside walls of any building, unless such building shall be supported by iron or other columns or supports of fire-proof material.

6. All end and party walls shall extend above the sheeting of the roof at least two and one-half feet, and in no case shall the planking or sheeting of the roof extend through or across any party or end wall, and in case of any opening in any party or end wall, the same shall be provided with iron or fire-proof doors, properly fitted and hung, so as to be easily and quickly closed in case of fire.

Sheds may be erected.

SEC. 3. Sheds not exceeding twelve feet in height at the peak or highest part, and privies not exceeding ten feet square and ten feet in height at the peak, may be constructed of wood, and shall not be subject to the provisions of this ordinance. But all depositories of ashes, within or without the fire limits, shall be built of brick, or other fire-proof material, without wood in any part thereof.

Wooden buildings not to be repaired or removed.

SEC. 4. No wooden building or part of building, within the fire limits, shall be raised, repaired, enlarged or removed to any other place within the same, nor shall any such building be removed into the fire limits; nor shall any wooden building within said limits which may hereafter be damaged to the extent of fifty per cent. of the value thereof, be repaired or rebuilt; nor shall such building, where the damages are less than fifty per cent. of its value, be so repaired as to be raised higher than the highest point left standing after such damage shall have occurred, or so as to occupy a greater space than before the injury thereto.

Damage, how ascertained.

SEC. 5. The amount of or extent of damage that may be done to any building, may be determined by three disinterested persons, residents of the city, one of whom shall be chosen by the owner of the building, the second by the Mayor, and the two so chosen shall select the third, and the decision of the persons so chosen shall be final and conclusive.

When deemed a nuisance.

SEC. 6. Any wooden building which may be erected, enlarged, removed or repaired, or in process of erection, enlargement, removal or repair, contrary to this ordinance, shall be deemed a nuisance, and upon information in writing it shall be the duty of the Mayor, after due notice to the owner or builder to abate the same, by an order in writing to require the Chief of the Police to raze such building to the ground; the expense thereof shall be reported by the Chief of the Police, and may be collected of the owner of such building by suit.

Penalty.

SEC. 7. Any owner, builder, or other person who shall own, build or aid in the erection of any building or part of building within the fire limits, contrary to, or in any other manner than authorized by the provisions of this ordinance, or who shall own, remove, or assist in removing any such building from without said limits into the same, or own, repair, or assist in repairing any damaged wooden building contrary in either case to any provisions of this ordinance, shall be subject to a penalty of not less than twenty-five dollars and not exceeding five hundred dollars, in the discretion of the court, for the first offence, and to a like penalty for every forty-eight hours such person shall fail to comply with the provisions of this ordinance. If any person shall violate any other provision of this ordinance, he shall be subject to a like penalty.

SEC. 8. In case of and during the continuance of a fire, no intoxicating liquors shall be allowed among the firemen, or be brought on to the ground for any purpose, except the same shall have been ordered by the Mayor or Chief Engineer, and any person or persons furnishing any intoxicating liquor or drink to firemen during a fire, except as herein provided, shall forfeit and pay a fine of not less than five, nor more than twenty-five dollars for every offence.

Liquors, when allow'd at fires.

SEC. 9. "An ordinance prescribing fire limits, and the construction of buildings therein," passed, November 18th, 1852, and the ordinances in amendment thereof, passed, March 3d, 1853, passed, September 8th, 1853, passed, September 14th, 1854, passed, July 10th, 1856, and passed, August 1st, 1856, are hereby repealed.

Passed, August 29, 1856.

AN ORDINANCE

To regulate Hackney Coaches, Cabs, Drays and Omnibusses.

The Mayor and Common Council of the City of Milwaukee, do ordain as follows:

SECTION 1. No person shall hire out, or keep, or use for hire, or cause to be kept or used for hire in the transportation of persons or property within the city, any hackney coach, cab, omnibus, or other carriage of any description, or

Coaches, cabs, &c., to be licensed.

any dray, cart or wagon, without a license from the city, under a penalty of twenty dollars for every offence.

Mayor to license.

SEC. 2. The Mayor is hereby authorized to license, under his hand, any resident of the city over twenty-one years of age, to keep a hackney coach, cab, omnibus or other public carriage, dray, cart or wagon, upon his entering into a bond, with one or more sureties to be approved by the Mayor, in the penalty of three hundred dollars, conditioned for the payment of all penalties which the applicant may incur, and all damages for which he may become liable.

Bond to be given.

Fees.

SEC. 3. When any application shall be granted, it shall be the duty of the City Clerk, upon the payment of one dollar to the Mayor for granting license and approving the bond, and one dollar to the Clerk, to issue a license and cause the same to be registered and numbered. Such license shall continue in force for one year from the date thereof.

No. of license and name of owner.

SEC. 4. Every person who may be licensed as aforesaid, shall forthwith cause the number of his license, together with his own name or the name which may be given to his vehicle, to be plainly painted on some conspicuous place on each side of the hack, cab, omnibus, coach or other carriage, cart, dray or wagon so licensed, under a penalty of three dollars, for every week he shall run or use the same without being so numbered and lettered.

When used in night time

SEC. 5. Every hackney coach, cab, omnibus or other carriage, when driven or used in the night, shall have fixed upon some conspicuous part of the outside of such vehicle, two lighted lamps, with plain glass fronts and sides, with the number of the license painted thereon with black paint, in legible figures at least two inches in length, so that they may be distinctly seen and known; and the owner or driver of any such vehicle, which shall be driven or used in the night without such lighted lamps, shall severally forfeit the sum of five dollars.

SEC. 6. The prices to be charged by the owner or driver of any hackney coach, cab, coach or other carriage or vehicle (except omnibusses) for the conveyance of passengers within said city, shall be as follows, to be regulated and estimated by the distance of the most direct routes, namely : Tariff of prices.

1. For conveying a passenger not exceeding one mile, 37½ cents.

For every additional passenger of the same family or party, 18¾ cents.

2. For conveying a passenger any distance exceeding a mile, and within the city limits, as follows :

For the first mile, 75 cents.

For each additional mile, 37½ cents.

For every additional passenger of the same family or party, 18¾ cents.

3. For conveying children between five and fourteen years of age, half of the above prices may be charged for the like distances, but for children under five years of age, no charge shall be made.

4. For the use, by the day, of any hackney coach or other carriage drawn by two horses, with one or more passengers, $4.50.

5. For the use of any such vehicle by the hour, with one or more passengers, with the privilege of going from place to place, and stopping as often as may be required, as follows :

For the first hour, $1.12½.

For the second hour, 62½ cents.

For each succeeding hour, 37½ cents.

6. For the use of any cab or other carriage drawn by a single horse, by the hour, with one or more passengers, with the privilege of going from place to place and stopping as often as may be required, as follows :

For the first hour, 75 cents.

For the second hour, 37½ cents.

For each succeeding hour, 30 cents.

7. For the use of any such cab or other carriage by the day, $3.00.

What baggage allowed.

8. Every passenger may be allowed to have conveyed upon such vehicle, without charge, his ordinary travelling baggage, not exceeding, in any case, one trunk, twenty-five pounds of other baggage. For every additional package, when the whole weight of baggage is over one hundred pounds, if conveyed to any place within the city limits, the owner or driver shall be permitted to charge 10 cents. If conveyed any greater distance, 15 cents.

Livery stables.

SEC. 7. Coaches drawn by two horses, kept by the keeper of a livery stable, for the conveyance of passengers in whole or in part within the city limits, shall be deemed to be included within the first section of this ordinance.

What streets are stands.

SEC. 8. The streets within the limits hereinafter mentioned, in the several wards of the City of Milwaukee, are hereby established as stands for drivers of hackney coaches, cabs, drays and omnibusses, while waiting with their vehicles for employment.

1st ward.

In the first ward, on the south side of Oneida and north side of Mason streets, between the east side of East Water and Main streets.

2d ward.

In the second ward, on Third street, south of Vliet street, and on Chestnut street, between Fifth street and the river.

3d ward.

In the third ward, on the south side of Wisconsin street, between East Water and Main streets, and on the south side of Michigan, Huron, Detroit, Buffalo and Chicago streets, between the Milwaukee river and the west side of East Water street.

4th ward.

In the fourth ward, on West Water street, north of Spring, on Second street, south of Clybourn street.

5th ward.

In the fifth ward, on South Water street, between Ferry and Barclay, on Lake between Ferry and the river.

Penalty.

Any hackman, cabman, omnibus driver, drayman or cartman who shall, while waiting for employment, or not being employed, place his hack, cab, omnibus, dray or cart upon any street, other than the streets or within the limits here mentioned, shall, on complaint before the Police Justice, be subject to a fine of not less than one nor more than five dollars for each and every offence.

Prices for goods, merchandize, &c

SEC. 9. The prices or rates to be taken by draymen, carmen or driver of any baggage wagon, for the carriage of any article, goods, wares, or merchandize, where the distance does not exceed half a mile, shall be as follows:

For every tierce of molasses or spirituous liquors, exceeding thirty and less than sixty gallons, fifteen cents when carried single; for every additional cask of like dimensions, five cents; for every hogshead of sugar, twenty-five cents; for every tierce of sugar, twenty cents; for every load of household furniture and housing the same, thirty-eight cents; if not requested to be housed, twenty-five cents; for every load of lumber, twenty-five cents; for every load of flour, consisting of six barrels or more, twenty-five cents; for a single barrel of flour, or other article not exceeding 300 pounds, twelve and a-half cents; for every load of dirt or filth removed out of any of the streets or alleys, ten cents; for loading, carting and unloading every load not above specified, twenty-five cents; for every load, where the distance between the points of receipt and delivery exceeds half a mile, and is not more than a mile, one-fourth more than the aforesaid rates; and if said distance exceeds one mile, one half more than the rates aforesaid may be received, in full compensation for any greater distance within the corporate limits of the City of Milwaukee.

Every violation of this section shall subject the offender to a penalty of not less than one nor more than five dollars for each and every offence.

Penalty for improper conduct.

SEC. 10. Any hackman, cabman, omnibus driver, drayman or cartman who shall, while waiting for employment on any stand, or while waiting for employment, or otherwise, at any rail road termination, steamboat or other boat landing, or elsewhere, leave such vehicle, except for the purpose of getting the baggage or other personal property of the person employing him, or who shall snap or flourish his whip, or use indecent or profane language, or be guilty of boisterous or loud talking or hallooing, or any disorderly conduct, or vex and annoy travellers and citizens, or obstruct any side-walk, shall be subject to a penalty of not less than two nor more than ten dollars in every case.

Policemen to arrest, &c.

SEC. 11. Any member of the Police department shall have power to arrest and commit any person offending in any manner against the provisions of this ordinance, who refuses or fails to desist from such offence when commanded; and they shall have power to give any direction which may be required for the preservation of good order and the equal convenience of the public, at any rail road termination and steam or other boat landing; and any hackman, cabman, drayman or other person who shall refuse or neglect to obey such directions, or who shall resist such officer in the discharge of any duty, shall be deemed guilty of a breach of the peace, and be subject to immediate arrest and commitment. On conviction, the offender shall be subject to a fine of not less than two dollars, and not exceeding one hundred dollars, and to imprisonment, in the discretion of the court, not exceeding twenty days.

What vehicles not to be licensed.

SEC. 12. Wagons and vehicles kept by merchants for the free delivery of goods sold by them, teams used for hauling earth and building materials, and coaches, wagons and other vehicles used exclusively for the transportation of persons or property beyond the city, or by public houses for the accommodation of their own business, shall not be deemed included in the first section of this ordinance.

Refusing to carry persons and baggage, &c.

SEC. 13. Any owner or driver of a hackney coach, cab, omnibus or other carriage, who shall refuse or neglect to convey any person with his baggage, when applied to for that purpose, or who shall ask, take or extort any greater price than those herein established, or who shall neglect or refuse to place the rates of fare inside of his vehicle, shall be subject to a penalty of not less than two nor more than twenty dollars for each and every offence.

SEC. 14. It shall be the duty of the City Clerk to keep a register of all licenses granted under this ordinance, wherein shall be stated the number of the license, to whom issued, and the date thereof. The licenses of the different kinds of vehicles, mentioned herein, shall be kept by distinct number, and in separate parts of said register. All licenses shall be subject to revocation for good cause. City Clerk to register licenses.

SEC. 15. "An ordinance to regulate hackney coaches, drays and omnibusses," passed, November 22, 1852, a supplemental ordinance to the same, passed, April 7, 1853, an ordinance to amend the same, passed, May 19, 1853, "an ordinance to regulate hackney coaches, cabs, drays and omnibusses," passed, July 9, 1855, and an ordinance to amend the same, passed, June 23, 1856, are hereby repealed.

Passed, August 29, 1856.

AN ORDINANCE

For the regulation of the Harbor of Milwaukee.

Be it ordained by the Mayor and Aldermen of the City of Milwaukee, in Common Council assembled :

SECTION 1. That the Harbor Master is hereby authorized and directed to give such orders and directions, from time to time, as he shall deem just and proper, relative to the location and change of situation of every steamboat, vessel or other craft or float in the harbor of Milwaukee. Harbor Master's powers.

SEC. 2. No person shall unload any steamboat, vessel or craft or float at or upon any of the public wharves or docks in this city, or otherwise place or deposit on any such Unloading of vessels.

wharf or dock, any stone, lumber, timber, firewood or other materials, without permission from the Harbor Master.

Steamers in the river. SEC. 3. All steamboats coming in or going out of the harbor, or passing up or down the river, shall be moved under a low pressure of steam, and slowly, so as not to endanger or injure any other boat or craft or the bridges or works in the harbor.

To carry lights. SEC. 4. All steamboats, brigs, vessels or other lake craft shall have kept on board during the night time, a conspicuous light or lantern.

Passing through bridges. SEC. 5. No sail vessel shall pass through the draw of any bridge in the City of Milwaukee, except it be towed, or under very light sail.

Penalty. SEC. 6. Any owner, master, or other person having in charge any steamboat, vessel or other craft or float violating any of the preceding provisions of this ordinance, shall forfeit, for the use of the City of Milwaukee, the penalty of twenty dollars, and every such steamboat, vessel or other craft or float, of which the owner, master, or other person having charge of the same, shall become liable as aforesaid, shall be chargeable therewith.

Obstructions not to be cast into the river SEC. 7. No person shall cast or deposit, or suffer to be cast or deposited in the harbor or navigable waters of this city, any earth or other heavy substances, filth, manure, logs or floating matter, or any obstructions, under the penalty of five dollars for each and every offence, and a like penalty for each and every day the same shall be suffered to remain therein, after notice to remove the same.

SEC. 8. Upon conviction of any person or persons of any of the offences hereinbefore set forth, the costs of the prosecution and conviction shall be added to the penalty, and for want of goods whereon to satisfy any execution issued therefor, the same shall require the offender to be committed to the county jail for ten days, for the penalty imposed in the sixth section of this ordinance, and for three days for the penalty named for each of the offences under the seventh section thereof.

SEC. 9. All persons owning or occupying any of the piers now, or which shall hereafter be erected in the Lake within the city bounds, and using the same for hire, for the landing of goods or passengers, or which are used for that purpose, shall cause the same to be securely railed on both sides, with a railing three feet and a half in height, consisting of posts and two horizontal slats, all to be of sufficient strength to prevent passengers or others from falling off from the same at night; and any persons occupying said piers, as aforesaid, shall cause to be kept up thereupon every night when any vessel or steamboat shall be lying thereto, at least three good lanterns, supplied with burning lights. Provided the above requirements shall not be applicable to the sides of the wide part of the outer end of any such pier.

Piers to be railed and lighted.

SEC. 10. Any person refusing or neglecting to comply with the provisions of the foregoing section, shall forfeit and pay for the use of the city, the penalty of ten dollars for each and every day they shall so refuse or neglect to comply.

Passed, September 24, 1846.

AN ORDINANCE

Relating to Penalties and Judgments.

Be it ordained by the Mayor and Aldermen of the City of Milwaukee, in Common Council assembled:

SECTION 1. That all ordinances prescribing penalties for their violation, shall be construed by the court to carry with such penalties all costs of prosecution and collection, and in entering up judgment in all cases, such costs shall be included as against the delinquent.

Judgment for penalties carry costs.

Duty of City Attorney.

SEC. 2. Whenever a judgment shall be rendered in favor of this city, for any cause, it shall be the duty of the City Attorney forthwith to take out an execution against the party, and proceed as speedily as possible to make collection of the same; and if the party against whom such judgment shall lie has not personal property to satisfy the same, but has real property in any county within the third judicial district, then it shall be the duty of said Attorney to file a transcript of such judgment in the Clerk's office, in the county where such real estate may be, and proceed without delay to collect the amount of such judgment out of such real estate.

Passed, October 5, 1846.

AN ORDINANCE

Establishing a Public Stand in the Third Ward.

Be it ordained by the Mayor and Aldermen of the City of Milwaukee, in Common Council assembled:

Hay and wood market

SECTION 1. That a public stand for the sale or disposal of wood, hay and other marketable articles, be, and the same is hereby established in the third ward, which shall consist of the following portions of Detroit street, namely: those between East Water street and the Milwaukee river, and between said East Water street and Main street.

Passed, February 8, 1847.

AN ORDINANCE

To compel the attendance of Members of the Common Council.

Be it ordained by the Mayor and Aldermen of the City of Milwaukee, in Common Council assembled:

Absentees fined.

SECTION 1. That when any Member of the Common Council shall absent himself from the sitting, after he shall have been in attendance, without the leave of the Common Council, he shall be fined in the sum of ten dollars.

Refusal to attend after notice fined.

SEC. 2. That when any Member of the Common Council shall refuse to attend a meeting of the Common Council, after a resolution shall have been passed by a majority of the members present, requiring his attendance forthwith, such Member shall be fined in the sum of twenty dollars.

Passed, February 18, 1847.

AN ORDINANCE

In relation to setting the Posts of the Erie and Michigan Telegraph Company.

Be it ordained by the Mayor and Aldermen of the City of Milwaukee, in Common Council assembled:

May erect posts.

SECTION 1. That the Erie and Michigan Telegraph Company shall hereby have the privilege of setting posts for the purpose of supporting their wire along such streets as may be necessary for the purposes and uses of said Company, provided that said Company shall erect in the bounds of the city fair and handsome poles.

How erected

SEC. 2. That the poles shall be erected on the outer side of the sidewalk in such a way as not to obstruct any passage or view, and that said posts shall be at least twenty feet high, and to be firmly and securely set so as not to injure or damage the side-walk or obstruct the use of the same, other than the size of the posts.

Unsightly poles to be removed.

SEC. 3. That if said Company shall erect crooked or unsightly poles, the Aldermen of the ward in which said poles are so erected, shall have the power to remove the same after notifying the agent or any one of the trustees of said Company, that such pole or poles must be removed, and another or others, in accordance with the requirements of this ordinance, be erected in its or their place, such pole or poles shall remain for six days after the giving of said notice, and the erection of all said poles shall be under the direction of the local committee of the ward in which such poles are erected.

Passed, August 28, 1847.

AN ORDINANCE

Relating to the appointment and duties of Sealer of Weights and Measures.

Be it ordained by the Mayor and Aldermen of the City of Milwaukee, in Common Council assembled :

How appointed.

SECTION 1. That there shall be appointed by the Common Council, a Sealer of Weights and Measures, who shall hold his office for one year, and until his successor shall be appointed and qualified, unless sooner removed by the Common Council, and the term of office of said Sealer shall expire on the first day of May in each year.

Standard weights, &c.

SEC. 2. The Sealer of Weights and Measures shall have the custody of the standard weights and measures belonging to the city, and shall take care that the same be not injured or in anywise impaired, and he shall not suffer the same to go out of his possession during his continuance in office. He shall enter into bonds to the City of Milwaukee, in the penal sum of one thousand dollars, conditioned for the faithful performance of the duties of his office, and that he will preserve the integrity of the standard committed to his care, and deliver the same to his successor in office, in as good condition as when received by him, necessary wear excepted.

Bond.

Duties.

SEC. 3. It shall be the duty of the Sealer of Weights and Measures to compare any weights and measures or implements used for weighing and measuring, that may be brought to him for that purpose, with the standard in his possession, and when found to conform thereto, he shall seal and mark the same, and he shall keep a register of all weights, measures, scale beams, patent balances, steel yards, or other implements used in weighing or measuring, sealed by him, with the name of the owners, and the date when sealed.

SEC. 4. A seal with some suitable device, and a brand and dies with the initials "M. C.," shall be procured at the expense of the city, for the use of the sealer, and a description of the seal and impress of the same shall be filed with the City Clerk. Seal.

SEC. 5. The sealer of weights and measures shall be entitled to demand and receive the following fees for his services: Fees.

For sealing and marking every scale, beam, patent balance, steel yard, or other instrument used for weighing in the City of Milwaukee, fifteen cents.

For sealing and marking measures of extension, at the rate of fifteen cents per yard, not to exceed fifty cents for any one measure.

For sealing and marking any weights under seven pounds, three cents; not less than seven pounds and under fourteen, five cents; not less than fourteen and under twenty-eight, ten cents; not less than twenty-eight and under fifty-six pounds, fifteen cents; fifty-six pounds and upwards, twenty-five cents.

For sealing and marking liquid and dry measures:

For every measure under one gallon, three cents; for one gallon and over, six cents.

For every measure of half a bushel, fifteen cents; for every measure of a bushel, twenty-five cents; for every measure of two bushels or upwards, one dollar.

The said sealer shall also be entitled to reasonable compensation for making such weights and measures conform to the standard.

SEC. 6. An inventory of the articles comprising the set of standard weights and measures, and the implements used in connection therewith, belonging to the city, shall be made out and filed with the Clerk, and the sealer of weights and measures first appointed, shall receipt to the City Clerk for the same, and each new incumbent shall receipt to his predecessor for the weights, measures and implements handed over to him, a duplicate of which receipt shall be filed with the said City Clerk.

Passed, November 11, 1847.

AN ORDINANCE

To regulate Trials of Impeachment before the Common Council of the City of Milwaukee.

Be it ordained by the Mayor and Aldermen of the City of Milwaukee, in Common Council assembled:

Parties to have process for witnesses

SECTION 1. That in all trials of impeachment before the Common Council of the City of Milwaukee, the complainant and respondent shall be entitled to have processes issued to compel the attendance of witnesses, to be issued by the Mayor, or acting Mayor, attested by the Clerk, which process may be served by the City Marshal or either of his deputies, or by any Constable of the city, to be made returnable at the meeting of the Common Council appointed for such trial.

Rules for trials.

SEC. 2. That any such trial may be adjourned from time to time, on good cause being shown either on the part of the complainant or respondent to the Common Council, and the same rules in relation to the examination of witnesses and arguments of council shall be observed, as are recognized in the District Court in and for the County of Milwaukee.

Penalties against.

SEC. 3. That after a witness has been served with a subpœna to appear before the Common Council in any trial for impeachment, such witness shall be subject to the same pains and penalties for non-attendance in accordance with said subpœna, as are by law provided against the non-attendance of witnesses after being duly subpœnaed in courts of record in Wisconsin, and that said pains and penalties may be enforced by prosecution or otherwise, in the name of the City of Milwaukee, and that said Common Council, according to section nineteen of the act aforesaid, shall have power to authorize an attachment to be issued by the Mayor, or acting Mayor, duly authorized by the Clerk, to compel the attendance of any witness who has been subpœnaed to attend on any trial as aforesaid and then pending before said Council.

SEC. 4. That the costs that may be taxed in trials of impeachment, as provided for in the act to incorporate the City of Milwaukee, are the following: the same fees for the attendance of witnesses shall be allowed as in courts of record of Wisconsin, and the same fees shall be allowed to officers for serving subpœnas, attachments, &c., as are allowed in civil actions at law in courts of record in Wisconsin. Costs.

Passed, March 6, 1848.

AN ORDINANCE

In relation to the report of Deaths within the City Limits.

Be it ordained by the Mayor and Aldermen of the City of Milwaukee, in Common Council assembled:

SECTION 1. That every sexton and keeper, or person or persons having in charge any cemetery, burial ground, or other place or places of burial within the limits of the City of Milwaukee, shall keep a book in which every such sexton, keeper, person or persons shall enter the name, age, place of residence, occupation, place of nativity, and the disease or other cause of death, of every person interred in the cemetery, burial ground, or other place or places of burial, under his or their charge, and make a detailed report of the same to the Common Council, at the first regular meeting in each month. Burials reports of.

SEC. 2. That all persons offending against the provisions of this section shall be fined ten dollars for each and every offence.

Passed, March 9, 1848.

AN ORDINANCE

Regulating the charge on Emigrants' and other Passengers' Goods landing on the Piers extending into Lake Michigan, in the City of Milwaukee.

Be it ordained by the Mayor and Aldermen of the City of Milwaukee, in Common Council assembled:

Rate of pierage. SECTION 1. That hereafter no owner or occupant of any pier extending into Lake Michigan, within the corporate limits of the City of Milwaukee, shall be entitled to receive from emigrants or other passengers, more than ten cents for every barrel bulk landed on such pier or piers.

Penalty for exacting more. SEC. 2. Any owner or occupant of any pier or piers extending into the Lake, who shall exact, suffer, allow or countenance a higher price to be charged or exacted on such pier or piers, shall be liable to a fine of fifty dollars, to be recovered by trial and conviction for such higher charge or charges on his pier.

Passed, May 3, 1849.

AN ORDINANCE

Regulating the Manufacture and Sale of Bread.

Be it ordained by the Mayor and Aldermen of the City of Milwaukee, in Common Council assembled:

Bakers to file Certificate. SECTION 1. Every baker or person who shall carry on the trade or business of baker, shall, on the first Monday of September, in each year, or within one month from the time of commencing such business, file with the Clerk of the city a certificate signed by him, stating his place of residence and business, under the penalty of five dollars for each and every neglect.

Assize o bread.

SEC. 2. All bread manufactured by the bakers of this city shall be made of good and wholesome flour or meal, into loaves of one, one and a-half, two or three pounds avoirdupois weight, and every loaf of such bread, except twisted loaves, shall be marked with the numbers indicating the weight of such loaf, and also with the initial letters of the baker thereof, under a penalty of ten dollars for each and every offence, to be recovered of the persons offering the same.

Passed, July 13, 1846.

AN ORDINANCE

Relating to Slaughter Houses in the City of Milwaukee.

Be it enacted by the Mayor and Aldermen of the City of Milwaukee, in Common Council assembled :

Animals not to be slaughtered within the city limits.

SECTION 1. That it shall not be lawful for any person or persons to keep a slaughter house or yard, for the purpose of slaughtering or dressing animals of any kind therein or about it, nor to slaughter or dress any animals in any building or yard within the corporate limits of the City of Milwaukee, and every person who shall violate the provisions of this section, shall forfeit the penalty of fifty dollars, with costs of prosecution for each and every day of such violation, and in default of payment shall be imprisoned in the county jail thirty days.

Penalty.

Notice to Butchers.

SEC. 2. This ordinance shall be and remain in force from and after its passage: *Provided always,* That no person now keeping a slaughter house or yard within the city, shall be liable to the penalty thereof, until he shall have had three days notice of its passage, which notice shall be either a printed or written copy of the ordinance, served upon the person or left at his place of abode.

Passed, August 9, 1849.

AN ORDINANCE

Supplemental to, and to amend the several Ordinances of the City of Milwaukee in relation to Fines, Penalties and Forfeitures.

Be it ordained by the Mayor and Aldermen of the City of Milwaukee, in Common Council assembled :

Imprisonment for non payment of penalties.

SECTION 1. That in all cases of conviction for the violation of any of the several ordinances of the city, except such ordinances as the term of imprisonment is now prescribed in the same, the imprisonment of the person or persons so convicted in case of the non-payment of any penalty, fine, or forfeiture, shall be in the Jail of Milwaukee county for the term of not less than one week, nor more than thirty days, in the discretion of the Court, and it is hereby made the duty of the Police Justice, in the execution for the collection of any such fine, forfeiture, or penalty and costs, when directing the imprisonment by law is allowed, to insert a clause directing the imprisonment of the offender or offenders, in the Jail aforesaid, for such length of time as may be specified in the ordinance under which the conviction is had, or for such length of time as may be determined by the Court under this supplemental and amended ordinance.

SEC. 2. This ordinance is hereby declared to be amendatory to the several ordinances of the City of Milwaukee which impose fines, forfeitures, or penalties, but do not provide for the imprisonment of the offenders in case of the non-payment of the same.

Passed, September 6, 1849.

AN ORDINANCE

For the preservation of Game within the city limits.

Be it ordained by the Mayor and Aldermen of the City of Milwaukee, in Common Council assembled:

SECTION 1. No person shall expose for sale, or have in his, her or their possession, in the City of Milwaukee, any woodcock, between the first day of January and the first Tuesday of July in any year, under the penalty of ten dollars for each woodcock so exposed for sale or had in possession. Woodcock, when not to be sold.

SEC. 2. That no person shall expose for sale, or have in his, her or their possession, in the City of Milwaukee, any pinnated grouse, (known as prairie hen or prairie chicken,) between the first day of February and the first Tuesday of August, in any year, under the penalty of five dollars for each grouse so exposed for sale or had in possession. Prairie chickens.

SEC. 3. That no person shall expose for sale, or have in his, her or their possession, in the City of Milwaukee, any partridge, between the first day of February and the first Tuesday of September, in any year, under the penalty of five dollars for each partridge so exposed for sale or had in possession. Partridges.

SEC. 4. That no person shall expose for sale, or have in his, her or their possession, in the City of Milwaukee, any quail, between the first day of February and the first Tuesday of October, in any year, under the penalty of five dollars for each quail so exposed for sale or had in possession. Quails.

SEC. 5. That no person shall expose for sale or have in his, her or their possession, in the City of Milwaukee, any fresh venison, between the first day of February and the first day of August, in any year, under the penalty of five dollars for each piece so exposed for sale or had in possession. Venison.

SEC. 6. The above penalties may be sued for and recovered before any Justice of the Peace, by any person or persons who will prosecute for the same, in which case one-half of the said penalty shall go to the person or persons who shall prosecute to conviction, and the other half to the commissioners of the Alms House, for the benefit of the poor.

Passed, February 12, 1852.

AN ORDINANCE

To regulate and restrain Runners and Solicitors for Boats, Rail Roads, Public Houses or other Establishments.

The Mayor and Common Council of the City of Milwaukee, do ordain:

Runners regulated.

SECTION 1. That any runner or solicitor for boats, rail roads, public houses, or other establishments, who shall, when engaged in his employment, make any unusual noise or disturbance, or make use of any profane, obscene or boisterous language, or use any language or be guilty of any act calculated to disturb the peace or the good order of the city, or harass, vex or disturb strangers or citizens, shall be subject for each offence, to a fine of not less than two dollars, and not exceeding twenty dollars.

Arrests for violation of ordinance.

SEC. 2. The Mayor, Marshal, or any other conservator of the peace, shall have power to arrest and commit any runner or solicitor for examination, who shall be engaged in the commission of any act made penal by this ordinance; they shall also have power to give any directions which may be required, for the preservation of the peace or the convenience of the public at any rail road termination, steamboat or other public landings. Any person who shall refuse to obey such directions, or resist any officer in the discharge of any duty, shall be subject to arrest and commitment, to answer to a charge of disturbing the peace, and to punishment by fine not exceeding fifty dollars.

Passed, March 20, 1852.

AN ORDINANCE

Defining the duties and fixing the compensation of the City Attorney

The Mayor and Common Council of the City of Milwaukee, do ordain as follows :

City Attorney, his duties.

SECTION 1. The City Attorney shall draft all ordinances, deeds, bonds, contracts and documents of whatever kind, which may be required of him by any ordinance, resolution or order of the Common Council, or any committee thereof, and to which the Common Council or any committee thereof may be a party ; he shall prosecute all actions and suits which the city shall direct to be brought in its own behalf or on behalf of any committee or officer thereof, and defend all suits against the city or any officer thereof, the defense of which shall be assumed by the city ; whenever required, he shall advise the Common Council, or any member, committee, or officer thereof, on all subjects touching their official duties ; he shall examine and inspect all tax and assessment rolls, and all proceedings predicated thereon, and advise how to correct the same if necessary ; he shall keep a register of all suits and legal proceedings to which the city is a party, and at the expiration of his term of office, and oftener if required, make a full report to the Common Council of all suits or other legal proceedings in which the city is interested, whether finished or pending, showing the names of the parties, the progress or results of the suits, and the disposition of all moneys, that may have come into his hands as such Attorney.

His compensation.

SEC. 2. The City Attorney shall receive, in full for his services, the sum of six hundred dollars per annum, and all travelling expenses, and ten per cent. on all sums by him collected on judgments or execution.

Passed, April 3, 1852.

AN ORDINANCE

Regulating the issue of City Orders.

The Mayor and Common Council of the City of Milwaukee, do ordain as follows :

Section 1. No funds shall be drawn from the Treasury, except the same shall have been duly allowed and appropriated by the Common Council.

Sec. 2. No funds shall be so drawn, except by an order signed by the Mayor and Clerk, which shall be made payable on the first day of February succeeding the issuing of the same, to the order of the person in whose favor the same may be issued ; such order shall specify the day and the purpose for which it was issued, and the account to which it is chargeable. All orders shall be receivable in payment of any taxes or assessments levied by authority of the city, or other dues payable to the city.

Orders to be received.

Sec. 3. No order shall be issued by the Clerk or Mayor until they have compared the same with the accounts as allowed by the Common Council.

Accounts not to be allowed at meeting when presented.

Sec. 4. No account shall be allowed at the same meeting on which the same may be presented, but the same, when presented, shall be referred, if a ward account, to the local committee of the proper ward, and if a city account, to the committee on finance and the comptroller, and the report of the committee or comptroller shall be endorsed upon or attached to the account.

Treasurer's duty.

Sec. 5. The Treasurer shall return to the Common Council, at each meeting thereof, all the orders he may have received previous to the last returns, with a schedule of the same, and the orders so returned shall be compared by the financial committee or comptroller, with the stubs of the orders so returned, and if found to be correct, the report thereof shall be entered upon the journal, and the said committee or comptroller shall, in the presence of the Common Council, cancel the orders so returned; the orders so cancelled shall be filed and preserved by the Clerk.

SEC. 6. The following shall be the form of orders hereafter to be issued: City orde :heir forı

$.......... No.........	CITY ORDERS................. No...........
Date........... 18......	*Milwaukee*,...................18.......
To.........................	The Treasurer will, on or before the first day of
For........................	February next, pay to the order of........................
....	..........................out of any funds in the Treas-
Received order as	ury belonging to the City, the same having this day
above.	been allowed for..
....	.........................*Clerk*. ....*Mayor*.

SEC. 7. All ordinances, or parts of ordinances, conflicting with the provisions hereof, are hereby repealed.

Passed, April 3, 1852.

AN ORDINANCE

Regulating the Assessing, Levying and Collecting of Taxes.

The Mayor and Common Council of the City of Milwaukee, do ordain as follows:

SECTION 1. The Assessors, within such time as the Common Council shall direct, shall make aut an assessment roll, which shall contain a description, as near as may be, of all the land, lots, or parcels of land within the city, sufficient to identify the same, and of all persons and bodies politic, liable to pay taxes on personal property; such assessment roll shall be so ruled as to show, in proper columns, a description of the real estate and of the cash value thereof, the value of any improvements thereon, the valuation of the real estate and improvements, and the corrected valuation thereof, and also the names of the persons or bodies politic liable to pay Assessors, :heir duties. Roll.

taxes on personal property, and the amount thereof for which they may be assessed.

Real estate. SEC. 2. On completing said roll, the Assessors shall proceed without delay to ascertain the cash value of all the real estate and improvements thereon within the city, and to enter the same opposite to the proper lot or tract, under the proper columns, and also to enter opposite to the name of each person or body politic, the amount for which they may be respectively assessed. Each column shall be added up by the assessors, and the several amounts carried forward, so as to show the total valuation of the real estate and personal estate respectively.

Personal property. SEC. 3. Personal property shall be assessed in the ward in which it may be found, bodies politic within the ward in which their office or place of business may be, and rights, credits and moneys in the ward in whieh the person to whom the same may be assessed shall reside.

Notice of completion of roll. SEC. 4. When the Assessors shall have completed and compared said assessment roll, they shall give notice thereof as required by law, and shall fix a time and place when and where they will hear the objections of parties deeming themselves aggrieved by such assessment, and any person failing or neglecting to present his objections to the Board of Assessors, within the time limited, shall be forever afterwards barred from objecting to the assessment made against him, or from receiving any redress from the Common Council.

Objections to roll. SEC. 5. It shall be the duty of the Assessors to attend at the time and place designated in their notice, and to hear such objections as may be made, and after hearing the same, shall alter, modify, or amend said roll, as to them shall seem just and proper; the hearing may be adjourned from day to day, but not beyond the time limited.

Return of roll. SEC. 6. Within one week from the time limited for the hearing of objections, the Assessors having completed and corrected said roll, shall return the same to the Common Council, with a certificate thereof signed by them or a majority of them.

Sec. 7. Should the Common Council refer the said roll back to the Assessors, they shall examine, revise and correct the same, as to them shall seem just and proper, and shall, within such time as the Common Council shall direct, return said roll to the Common Council with a certificate thereof.

Sec. 8. When the said roll shall have been revised and corrected by the Common Council, the same shall be filed with the Clerk, and an order confirming the same shall be entered among the proceedings of the Common Council. Roll filed and confirmed.

Sec. 9. In describing real estate, or in stating the amount of taxes, severally or collectively, upon any real or personal estate, figures and the usual abreviations used in the description of real estate may be used in any roll, tax list, warrant or other proceeding in reference to the levying, assessing or collecting of taxes.

Sec. 10. When the Assessors shall be unable satisfactorily to ascertain the amount to assess any person or body politic, they shall assess such sum as they may deem just and proper, unless the proper party shall show by affidavit the true sum which should be assessed.

Passed, April 3, 1852.

AN ORDINANCE

Regulating the sale of Hay and Wood in the First Ward.

The Mayor and Common Council of the City of Milwaukee, do ordain:

Section 1. All that part of East Water and Market streets, lying between the hay scales and the Market House, and also the Market Square, and that west twenty feet of Market street, from Oneida to Biddle streets, all situated in Hay and wood market.

the first ward of the City of Milwaukee, is hereby declared to be and made a public stand for the sale of loads of wood and hay.

SEC. 2. No person or persons shall be allowed to expose for sale any hay or wood on any part of Market Square or on any part of East Water or Market streets, lying between the south line of Mason street and said hay scales ; nor shall any person permit his or her team, sleigh, wagon or other vehicle, unless the same shall be loaded with hay or wood, to stand on that part of East Water and Market streets, or on the Market Square, mentioned in the first sections of this ordinance, more than ten minutes at any one time.

Penalty for violation.

SEC. 3. Any person or persons violating the provisions of this ordinance, shall forfeit and pay the sum of one dollar for each and every offence, together with the costs of prosecution.

SEC. 4. It is hereby made the duty of the Aldermen of the first ward, the City Marshal and his deputies, and also the person appointed to superintend the sale of hay and wood in the first ward, to prosecute, before the Police Justice, any and all persons who may violate the provisions of this ordinance.

SEC. 5. The provisions of any ordinance or resolution heretofore passed, which may conflict with any thing herein contained, are repealed.

Passed, April 29, 1852.

AN ORDINANCE

To regulate the time, place and manner of holding Auctions and Vendues.

The Mayor and Common Council of the City of Milwaukee, do ordain :

Auctions, certain places designated.

SECTION 1. The Market Square, in the first ward, the foot of Michigan, Huron, Detroit and Buffalo streets, in the third ward, are hereby designated as places at which merchandize or other articles may be sold or exposed for sale at public auction or vendue in said wards, but no such merchandize or other article shall be exposed for sale or placed within thirty feet of any side or cross walk on East Water or Market streets.

Sec. 2. No goods, wares, or merchandize or other thing whatever, shall be placed, sold, or exposed for sale, at public auction or vendue, in any streets, side-walk, alley or public ground in said first and third wards, other than such as are herein designated. Any person who shall violate the provisions of this section, shall forfeit and pay for each and every offence, the sum of twenty-five dollars, together with costs of prosecution.

Crying in the streets prohibited.

Sec. 3. No bell-man or crier, or any drum, fife, or other instrument of music, or any show or signal, noise or other means of attracting the attention of the public, other than a sign or flag, shall be employed, suffered or be permitted to be used at or near any place of sale or auction, or at or near any auction room or place in said wards, for the purpose of attracting attention to such sale or auction, under a penalty of five dollars for each and every offence together with costs of prosecution.

Sec. 4. No auctioneer, his agent or servant, nor any person engaged or employed in selling goods, or other things at auction, shall expose for sale at public auction or vendue, any goods, wares or merchandize or other thing whatsoever, to any person or persons who, at the time of bidding for the same or whilst examining the same, shall be on the sidewalk of any street in the said wards, under the penalty of one dollar for each and every offence.

Sec. 5. All fines and penalties for the violation of any of the provisions of this ordinance, shall be sued for and recovered from the auctioneer, his agent or servant, or other person violating or permitting the same to be violated.

In force, 1st and 3d wards. SEC. 6. This ordinance shall be in force in the first and third wards of said city only.

Passed, May 6, 1852.

AN ORDINANCE

To provide for the compensation of the City Printers.

The Mayor and Common Council of the City of Milwaukee do ordain :

City Printer's compensation. SECTION 1. That there shall be paid to the City Printer, in the German language, the sum of fifteen cents per square for the first insertion, and five cents per square for each subsequent insertion, and that there shall be paid to the City Printer, in the English language, the sum of ten cents per square for the first insertion, and five cents per square for each subsequent insertion of any ordinance, resolution or notice which, by the charter or ordinance of the Common Council, may be required to be published in a daily newspaper; such compensation to be paid quarterly by orders on the treasury in the usual form, but no payment to be made, until the proper affidavit of such publication shall be first made and filed.

SEC. 2. All notices shall be published such time as may be required by the charter or ordinances, and all ordinances three insertions : *provided however,* that ordinances shall be deemed and considered in force from and after their first publication.

Passed May 6, 1852.

AN ORDINANCE

Relating to the exhibition of Shows and Showmen.

The Mayor and Common Council of the City of Milwaukee do ordain :

Exhibitions regulated. SECTION 1. That it shall not be lawful for any person or persons to exhibit to public view for gain, within the city, any animal or animals, wax or other figures, or painting, feats of circus riding, rope or wire dancing, slight of hand, or any theatrical or musical entertainments, without first having obtained a license therefor, and if any person shall offend against the provisions of this section, he shall pay for each offence a sum not less than fifteen dollars, nor more than fifty dollars, and costs of prosecution, and in default of the payment of such fine and costs, shall be imprisoned in the Jail of Milwaukee county not less than one or more than thirty days at the discretion of the Court or Justice rendering judgment. **Penalty.**

SEC. 2. It shall be the duty of the Mayor to grant the license herein provided for, if (in his opinion) the exhibition will not injuriously effect the morals of the people or offend against the rules of decency and good order, and he shall, at his discretion, fix the sum to be paid for such license, but no license shall be issued until the person applying for the same shall present to the Mayor and Clerk the Treasurer's receipt for the amount so fixed by the Mayor, and the Clerk shall preserve said receipt and make an entry thereof. **License by Mayor.**

SEC. 3. Every license granted in pursuance of this ordinance shall specify the time of its duration, and shall be of no validity after the expiration of such time, and no such license shall be assignable for the benefit of any other person.

SEC. 4. It shall be lawful for citizens of the city to give concerts or musical entertainments without charge. **Concerts, &c. by citizens without license.**

Passed May 20, 1852.

AN ORDINANCE

Regulating to Licensing and Taxing Auctioneers.

The Mayor and Common Council of the City of Milwaukee, do ordain :

SECTION 1. There shall be paid into the City Treasury for the use of the City of Milwaukee, upon all sales by auction, **Auctioneers to pay 2 per cent. of sales** of goods, wares, or merchandize, two per cent. of the moneys accruing from such sales out of said moneys: *provided*, that nothing herein contained shall extend to any sale by auction, of goods, wares or merchandize, made by virtue of any rule, order, decree or judgment of any Court, or made by virtue of any laws respecting the collection of taxes or to any sale, by auction, of property belonging to the United States, or this State, or made in consequence of any general assignment of property or effects for the benefit of creditors, or made by or on behalf of any executor or administrator.

Not required in certain cases.

Auctioneers, licenses.

SEC. 2. No person shall hereafter act as auctioneer, or sell or exhibit for sale at public auction or vendue, within the City of Milwaukee, any goods, wares or merchandize, unless such persons shall have a license therefor from the Mayor; any person violating the provisions of this section, shall forfeit and pay to the city, for each and every offence, and for each and every day he may so act as auctioneer, or exhibit and sell, at public auction or vendue, any goods, wares or merchandize, the sum of thirty dollars, besides costs of suit, in addition to the tax imposed by this ordinance; *provided*, that no license shall be required for sale at auction of any goods, wares or merchandize, which, by this ordinance, are not made liable to tax or duty.

Bond.

SEC. 3. The Mayor is authorized to license any person residing in the city to act as auctioneer, provided that the person, desiring to be licensed, shall first pay the sum of fifty dollars, and execute to the City of Milwaukee, a bond, in the penal sum of five hundred dollars, with two sureties, to be approved by the Mayor, conditioned that the person so licensed shall pay the tax or duty imposed by this ordinance and comply with the provisions of the same.

Monthly report.

SEC. 4. Every person so licensed, shall, monthly, on the first Monday of each month, render, under oath, to the City Comptroller, a true and full account of all goods, wares or merchandize, liable to pay the duty or tax imposed by this ordinance, sold by him during the preceding month, or subsequent to the last monthly statement, and shall, at the same time, pay over to the Comptroller the amount of such duty or tax.

SEC. 5. It shall be the duty of the Comptroller, on the first Monday of each month, to demand from each auctioneer or person employed in the auction business, the statement and the tax or duty specified in the foregoing section, and he shall pay over to the Treasurer the sum so received, and file such statement with the Treasurer. Comptroller to demand payment and report.

SEC. 6. No license shall be granted for a term less than one year. Limit of license.

SEC. 7. In all cases, where the auctioneer or owner of the property sold, or any person employed by them, or either of them, shall become the purchaser of the property sold at such sale, it shall be subject to the same tax or duty as if any other person had become the purchaser.

SEC. 8. The sale book of any auctioneer shall be open to the inspection of the Comptroller, and in case the Comptroller shall have reason to believe that the monthly statement of the auctioneer is untrue or incorrect, he shall charge such auctioneer such sum as he may deem just and proper, according to the provisions of this ordinance. Sale book to be open to Comptroller

Passed, May 28, 1852.

AN ORDINANCE

Fixing the Compensation of the City Comptroller and City Clerk, and imposing additional duties on the City Clerk.

The Mayor and Common Council of the City of Milwaukee, do ordain as follows:

SECTION 1. The City Comptroller shall be paid the sum of two thousand dollars, as an annual salary for all services Comptroller's compensation.

rendered and imposed on him by the provisions of the City Charter or by the Common Council.

SEC. 2. The annual salary of the City Clerk shall be fifteen hundred dollars for all services performed either by himself or deputy, and he shall execute to the City of Milwaukee a bond in the penal sum of five hundred dollars, with at least two sureties, as provided in section one of chapter three of the City Charter, and he shall also, quarterly, in the months of June, September, December and March, render an accurate statement to the Common Council, verified by his oath, of all moneys or fees received by virtue of his said office, which sums shall be deducted from each quarter's salary.

Clerk to copy assessment roll.

SEC. 3. Immediately after the revisal and confirmation of the assessment roll, it shall be the duty of the City Clerk to copy such assessment roll into a suitable book to be provided for that purpose, and to set opposite to each tract or parcel of land or person named therein, such sum or sums as may have been levied on such tract or parcel of land or person, for the current year, at the rate per cent. or amount for city, ward or other purposes directed by the Common Council, and duly to record such tax list; it shall also be the duty of the Clerk to make out and transmit to the Clerk of the Board of Supervisors, of the County of Milwaukee, an accurate copy of such revised assessment roll, as provided in section twenty-seven of chapter eight of the City Charter.

To send copy of roll to Board of Supervisors.

Clerk's Deputy.

SEC. 4. The City Clerk may nominate, and by and with the advice and consent of the Common Council, may appoint a deputy, and such Deputy Clerk, before entering upon the discharge of his duties, shall take and subscribe an oath of office and file the same, duly certified, with the City Clerk.

Passed, June 10, 1852.

AN ORDINANCE

In addition to an ordinance, relating to the appointment and duty of Sealer of Weights and Measures, passed, November 11th, 1847.

The Mayor and Common Council of the City of Milwaukee, do ordain as follows :

SECTION 1. The Sealer of Weights and Measures shall, in the months of January and July in each year, call on all persons in the City of Milwaukee using any weights, measures or implements in the purchase or sale of any merchandize or commodity, and compare all the weights, measures or implements used for the purpose aforesaid, with the standards in his possession, belonging to the city, and if the same, on careful inspection, are found to conform thereto, he shall seal and mark such weights, measures or implements with his official seal or brand.

Sealer of Weights and Measures, his duties.

SEC. 2. Any person or persons in the City of Milwaukee, found using any weights, measures or implements for the purchase or sale of any merchandize or commodity which are not in conformity with the city standards, and who shall refuse to have their weights, measures, or implements used for the purpose aforesaid, inspected when called upon by the City Sealer, shall, for each offence, forfeit and pay the sum of ten dollars, for the use of the city, to be collected as is provided in sections four, five and six of chapter ten of an act to consolidate and amend the act to incorporate the City of Milwaukee, and the acts amendatory thereto, approved, February 20th, 1852.

Penalty for using illegal weights and measures.

SEC. 3. The Sealer of Weights and Measures may appoint a deputy, by and with the consent and advice of the Common Council, and such deputy, before entering upon the discharge of his duties, shall take and subscribe an oath of office and file the same, duly certified, with the City Clerk.

Deputy.

,, s, who to pay them.

SEC. 4. The fees for services, to which the Sealer of Weights and Measures is entitled by virtue of section five of the ordinance to which this is additional, shall be paid by the owners of the weights and measures inspected.

SEC. 5. In addition to the set of standard weights and measures in the office of the City Sealer, the following implements may be procured for his use, viz : one drilling machine and drills, three punches, one drawing knife, one hammer, one hopper frame, cut steel stamp, and one iron branding iron.

Passed, June 24, 1852.

AN ORDINANCE

Regulating the Storage and Sale of Gunpowder within the City of Milwaukee.

The Mayor and Common Council of the City of Milwaukee, do ordain as follows :

Gunpowder, regulations for keeping.

SECTION 1. All gunpowder which now is, or hereafter may be brought within the corporate limits of this city, shall be deposited and kept in such powder magazine as may be approved of by the Common Council, and no person shall keep or have, or suffer to be kept or had, in any building or place by him or her owned and occupied in the city, except in the said powder magazine, any greater quantity of gunpowder than ten pounds, for any longer period than ten hours ; nor ten pounds, or any less quantity, unless the same is securely kept in a tin canister with a tin cap or cover, and no such canister shall be opened after candle light, under a penalty of twenty-five dollars for each and every offence.

Keeper of magazine.

SEC. 2. All gunpowder kept within the corporate limits of this city, except as above excepted, shall be deposited and stored in said magazine, which said magazine shall be under the direction of a keeper or overseer, to be appointed by the

Common Council, and subject to such rules, regulations and ordinances as they may think just and equitable.

SEC. 3. The keeper or overseer of said powder magazine shall receive all gunpowder delivered to such magazine, on each and every day, except Sunday, from eight o'clock in the morning till sundown, and shall be deemed responsible for all powder so delivered to his care, and shall give his receipt for the same, specifying marks and quantity and quality whenever required, and shall deliver the same out from eight o'clock in the forenoon until three o'clock in the afternoon, when demanded by the owners or those legally entitled to the possession thereof.

SEC. 4. The keeper or overseer of the said powder magazine shall be authorized to receive and collect of the owners or persons depositing or storing powder in said magazine, the sum of fifteen cents for each keg of powder received, stored and delivered by him, which said sum shall be a lien upon the powder so stored, until the same is fully paid. Fees of keeper.

SEC. 5. No boat, sloop, schooner, vessel or wagon or other conveyance with gunpowder on board, shall be allowed to enter and remain within the corporate limits of the city, under any circumstances, for a longer period than three hours, without reporting the same to the keeper of the powder magazine, and taking his order in relation thereto, in writing, under a penalty of ten dollars for each and every offence.

SEC. 6. No person shall be allowed to enter the said magazine without permission from the keeper or overseer; and the said keeper or overseer shall provide slips of coarse carpeting or cloth to be laid upon the floor to walk upon in passing in and out.

SEC. 7. The Mayor, or either of the Aldermen, the Marshal and Deputy Marshals of the respective Wards, or Fire Wardens, or any person deputed by the Common Council, may enter into and upon any building, boat, sloop, schooner, vessel, wagon, or other conveyance, wharf, or other place or Powers of city officers.

places whatsoever, within the corporate limits of said city, where powder shall be kept, and if any greater quantity than is hereby allowed to be kept, shall be found therein, he shall remove or cause to be removed, such excess to the powder magazine, at the expense of the owners thereof. Any person or persons who shall offer any resistance whatever to the execution of the authority herein granted, shall forfeit the sum of fifty dollars, for each and every offence.

Sec. 8. All ordinances heretofore passed regulating the storage and sale of gunpowder are hereby repealed.

Passed November 22, 1852.

AN ORDINANCE

For the Prevention of Fire.

The Mayor and Common Council of the City of Milwaukee, do ordain as follows :

Ashes.

Section 1. No person shall keep or deposit, or allow to be kept or deposited, any ashes in any wooden vessel, within the limits of this city, nor shall any person throw or deposit any ashes, or allow them to be deposited, on his, her or their premises within fifty feet of any wooden structure, unless in a secure stone or brick ash-room, under the penalty of ten dollars for each and every offence.

Carrying fire

Sec. 2. No person shall carry any fire in or through any street, lot, land or alley within this city, except the same be carried or placed in some close secure pan or vessel, under the penalty of five dollars for each and every offence.

Fire-crackers, bon-fires, &c.

Sec. 3. No person shall fire or set off any squib, cracker, or gunpowder or fire-work, or build any bon-fire within one hundred feet of any building in this city, under the penalty of five dollars for each and every offence ; and the Mayor, Marshal or any Alderman or Fire Warden may restrain or prohibit any firework or bon-fire in any part of the city, whenever, in their opinion, there shall be danger therefrom.

SEC. 4. It shall not be lawful to burn any shavings in any street, road or lane, or to kindle any fire or any other combustible matter, in any street, road or lane, or on any wharf in this city, within one hundred yards of any building or pile of lumber, under the penalty of ten dollars for each and every offence; nor shall any person have, put or keep any hay or straw, uncovered in stack or pile, within the like distance of any building, nor put or keep, allow to be put or kept, any hay, straw, hemp, flax, tow, shavings, in any stable or other building, within such distance from any chimney, hearth or fire-place, or place for depositing ashes, as may be deemed unsafe or dangerous by the Fire Wardens of the proper ward, under the penalty of ten dollars for every hour the same shall so remain after notice to the offender, by the Fire Warden to remove the same. Burning shavings. Piles of hay, straw, &c.

SEC. 5. No pipe of any stove or franklin shall be put up in any house or building unless it be conducted into a chimney, made of brick or stone; nor shall any person at any time set fire to any chimney for the purpose of cleaning the same, without previous consent of the Fire Warden of the proper ward; and any person putting up or procuring to be put up, the pipe of any stove or franklin, or doing any other act contrary to this section, shall, for every offence, forfeit five dollars, and the further sum of one dollar for every twenty-four hours the same shall remain so put up, after notice by any Fire Warden to alter the same. Stove pipes.

SEC. 6. Every chimney, hereafter to be erected, and all chimneys whatsoever, shall be plastered with lime and sand on the inside thereof, under the penalty of twenty-five dollars, and a further penalty of ten dollars for every fifteen days neglect to alter or take down the same, after a notice given by any Fire Warden for that purpose. It shall be the duty of the Engineers and Fire Wardens to take notice of all chimneys where the same are being constructed, and ascertain whether they are in conformity with the require- Chimneys.

ments of this chapter, and if not, make report to the Common Council. Chimneys shall be so constructed or altered as to admit of the flues therein being swept or cleaned from top to bottom, under the penalties, for neglect or refusal, of five dollars for each offence.

Scuttles.

SEC. 7. Every dwelling house or other building more than one story in height, within this city, shall have a scuttle through the roof and a convenient and suitable stairway or ladder leading to the same; and any person constructing such dwelling house or building, without such a scuttle, and every owner of any such house or building now erected, (not having other permanent and convenient means of access to the roof,) neglecting to comply with the requisitions of this section for the space of thirty days after notice from a Fire Warden, shall forfeit twenty-five dollars, and the further sum of five dollars for every ten days the non-compliance shall continue to exist.

Lights in stables.

SEC. 8. No owner or occupant of any livery or other stable within this city, nor any person in the employment of such owner or occupant, shall use therein any lighted candle or other light, except the same be securely kept within a bone, tin or glass lantern, under a penalty not exceeding ten dollars for each offence, to be recovered with costs of suit.

Fire wardens

SEC. 9. It shall be the duty of the Fire Wardens, or either of them, in their respective wards, twice in each year, viz: in the months of May and November, and as much oftener as may be deemed proper, between sunrise and sunset, to enter into any house or building, lot, yards or premises in said city, and examine the fire-places, hearths, chimneys, stoves and pipes thereto, ovens, boilers or other apparatus likely to cause fire; also the places where ashes may be deposited, and all places where any gunpowder, hemp, flax, tow, hay, straw, rushes, shavings, or other combustible materials may be lodged, and the said Fire Wardens shall give such directions in regard to the several foregoing matters as they or any of them may think expedient, either as to the removal and alteration, or better care and management thereof, which directions shall be obeyed and complied with by the person or persons directed in that behalf, and at their expense.

SEC. 10. If any person or persons shall neglect or refuse so to comply with any such directions, as any of said Fire Wardens may give in the premises, or shall obstruct or hinder any Fire Warden or his assistants, in the performance of his duty, the person so offending shall forfeit and pay for every such neglect, non-compliance or hindrance, a sum not exceeding fifty dollars, and for every day which shall elapse after the time allotted for such removal, alteration, better care or management, without compliance with such directions, the said person shall also forfeit and pay a further and additional sum of five dollars; and all expenses caused in carrying into effect the directions of the Fire Wardens, shall, in the first instance, be paid by the occupant of the premises, and shall be deducted from the rent payable by him, her or them, unless such directions were rendered necessary by the act or default of the said occupant, or there be a special agreement to the contrary between the landlord and said occupant; and it shall also be the duty of said Fire Wardens to ascertain whether or not their directions are duly complied with, and in case of non-compliance, or in case of any violation of this chapter, to report the names of all the offenders, with the particular circumstances, to the Common Council, who may thereupon cause such offenders to be prosecuted for the recovery of the penalties incurred by them.

SEC. 11. The provisions of any ordinance heretofore passed, which may conflict with this ordinance, are hereby repealed.

Passed, November 22, 1852.

AN ORDINANCE

Relating to the First Ward Market, and to License and regulate Butcher's Stalls, Shops and Stands for the sale of Butcher's Meat, Poultry, Game and Fresh Fish.

The Mayor and Common Council of the City of Milwaukee, do ordain as follows :

Location of market.

SECTION 1. The building situated on lots numbered five and six, (5 and 6), in block numbered fifty-five, (55), in the first ward of the City of Milwaukee, is hereby established as a public Market, to be known and called the "First Ward Market."

SEC. 2. The said Market House shall be under the entire control and management of the Aldermen of the first ward, for the time being, and they are hereby authorized and empowered to lease and manage said property in such way and manner as will be most conducive to the interests of said ward.

Penalties against selling out of market.

SEC. 3. Any person or persons who shall expose for sale, or sell any butcher's meat, game, poultry or fresh fish, in or on any of the streets or alleys, or on any lot, or in any store, building or place within the limits of the first ward, in the City of Milwaukee, other than the First Ward Market House, without first having obtained a license therefor, as hereinafter provided, shall forfeit and pay the sum of ten dollars for each and every offence ; *Provided,* That nothing herein contained shall be construed to prohibit sales by public auction, in pursuance of any law of this State, or of the United States.

SEC. 4. License may be granted to such person or persons as may apply for same to the City Clerk, for the sale of butcher's meat, game, poultry and fresh fish in other places in said ward than the First Ward Market House, on payment of the sum hereinafter specified to the City Treasury.

License.

SEC. 5. No license shall be granted for a term exceeding one year, nor for a less term than six months, and the amount to be paid therefor shall be two hundred and fifty dollars per year, and at that rate for the less time.

SEC. 6. Any person desirous of obtaining a license for the purpose mentioned in the third section of this ordinance, shall pay into the City Treasury such sum as is herein provided, for the longer or shorter term, and on the presentation of the Treasurer's receipt therefor to the City Clerk, it shall be the duty of said Clerk, on payment of the usual fees therefor, to issue to such person a license, in which shall be set forth the place for selling butcher's meat, game, poultry and fresh fish, and the time for which the same was granted.

SEC. 7. All moneys paid into the City Treasury, arising from license duties or penalties imposed by the provisions of this ordinance, shall be placed to the credit of the first ward, and shall be used for the sole benefit of said ward.

Superintendent of market.

SEC. 8. William Stupenski is hereby appointed Superintendent of the First Ward Market, on the condition that he complies with such restrictions in relation to the management thereof, and his compensation, as the Aldermen of said ward, for the time being, may impose.

SEC. 9. It shall be the duty of the City Marshal and the Superintendent of the First Ward Market, or either of them, to enforce this ordinance against all and any person who may violate the provisions thereof.

SEC. 10. All ordinances, rules or regulations conflicting with the provisions of this ordinance are hereby repealed.

Passed, December 2, 1852.

AN ORDINANCE

To provide for repairs to Engines and other property belonging to the City, connected with the Fire Department, and for placing said Department in a more efficient condition, &c.

The Mayor and Common Council of the City of Milwaukee, do ordain as follows :

Who to contract for repairs.

SECTION 1. The City Comptroller and Chief Engineer of the Fire Department, by and with the advice and consent of a majority of the committee on said department, are hereby authorized and empowered to contract, for and in behalf of the city, for all repairs necessary to be made from time to time to any engine or other property connected with said department, belonging to the city.

SEC. 2. All bills or claims for such repairs shall be presented to the Common Council, and referred to the committee on the Fire Department, and if certified by such committee to be correct, shall be passed over to the City Comptroller for approval, and by him returned to the Common Council for final action.

Purchase of new engines, &c.

SEC. 3. Whenever it may be necessary to purchase a new engine, hose, or hook and ladder carriage, or any other property, in order to render said Fire Department more efficient and useful, the Chief Engineer, in conjunction with the committee on the Fire Department, shall prepare a list of such articles as by them may be deemed necessary, and submit the same to the Common Council.

Yearly appropriation.

SEC. 4. From and after the thirty-first day of December, eighteen hundred and fifty-two, the sum of one hundred dollars shall be annually paid to each of the companies belonging to the Fire Department, that are in active service, for the purpose of aiding in the purchase of suitable equipments for the members and furniture for the engine and other houses ; said sum to be appropriated semi-annually, and to be drawn by the foreman of each company, on the presentation to the Common Council of a certificate from the Chief Engineer, that such company is in good condition, and has been ready for service at any call during the preceding six months.

SEC. 5. In case of any alarm of fire, the bells on the churches and public buildings in this city shall be rung in the manner provided in an ordinance for the prevention and extinguishment of fires, now in force, and if such alarm is made between the hours of six o'clock in the evening and six o'clock in the morning, the person ringing the first bell shall be entitled to the sum of one dollar and fifty cents therefor, and each of the other bell ringers the sum of one dollar; but if at any other time during the twenty-four hours of each day, the first bell ringer shall be paid one dollar, and other ringers fifty cents therefor. Alarm bells.

SEC. 6. All accounts for services in ringing bells at fire alarms, shall specify the time when such service was rendered, and the name of the owner or occupant of the property destroyed or damaged, and shall be verified by the oath of the claimant before presentation to the Common Council for payment.

SEC. 7. All ordinances, rules or regulations in any manner conflicting with the provisions of this ordinance are hereby repealed.

Passed, December 2, 1852.

AN ORDINANCE

To provide for Licensing and Regulating the Vending and Dealing in Vinous, Spirituous or Fermented Liquors.

The Mayor and Common Council of the City of Milwaukee, do ordain as follows:

SECTION 1. No person shall deal in, sell, or deliver for money or other valuable thing, or give away, within the Liquors not to be sold without license.

limits of the City of Milwaukee, any vinous, spirituous or fermented liquors, without first having licensed thereto, as herein prescribed.

Form of license. SEC. 2. All licenses shall be signed by the Mayor and Clerk, and shall specify the place where the business of selling or dealing in such liquors shall be carried on, and no license shall be issued for less than six months, nor shall the Not assignable. same be assignable or in use to the benefit of any person other than the one to whom the same may be issued.

City Treasurer to give a receipt. SEC. 3. Any person paying to the City Treasurer the sum of fifteen dollars in money, or in city orders, due or to City Clerk's duty. become due within a year, may, on presentation to the Clerk, of the Treasurer's receipt therefor, receive a license, as herein prescribed, for the term of one year from the date thereof, and any person applying for a less term than one year shall pay therefor at the rate of fifteen dollars a year for the term of such license.

Gaming prohibited. SEC. 4. No person licensed under this chapter, nor any person employed by or acting for him, her or them, shall at any time permit any gaming for money or other value within his, her or their premises, or suffer any drunkenness, reveling, quarreling, fighting, or any other disorderly or immoral conduct, or sell or give any vinous, spirituous or fermented liquors to any minor, apprentice or servant, except upon the authority of such persons parent, master, mistress or guardian, nor sell or give any such articles to any person in a Penalty. state of intoxication or bordering thereon ; and any person or persons offending against this section shall, upon conviction thereof, forfeit and pay for every such offence, for the use of said city, a sum not exceeding fifty dollars, with costs of prosecution, and liable to have his, her or their license suppressed and declared void.

Penalty for evading ordinance. SEC. 5. Every person who shall, within the limits of the City of Milwaukee, directly or indirectly, deal in, sell, or with intent to evade the provisions of this ordinance, give to any other person any vinous, spirituous or fermented liquors without first having obtained a license therefor, according to the provisions hereof, shall, upon conviction thereof, be fined in a sum of not more than one hundred dollars nor less than twenty-five dollars.

City Clerk to keep a list.

SEC. 6. It shall be the duty of the City Clerk to keep a list of all persons to whom licences shall issue under this ordinance, and give a copy thereof to the Marshal, whose duty it shall be to notice and inquire into all infractions of this ordinance that may come to his knowledge, and report the same to the Common Council and City Attorney.

Marshal's duty.

Certain persons to retain privileges.

SEC. 7. All persons now holding licenses, under the authority of the City of Milwaukee, shall retain all the privileges thereof, during the full time for which they were issued, any thing in this ordinance to the contrary notwithstanding.

SEC. 8. All ordinances heretofore passed, regulating and licensing the vending and dealing in vinous, spirituous or fermented liquors, are hereby repealed.

Passed, May 5, 1853.

AN ORDINANCE

Fixing the compensation of Inspectors and Clerks of Election, and providing for the payment thereof.

The Mayor and Common Council of the City of Milwaukee, do ordain as follows :

Compensation of clerks and inspectors of elections.

SECTION 1. Hereafter there shall be paid to the Inspectors and Clerks of election in the several wards of the City of Milwaukee, the following sums for their services:

Of general elections.

To each of the Inspectors at any general elections held for State and County Offices, or at any annual election for City Officers, the sum of six dollars, and to each of the Clerks of such elections the sum of four dollars.

Of special elections.

To each of the Inspectors at any special election held for City, County or Ward Officers, or any other special elections, the sum of four dollars, to each of the Clerks of such election the sum of three dollars.

Services paid out of general city fund.

SEC. 2. Any services performed under the preceding section, shall be chargeable to the City of Milwaukee, and shall be paid out of the general city fund.

Passed, May 5, 1853.

AN ORDINANCE

Regulating the mode of Procedure in the Removal of City Officers, and for other purposes.

The Mayor and Common Council of the City of Milwaukee, do ordain as follows:

City officers may be removed for cause.

SECTION 1. Whenever any officer or agent under the city government shall be guilty of any official misconduct or neglect of duty, or for any due cause, he may be removed from any such office or agency by the Common Council.

Complaint to be signed by complainant

SEC. 2. No officer or agent shall be removed from office, for any cause, until a complaint, with the signature of the complainant attached thereto, specifying the misconduct or neglect of duty, shall be submitted to the Common Council.

Notice to be given to accused.

SEC. 3. Whenever a complaint shall be made against any officer or agent, as provided in the preceding section of this ordinance, it shall be the duty of the Common Council to fix on a day and place for the hearing of such complaint, and to direct their Clerk to cause notice to be given to the accused person of the pending of the same, by serving a copy thereof on him personally, or leaving such copy at his last and usual place of abode, with some person of discretion, and appending thereto the time and place of the hearing of such complaint.

Common Council to hear and determine.

SEC. 4. On the day fixed for the hearing and the appearance of the accused, either in person or by counsel, the Common Council shall proceed to hear the evidence adduced, both on the part of the complainant and respondent, and determine the matter according to the right of the case: *Provided, however,* That the accused person shall not be removed from office unless two-thirds of all the members of the Common Council, present at such hearing, shall concur in such removal, and the question determined by a call of the yeas and nays.

SEC. 5. No member of the Common Council shall be expelled therefrom, until charges are made in writing, signed by one or more members of said Common Council, specifying the particular neglect of duty or misconduct of such member. Charges to be made in writing.

SEC. 6. Whenever any charges are made against any member of the Common Council, as provided in the preceding section, it shall be the duty of the Council to cause notice to be given to the accused, and the time fixed for the hearing, as is provided in section three of this ordinance, and like proceedings shall be had as in case of a complaint preferred against any officer or agent of the city government: *Provided,* That no member of the Council shall be expelled therefrom unless two-thirds of the whole Board, on a call of the yeas and nays, shall concur in the passage of a resolution for such expulsion. Notice to be given to the accused of the time of hearing.

Passed, May 19, 1853.

AN ORDINANCE

To provide for the Compensation of the City Printers.

The Mayor and Common Council of the City of Milwaukee, do ordain:

SECTION 1. That there shall be paid to the City Printers in the German languge, the sum of thirty cents per square for the first insertion, and twelve and one-half cents per square for each subsequent insertion; and that there shall be paid to the City Printer, in the English language, the sum Rates to be paid city printers.

of twenty-five cents per square for the first insertion, and twelve and one-half cents per square for each subsequent insertion, for any ordinance, resolution or notice which, by the charter or ordinance of the Common Council, may be required to be published in a daily newspaper ; such compensation to be paid by orders on the Treasury in the usual form, but no payment to be made until the proper affidavit of such publication shall be first made and filed.

Number of insertions.

SEC. 2. All notices shall be published such time as may be required by the charter or ordinances, and all ordinances three insertions : *Provided, however,* That ordinances shall be deemed and considered in force from and after the first publication.

Former ordinance repealed.

SEC. 3. An ordinance to provide for the compensation of City Printers, passed, May 6th, 1852, is hereby repealed.

Passed, June 2, 1853.

AN ORDINANCE

To regulate the sale of Hay and the measuring and selling of Fuel, and to appoint an Inspector of Fuel.

The Mayor and Common Council of the City of Milwaukee, do ordain as follows :

Hay to be weighed.

SECTION 1. No person shall offer for sale, or sell within the limits of the City of Milwaukee, any hay loaded upon any wagon, sled or other vehicle, without first having obtained a written ticket or certificate of the weight or quantity of hay upon such sled or other vehicle, from the owner or attendant of some established and sealed hay scale within the city limits aforesaid, which ticket shall be signed by the owner or attendant of such scale.

Ticket to be exhibited.

SEC. 2. Any person offering hay for sale, shall exhibit his ticket of the weight of the same to the purchaser thereof, before being entitled to receive pay therefor, under the penalty hereinafter provided.

SEC. 3. All fire-wood offered for sale within the limits of the City of Milwaukee, loaded upon any wagon, sled or vehicle, shall be first inspected and measured by an Inspector to be appointed as hereinafter provided, and such Inspector shall give to the owner thereof a written ticket, with his signature attached thereto, of the quantity of wood contained in such load. Fire wood to be inspected.

SEC. 4. Any person or persons who shall offer for sale any wood or hay, contrary to the provisions of the preceding sections of this ordinance, shall forfeit and pay for each and every offence the sum of one dollar, together with the cost of prosecution. Penalty.

SEC. 5. The attendent upon hay scales shall be entitled to receive, for weighing each load of hay, the sum of twelve and a-half cents, and the Inspector of wood, five cents for each load of wood, to be paid by the person to whom the ticket for such weight or measurement shall be delivered. Fees.

SEC. 6. The Common Council, at the present session of this board, shall elect, by ballot, one Inspector of Wood; and such Inspector, before entering upon the duties of his office, shall take and subscribe an oath of office and file the same with the City Clerk. Inspector, how appointed.

SEC. 7. The Inspector of Wood may appoint a deputy in any ward in the city in which such Inspector does not himself reside, which appointment shall be reported to the Common Council, and shall be subject to confirmation or rejection. May appoint deputies.

Passed, December 15, 1853.

AN ORDINANCE

To provide for the compensation of Judges, Jurors, and other persons who may render services in the laying out or opening Streets or Alleys and Public Grounds.

The Mayor and Common Council of the City of Milwaukee, do ordain as follows:

Compensation of Judge Jurors, &c.

SECTION 1. There shall be paid for the services, required in chapter six of an act entitled "an act to consolidate and amend the act to incorporate the City of Milwaukee, and the several acts amendatory thereof," approved, February 20th, 1852, in the opening of streets, alleys and public grounds, the following sums, to wit:

To the Judge of the County or Circuit Courts, for the appointment of a Jury in each case, one dollar.

For issuing precept for Jury, fifty cents.

For the appointment of substitutes, twenty-five cents each.

To the City Marshal, for service of the precept on each Juror, twelve and a-half cents, and six cents per mile for actual travel in the service of such precept.

For attending upon a Jury, for each day, when requested, two dollars, and for each half day, one dollar.

To each Juror for every day actually and necessarily employed in the discharge of their duties, two dollars, and for each half day when so employed, one dollar.

To the persons employed to prepare the reports of the Jury, for each folio, twenty-five cents.

To the person administering the oath to Jurors and certifying the same, for each Juror, ten cents.

Duty of Jury to make bill of Fees, &c.

SEC. 2. It shall be, and hereby is made the duty of the Jury, before making the apportionment and assessment required by section fourteen of chapter six, referred to in the preceding section of this ordinance, to make a bill of fees and expenses, according to section one of this ordinance, and present the same to the City Comptroller to be audited, and the same, when audited by the City Comptroller, shall be apportioned and assessed by them, together with the damages upon the real estate benefitted, as provided in said section fourteen.

Passed, January 26, 1854.

AN ORDINANCE

To provide for the offering and payment of Rewards for the detection of Incendiaries in the City of Milwaukee.

The Mayor and Aldermen of the City of Milwaukee, in Common Council assembled, do ordain as follows :

SECTION 1. The Mayor of the City of Milwaukee shall be, and is hereby authorized, in behalf of said city, to offer such reward as he shall, from time to time, think proper, (not exceeding in any one case the sum of five hundred dollars), for the detection and conviction of any person or persons who may have been guilty of committing any act within the said city constituting such person an incendiary.

Mayor may offer reward for detection of incendiaries.

SEC. 2. Such reward shall be paid by the City of Milwaukee, out of the general city fund, to the person entitled to the same, upon clear and satisfactory proof being made to the Mayor, and upon his certificate that such proof has been duly and satisfactorily made, and that said claimant is entitled to said reward.

To be paid from general city fund.

Passed, December 28, 1854.

AN ORDINANCE

To authorize the appointment of Special Constables.

The Mayor and Common Council of the City of Milwaukee, do ordain as follows :

SECTION 1. The Mayor is hereby authorized and empowered to appoint any number of special constables which he may

Mayor may appoint special constables.

deem expedient, at any time when he may deem the safety, peace or interest of the city may require the aid of such additional and special police.

Passed, October 5, 1854.

AN ORDINANCE

To provide for the compensation of Judges, Jurors and other persons who may render services in laying out, or opening Streets or Alleys and Public Grounds.

The Mayor and Common Council of the City of Milwaukee, do ordain as follows :

SECTION 1. There shall be paid for the services, required in chapter six of an act entitled "an act to consolidate and amend the act to incorporate the City of Milwaukee, and the several acts amendatory thereof," approved, February 20th, 1852, in the opening of streets, alleys and public grounds, the following sums :

Fees of Judges. To the Judge of the County or Circuit Court, for the appointment of a Jury in each case, for issuing precept for Jury, three dollars ; for the appointment of substitutes, fifty cents each.

Marshal's fees. To the City Marshal, for the service of a precept on each Juror, twenty-five cents, and ten cents each Juror for notifying them to attend any meeting, and ten cents per mile for actual travel in the service of such notice, and for attending upon a Jury, for each day, when requested, three dollars.

Fees of Jurors. To each Juror, for every day actually employed in the discharge of their duties, three dollars.

Amount to be paid preparingreport To the persons employed to prepare the report of the Jury, for each folio, twenty-five cents.

Fees of officer administering oath. To the persons administering the oath to Jurors and certifying the same, for each Juror, twenty-five cents.

Jury to make a bill of fees and expenses SEC. 2. It shall be, and hereby is made the duty of the Jury, before making the apportionments and assessment required by section fourteen of chapter six, referred to in the preceding section of this ordinance, to make a bill of fees and expenses, according to section one of the ordinance, and present the same to be audited, and the same, when so audited by the City Comptroller, shall be appropriated and assessed by them, together with the damages upon the real estate benefitted, as provided in said section fourteen. Bill must be presented to Comptroller to be audited When audited, shall be appropriat'd Damages to be assessed by Jury.

Sec. 3. All ordinances heretofore passed, contravening the provisions of this ordinance, are hereby repealed.

Passed, October 21, 1854.

AN ORDINANCE

To prevent the discharge of Fire-arms in the City of Milwaukee.

The Mayor and Common Council of the City of Milwaukee, do ordain as follows:

Section 1. No person shall discharge any fire-arms within the limits of the city, except on the fourth day of July, or in the performance of military duty, and under the command of the Commandant of a regularly organized military company, under the penalty of not exceeding ten dollars nor less than one dollar. Prohibiting discharge of fire-arms in city limits.

Sec. 2. It shall be, and is hereby made the duty of any and all Police Officers and Constables, having knowledge of the violation of this ordinance, to arrest any and all persons who shall violate this ordinance, and take them before the Police Justice, to be dealt with according to law for the violation of said ordinance. Duty of police to enforce ordinance.

Passed, April 30, 1855.

AN ORDINANCE

To preserve the Health of the City of Milwaukee.

The Mayor and Common Council of the City of Milwaukee, do ordain as follows:

Section 1. The Aldermen of said city shall constitute a Board of Health, of which the Mayor shall be a member, and Aldermen to constitute board of health.

ex-officio presiding officer when present; in the absence of the Mayor, the said Board may choose one of its members as presiding officer. Such Board of Health shall exercise all the powers for the preservation of the health, and perform all the duties conferred by the Charter of the City of Milwaukee and this ordinance, within the limits of the said City of Milwaukee, and may take such measures and make such rules and regulations as they may deem most effectual for the preservation of the public health. They may, from time to time, appoint such Health Officers, and the same at pleasure remove, as they may deem necessary to aid them in the execution of their powers and duties.

To appoint health officers and make rules.

Marshal, Deputy and Health Officers to obey rules of the board.

SEC. 2. It shall be the duty of every Marshal and Deputy Marshal, and such Health Officer and Officers as may be appointed and designated, to obey and perform implicitly every order, regulation and direction of said Board, in all matters pertaining to the duties of said Board, and in any matter relating to the health of the city; and each and any of said Officers who shall refuse or neglect to perform faithfully any such order, regulation or direction, shall forfeit a penalty of ten dollars for each and every offence.

To remove cause of sickness.

SEC. 3. It shall be the duty of the Board of Health, and of each member thereof, to investigate and ascertain, if practicable, causes tending to create sickness, and to take the necessary steps for the removal of such causes, and for this purpose each member of the Board within the ward where he resides, and the Marshal or Deputy Marshal, or Health Officer, shall have the power to direct the removal or purification of all filthy or nauseous places or substances producing disagreeable smell or tending to produce disease, and in case the owners, or persons occupying premises on which such places or substances may be, should not remove or purify the same, when directed by such member of the Board, or by the Marshal, Deputy Marshal or Health Officer, shall have power to remove or purify all causes as aforesaid, and

Owners to remove filth when directed.

any such person refusing or neglecting to remove or purify the causes aforesaid, when so directed by a member of said Board, or by the Marshal, Deputy Marshal or Health Officer, such person shall forfeit a penalty of not exceeding twenty dollars nor less than one dollar for each and every such offence, together with the costs and expense of removing or purifying the offensive places or causes aforesaid.

Penalty for not complying.

SEC. 4. The Board of Health, or any member thereof, or any officer under their direction, shall have power to enter upon the premises and into the house of every person in the city, as often as he shall deem it necessary, or the Board of Health shall order, and examine into the health, cleanliness, and the number of persons inhabiting such house, and inspect the cellars, vaults, privies and sewers of such premises. Any person or persons who shall wilfully hinder or molest any officer in the performance of his duties, required by this or any other general ordinance of the city, shall forfeit a penalty not exceeding twenty-five dollars.

Power given to enter premises to inspect.

Penalty for molesting the inspector

SEC. 5. Whenever any contagious disease shall break out, or be found to infest the city, it shall be the duty of said board to provide a hospital or place for the reception of all persons inflicted with such disease, and remove all such persons to such hospital, without delay, as can be so removed, and also to provide, at the expense of the city, all necessary comforts and medical aid for the inmates of the hospital, and, for this purpose, the said board may command the services of the alms-house physicians, who shall be *ex-officio* hospital physicians, and also employ such other medical aid as they may deem necessary, and employ all such nurses, cooks, and other help, as may be necessary for the proper police of the hospital. *Provided, however,* That in case any persons shall be sent to said hospital, who are not in indigent circumstances, such persons shall pay, to the city, all expenses which may have been incurred in their behalf, in-

To provide hospital.

Physicians to be empowered.

Persons not in indigent circumstances to pay

expenses incurred.

cluding pay to physicians, nurses, boarding, and expenses of every kind.

Penalty for bringing persons infected with disease.

SEC. 6. If any person shall bring, or cause to be brought, into this city, any person who shall at the time be infected with Asiatic cholera, commonly so called, small-pox, or other virulent, contagious disease, such person shall forfeit a penalty of fifty dollars. And if any person, infected by any such disease, shall, by his own act, come into the city, or be brought into it by his own direction, such person shall forfeit a penalty of fifty dollars for such offence, and shall, if practicable, be removed, under the direction of the Board of Health, to the place from which such person shall have come.

Powers of health officers.

SEC. 7. The Board of Health, or any officer thereof, shall have power to stop, detain and examine, and by order, to direct to be stopped, detained and examined, for the purpose of preventing the entrance of any pestilential or infectious disease into the city, any person coming from any place infected or believed to be infected with such diseases.

Owners or drivers of public conveyances not to bring any infected person in city limits.

SEC. 8. The owner, driver or person in charge of any stage or other public conveyance, which shall enter the city, having on board any person sick of any malignant fever, or pestilential or infectious disease, (unless such person became sick on the way, and could not be left), shall forfeit the penalty of fifty dollars. Such owner, driver or person in charge, shall, within two hours after the arrival of such sick person, report, in writing, the fact, with the name of such person, if known, and the place or house where such person was put down in the city, to the Mayor, City Clerk, Marshal or Aldermen, and for each and every neglect to comply with those provisions, such person shall forfeit the penalty of fifty dollars.

Masters of vessels not to land any infected person in city limits.

SEC. 9. If any captain or master of a steamboat, vessel or lake craft of any kind, or person in charge thereof, shall land, or suffer to be landed from such steamboat, vessel or lake craft any person or persons infected with Asiatic cholera, commonly so called, small pox, or other virulent, contagious diseases, on any pier, wharf, scow, boat, lighter, landing or place of any kind, within the corporate limits of this city, such person, captain, master, or person in charge thereof shall forfeit the penalty of fifty dollars for each and every person so landed within the limits of the city. *Provided, however,* That persons destined to this port, who are apparently in good health when coming on board at the port whence such steamer, vessel or lake craft may have sailed, may be landed at such time and place, and in such manner as may be directed by the Board of Health, or by the Mayor, Marshal or other health officer acting under their direction, but for any deviation from, or violation of any order or direction of said board, or of the Mayor, Marshal, or other officers acting under their direction, the captain, master, or person having command on board, shall forfeit the penalty of fifty dollars.

Infected persons to remain where landed until board of health notified.

SEC. 10. In case any person or persons infected with disease as aforesaid, shall, in contravention of ordinance, be landed and left on any pier, wharf or other place, before the proper authority shall have notice thereof, such person shall remain on the pier, wharf or other place where landed, until the Board of Health or health officer shall have been notified, and some action had by said board or health officer for suitably disposing of such persons, and if the owner or keeper of such pier, wharf or other place of landing, on which such person or persons shall have been landed, shall, in any manner, move, or cause such person or persons to be removed off such pier, wharf or other place of landing without the order and sanction of the Board of Health or health officer, such owner or keeper shall forfeit the penalty of fifty dollars for each and every person so removed by him, or by his order or direction, from the place where such person was landed.

Penalty.

Penalty for neglect of not complying with order of health officers.

SEC. 11. Every person, master or captain in charge of any steamboat or other craft or vessel which shall enter the city, or touch at any of the piers or landing in the city, having on board thereof any person sick of any malignant fever or other pestilential or infectious disease, (unless the person, so diseased, became so on the way, and could not be left), shall forfeit the penalty of fifty dollars. It shall be the duty of such captain, master or person in charge, within six hours after his arrival, to report, in writing, to the Mayor, City Clerk or health officer, the fact of such sick person being on board, and the name, description and location of his craft, and he shall not permit such sick person to land, or be landed, or to communicate with the shore in any way, until the Board of Health or health officer shall give permission, in writing, to that purpose ; for any neglect or violation of these provisions, or either of them, the person so violating shall forfeit the penalty of fifty dollars.

Duties of harbor master and health officer.

SEC. 12. It shall be the duty of the Harbor Master, or health officer, as often as he may deem it necessary, to enter upon every steamboat, vessel or other lake craft, entering, or being in the Port of Milwaukee, immediately upon such boat, vessel or other craft nearing the shore, and, by strict search and diligent inquiry, ascertain if any persons are on board infected with Asiatic cholera, commonly so called, small pox, or other virulent, contagious disease, and if so, to forbid such person being landed until the Board of Health shall have been notified, and taken order relative to any such persons which it may be proposed to land, and such order shall be conclusive, in regard to the boat, vessel or other craft on which such passengers may be. *Provided, however*, That the Board of Health shall in no case suffer to be landed any persons who are infected with such disease previous to coming on board at the port whence such boat, vessel or other craft shall have been sailed, but such persons shall be absolutely kept on board such boat, vessel or other

No infected person to land.

craft, and prevented from landing within the limits of the city.

SEC. 13. To enforce the provisions of this ordinance, and to prevent any infectious persons being landed in contravention thereof, the Mayor and Aldermen, each member of the Board of Health, the Marshal and each Deputy Marshal and Health Officer shall severally have power to command the services of all by-standers to prevent, by force and arms, any person from being landed from any steamboat, vessel or other craft, in violation of this ordinance, and if any person whose services be so commanded shall refuse or neglect to aid such officers in the discharge of the duties so demanded of him, every person so refusing or neglecting shall forfeit the penalty of fifty dollars, and in case any person or persons shall have been landed in contravention of the provisions of this ordinance, without the knowledge of any of said officers, it shall be the duty of each and every of said officers, immediately upon being informed of such fact, to cause such person or persons to be immediately returned on board such boat, vessel or other craft, if still in port, by force, if necessary, there to remain until the order of the Board of Health shall be had for the further disposal of such persons; such return of such persons to the boat, vessel or other craft shall in no wise exempt the captain, master or person in charge, nor the boat, vessel or other craft from the penalties herein specified, for the unauthorized landing of such infected persons.

Health officer to command assistance.

Penalty for not rendering assistance when called on.

Infected persons to be retained on board of vessels.

SEC. 14. Each and every physician, who may be called upon to attend any case of small pox, Asiatic cholera, malignant fever, pestilential or infectious disease, or shall at any time hereafter attend any such case, shall, within twenty-four hours after first seeing any such case, report the same to the Mayor or some member of the Board of Health, Health Officer or City Marshal, stating the house or location where such case exists, in order that precautionary measures may

Physicians to report cases of small pox, &c., to Mayor.

be taken to protect the community against the spread of any such disease, and every such physician, attending any such case, within the city limits, who shall neglect or refuse to report the same, as is herein provided, shall forfeit the penalty of fifty dollars.

Penalty for neglect to report to Mayor.

SEC. 15. All ordinances and resolutions, the provisions of which are contrary to, or in contravention with those herein contained, are hereby repealed.

Passed June 25, 1855.

AN ORDINANCE

To provide for Licensing and Regulating Billiard Tables and Nine or Ten-Pin Alleys.

The Mayor and Common Council of the City of Milwaukee, do ordain as follows :

Billiard tables and bowling alleys to be licensed.

SECTION 1. No person shall erect or keep, or permit to be erected, placed or kept upon his, her or their premises, within the limits of the city, any billiard table, bowling alley, nine or ten-pin alley, used and kept for hire, without first having obtained a license therefor, under the penalty of ten dollars for each day the same is so kept.

Amount of license and when paid.

SEC. 2. No such license shall be granted, except upon the written application of the person desiring the same, which application shall state the place where such billiard table, bowling alley, nine or ten-pin alley, and the number of each are to be kept, nor unless the applicant shall pay into the city treasury the sum of twenty dollars for one table or alley, and the additional sum of ten dollars for each additional table or alley so kept for use by such applicant in the same place or building.

Penalty for not complying with ordinance.

SEC. 3. If any person licensed to keep a billiard table, bowling alley, nine or ten-pin alley, shall, without license therefor, keep a bar for the sale of vinous, spiritous or fermented liquors, or shall allow or permit any kind of rioting or reveling, drunkenness, lewed or disorderly conduct, on his, her or their premises, or shall use the billiard table, nine or ten-pin alley, so kept by him, for the purpose of gaming, or permit the same to be used for gambling, he shall, on conviction thereof, forfeit to the city the sum of one hundred dollars, and shall be liable to have his, her or their license revoked and annulled.

SEC. 4. All ordinances heretofore passed providing for licensing and regulating billiard tables and nine or ten-pin alleys are hereby repealed, but shall not effect or invalidate any license heretofore given.

Passed, September 3, 1855.

AN ORDINANCE

For the Appointment of Superintendent of Bridges in the City of Milwaukee.

The Mayor and Common Council of the City of Milwaukee, do ordain as follows:

SECTION 1. The Common Council shall annually appoint a competent person, to be styled "Superintendent of Bridges," whose duty it shall be to see that all the bridges in said city are kept in good repair, and when out of repair to cause the same to be repaired, and also to inspect all bridges that may be in process of being built, and give directions in relation to the same, and to report to the Common Council, as often as he may deem proper, or when called upon by the Bridge Committee, the state of the bridges and the repairs to be made, and whether the bridges, being built at any time, are being built in a good and workmanlike manner, and in accordance with the contracts entered into with the contractor.

Superintendent of bridges appointed.

Duties of superintendent.

SEC. 2. The Superintendent of Bridges shall receive an annual salary of four hundred dollars for his services, and shall

Compensation of superintendent

notify the City Attorney of any violation of law in relation to bridges, and of damages done by any person or vessel to any bridge in said city, and see to procuring testimony in relation to any suit which may be brought for injuries to any bridge in the city.

Passed, November 23, 1855.

AN ORDINANCE

Relating to the duties of the Marshal and the Police.

The Mayor and Common Council of the City of Milwaukee, do ordain as follows :

Marshal's salary.

SECTION 1. The Marshal shall perform the duties required by the ordinances or regulations of the Common Council, and shall receive an annual salary therefor of two hundred dollars, in addition to his fees for collecting license moneys, and summoning and attending Juries, and the compensation for his services as Policeman, which shall be the same as any member of the Police Department.

To collect licenses.

SEC. 2. The Marshal shall perform the duties of Messenger to the Common Council and of the Board of School Commissioners, and when he shall collect any unpaid license moneys he shall immediately pay over such moneys to the City Treasurer, and take his receipt for the same ; he shall report all such collections to the Common Council at their next meeting ; he shall also, unless the Common Council should otherwise direct, summon all Juries appointed to determine the necessity of taking lands for public use, and may, on his petition, be appointed Policeman during his term of office as Marshal, but, in such case, shall be in subordination to, and under the control and direction of, the Chief of Police, and be liable to suspension and removal as other members of the Police Department.

May be policeman.

SEC. 3. All duties required by any ordinance now in force to be performed by the Marshal, except those herein mentioned, shall hereafter devolve upon, and be performed by, the Police Department, and when such duties shall be performed by any member of the Police Department, all penalties prescribed for the breach of any such ordinance shall accrue and be recoverable as if such duties had been performed by the Marshal.

Chief of Police to enforce ordinance.

SEC. 4. The ordinance entitled "an ordinance to authorize the Marshal to appoint deputies," passed, July 13, 1846, and the ordinance entitled "an ordinance defining the duties of Marshal," passed, May 6, 1852, and the provisions of any other ordinance heretofore passed, which may conflict with this ordinance, are hereby repealed.

Passed, April 24, 1856.

AN ORDINANCE

Relating to Camphene and other Burning Fluid in the City of Milwaukee.

The Mayor and Common Council of the City of Milwaukee, do ordain as follows:

SECTION 1. The sale, storage and manufacture of camphene and other burning fluids, in the different wards of the city, within what is known and designated as the fire limits of said city, is hereafter forbidden and prohibted, with the exception that a license may be obtained for the sale of the same in small quantities, in the day time, as hereinafter provided. Any person guilty of a violation of this provision, shall forfeit and pay a penalty of one hundred dollars for each and every offence.

Camphene and other burning fluid how regulated.

Penalty.

SEC. 2. The Aldermen in each ward, or a majority of them, are hereby authorized to give a written license, in their ward, for a term not exceeding one year, to one or more persons, to keep for sale and retail, within said fire limits, cam-

Aldermen may license small quantities.

phene or other burning fluid, in a quantity not greater at any one time than thirty gallons, the same to be kept in tin cans or stone jars, well stopped, and on no occasion to be sold, retailed or opened after dark or by candle light. Any person having such license, who shall violate the provisions of this section, shall pay a penalty of twenty dollars for each and every offence.

Passed, June 16, 1856.

AN ORDINANCE

To provide for the Abatement of certain Nuisances.

The Mayor and Common Council of the City of Milwaukee, do ordain as follows:

Aldermen to order the removal of buildings from streets and sidewalks.

SECTION 1. Whenever two or more of the Aldermen of any ward shall make an order, directing the owner or occupant of any dwelling-house or building, situated, in whole or in part, in any street, alley or side-walk, in such ward, to remove such dwelling-house or other building from such street, alley or sidewalk by a certain day, to be not less than three nor more than thirty days from the date of such order, which shall be dated on the day of the making thereof; it shall be the duty of the Clerk of the Aldermen and Street Commissioners of such ward, within three days after the date of such order, to make and deliver to the Chief of the Police, a certified copy of such order, whose duty it shall be to endorse thereon the time of receiving such copy, and, within three days after the receipt of such copy, to serve, or cause to be served, by a policeman, a copy of such order upon such owners or occupant, by delivering to him or her a copy of such order, or by leaving the same at such dwelling-house or other building with some person of suitable age and discretion, who shall be informed of its contents.

Chfef of Police to servè the order.

If owner does not remove the

SEC. 2. In case the owner or occupant of such dwelling-house or other building, after being notified as aforesaid of such order, should not remove such dwelling-house or other building from such street, alley or side-walk, within the time limited in such order, then the Chief of the Police shall have power to take down and remove, or remove without taking down, such dwelling-house or other building from such street, alley or side-walk, to some suitable place, and the owner or occupant of such dwelling-house or other building, refusing or neglecting to remove the same from such street within the time limited in such order, after being notified as aforesaid, shall forfeit and pay not exceeding the sum of fifty dollars for each and every such offence, together with all costs of removal and abatement, and every forty-eight hours such dwelling-house or other building shall stand in such street, alley or side-walk, after the expiration of the time limited in such order for the removal thereof, shall constitute a new offence by such owner or occupant.

building, then Police to do it.

Penalty.

SEC. 3. Whenever any building or tenement, situated on any lot or tract of land within the limits of this city, shall be used or occupied for a slaughter-house, bone factory or any other business that is nauseous and detrimental to the health of the city, the Common Council shall declare the same a common nuisance, and the City Clerk shall thereupon make out a certified copy of such order or resolution and give the same to the Aldermen of the ward in which said nuisance may be situated ; the Aldermen of said ward shall then, and they are hereby authorized to order the same to be abated and removed, which shall be done by the Chief of the Police, in the same manner as is provided in the second section of this ordinance for the removal of any dwelling-house or other building situated in any street, alley or side-walk of said city.

Slaughter houses to be declared a public nuisance.

How removed.

SEC. 4. If the owner or occupant of any building or tenement, so declared a public nuisance, shall neglect or refuse to abate and remove the same within the time limited by the

Penalty.

order of said Aldermen, he shall forfeit and pay the penalty provided in the second section of this ordinance.

Sec. 5. This ordinance shall not be construed as repealing or amending any ordinance now in force for abating and removing nuisances.

Passed, June 23, 1856.

AN ORDINANCE

To authorize an Issue of City Bonds for the Construction of Bridges.

The Mayor and Common Council of the City of Milwaukee, do ordain as follows :

City bonds authorized for a bridge.

Section 1. The Mayor and City Clerk are hereby authorized and directed to sign and execute fifteen thousand dollars in Milwaukee City Bonds, of one thousand dollars each, payable in twenty years from the date thereof at the office of Messrs. Duncan, Sherman & Co., in New York City, with interest, semi-annually, at the rate of seven per cent. per annum, payable at the same place ; said bonds to be issued for the purpose of constructing bridges across the Milwaukee river, according to the provisions of an act of the Legislature of the State of Wisconsin, entitled "an act relating to the City of Milwaukee," approved Oct. 6, 1856.

Sec. 2. The City Clerk is hereby authorized and directed to deliver the City Bonds named in the first section of this ordinance to James B. Cross, Mayor, and take his receipt for the same.

Mayor authorized to sell the bonds.

Sec. 3. The Mayor of the City is hereby authorized and directed to negotiate and sell the City Bonds named in this ordinance, and place the proceeds thereof in the City Treasury, to be paid out by the City Treasurer on City Orders for work done under the contracts for constructing bridges.

Mayor may hypothecate them.

Sec. 4. The Mayor, in his discretion, may, instead of selling at once the City Bonds to be issued under the provisions of this ordinance, hypothecate them, in whole or in part, and raise the money necessary for immediate use in said bridge contracts, and thereafter sell the bonds to replace such money at such time and place as he may deem for the best interests of the city.

Passed, October 9, 1856.

AN ORDINANCE

To repeal part of an Ordinance entitled "An Ordinance to restrain Horses, Cattle, Sheep, Goats, Dogs, Mules, Jackasses and other animals and Fowls from running at large," passed August 18, 1856.

The Mayor and Common Council of the City of Milwaukee, do ordain as follows :

Repealed as to horses, cattle and hogs.

SECTION 1. So much of the ordinance entitled "an ordinance to restrain horses, cattle, sheep, goats, dogs, mules, jackasses and other animals and fowls from running at large," passed August 18, 1856, as relates to horses, cattle and hogs, be, and the same is hereby repealed.

Passed, November 8, 1856.

RULES

OF THE

COMMON COUNCIL.

RULES.

RULE 1. The regular meetings of the Common Council shall be held on Monday of every other week, at seven o'clock in the evening, during the year. Special meetings may be called at such times as the Mayor, or a majority of the Council, when in session, may direct.

RULE 2. The Mayor, or in his absence, the President of the Board, shall take the Chair, at the hour above named, or at the hour to which the Council is adjourned, and if a quorum be present, shall direct the journal of the preceding meeting to be read. The presiding officer, for the time being, shall preserve order and decorum, and decide questions of order, subject to an appeal to the Council.

RULE 3. When the presiding officer shall have called the members to order, the Clerk shall proceed to call the roll in alphabetical order, noting who are present, and who absent, and if, after having gone through with the call, it shall appear that a quorum is not present, the fact shall be entered on the journal and the Council shall stand adjourned to the time appointed for the next regular meeting.

RULE 4. Any member who shall not appear and answer to his name, when the roll is called at any regular meeting, or at any special or adjourned meeting when duly notified thereof, and who shall not thereafter render a sufficient excuse for his non-appearance, shall pay to the Clerk the sum of one dollar for the use of the Board.

RULE 5. In case of the absence of the Mayor and President of the Board, the Council shall, at any regular or special meeting, proceed to elect one of their number to preside at the meeting.

Rule 6. Every ordinance, or resolution in the nature of an ordinance, shall receive three several readings, previous to its passage ; but no such ordinance or resolution shall have its third reading on the same day that it is first read, unless by a suspension of the rules, as hereinafter provided.

Rule 7. All demands, claims, or accounts against the city, shall be presented and referred to the Comptroller, and if reported on favorably, shall, before they are allowed by the Council, be approved by the appropriate Committee.

Any claim, demand or account for work done, or materials found, on contract, or otherwise, by order of the Street Commissioners of any ward, shall first be examined by such Street Commissioners, and certified by them as correct, and when presented to this Board, shall be referred to the Comptroller, and by him returned to the Council for allowance.

Rule 8. All petitions, remonstrances and accounts, when presented, shall be read at length by the member presenting the same, or by the presiding officer, or clerk, unless otherwise ordered.

Rule 9. All resolutions, and amendments to any document before the Council, shall be reduced to writing before they shall be acted on.

Rule 10. Every member, previous to his speaking, shall rise and address the presiding officer, and shall not be interrupted except by a call to order.

Rule 11. When a member is called to order by the presiding officer, he shall take his seat, and shall not be suffered to proceed without leave of the Board.

Rule 12. No member shall speak more than twice on any question without first obtaining leave of the Board.

Rule 13. The ayes and noes shall be ordered upon any question at the request of a member, and the Clerk shall call the roll in alphabetical order.

Rule 14. When a motion has once been decided, it shall be in order for any member who voted in the majority, to move a reconsideration thereof, at the same, or next succeeding meeting, and if a majority of the members present shall be in favor of a reconsideration, the subject shall be before the Board for further action.

Rule 15. The following standing committees, consisting of three members each, shall be appointed by the Mayor, viz :—1, Finance ; 2, Judiciary ; 3, Schools ; 4, Police ; 5, Fire Department ; 6, Printing ; 7, Licenses ; 8, Rail Roads ; 9, Harbors ; 10, Old Taxes ; 11, Gas Light.

There shall also be appointed a Committee on Bridges, to consist of one member from each ward in the city.

Rule 16. The Committee on Printing shall carefully examine all ordinances and resolutions required to be published, after the same have been passed, and shall superintend the printing of the same, and no such ordinance or resolution shall be signed by the Mayor until such examination is made.

Rule 17. The order of business shall be as follows :—1st, The presentation of petitions, memorials and accounts ; 2d, Reports of Standing Committees ; 3d, Reports of Select Committees ; 4th, The presentation of Ordinances, or Resolutions ; 5th, The consideration of unfinished business.

Rule 18. It shall be the duty of the Clerk of this Board, in addition to the duties prescribed in the City Charter, to record all ordinances passed by the Common Council, in a suitable book, and to furnish the Chairman of Committees, Comptroller, and other city officers, with the resolutions and other matters that may be referred to them, and to perform all such other clerical duties as may be required by this Board.

Rule 19. No rule shall be suspended, recinded or amended, without the concurrence of two-thirds of the members present at any meeting.

Rule 20. The rules of parliamentary practice, comprised in Jefferson's or Cushing's Manuals, shall govern the proceedings of this Board in all cases to which they are applicable, and in which they are not inconsistent with these rules, or the laws of the State.

INDEXES.

INDEX.

INDEX TO CITY CHARTER.

INDEX TO LAWS.

INDEX TO ORDINANCES.

Page.

APPENDIX.

APPENDIX.

THE FOLLOWING ORDINANCES AND ACT OF THE LEGISLATURE WERE NOT PASSED IN TIME TO BE INCORPORATED IN THE FOREGOING PAGES.

AN ORDINANCE

To regulate the Sale of Hay in the Seventh Ward of the City of Milwaukee.

The Mayor and Common Council of the City of Milwaukee, do ordain as follows:

Section 1. All that part of Biddle Street, between Water and Market Streets, and the west side of Market Street, between Biddle and Division Streets, in the Seventh Ward of the City of Milwaukee, is hereby declared to be, and made a public stand for the sale of hay. **Stand for hay in 7th ward.**

Sec. 2. No person shall be allowed to expose for sale any hay, or load of hay, in any portion of the Seventh Ward of said city, except in the places designated in the first section of this ordinance; and any person who shall suffer his team, sleigh, wagon, or other vehicle, with a load of hay, to remain more than ten minutes in any other part of said Seventh Ward, shall be liable to a penalty of not less than one, nor more than five dollars. **Penalty for selling hay elsewhere.**

Sec. 3. It is hereby made the duty of the Inspector and Superintendent for the sale of wood and hay in this city, to enforce the provisions of this ordinance, and to make complaint for any violations of the provisions thereof. **Duty of Inspector.**

Passed, November 24, 1856.

AN ORDINANCE

To authorize an issue of City Bonds to make repairs and additions to the several Common School Houses in the City of Milwaukee.

The Mayor and Common Council of the City of Milwaukee, do ordain as follows:

Bonds authorized for school houses.

SECTION 1. The Mayor and City Clerk are hereby authorized and directed to sign and execute seven thousand dollars in Milwaukee city bonds, of one thousand dollars each, payable in ten years from the date thereof, at the office of Duncan, Sherman & Co., in New York City, with interest, semi-annually, at the rate of seven per cent. per annum, payable at the same place; said bonds to be issued for the purpose of making additions to and repairing the several Common School Houses in the City of Milwaukee.

SEC. 2. The City Clerk is hereby authorized and directed to deliver the city bonds named in the first section of this ordinance to James B. Cross, Mayor, and take his receipt for the same.

Mayor to negotiate the same.

SEC. 3. The Mayor of this City is hereby authorized and directed to negotiate and sell the city bonds named in this ordinance, and place the proceeds thereof in the City Treasury, to be paid out by the Treasurer on city orders, for work done under the contracts for the additions and repairs to the several Common School Houses in the City of Milwaukee.

May hypothecate the same.

SEC. 4. The Mayor may, in his discretion, instead of selling at once the city bonds to be issued under the provisions of this ordinance, hypothecate them, in whole or in part, and raise the money necessary to continue and complete the work named in this ordinance, and thereafter sell the bonds to replace such money, at such time and place as he may deem for the best interests of the city.

Passed, November 24, 1856.

AN ORDINANCE

To authorize an issue of City Bonds for the construction of Bridges.

The Mayor and Common Council of the City of Milwaukee, do ordain as follows:

SECTION 1. The Mayor and City Clerk are hereby authorized and directed to sign and execute fifteen thousand dollars in Milwaukee city bonds, of one thousand dollars each, payable in twenty years from the date thereof, at the office of Messrs. Duncan, Sherman & Co, in the City of New York, with interest, semi-annually, at the rate of seven per cent. per annum, payable at the same place; said bonds to be issued for the purpose of constructing bridges across the Milwaukee River, according to the provisions of an act of the Legislature of the State of Wisconsin, entitled "An act relating to the City of Milwaukee," approved October 6, 1856. Bonds authorized for the construction of bridges.

SEC. 2. The City Clerk is hereby authorized and directed to deliver the city bonds named in the first section of this ordinance to James B. Cross, Mayor, and take his receipt for the same.

SEC. 3. The Mayor of the City is hereby authorized and directed to negotiate and sell the city bonds named in this ordinance, and place the proceeds thereof in the City Treasury, to be paid out by the City Treasurer on city orders, for work done under the contracts for constructing bridges. Mayor to negotiate the same.

SEC. 4. The Mayor, in his discretion, may, instead of selling at once the city bonds, to be issued under the provisions of this ordinance, hypothecate them, in whole or in part, and raise the money necessary for immediate use on May hypothecate them said bridge contracts, and thereafter sell the bonds to replace such money, at such time and place as he may deem for the best interests of the city.

Passed, November 24, 1856.

AN ORDINANCE

Authorizing the purchasing, improving and establishing a Market Square in the Third Ward of the City of Milwaukee.

The Mayor and Common Council of the City of Milwaukee, do ordain as follows:

Market Square in 3d ward.

SECTION 1. More than twenty-five freeholders, residents of the third ward of the City of Milwaukee, having by petition represented to the Common Countil, that it is necessary to take for a Market Square all of block twenty-five (25), in said ward; authority, therefore, is hereby given to the Aldermen of said third ward to purchase said premises, or any part thereof, of the owner or owners thereof, with whom they can agree for such purchase, or to take the same, or any portion thereof which they may be unable to purchase, in accordance with and according to the provisions of an act of the Legislature, entitled "an act to authorize the several wards, in the City of Milwaukee, to purchase grounds for Market and Public Squares," approved, March 19, 1856.

SEC. 2. The premises described in the foregoing section, are hereby set off and established as a Market Square in said third ward, to be under the control of the Aldermen of said ward, and to be kept and regulated for the public use, and hereafter to be called and known by and under the name of the Third Ward Market Square.

Bonds authorized.

SEC. 3. For the purpose of purchasing and improving said Market Square, the Aldermen of said ward are hereby authorized, for and in the name of said ward, to issue bonds, not exceeding in amount the sum of fifty thousand dollars, on such terms, for such time and drawing such interest as to them shall seem advisable; but to be issued in accordance with and within the restrictions imposed by said act of the Legislature.

Survey and profile to be made.

SEC. 4. The Aldermen of the said ward shall cause an accurate survey and profile, or map, of said Market Square to be made by the City Surveyor, and filed in his office, and before proceeding to improve the same, they shall cause a plan and specifications of such improvement to be drawn, and a copy thereof deposited in the office of the City Comptroller.

Proceedings to be recorded.

SEC. 5. All the proceedings of said Aldermen, under this ordinance and said act of the Legislature, shall be entered at length in the records of said ward, and they shall make out a certified list of all the bonds so issued, specifying the amount, the rate of interest they draw, and the time when the interest and principal thereon become due, which shall be filed with the City Comptroller, and entered on the records in his office.

Submitted to the voters.

SEC. 6. This ordinance shall not be in force until submitted to the legal voters of the Third Ward of the City of Milwaukee, at an election to be held for that purpose, at the time hereinafter provided, and adopted by a majority of the whole number of votes given at such election.

Time of election.

SEC. 7. An election shall be held on the nineteenth day of December, 1856, between the hours of two and seven o'clock in the afternoon of said day, at the usual place in said ward for holding elections, for the purpose of the adoption or rejection of this ordinance, and such election shall be conducted, and the votes canvassed and returned in the same manner, and by the same officers, as at other city elections.

SEC. 8. On the ballots which shall be received by the Inspectors at said election, shall be either written or printed the words, "For the Market Square," or the words, "Against the Market Square."

Votes, how canvassed.

SEC. 9. At the next regular or special meeting of the Common Council, after the returns of the election from said Ward are made to the City Clerk, the Common Council shall proceed to canvass said returns ; and if it is found that a majority of all the votes taken are in favor of said Market Square, it shall be the duty of the Mayor to make proclamation thereof in the official papers of the city, and this ordinance shall be in force from and after its first publication, subsequent to the date of such proclamation.

Notice, how given.

SEC. 10. It is hereby made the duty of the City Clerk, to cause a certified copy of the petition on file in his office for this Market Square, together with a notice of the time and place of holding the election specified in this ordinance, to be published in the official papers of this city three several times, one of which publications shall be made in each of said newspapers, at least fifteen days previous to the time of holding said election.

Passed, December 1, 1856.

AN ORDINANCE

To authorize an issue of City Bonds to make repairs and additions to the several Common School Houses in the City of Milwaukee.

The Mayor and Common Council of the City of Milwaukee, do ordain as follows :

Bonds authorized to make repairs to school houses.

SECTION 1. The Mayor and City Clerk are hereby authorized and directed to sign and execute twenty-five thousand dollars in Milwaukee city bonds, of one thousand dollars each, payable in twenty years from the date thereof, at the office of Messrs. Duncan, Sherman & Co., in New York City, with interest, semi-annually, at the rate of seven per cent. per annum, payable at the same place ; said bonds to be issued for the purpose of constructing new School Houses in the Second and Seventh Wards.

SEC. 2. The City Clerk is hereby authorized and directed to deliver the city bonds named in the first section of this ordinance to James B. Cross, Mayor, and take his receipt for the same.

SEC. 3. The Mayor of this city is hereby authorized and directed to negotiate and sell the city bonds named in this ordinance, and place the proceeds thereof in the City Treasury, to be paid out by the Treasurer on city orders, for work done under the contracts for the construction of said School Houses in the Second and Seventh Wards of the City of Milwaukee. Mayor to negotiate the same.

SEC. 4. The Mayor may, in his discretion, instead of selling at once the city bonds to be issued under the provisions of this ordinance, hypothecate them, in whole or in part, and raise the money necessary to continue and complete the work named in this ordinance, and thereafter sell the bonds to replace such money, at such time and place as he may deem for the best interest of the city. May hypothecate them

Passed, December 4, 1856.

AN ORDINANCE

To authorize an issue of City Bonds to the Milwaukee and Beloit Rail Road Company.

The Mayor and Common Council of the City of Milwaukee, do ordain as follows:

SECTION 1. The Mayor of the city and the City Clerk are hereby authorized and directed to execute and deliver to the Milwaukee & Beloit Rail Road Company, Milwaukee city bonds to an amount not exceeding one hundred thousand dollars, in the manner and upon the conditions hereinafter mentioned, said bonds to be used in the completion and equipment of the rail road now being constructed by said company, from the City of Milwaukee to the City of Beloit, via the villages of East Troy, Elkhorn and Delavan, in the County of Walworth, in this state, as mentioned in the pro- Bonds issued to the Mil. & Beloit R. R. Co.

visions of an ordinance authorizing an issue of city bonds to the Milwaukee & Beloit Rail Road Company, passed June 16, 1856, and adopted by a vote of the people July 14, 1856.

Co. to give security.

SEC. 2. Such bonds may be delivered by the Mayor and Clerk of this Board, at any time after the securities from said rail road company, for the payment of the principal and interest on said bonds are executed and delivered to the city, in accordance with the requirements of the conditions of the report of the committee on rail roads, submitted and approved by the Common Council, December 4, 1856.

Passed, December 4, 1856.

AN ORDINANCE

To authorize an issue of City Bonds to I. A. Hazbrook, to apply on his contract to construct the Harbor at the "Straight Cut."

The Mayor and Common Council of the City of Milwaukee, do ordain as follows:

Bonds issued for the Harbor at the Straight Cut.

SECTION 1. The Mayor of the City, and the Clerk of this Board, are hereby authorized to execute and deliver to Isaac A. Hazbrook, eighteen thousand dollars in Milwaukee city bonds, to apply on his contract for the construction of the Harbor at the Straight Cut, and endorse the amount on his contract, when so executed and delivered to him.

Passed, December 4, 1856.

AN ORDINANCE

To amend an ordinance entitled "An ordinance to amend an ordinance permanently to establish the grade of certain streets in the First Ward of the City of Milwaukee," passed August 1, 1856.

The Mayor and Common Council of the City of Milwaukee, do ordain as follows:

Grade of Milwaukee street, in the 1st ward.

SECTION 1. The first section of "An ordinance to amend an ordinance permanently to establish the grade of certain streets in the First Ward of the City of Milwaukee," passed

August 1, 1856, is hereby so amended as to fix the elevation of Milwaukee Street, at a point half way between Knapp and Ogden Streets, at fifty-five feet, and the grade of said Milwaukee Street is hereby fixed and permanently established at fifty-five feet, at a point half way between Knapp and Ogden Streets, and all parts of any ordinance or ordinances conflicting with this ordinance, as to the elevation of Milwaukee Street, at the point herein specified, are hereby repealed.

Passed, December 4, 1856.

AN ACT

To amend an Act entitled "An Act to Incorporate the City of Milwaukee, and the several Acts amendatory thereof," approved February 20, 1852.

The People of the State of Wisconsin, represented in Senate and Assembly, do enact as follows :

Fifth Ward divided.

SECTION 1. All the territory now included in the Fifth Ward of the City of Milwaukee, which lies east of the center of Monroe Street, and the quarter section line through section thirty-two, running through the center of said street to the south line of said Ward, shall hereafter constitute and be the Fifth Ward of the City of Milwaukee ; and all the territory now included in the Fifth Ward of the City of Milwaukee, which lies west of the center of Monroe Street, and the quarter section line above referred to, shall hereafter constitute and be the Eighth Ward of the City of Milwaukee ; and said Fifth and Eighth Wards hereby created shall have all the rights and privileges, and be subject to the same regulations, laws and ordinances, as the other wards in said city.

Eighth Ward established.

Aldermen and officers, how elected.

SEC. 2. At the next annual charter election in the City of Milwaukee, there shall be elected in the 5th Ward hereby created, one Alderman, who shall hold his office for two years, and one Alderman, who shall hold his office for one year ; and there shall be elected in the Eighth Ward hereby created, one Alderman, who shall hold his office for two years, and two Aldermen, who shall hold their respective offices for one year ; and, annually thereafter, there shall be elected in each of the aforesaid Fifth and Eighth Wards, one Alderman, who shall hold his office for two years, and one Alderman, who shall hold his office for one year ; and the Alderman elected for two years, in the Fifth Ward, at the last city election, shall continue and be Alderman for the said Fifth Ward, hereby created, for the remainder of his term of office; and it shall be the duty of the Common Council, at the next city election, to appoint three Inspectors of Election in each of said Fifth and Eighth Wards, and to designate the places for holding the election in said wards.

City Comptroller to apportion the indebtedness

SEC. 3. It shall be the duty of the City Comptroller to apportion the amount of city indebtedness now charged to the fifth ward, between the fifth and eighth wards hereby created, in proportion to their respective equalized assessment rolls for the year 1857; and all property, real or personal, which, prior to the passage of this act, belonged to the fifth ward of the City of Milwaukee, shall thereafter belong jointly to the fifth and eighth wards of said city.

When act to take effect.

SEC. 4. The foregoing sections, one, two and three, of this act, shall take effect and be in force from and after the thirty-first day of March, A. D. 1857.

Corporate limits extended and 6th Ward enlarged.

SEC. 5. The corporate limits of the City of Milwaukee are hereby enlarged and extended so as to include within the limits of said city all of section seventeen (17), and all of section eighteen (18), town seven (7), north of range twenty-two (22) east, and the territory hereby added to said city shall constitute and become a part of the sixth ward thereof, and shall be subject to the laws, regulations and ordinances governing said ward and city.

City indebtedness hereafter to be ascertained.

SEC. 6. Hereafter, annually, it shall be the duty of the Common Council of the City of Milwaukee to ascertain the total amount of the general city indebtedness, over and above any floating debt that is to be paid out of the taxes of the current year, and not to include any bonds issued to rail road or other companies, for the final payment of which the city has taken security.

Sinking fund created, and tax to be levied.

SEC. 7. Hereafter, annually, at the time of raising and levying a tax for city and ward purposes, the Common

Council are hereby authorized to levy a tax on all the property in said city liable to taxation, at a rate per cent. sufficient to raise a sum equal to five per cent. of the then city indebtedness—the same to be enforced and collected in the same manner as other city taxes are collected, and to be known as a sinking fund, for the ultimate redemption of the whole city indebtedness.

Tax, how levied.

SEC. 8. The tax annually provided for in the preceding section, it shall be the duty of the said Common Council to apply in such manner as they may deem advisable for the payment, each year, of five per cent. of the city indebtedness, and the same shall be applied for no other purpose. *Provided,* The Common Council are hereby authorized to issue city bonds, to have the benefit of this act to pay off any present city indebtedness that has never been funded, and also, to issue new bonds under this act, to take up and pay any outstanding city bonds when they become due. All bonds hereafter issued to draw interest, not exceeding seven per cent. payable semi-annually, the principal to be paid twenty years from date in the City of New York.

Old bonds may be taken up.

SEC. 9. This act, except sections one, two and three, shall take effect and be in force from and after its passage.

Approved, October 11, 1856.

INDEX TO APPENDIX.

www.ingramcontent.com/pod-product-compliance
Lightning Source LLC
LaVergne TN
LVHW021242110826
845150LV00002B/383